This book provides a radical new interpretation of the aims of the lesser German princes during the seventeenth and eighteenth centuries through the example of the duchy of Württemberg. Arguing that the princes' political ambitions were fundamental in shaping the internal development of their territories, the author sheds new light on the political importance of the notorious German 'soldier trade' and its role in international diplomacy.

The wider social and political impact of these policies is also investigated in a comparative framework, while traditional interpretations of the dramatic struggle between duke and estates are challenged in a reassessment of the role of early modern representative institutions in German state development. The relationship of these internal political struggles to the different elements of the Holy Roman Empire is revealed, opening up new perspectives on the role of the German states within the imperial structure and revealing the empire as a flawed but functioning political system.

CAMBRIDGE STUDIES IN EARLY MODERN HISTORY

War, state and society in Württemberg, 1677–1793

CAMBRIDGE STUDIES IN EARLY MODERN HISTORY

Edited by Professor Sir John Elliott, University of Oxford, Professor Olwen Hufton, Harvard University, and Professor H. G. Koenigsberger

The idea of an 'early modern' period of European history from the fifteenth to the late eighteenth century is now widely accepted among historians. The purpose of Cambridge Studies in Early Modern History is to publish monographs and studies which illuminate the character of the period as a whole, and in particular focus attention on a dominant theme within it, the interplay of continuity and change as they are presented by the continuity of medieval ideas, political and social organisation, and by the impact of new ideas, new methods and new demands on the traditional structure.

For a list of titles published in the series, please see end of book

War, state and society
in Württemberg, 1677–1793

PETER H. WILSON

University of Newcastle upon Tyne

CAMBRIDGE
UNIVERSITY PRESS

Published by the Press Syndicate of the University of Cambridge
The Pitt Building, Trumpington Street, Cambridge CB2 1RP
40 West 20th Street, New York, NY 10011–4211, USA
10 Stamford Road, Oakleigh, Melbourne 3166, Australia

© Cambridge University Press 1995

First published 1995

Printed in Great Britain at the University Press, Cambridge

A catalogue record for this book is available from the British Library

Library of Congress cataloguing in publication data
Wilson, Peter H.
War, state and society in Württemberg, 1677–1793
Peter H. Wilson.
p.   cm. – (Cambridge studies in early modern history)
Includes bibliographical references.
ISBN 0 521 47302 0
1. Württemberg (Germany) – History, Military. 2. Württemberg
(Germany) – Politics and government. 3. Social classes – Germany –
Württemberg – History – 18th century. 4. Holy Roman Empire –
History – 1648–1805. I. Title. II. Series.
DD801.W76W55 1995
943'.47–dc20   94–16546 cip

ISBN 0 521 47302 0 hardback

For my parents

Contents

Illustrations

Tables

Preface

This book now bears little resemblance to its earlier form as a doctoral thesis, which was more limited in scope and took events only up to 1770. During both the research and the transformation of my thesis into a book it has been my good fortune to benefit from the advice and assistance of a large number of people and institutions. I would like to thank particularly my supervisor Professor T. C. W. Blanning, Sidney Sussex College Cambridge, for his constant help and guidance, and my examiners Drs Jonathan Steinberg, Trinity Hall and Derek McKay, LSE, for their constructive criticism. Invaluable assistance and encouragement during my extended stay in Germany in 1986–9 was provided by Professor Volker Press of Tübingen, whose recent sad death represents a great loss for German scholarship. I am also indebted to the late Professor James Allen Vann for his encouragement and advice during the initial stages of my research.

I acknowledge the gracious permission of HRH The Duke of Württemberg to make use of papers in the family Hausarchiv, Stuttgart. I owe a great debt of thanks to Dr Hans-Martin Maurer and his staff at the Hauptstaatsarchiv, Stuttgart, where most of my research was conducted, for their unflagging assistance, and to the archivists and librarians at the Landesbibliothek, Stuttgart, the Wehrgeschichtliches Museum, Rastatt, the British Library Bloomsbury, the Public Record Office, Chancery Lane, London, and Sunderland University Library whose inter-library loans section provided valuable assistance during the final stages of my work. I am also indebted to the late Dr Hans Bleckwenn of Münster, who kindly allowed me to draw on papers in his private collection.

For reading and commenting upon sections of the original thesis I would like to thank especially Dr Gaby Haug-Moritz of Tübingen and Daniel Hohrath of Esslingen, to whom I owe much for their insight into the Württemberg estates and the nature of eighteenth-century warfare. Professor Jeremy Black of Durham kindly allowed me to see the typescript of his book on British foreign policy 1783–93 prior to publication and provided much general advice and encouragement.

I owe substantial thanks to the British Academy for funding my Major State Studentship and to the German Historical Institute, London, Jesus College Cambridge, and the managers of the Prince Consort and Thirwell Fund for providing additional financial assistance during the completion of my thesis.

Preface

Sunderland University provided a term's sabbatical which proved invaluable in the later stages of revising this work. Roger Cullingham and the staff of Thameslink, Windsor, efficiently turned numerous handwritten drafts into clear, legible text.

Finally, I wish to thank Eliane for her understanding, support and good humour throughout the completion of this work.

Note on form

All dates are given throughout in the New Style. Names of places and people have been left in their German form unless there is a commonly used Anglicised version, when this is used instead. Titles and technical terms are given in English except in cases where there is either no translation or the translation can be misleading. In such cases the German has been used throughout, but italicised and explained the first time the word appears. Money is expressed in *Rheinische Gulden* (Rhenish florins), the currency then in use in Württemberg. Where other currency is cited in the text, a conversion into florins is given wherever possible in the footnotes. One florin (fl.) was subdivided into 60 *Kreuzer* (xr.), each worth six *Heller* (h.). Conversion into modern values is always approximate at best, but the rates most commonly cited are that one florin was worth 1.71 pre-1914 *Mark* or ten *Reichsmark* in 1933. Contemporary conversion rates for the most common currencies are set out below:

1fl. Rhenish =	1.25fl. Dutch
1.5fl. =	1 Taler
1fl. =	2 French Livre (*c.* 1700–1750)
1fl. =	2.5 French Livre (post-1750)
1fl. =	5 Venetian Lire (1680s)
7.5fl. =	£1 sterling (1680s)
8fl. =	£1 sterling (1730s)
9fl. 9xr. =	£1 sterling (1780s)

Abbreviations

ADB	*Allgemeine deutsche Biographie* (issued by the historische Commission bei der Königl. Akademie der Wissenschaften, 56 vols., Leipzig, 1875–1912)
BBSAW	*Besondere Beilage zum Staatsanzeige für Württemberg*
BMWB	*Beiheft zum Militär-Wochenblatt*
bn	battalion
BWKG	*Blätter für württembergische Kirchengeschichte*
cav	cavalry
coy	company
DBKH	*Darstellungen aus der bayerischen Kriegs- und Heeresgeschichte*
DR	Dragoon Regiment
HDM	*Handbuch zur deutschen Militärgeschichte 1648–1939* (issued by the Militärgeschichtliches Forschungsamt, 11 vols., Frankfurt am Main, 1964–81)
Hie gut Württemberg	*Beilage zur Ludwigsburger Kreiszeitung*
HKE	*Herzog Karl Eugen und seine Zeit* (issued by the Württembegischer Geschichts- und Altumsverein, 2 vols., Esslingen, 1907–9)
HSAS	Hauptstaatsarchiv Stuttgart
inf	infantry
IR	Infantry Regiment
JRA	*Jüngster Reichsabschied*, or last recess of the imperial diet 1654
KR	Kürassier Regiment
LBGB	*Ludwigsburger Geschichtsblätter*
LBS	Landesbibliothek Stuttgart, Handschriftliche Abteilung
LBSAW	*Literärische Beilage zum Staatsanzeige für Württemberg*
NF	Neue Folge
PJb	*Preussischer Jahrbücher*
PRO	Public Record Office
rgt	regiment
VKGLK	*Veröffentlichungen der Kommission für Geschichte und Landeskunde in Baden-Württemberg*

Abbreviations

WJb	*Württembergische Jahrbücher für vaterländische Geschichte, Geographie, Statistik und Topographie*
WJSL	*Württembergische Jahrbücher für Statistik und Landeskunde* (continued from 1954 as *Jahrbücher für Statistik und Landeskunde in Baden-Württemberg*)
WNJB	*Württembergische Neujahrsblätter*
WVJHLG	*Württembergische Vierteljahreshefte für Landesgeschichte*
ZGO	*Zeitschrift für die Geschichte des Oberrheins*
ZWLG	*Zeitschrift für württembergische Landesgeschichte*

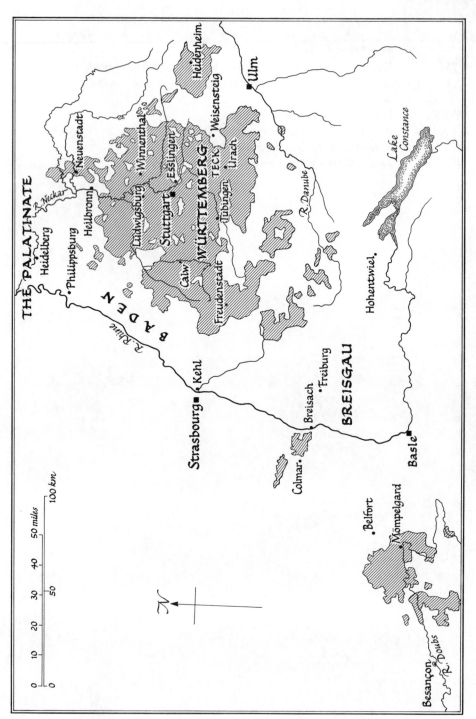

The Württemberg territories in the eighteenth century

Introduction

This book is about the interrelationship between war, society and political ambition in absolutist state-building in the German south-west. It focuses on the duchy of Württemberg as a case study to test existing theories on the development of states and to provide an insight into the structure of the Holy Roman Empire (*Reich*). The first three chapters approach these issues thematically and comparatively. The following five examine the Württemberg experience between 1677 and 1793. Though these dates mark the accession and death of particular Württemberg dukes, they also coincide with the major historical shifts that form the parameters of this study. The first is when the move towards absolutism began in earnest in both Württemberg and many other smaller German territories. The second saw the onset of the French Revolutionary Wars and the progressive collapse of the Reich. The ground rules governing the political actions of the participants in this story were irrevocably altered and a new set of circumstances was introduced under which future German state development was to take place.

In testing the validity of the theories of motive forces behind state development, Württemberg is of particular interest as it is smaller than the states normally chosen as examples of the two most widely accepted theories. It is also the prime example for the recent theory advanced specifically to explain the development of the smaller states.

The older of these two theories puts forward the 'primary of foreign policy' (*Primat der Aussenpolitik*) as the driving force behind the development of the state.[1] In order to defend itself against foreign aggression and compete with other states, the emergent modern state had to develop a larger, centrally ruled and administered territory sufficient to maintain an adequate level of constant military preparedness. This link between military and state organisation is now widely accepted by historians, especially those in Germany, as a truism. A state without military power is considered 'an absurdity' and 'especially the modern state as it developed, in the absolutist epoch', is seen to have been largely – if not wholly – determined by its

---

[1] O. Hintze, 'Military organisation and the organisation of the state' and 'The formation of states and constitutional development', both in F. Gilbert (ed.), *The historical essays of Otto Hintze* (Oxford, 1975), pp. 157–77, 180–215. See also G. Oestreich, 'Zur Heeresverfassung der deutschen Territorien vom 1500 bis 1800', in R. Dietrich and G. Oestreich (eds.), *Forschungen zu Staat und Verfassung. Festgabe für Fritz Hartung* (Berlin, 1958), pp. 419–39.

military organisation.[2] Absolute monarchy is regarded as synonymous with a standing army.[3]

The second theory sees the drive towards a well-ordered state (*eine gute Polizei*) as being responsible for the development of the modern state. According to this theory, the need to control those elements of the population considered dangerous to the ruling elites prompted the state to develop a bureaucratic apparatus to regulate all aspects of society and the economy.

Within the literature on both theories there is a debate over the respective weight to be assigned to the role of impersonal forces, often defined in Marxist socio-economic terms, and that of the individual. The emphasis on the latter heightens the role played by individual rulers and sees their personal characteristics as instrumental in shaping wider events. The former sees individual actions as largely predetermined by the underlying socio-economic structure. In its classic, Marxist, form, this tendency views the creation of absolutism as the product of the transition from feudalism to capitalism. The monarch is seen as essentially part of the nobility, who either emancipates himself from their control by a temporary alliance with the 'bourgeoisie' (Western model), or collaborates with them, gaining the nobles' support for centralisation by extending their control over the peasantry (Eastern model).[4]

A more watered-down version eschews such class analysis, but still sees state-building as essentially a group rather than an individual activity. These groups, often rather imprecisely termed 'elites', helped push forward state development through their interaction, either in conflict, or collaboration, with the ruler. The two most important elite groups were the bureaucrats and the estates, or leading notables who were nominally the representatives of the entire population and who sat in an assembly with varying powers over policy-making and taxation.

A recent example of this concept is Marc Raeff's idea of an inner dynamism of the bureaucracy. This is said to have propelled it to assume ever more functions as a result of the decline and withdrawal of the church and the consequent movement of the secular power into the vacuum. The projects for all kinds of reforms and improvements, along with the tendency towards ever-increasing supervision and regulations associated with German cameralism, seems to provide evidence for this view.[5] Though sometimes overstated, it does have the advantage that it

---

[2] H. Schmidt, 'Staat und Armee im Zeitalter des "miles perpetuus"', in J. Kunisch and B. Stollberg-Rillinger (eds.), *Staatsverfassung und Herresverfassing in der europäischen Geschichte der frühen Neuzeit* (*Historische Forschungen*, 28, Berlin, 1986), pp. 213–48 at p. 214; also G. Best, *War and society in revolutionary Europe, 1770–1870* (London, 1982), p. 8.

[3] J. Childs, *Armies and warfare in Europe 1648–1789* (Manchester, 1982), p. 28.

[4] P. Anderson, *Lineages of the absolutist state* (London, 1974); A. Dorpalen, *German history in Marxist perspective. The East German approach* (London, 1985), pp. 138–67.

[5] M. Raeff, *The well-ordered police state. Social and institutional change through law in the Germanies and Russia 1600–1800* (New Haven/London, 1983); C. W. Ingrao, *The Hessian mercenary state. Ideas, institutions and reform under Frederick II 1760–1785* (Cambridge, 1987), esp. pp. 23–37.

takes account of the influence of ideas such as mercantilism and enlightenment philosophy in policy-making.

Often the two main theories are linked together with the standing army being regarded as 'a coercive policy instrument used in internal affairs as well as in wars against foreign opponents'.[6] Indeed, the link is already inherent in the theory of the primacy of foreign policy. The 'pushing and pressing' of states against each other forced each state to seek appropriate military organisation and consequently to shape its internal structure. Those forces within the state that opposed this development, such as territorial estates, had to be crushed or, at least, coerced into co-operating, otherwise the state would be unable to compete with its rivals and so risk losing its independence.[7]

Again, this is seen as being especially true of the absolutist era, or, as the Marxists prefer it, 'the late feudal epoch'. Some go so far as to mirror Eckart Kehr's work on Wilhelmine Germany and transform the concept of primacy of foreign policy into one of domestic policy.[8] The domestic security considerations of the ruling elites thus become the primary factor behind bureaucratic centralisation and military development. Dangerous social elements could be intimidated by the new standing armies. The supposedly high proportion of 'foreign mercenaries' in these armies is taken as proof of their deployment as instruments of social control used by an absolutist ruler to suppress his own subjects. Potential opposition from traditional elites could be avoided by integrating them into the officer corps and so making them a part of the absolutist state's system of control. These elites were thus given a role that both enabled them to maintain their material position and compensated them for their loss of political independence. The standing army also served to protect their control of the means of production from attacks by the lower orders.[9] This has been seen as being particularly true of those lands east of the river Elbe, especially Prussia,[10] and has led Marxist historians to characterise 'the standing army as the pillar of feudal reaction'.[11]

The Thirty Years War (1618–48) is regarded as providing a major impetus for these developments. The brutality of the conflict left a deep imprint on the German

[6] Childs, *Armies and warfare*, p. 27.
[7] Hintze, 'Military organisation'.
[8] E. Kehr, *Der Primat der Innenpolitik: gesammelte Aufsätze zur preussisch–deutschen sozialgeschichte im 19 und 20 Jahrhundert* (Berlin, 1970).
[9] H. Schnitter and T. Schmidt, *Absolutismus und Heer* (Berlin, DDR, 1987); H. Schnitter, 'Zur Funktion und Stellung des Heeres im feudalabsolutistischen Militarismus im Brandenburg–Preussen', *Zeitschrift für Militärgeschichte*, 10 (1971), 306–14; V. G. Kiernan, 'Foreign mercenaries and absolute monarchy', *Past and Present*, 11 (1957), 66–86.
[10] The most cogent and balanced example of this argument is O. Büsch, *Militärsystem und Sozialleben im alten Preussen 1713–1807. Die Anfänge der sozialen Militärisierung der preussisch–deutschen Gesellschaft* (Berlin, 1962).
[11] O. Rocholl, 'Das stehende Heer als Stütze der feudalen Reaktion. Ein Beitrag zur Heeresgeschichte vornehmlich des 17. Jahrhunderts', *Wissenschaftliche Zeitschrift der Karl-Marx-Universität Leipzig. Gesellschafts- und staatswissenschaftliche Reihe*, 1, 9/10 (1952/53), 499–510.

consciousness, heightening both the desire for strong government and the fear of future conflict. This was especially the case among the smaller states which, like Württemberg, had been powerless to prevent their territory becoming a common battlefield.

The lesson of the war was clear: 'A poor state was a victim state.'[12] Only a ruler who could establish firm fiscal control and maximum exploitation of available resources could survive and increase his power. The way forward appeared to be to prolong the emergency situation created by the war and make it the basis of government. Those, like the Prussian Hohenzollerns, who managed to do this were able to bypass their estates and were well on the way to establishing absolutism by 1700. However, the war had left many princes heavily in debt and compelled them to grant further concessions to their estates in return for financial assistance. The resumption of prolonged warfare in the 1670s following the aggression of Louis XIV and the Turks gave these princes a second chance. One such ruler was the duke of Württemberg and the degree to which he was able to exploit these circumstances to introduce absolutism will be the subject of Chapters 4 and 5.

If the importance of war in the creation of absolutism has long been recognised, the exact nature of the link is still the matter of some debate. Followers of Michael Roberts' thesis of a 'Military Revolution' see late seventeenth-century absolutism as the product of military change taking place between 1560 and 1660. Changes in weaponry and tactics resulted in armies becoming not only larger but more expensive. To cope with these changes, rulers were forced to reform and expand their administrations, resulting in a drive to absolutism. Recently, this theory has been stood on its head by Jeremy Black, who correctly points out that the major increase in army size occurred in the last third of the seventeenth century, after absolutism had been introduced in many major European states. This increase, he argues, was the product, not the cause, of absolutism and resulted from the greater degree of internal political stability which absolutism had created.[13]

With regard to both views, it is worth remembering that the connection between absolutism and military growth was never uniform, nor inevitable. Often, military needs proved so pressing that princes were compelled to contract out to private 'military enterprisers' who carried out organisational tasks in the absence of permanent state employees.[14] Though the state clawed back these functions

---

[12] M. Hughes, *Early modern Germany 1477–1806* (London, 1992), p. 102.

[13] M. Roberts, 'The military revolution 1560–1660', in his *Essays in Swedish history* (London, 1967), pp. 195–225; G. Parker, 'The military revolution 1560–1660 – a myth?', *Journal of Modern History*, 47 (1976), 195–314 and his *The military revolution. Military innovation and the rise of the west 1500–1800* (Cambridge, 1988); J. Black, *A military revolution? Military change and European society 1550–1800* (London, 1991).

[14] F. Redlich, *The German military enterpriser and his workforce. A study in European economic and social history* (2 vols., Wiesbaden, 1964–5).

whenever it could, the creation of a large fiscal and military bureaucracy did not automatically enhance princely control. Fiscal pressures frequently forced a ruler to tolerate, or even encourage, the growth of a venal bureaucracy through the sale of public office. In any case, the incumbents of such posts often developed a will of their own and professional ethos that was sometimes at odds with princely policy. Moreover, the constant need for money strengthened the influence of the estates and other institutions whose approval was necessary for taxation. If anything, war hindered as much as encouraged the development of absolutism. Württemberg provides a good example of this, as the discussion of the relative position of the estates and bureaucracy in Chapter 2 will show.

Partly because these theories of state development appear to fit so well within the situation identified in Prussia and partly because of that state's later role as leader of a united Germany, there has been a tendency to use Prussian examples as the basis of generalisations for the rest of Germany. P. G. M. Dickson's recent work now provides an excellent analysis of the relationship of fiscal and military policy to bureaucratic change in Austria. However, there is a noticeable lack of such investigations for the smaller states.[15] The military creations of the small German princes are still generally dismissed as 'playing with soldiers' (*Soldatenspielerei*). Their main function is seen as a source of revenue for their despotic – enlightened or otherwise – creators. Alongside Hessen-Kassel, Württemberg is regarded as the prime example of this 'soldier trade' (*Soldatenhandel*).[16]

This view of the military establishments of the small states appears to support the third and most recent theory on the driving force behind state-building. This is the idea of 'cultural competition', which was first advanced by James Allen Vann in connection with Württemberg and has recently been linked to Hessen-Kassel.[17] 'Unable even to contemplate cutting a dash on the international stage' owing to the inadequacy of their resources, the rulers of such states are said to have found an outlet for their desire for prestige in attempting to establish their territories as 'the most cultured in the Holy Roman Empire'.[18]

Like the primacy of foreign policy, the idea of cultural competition identifies the desire for money as the driving force behind the state-building of the absolutist

---

[15] P. G. M. Dickson, *Finance and government under Maria Theresia 1740–1780* (2 vols., Oxford, 1987). For a rare attempt to assess these issues in a small German state, see H. Caspary, *Staat, Finanzen, Wirtschaft und Heerwesen im Hochstift Bamberg (1672–1693)* (Bamberg, 1976).

[16] For example: 'Perhaps the epitome of small standing armies, excessive military expenditure and militaristic absolutism is to be found in the history of the Duchy of Württemberg during the eighteenth century': Childs, *Armies and warfare*, p. 35. The literature on the *Soldatenhandel* is discussed on pp. 74–7 below.

[17] J. A. Vann, *The making of a state. Württemberg 1593–1793* (Ithaca/London, 1984). Vann's theory of cultural competition has not found a favourable reception among German historians; see the reviews of his book by B. Wunder, *ZWLG*, 45 (1986), 393–6; and H. M. Maurer, *ibid.*, 47 (1988), 511–12; Ingrao, *Hessian mercenary state*.

[18] Review of Ingrao's work by T. C. W. Blanning in *German History. The Journal of the German History Society*, 6 (1988), 191–2.

monarchs. The difference between the two theories is the motive for demanding the money. The former maintains it was required for military competition – the latter, as its name indicates, for cultural competition. This implies that the rulers of the small states placed the buildup of their prestige above the achievement of their political aims. The evidence advanced in Vann's book seems to suggest that Württemberg was indeed a classic exampile that supports this theory. The court was always dazzling and often at the forefront of contemporary culture. The high point appears to be reached under Duke Carl Eugen (1737/44–93) who is universally depicted as having used the money he obtained from foreign subsidy treaties to finance his 'cultural competition' rather than raise the troops he was supposed to provide.

The nature of these treaties and their role in princely policy is the subject of Chapter 3. As Dickson points out, one of the major problems in evaluating their importance is that 'little is known about the use made of subsidies once they were received'.[19] With few rare exceptions,[20] no one has bothered to work out what the German princes really spent the money on. Chapters 5, 6 and 8 attempt to do this for Württemberg, the most notorious case throughout the secondary literature for the most blatant misuse of subsidies.

Money, for whatever purpose, was certainly a cause of prince–estate conflict. Württemberg internal relations from the 1670s to the 1790s were dominated by the dispute between duke and estates over fiscal control. However, money was not the ultimate object of the battle, but rather the trigger for a wider struggle for power. As Chapter 2 will show, money provided the starting-point, because it represented the means for a prince to achieve his dynastic aims (outlined in Chapter 1). Conversely, control over taxation ensured the continued influence of those socio-economic groups represented in the estates and limited the effects of the duke's more reckless policies which were detrimental to their wider interests.

An analysis of the course of this conflict opens up a further dimension for the issue of state-building. Rulers such as the duke of Württemberg, whose estates had effective control over taxation, had an incentive to reform. These reforms could range from efforts to maximise returns on what sources of income were directly available to attempts to seize immediate control of those that were not. This raises the issue of whether early modern representative institutions acted as a positive or negative force in state development.

The Anglo-Saxon Whiggish tradition sees the estates as assisting positively in the development of their state by defending popular freedoms and sharing in administrative tasks. This is a view which is shared by the older folksy–patriotic Württemberg historians, who portray the estates as fighting an unceasing battle in

[19] Dickson, *Finance and government*, II, pp. 157–8, 183.
[20] P. C. Hartmann, *Geld als Instrument europäischer Machtpolitik im Zeitalter des Merkantilismus 1715–1740* (Munich, 1978).

the duchy's best interests against the actions of arbitrary and irrational dukes.[21] The wider German literature, on the other hand, tends to see the estates as impediment (*Hemmschuh*) to the 'progressive' centralising tendencies of the monarch.

Regardless of opinion, however, both views have similar implications. Both see state development as the product of prince–estate dualism and not the sole creation of the prince and his bureaucracy. Further, both see this dualism primarily as a conflict relationship, with prince and estates as mutually hostile and a struggle for power as inevitable.

Recently, this interpretation has come under criticism. Prince–estate relations were not automatically hostile but were characterised as much by co-operation as conflict. The perennial complaints of princely transgressions on traditional rights and privileges represent the rhetoric of contemporary political debate and were not in themselves evidence of permanent estrangement of the two parties. Real conflict only arose when the sides could no longer reach a compromise with each other.[22]

As the investigation of the long conflict in Württemberg will show, this happened when a threat to the vital interests of one party posed by the policies of the other coincided with the absence of a convergence of general interests. This became progressively more common in Württemberg from the 1670s as the adoption of an alien baroque court culture was followed in 1733 by the rule of a Catholic duke over Lutheran subjects. After the European 'reversal of alliances' in 1756 removed the potential of a French invasion as a common threat, the duke sought to free himself from domestic constraints by ambitious military expansion. The failure of this policy between 1759 and 1765 did not result, as previously believed, in a new spirit of co-operation after the final settlement (*Erbvergleich*) of 1770. Instead, conflict continued, though on a reduced scale because of the diminished possibilities for ambitious ducal policies.

The examination of this conflict, together with ducal efforts to realise long-term dynastic aims, also opens up new perspectives on the position of the smaller German territories within the system of the old Reich. In the past, the presence of these small states was seen by nationalist historians as a hindrance to German unification under Prussian leadership. Keen to champion this unified state, such writers sought to paint the military and political organisations that preceded it in as bad a light as possible. Thus, the political structure of the Reich was portrayed as weak and ineffective and the myriad of small states was criticised as *Kleinstaaterei*.

---

[21] F. L. Carsten, *Princes and parliaments in Germany from the fifteenth to the eighteenth century* (Oxford, 1959). For the older Württemberg view, see the works of Karl Pfaff whose influence is to be found in those of A. E. Adam, A. Pfister and many others.

[22] J. Gagliardo, *Germany under the old regime 1600–1790* (Harlow, 1991), pp. 101–3. See also the useful discussion of these issues in G. Haug-Moritz, *Württembergischer Ständekonflikt und deutscher Dualismus. Ein Beitrag zur Geschichte des Reichsverbands in der Mitte des 18. Jahrhunderts* (*VKGLK*, Reihe B, vol. 122, Stuttgart, 1992), pp. 5–14.

Though this so-called Borussian legend still persists in some general works, it has been extensively revised in the specialist literature since the 1960s.

Increasingly, the Reich is seen as a flawed but functioning political system which acted relatively effectively to protect its weaker components from the transgressions of the stronger parts. This system is regarded as having operated on a number of levels: national (Reich), regional (*Kreis*), and local (territorial state).[23] The relationship between each level and between all three and the emperor was regulated by the complex system of checks and balances built into the post-1648 imperial constitution. There has been a tendency to ignore the relationship between the various parts of this system in favour of detailed studies of the individual components. The present study is intended to redress this. By studying the course of princely policy at all levels, the relationship of each part to the whole can be better understood.

In particular, it aims to open up the complex matrix of emperor–Kreis–territorial state, and the relationship of the first two to the key components of the latter: duke, estates and bureaucracy. In doing so, I aim to explain why it proved so difficult for small and medium princes such as the dukes of Württemberg to realise their aims as long as the system of the Reich continued to function. This will shed light on the relative effectiveness of various parts of the system and on the ability of the emperor to exploit both the system and the princes' weakness to advance his own aims.

This will involve a reassessment of the relationship of both Württemberg and the emperor to the Swabian Kreis. Apart from the imperial courts,[24] much of the recent historiography has focused on the Kreise in general and Swabia in particular. Swabia is widely regarded as having been the best-functioning of all ten Kreise. Its member states are depicted as co-operating effectively to maintain a common defence force, regulate trade and tariffs, stamp out vagrancy and enforce imperial legislation. In Vann's very positive assessment of the period 1648–1715, the Kreis is portrayed as overcoming confessional differences between Protestants and Catholics and working harmoniously with the emperor. Even in Heinz–Günther Borck's investigation of the period its final collapse between 1792 and 1806, the Kreis emerges as a functioning institution, albeit one that was cracking under the strain of immense upheaval.[25] Recently, Vann's optimistic view has been toned down by Graf von Neipperg, who argues that the much-vaunted Swabian efficiency was as much a product of discord as accord. Internal divisions, such as those between Württemberg and Constance, Protestants and Catholics, as well as often hostile relations with both the emperor and the nearby Austrian authorities, proved

---

[23] This system is further explained on pp. 17–23.

[24] M. Hughes, *Law and politics in eighteenth-century Germany. The Imperial Aulic Council in the reign of Charles VI* (Woodbridge, 1988).

[25] J. A. Vann, *The Swabian Kreis. Institutional growth in the Holy Roman Empire, 1648–1715* (Brussels, 1975); H. G. Borck, *Der schwäbische Reichskreis im Zeitalter der französischen Revolutionskriege (1792–1806)* (*VKGLK*, Reihe B, vol. 61, Stuttgart, 1970).

a constant source of conflicts. These produced varying coalitions of disparate forces which tended to balance each other out. This helped as much to maintain an equilibrium as any genuine convergence of interest between the parties.[26] The extent to which these findings are borne out and to which they represent in microcosm the workings of the entire Reich will be revealed in the following chapters.

---

[26] R. Graf von Neipperg, *Kaiser und schwäbischer Kreis (1714–1733). Ein Beitrag zu Reichsverfassung. Kreisgeschichte und kaiserlicher Reichspolitik am Anfang des 18 Jahrhunderts (VKGLK,* Reihe B, vol. 119, Stuttgart, 1991).

Princely aims and policy-making

CHARACTERISTICS OF THE SMALLER GERMAN STATES

In determining princely aims and how these affected policy-making, we must avoid the trap of reducing the motivation for every action to one cause. Clearly, individual character, upbringing and religion, not to mention the shape and location of territory and the general intellectual atmosphere, created a different set of criteria for each prince. Clearly also, these criteria changed in response to inter-action with other individuals, groups and states. In some cases, pursuit of 'higher ideals' through patronage of the arts, or the desire to benefit the population by benevolent reforms, looms large. Never absent, however, are dynastic and political goals, and it is upon these that this chapter will concentrate. In doing so we need to beware of automatically regarding all other aspects of princely policy as subordinate to these ends.

It is a popular but fallacious criticism of the notion of absolutism, especially the 'enlightened' sort, that all reforms were designed to strengthen the state's potential to achieve political ends. Furtherance of political aims and the advancement of the 'common good' were not necessarily mutually exclusive. A tax reform might both introduce a fairer distribution of financial burdens and raise more money for the army. Assessing just which motive was foremost in a particular ruler's mind at the time is always problematical, and is probably best left to the biographer. Our concern is with those aims that had the greatest impact on the shaping of the internal structure of the state. As will become apparent, these were the dynastic and political aims of the prince.

A word or two needs to be said here about the terms 'absolutism' and 'state'. None of the rulers of the so-called absolutist era of the late seventeenth and eighteenth centuries was actually absolute. All were hindered to a greater or lesser extent by estates, bureaucracies and other obstacles. The extent of these limits forms a major theme of this book, and we will return to it during our investigation of Württemberg's internal political structure in the next chapter. It has, however, often been said that the 'enlightened' form of absolutism worked best in the type of small German state that forms the centre of this study.[1] These are said to have been

---

[1] Ingrao, *Hessian mercenary state*, p. 6.

'insulated' from power politics and less interested in pursuing ambitious political goals. The structure of the Reich is supposed to have 'provided military security' which 'permitted them to concentrate on domestic policy'. The assumed lack of large standing armies is taken as proof of this, while where these armies existed, their primary purpose is given as earning money to fund such policy, whether of the truly 'enlightened' sort – furtherance of the common good (economic reforms, hospitals, etc.) – or the narrower cultural competitive variety (opera, theatre, public libraries).

While this may well have been true for Hessen-Kassel in the latter half of the eighteenth century, it was not typical for the other small states. First, its ruler actually had money from subsidy treaties that was surplus to the costs he had incurred, and this permitted him to finance a reform programme. Second, both ruler and potential opposition groups (estates, nobility) co-operated to a degree seldom found elsewhere. As this and the following two chapters will demonstrate, the small states of the Reich were not lacking in dynastic and political ambitions; it was merely that their ambitions were usually in inverse proportion to their ability to achieve them.

The term 'state' is used here as a convenient shorthand for the territorial entities that made up the old Reich. These were known at the time as the *Reichsstände* or estates of the empire as represented in the imperial diet (*Reichstag*). In reality, none was a state in the modern sense, as they were neither fully sovereign nor were their judiciaries separate from their administrations. The Peace of Westphalia in 1648 accorded the German princes the *ius territorii et superioritatis* which was defined as territorial sovereignty (*Landeshoheit*) and not full *souveraineté* which was reserved exclusively for the emperor. Landeshoheit permitted the princes to maintain armed forces and to make treaties with foreign powers, provided these were not directed against the Reich. However, all princes remained subject to a certain extent to imperial law and all acknowledged, with varying degrees of sincerity, the emperor as their overlord.

Although during the course of the eighteenth century some of the larger territories did develop attributes of a modern state, the concept of the state in the smaller territories remained, in practice, that of the so-called 'classical absolutist'. According to this, state power was inseparable from princely authority and the state was an extension of the prince's dynastic lands. His authority was based on divine right as expressed in the heading of decrees: 'By the Grace of God . . . ' (*'Von Gottes Gnaden'*). While both princely office and territory were seen as public trusts for whose well-being the ruler was responsible to God, the concept of the ruler as the servant of some larger, impersonal 'State' remained alien to most of the lesser princes. Of course, this view was neither unchanging nor uniform across the German territories. As one would expect, traditional, even medieval, conceptions of the state coexisted alongside newer ideas. Thus, while eighteenth-century Württemberg bureaucrats were developing a sense of loyalty to an impersonal state,

Carl Eugen could still echo Louis XIV and exclaim: 'What fatherland? I am the fatherland'.[2] The continued identification of prince and state naturally had implications for the internal structure and policy-making of the smaller territories, though we should not underestimate the influence of other groups, such as estates and bureaucrats, on both.

At this time the territories, particularly the smaller ones, were run very much as family concerns in the manner of a landlord running a country estate. The central administration still displayed its origins as the management bureau for the prince's private household and domains. Similarly, the standing armies, which are taken as so characteristic of the absolutist era, developed not from territorial militias, but from units raised under agreements between the ruler and private contractors.[3] The prince, not the state, was the 'owner' of the army. The soldiers swore an oath of allegiance to him and not to the state.[4]

Therefore, we cannot really speak of a 'state's policy', but rather that of a particular prince or, at the most, a family and its servants. The armies of the small states fought chiefly for the dynastic interests of their prince, though sometimes these interests coincided with what might be considered those of the bulk of the population: for example when resisting foreign invasion.

The word 'small' refers not so much to the physical size of the states in question, but rather to their political weight within the Reich. This was determined by a combination of the status of the ruler, the resources of his territories and their strategic position.

Surveying the Reich in 1700, only one state could be described as 'large'. This was the conglomerate of Habsburg territories collectively known as Austria. After the successful conquest of Hungary (1683–99), Austria had taken its position as the second European superpower alongside France. However, this conquest had begun the process of the shifting of Habsburg interests outside the Reich and the subordination of their role as emperor to their *Hauspolitik* (dynastic policy). This process continued throughout the eighteenth century.

---

[2] Quoted in E. Marquardt, *Geschichte Württemberg* (Stuttgart, 1985 edn), p. 208. For bureaucratic loyalty see B. Wunder, *Privilegierung und Disziplinierung: Die Entstehung des Berufsbeamtentums in Bayern und Württemberg 1780–1825* (Munich, 1978), pp. 36–91.

[3] Hintze, 'Military organization'; G. Papke in *HDM*, I, p. 209. For these private contractors see Redlich, *German military enterpriser*.

[4] The Württemberg dukes regularly spoke of the regiments as their 'property' (*Eigenthum*). In the *Articuls-Brieff* of 25 June 1727 the soldiers swore an oath to Eberhard Ludwig 'als Ihren FeldHerrn, und Unsern Land und Leuthen getreu und hold zu seyn'. Under Carl Eugen (*Kriegsartikeln*, 11 Feb. 1758 and 1 Jan. 1769) this formula was reduced simply to loyalty to 'Sr. Herzoglichen Durchlaucht zu Württemberg'. The Kreistruppen swore on the basis of the *Articuls-Brieff* of 15/25 Oct. 1694 and 21 Nov. 1710 loyalty to the 'Fürsten und Ständen des Hoch: Löblichen Schwäbischen Crayses': HSAS, A30c: Bü. 1 and 2; A202: Bü 2302. The prince was also supreme commander: see F. Hossbach, *Die Entwicklung des Oberbefehls über das Heer in Brandenburg. Preussen und im Deutschen Reich von 1655–1945. Ein kurzer Überblick* (Würzburg, 1957).

The other states fall roughly into three categories: medium, small and minor. The boundaries between these groupings were blurred and in a constant state of flux. The members of a particular category were not completely identical in status and influence. Moreover, it should be stressed that this categorisation is based on the modern criteria of power politics and not on contemporary legal theory which assigned the states quite a different order of precedence. The categories do, however, accord with the way outsiders were beginning to view the internal power balance of the Reich.[5]

The medium states in 1700 were five in number: Brandenburg-Prussia, Hanover, Saxony, Bavaria and the Palatinate. All owed their importance to their status as electorates and to their resources.[6] During the course of the century, Brandenburg-Prussia was to rise to major-power status, while the others barely managed to maintain their existing positions. Below this group was the small state category, headed by the three ecclesiastical electorates: Mainz, Cologne and Trier. These owed their importance to their status as electorates rather than to their resources, though Cologne was temporarily powerful through the simultaneous holding of other bishoprics (chiefly Münster) by its archbishop.[7] Roughly equal to these were the duchy of Württemberg and the landgraviate of Hessen-Kassel. Although larger in terms of resources than the three archbishop-electors, both lacked their electoral status. Below them in terms of importance came a series of states which were hard put to keep up. These were primarily: Hessen-Darmstadt, Brunswick-Wolfenbüttel, Baden and Ansbach-Bayreuth (after their respective unifications in 1771 and 1769), Holstein and Mecklenburg and Saxon duchies. Of these, Holstein and Mecklenburg had effectively ceased to keep pace by about 1720, because of internal squabbles and the adverse influence of their more powerful neighbours. Finally, there was the mass of minor states which, although numerous, were politically of little weight. Of these, Zweibrücken, Waldeck and the archbishopric of Salzburg were perhaps the most important. Collectively, these medium, small and minor states are sometimes described as a 'third Germany' alongside the two major powers, Prussia and Austria.

The dynastic and political ambitions of this third Germany roughly fall into three categories: preservation of the dynasty, defence of existing possessions, and increase in status and territory. Obviously, here too there were overlaps between the categories. However, for our purposes, this categorisation is sufficient.

---

[5] For example, France in 1748: O. C. Ebbecke, *Frankreichs Politik gegenüber dem deutschen Reiche in den Jahren 1748–1756* (Freiburg i. Br., Ph.D., printed 1931), pp. 27–41.

[6] The old Reich was not a hereditary monarchy. Instead, the emperor was chosen by those princes with the electoral title (*Kurwürde*).

[7] The formal legal structure of the Reich gave the elector of Mainz second place to the emperor himself. This was not without practical political influence, see T. C. W. Blanning, *Reform and revolution in Mainz 1743–1802* (Cambridge, 1974), pp. 46–8.

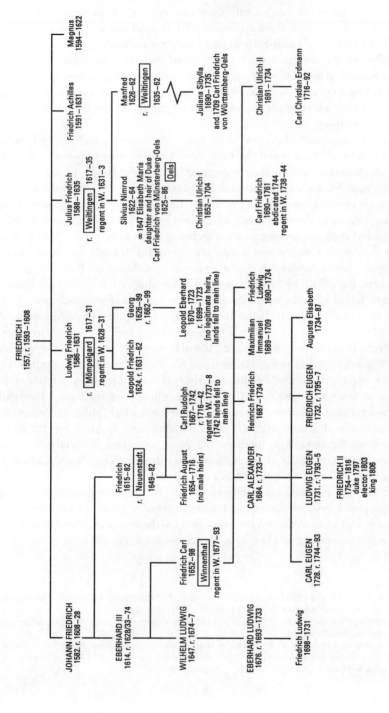

Fig. 1: A simplified family tree of the House of Württemberg

Princely aims and policy-making

PRESERVATION OF THE DYNASTY

Preservation of the dynasty almost always featured in major policy decisions as it directly concerned the prince's own family. The Pragmatic Sanction is perhaps the most outstanding example of how this aim could affect a state's entire foreign policy.[8] The numerous wars of succession between 1655 and 1778 provide other examples. Survival of the dynasty was important, because it secured not only the material well-being of the eldest son and heir, but also that of the other family members and their servants.

A judicious marriage policy represented the best method of securing dynastic survival and generally advancing family fortunes. No dynasty could escape the grim realities of early modern demography. Failure to produce an heir or simply live long enough opened the door to political instability, succession disputes and all the dangers inherent in a regency. The experience of Württemberg, especially the weak regency of 1737–44, provides a good example of just how far dynastic ambition could be set back by such misfortunes.

However, over-profligacy raised the problems of how to provide for additional family members. The traditional method of dividing the territory among all sons and heirs had created the fragmented pattern that so characterised the Reich and hindered the development of the territories as modern states. To counter this, the princes had begun to adopt the law of primogeniture. Württemberg introduced this relatively early, in 1482, and had it confirmed in imperial law in 1495 when the territory was raised to the status of a duchy. However, primogeniture complicated the task of providing for the material well-being of junior family members. As existing territory could no longer be alienated, additional land had to be acquired to provide them with a status and income appropriate to their noble birth. Land was in short supply and correspondingly expensive. The increasing difficulty encountered in acquiring it is illustrated by the genealogy of the six Württemberg lines which existed in 1700[9] (see fig. 1).

The senior line ruled the duchy itself. The next two most senior branches were created in 1617 by Duke Johann Friedrich (1608–28) to provide for his two brothers who could not inherit Württemberg itself. Ludwig Friedrich was given the county of Mömpelgard (Montbéliard) on the left bank of the Rhine which had always been considered separate from the duchy, while Julius Friedrich was

---

[8] The Pragmatic Sanction was a special decree passed by Emperor Charles VI designed to ensure the inheritance of Habsburg possessions in the female as well as the male line. See W. Brauneder, 'Die Pragmatisch Sanktion – das Grundgesetz der Monarchia Austriaca', in K. Gutkas (ed.), *Prinz Eugen und das barocke Österreich* (Salzburg/Vienna, 1985), pp. 141–50.

[9] On these problems see B. Wunder, 'Der Administrator Herzog Friedrich Karl von Württemberg (1652–1698)', *ZWLG*, 30 (1971), 117–63 at pp. 117–19; Vann, *Making of a state*, pp. 139–41. On this genealogy see R. Uhland, 'Die Genealogien des Hauses Württemberg', in Uhland (ed.), *900 Jahr Haus Württemberg* (Stuttgart, 1985 edn), pp. 397–411.

assigned the fief Weiltingen which had been bought in 1616.[10] A fourth line was created in 1649 when Duke Eberhard III (1628/33–74) gave his younger brother the revenues and lesser jurisdiction of the district of Neuenstadt.[11] This method was nominally in compliance with the law of primogeniture as the Neuenstadt line was not fully sovereign. Nonetheless, it weakened the capital base of the duchy and was ruled out for future generations by Eberhard himself in his wills of 1653 and 1664. Just how difficult it had become by the late seventeenth century to purchase adequate land is demonstrated by the creation of the fifth line on Eberhard's death in 1674. All that was available for the late duke's second son was the castle of Winnenthal which had been bought from the Teutonic Knights in 1665.[12] The creation of the sixth line in 1649 was a happy accident that occurred all too seldom: a junior member of the Weiltingen branch inherited the duchy of Oels in Silesia upon the extinction of the previous male line.[13]

These difficulties forced the princes to find some other way to provide for the material well-being of junior sons. The standard practice among Catholic families was to engineer the election of their offspring to high church posts. As bishops, even as lowly abbots, they would become independent princes of the Reich in their own right. This was, for example, a long-established practice of the Bavarian Wittelsbachs. However, it ran up against competition from the families of imperial knights (*Reichsritter*) who were pursuing similar aims. Further, this possibility was closed to a Protestant house such as that of Württemberg.[14]

The next best path lay in military service, either in the army of a more powerful prince – usually the emperor – or as an independent 'military enterpriser'. Not only was such service a traditional and respected occupation for those of noble birth, it also offered the possibility of lucrative financial reward which would enable the purchase of territory. It was also not unknown for great potentates such as the emperor to make gifts of such territory outright to successful generals. For example, Marlborough was given the Bavarian lordship of Mindelheim in 1706 and so became, like the duke of Württemberg, an estate of the Swabian Kreis. Two years previously, the victorious General Ludwig Wilhelm von Baden-Baden was enfiefed

---

[10] Mömpelgard had been ruled by a line founded in 1553 by Duke Friedrich I's father. It had 56,000 inhabitants at the end of the old Reich. Weiltingen had been bought in 1616 and in 1787 had 832 inhabitants. The line also ruled the district of Brenz (733 inhabitants). On its extinction in 1705 these lands returned to the senior line.

[11] This line had the districts of Neuenstadt, Mockmühl and half of Weinsberg (total population in 1787: *c.* 12,140), and died out in 1742.

[12] For details of this inheritance, see Vann, *Making of a state*, p. 139 n. 16. On the death of Eberhard Ludwig (1733) the senior Württemberg line died out and Carl Alexander of the Winnenthal branch became duke.

[13] The territory of the Oels branch covered 1,650 km² with 70,000 inhabitants. On this branch see H. Schukraft, 'Die Linie Württemberg–Oels', in Uhland (ed.), *900 Jahre Haus Württemberg*, pp. 379–89.

[14] L. G. Duggan, 'The church as an institution of the Reich', in J. A. Vann and S. W. Rowan (eds.), *The old Reich. Essays on German political institutions 1495–1806* (Brussels, 1974), pp. 149–64.

with the Ortenau. It is, therefore, not surprising that virtually all the twenty-two junior sons of the main Württemberg line born in the seventeenth century followed this path.[15]

This form of military activity gave a considerable impetus to the development of standing armies within the small states as the discussion of the Regent Friedrich Carl (1677–93) and Duke Carl Alexander (1733–7) will show. It also provided the emperor with an opportunity to exert pressure on these states through his monopoly of appointments to the Austrian and imperial armies (*Reichsarmee*), and his considerable influence within the church.

In the case of Württemberg, the emperor also had considerable influence over the duchy derived directly from the establishment of primogeniture. In his recognition of the indivisibility of the duchy in 1495, the emperor had proclaimed Württemberg an imperial fief (*Reichslehen*) which would fall to his free disposition if the ruling house died out. In 1534 and 1552 the dukes had been forced to recognise the transference of these claims from the emperor in his capacity as head of the Reich to him as head of the House of Habsburg: a small but important distinction. Although the duke managed to buy off part of the Austrian claim at great expense in 1599, the threat of disinheritance of the rest of the family in the event of the extinction of the male line still had a considerable effect on Württemberg policy and provided a convenient pressure point for Austrian influence.[16]

DEFENCE OF EXISTING POSSESSIONS

A second important policy aim was defence of existing titles and possessions. This was taken seriously, as defence of his subjects was considered a major reason for a prince's existence and justification for absolute rule. The lessons of the Thirty Years War proved that the best means of defence lay in a permanent force of professional soldiers. As has already been indicated at the start of this chapter, it has often been said that the Reich worked as a protective structure, enabling the small states to dispense with such forces. This is somewhat misleading, as in many ways this structure encouraged them to raise and maintain troops in the first place.

The organisation of the Reichsarmee in 1681 made each state directly responsible for raising and maintaining a fixed quota of soldiers which would combine with

---

[15] Wunder, 'Der Administrator', 119.
[16] The districts of Neuenburg, Beilstein and Bottwar were in any case fiefs of the kingdom of Bohemia, a Habsburg possession since 1526. The district of Blaubeuren was a fief of their county of the Tirol while other smaller parts of Württemberg were fiefs of their Austrian lordship of Hohenburg in Swabia. Under the 1599 agreement the Habsburgs retained a claim (*Anwartschaft*) on the rest of Württemberg. On these complexities see P. L. H. Röder, *Geographie und Statistik Wirtembergs* (2 vols., Laibach in Krain/Ulm, 1787–1804), I, pp. 137–40; A. Dehlinger, *Württembergs Staatswesen in seiner geschichtlichen Entwicklung bis heute* (2 vols., Stuttgart, 1951–53), I, pp. 39–41.

other contingents to form the various regiments of the Reichsarmee. Power to supervise and co-ordinate this was devolved from the central organs of the Reich (Reichstag and emperor) to the intermediate level of the imperial circles (*Reichskreise*). These had originally been established in the early sixteenth century to oversee maintenance of law and order. While this system had been developing prior to 1681, the ordinances passed by the Reichstag in that year consolidated it and gave a considerable boost to the development of the Kreise.[17] The emperor was merely left with the appointment of the Reichsarmee's general staff and direction of its military operations. These were to be financed by the payment of contributions called Roman months (*Römer Monate*) based on a scale drawn up in 1521.[18]

As this was a collective system of defence it was only effective when at least the majority of the member states co-operated and refrained from following their own interests. As the larger ones such as Brandenburg-Prussia and Hanover almost immediately refused to co-operate fully, it was left to the smaller states to make the system work. This was done by seeking closer ties with those Kreise where the system had not already broken down completely. These ties were cemented in the associations (*Associationen*) of two or more Kreise providing for military co-operation. Significantly it was the Swabian and Franconian Kreise – the two where territorial fragmentation was most pronounced – that were the driving force behind the Associationen of the late seventeenth and early eighteenth centuries.[19] Further, it was their decision in 1694 to retain at least part of their forces permanently in peace as well as wartime that led to the introduction of standing forces in many of the small states for the first time. These forces were the so-called *Kreistruppen* which thereafter existed alongside the household troops (*Haustruppen*) of the prince. Only the very small states continued the

---

[17] For an overview of these developments see G. Papke in *HDM*, I, pp. 236–56; M. Jähns, 'Zur Geschichte der Kriegsverfassung des deutschen Reiches', *PJb*, 39 (1877), 1–28, 114–40, 443–90. For regional studies see B. Sicken, *Das Wehrwesen des fränkischen Reichskreises. Aufbau und Struktur (1681–1714)* (2 vols., Würzburg Ph.D., printed Nuremberg, 1967); P. C. Storm, *Der schwäbische Kreis als Feldherr. Untersuchungen zur Wehrverfassung des schwäbischen Reichskreises in der Zeit von 1648–1732* (Berlin, 1974). For an example of pre-1681 developments see H. Forst, 'Die deutschen Reichstruppen im Türkenkriege 1664', *Mitteilungen des Instituts für österreichische Geschichtsforschung, Ergänzungsband*, 6 (1901), 635–48. For the eighteenth century see A. G. W. Kohlhepp, *Die Militärverfassung des deutschen Reiches zur Zeit des siebenjährigen Krieges* (Greifswald Ph.D., printed Stralsund, 1914).

[18] This scale was called the *Wormser Matrikel* and is printed in G. Schreiber, *Der badische Wehrstand seit dem 17. Jahrhundert bis zu Ende der französischen Revolutionskriege* (Karlsruhe, 1849), pp. 47–61. The scale expressed each territory's troop contingent in monetary terms counting one horseman as 12fl. and one footsoldier as 4fl. On this basis, one Römer Monat was nominally 129,280fl. of which Württemberg (60 horse, 277 foot) was liable for 1,838fl. In practice in the eighteenth century the duchy paid only 1,400fl.

[19] G. Papke, *HDM*, I, pp. 246–53; R. Fester, *Die armirten Ständen und die Reichskriegsverfassung 1681–1697* (Frankfurt am Main, 1886).

old practice, whereby the princely bodyguard served as the Kreistruppen in wartime.[20]

The Associationen were an expression of the idea of *Reichspatriotismus*, a concept which embraced the protective and preserving character of the Reich. Reichspatriotismus implied loyalty to the Reich and to the emperor as its head, but not to him as head of the House of Habsburg. This important distinction was often missed by nineteenth-century historians, who saw champions of Reichspatriotismus such as Bishop Friedrich Carl von Schönborn as advocates of a strong, centralised Reich under Austrian leadership. In fact, their support for the emperor was qualified by the proviso that he did not disturb the system of checks and balances established by the Peace of Westphalia of 1648. When he appeared to be doing so in order to advance Austrian interests, they did not hesitate to oppose him by calling on the support of the guarantors of the Peace (France and Sweden) as in the Rhenish Alliance of 1658–68.

The system they were seeking to defend was one that protected the weak against the strong and guaranteed the rights of each constituent member against arbitrary action.[21] These 'members' included not only what we have termed the 'states', but also the territorial estates within them and indeed virtually any region, town, guild or special group that had privileges or 'liberties' guaranteed in charters recognised somewhere in the complex of imperial law. These charters shielded the vested interests of each from encroachments of those further up the hierarchy. Therefore, just as the territorial estates were protected from arbitrary action by their prince, the prince was protected from the acquisitiveness of his larger neighbours.

This gave the system considerable strength as it ensured a multitude of opportunities for appeal and intervention and made defence of one's own interests identical with preserving the liberties of others. An example of this was the intervention of Hanover and Brunswick in 1719 to prevent the duke of Mecklenburg from crushing the local autonomy of his towns and nobility. In doing so, these states not only saved this autonomy from destruction, but simultaneously prevented the duke from developing as a rival to their territorial expansion.

However, within the very element that gave the system its strength lay the roots of its ultimate collapse. All the princes were to a greater or lesser extent trying to emancipate themselves from the restraints placed on their power by the autonomy

---

[20] On the nature of these obligations see Wilson, 'The power to defend, or the defence of power: the conflict between duke and estates over defence provision, Württemberg 1677–1793', *Parliaments, Estates and Representation*, 12 (1992), 25–45 at pp. 28–30.

[21] The literature on this system is now extensive. For good introductions see J. Sheehan, *German history 1770–1866* (Oxford, 1989), pp. 11–41; J. G. Gagliardo, *Reich and nation: the Holy Roman Empire as idea and reality 1763–1806* (Bloomington, 1980), chs. 1–3; Hughes, *Early modern Germany*, pp. 114–38; H. Duchhardt, *Deutsche Verfassungsgeschichte 1495–1806* (Stuttgart, 1991), pp. 143–259.

of their territorial estates and other privileged groups. In order to do so they ultimately had to free themselves from the Reich itself as this protected that autonomy. Already in 1648 the electors had secured the right of *non appellando* and so prevented the potential opposition groups within their territories from appealing to the imperial courts when their liberties were curtailed. Other princes also tried to obtain such rights. However, it is within the area of the Reich's military system rather than its legal structure that this development had the most serious consequences. This manifested itself in two ways.

First, the Reichspatriotismus, that is the loyalty of the Reichsstände to this system, was always limited by the proviso that their support for it did not involve them in great expense or endanger their own defence. As early as 1700 this characterised the attitude of the Swabian Kreis towards the question of common defence, and this was to grow more pronounced as the century wore on.[22] A typical example of this was the refusal of most of the princes to contribute to the upkeep of the two imperial fortresses, Kehl and Philippsburg, on the grounds that, as these lay far from their own borders, they were of no use to them.

This reluctance to contribute to the common cause was least pronounced among the ecclesiastical states and the imperial knights and cities precisely because these benefited most from the system. Ever since the Reformation, the ecclesiastical princes had feared secularisation by their secular neighbours, and these fears grew after 1648 when this actually occurred with a number of bishoprics. The imperial knights and cities also feared the incorporation (*Mediatisierung*) of their possessions into the expanding territorial states. As the system guaranteed their continued existence, they, together with the ecclesiastics, tended to feature prominently among the supporters of the imperial ideal.[23]

Second, Reichspatriotismus provided a convenient vehicle for the furtherance of dynastic ambitions. The appropriation of the cause of 'imperial liberties' by Frederick II of Prussia to oppose Austria is already well known.[24] Previously overlooked, however, has been the manipulation of the Reich's military system by the small states to build up their standing armies. These states were quick to make use of the eagerness of their even smaller neighbours to pay cash rather than provide their contingents to the Reichsarmee. These payments, called *Relutionen*, were then used to hire troops to take the place of the missing contingent. Such money provided a golden opportunity for princes such as the dukes of Württemberg and Celle (Hanover), whose estates consistently refused to provide sufficient funds to

---

[22] R. Gebauer, *Die Außenpolitik der schwäbischen Reichskreises vor Ausbruch des spanischen Erbfolgekrieges (1697–1702)* (Marburg Ph.D., printed 1969), p. 178.

[23] Duggan, 'The church'; V. Press, 'Der württembergische Angriff auf die Reichsritterschaft 1749–1754 (1770)', in F. Quartal (ed.), *Zwischen Schwarzwald und Schwäbischer Alb* (Sigmaringen, 1984), pp. 329–48, esp. pp. 329–36; K. S. Bader, 'Die Reichsstädte des schwäbischen Kreises am Ende des Alten Reiches', *Ulm und Oberschwaben*, 32 (1951), 47–70.

[24] See pp. 104–5.

raise large armies.[25] These armies were necessary if the princes were to be able to achieve the coveted status of 'armed estate' (*Armierter Stand*).[26] This status entitled their territories to dispensation from quartering of Reichsarmee and Austrian soldiers, on the grounds that they were already contributing enough to the common cause by providing an army of their own. Such a dispensation was of considerable value, because the quartering of foreign troops was a considerable burden. Apart from the impairment of a prince's pretensions to sovereignty by having foreign troops over which he had no control quartered on his territory, such troops were notoriously bad at paying for the food and accommodation they received. In addition, by having an armed force at his disposal, a prince was able to make alliances that enhanced the defence of his territory and helped him achieve his other political aims.

Paradoxically, although the princes were keen to exploit the system of common defence to further their own ends because it was useful to them, they were also interested in ensuring it functioned efficiently. Not only would their territories benefit from the better protection provided by the Reichsarmee, but this army also gave them lucrative command posts for themselves and their sons. Thus, the dukes of Württemberg, for example, were always eager to ensure that the institutions of the Swabian Kreis functioned smoothly and were even prepared occasionally to abide by decisions of the Kreis Assembly (*Kreistag* or *Konvent*) that went against their interests.[27] However, when the effect of the Kreis as a restraining element on their dynastic ambitions began to outweigh the advantages it offered them, they gradually lost interest in it; in 1757 Carl Eugen failed to provide half of his contingent of Kreistruppen, as he needed the money for the Haustruppen which better served his interests. With the total disbandment of Württemberg's contingent in 1763, the Swabian Kreistruppen effectively ceased to exist as the others followed the duchy's example.[28] Although the troops were re-formed at the start of the Revolutionary Wars, Württemberg became increasingly dissatisfied as the Kreis majority involved the duchy in a war it did not want to fight. After the

[25] For Celle's provision of Mecklenburg's contingent between 1677 and 1697 see G. Tessin, *Mecklenburgisches Militär in Türken und Franzosenkriegen 1648–1718* (*Mitteldeutsche Forschungen*, 42 (Cologne/Graz, 1966), pp. 25–9. For Württemberg see pp. 118 and 171–2 below.

[26] Fester, *Die armirten Stände*, pp. 23–31.

[27] For examples see Vann, *Swabian Kreis* and pp. 136, 148–9 below. On the Kreistag see Storm, *Feldherr*, pp. 128–50. On the structure of the Swabian Kreis see also F. Kallenberg, 'Spätzeit und Ende des Schwäbischen Kreises', *Jahrbuch für Geschichte der oberdeutschen Reichsstädte*, 14 (1968), 61–93.

[28] HSAS, A8: Bü 8; A202: Bd. 154–215; C14; Bü. 77, 87/I, 87/II, 87a, 530a, 568. This fact has previously been completely overlooked in the Württemberg literature. The duchy's cavalry contingent (half of the Swabian DR Württemberg) was entirely disbanded in April 1763 while the infantry (86 per cent of Swaiban IR Württemberg) became the Haus IR Augé, which was disbanded in August 1765. The two Swabian regiments continued nominally to exist, because a few of the other contributory territories, such as the imperial city of Heilbronn (for the cavalry), still maintained their contingents and because Carl Eugen still appointed officers to the non-existent Württemberg contingent.

bishop of Constance had successfully blocked his attempts to hijack the Kreis as a vehicle for Württemberg Hauspolitik, the duke finally followed the lead of the larger states a century before and *de facto* seceded. Just as the withdrawal of Hanover and Brandenburg from the Lower and Upper Saxon Kreise respectively had led to the collapse of these as effective institutions, the secession of Württemberg signalled the end of the Swabian Kreis.[29] Immediately after the withdrawal of the duchy's military contingent in 1796, the remaining Kreistruppen were disarmed by the Austrians.[30] Although the Kreis remained in existence until the final collapse of the Reich ten years later, it had effectively ceased to function.

INCREASE IN STATUS AND TERRITORY

It is now time to turn to the third category of princely ambitions, namely the desire for increased status and territory. It has often been said that the lesser princes of the Reich lacked such ambitions. This was not the case. Not only were they just as ambitious as their larger neighbours, they were also consistent to the point of obduracy.

The Württemberg dukes were no exception to this. Underlying their seemingly changeable, often erratic, policies was a set of consistent political goals. While these varied in detail from time to time, the basic components remained unchanged for all three dukes that feature in this study. By an increase in status they envisaged an elevation from duke to elector which would give them a greater say in imperial politics. Their main rival, the landgrave of Hessen-Kassel, wanted the same, as did the bishops of Augsburg and Würzburg, who put in a claim for the Bavarian electoral title during the War of the Spanish Succession. Two of the three Württemberg dukes were not prepared to stop at just that. Eberhard Ludwig tried in 1711 to crown himself 'King of Franconia' with French assistance, while between 1758 and 1759 Carl Eugen sounded out the possibility of being made king of Poland.[31] Again they were not alone in having such ambitions. Margrave Ludwig Wilhelm von Baden-Baden (1677–1707), the famous Türkenlouis, had tried to buy his election as king of Poland in 1697. At the very time that Carl Eugen was intriguing in Warsaw, his rival the landgrave was doing the same.[32] Even more extreme than these schemes was the plan of Max Emanuel of Bavaria (1679–1726)

[29] Borck, *Schwäbische Reichskreis*, pp. 68–250.

[30] H. Hahn, 'Das Ende des schwäbischen Kreiskontingents', *Zeitschrift für Heereskunde*, 37 (1973), 52–7, 123–31; A. von Schempp, 'Die Entwaffnung und Auflösung des schwäbischen Kreiskorps am 29. Juli 1796', *BBSAW*, 14 (1911), 209–15.

[31] For Württemberg see Chapters 4–8; Ingrao, *Hessian mercenary state*, pp. 125–6; B. Wunder, 'Die französisch–Württembergischen Geheimverhandlungen 1711', *ZWLG*, 28 (1969), 363–90; HSAS, G230: Bü. 54.

[32] HSAS, A74: Bü. 147, rescript to Legationsrat Straube 21 Oct., 13 Nov. 1763; Ingrao, *Hessian mergenary state*, p. 126. The Württemberg representative was Ernst Friedrich von Heimenthal, who was Hessian ambassador to the Franconian Kreis.

to exchange his electorate for part of the inheritance of the Spanish Habsburgs as long as this included a royal crown. His cousin, Johann Wilhelm of the Palatinate (1685–90), whose sisters were already queens in Madrid, Lisbon and Vienna, dreamt of becoming king of Armenia, having failed to win the Polish crown.

Although such plans appear as wild dreams to modern eyes, they were considered by contemporaries to be realisable. Moreover, there were sufficient precedents to prove this. In 1692 the duke of Calenberg had been raised to elector of Hanover by the emperor despite considerable opposition from neighbouring princes. Ten years later, the emperor gave the Brandenburg elector permission to call himself 'King in Prussia', while the Saxon electors managed twice to make themselves kings of Poland (1697, 1733). By successful marriage policies, Elector George Louis of Hanover succeeded to the English crown in 1714, while Landgrave Friedrich I von Hessen-Kassel became king of Sweden six years later. Even Carl Gustav of tiny Pfalz-Zweibrücken had become a king, also of Sweden, in 1654. Finally and perhaps most spectacular of all, Elector Charles Albert of Bavaria (1726–45) actually became emperor between 1742 and 1745, albeit only with French support.

The reason for all attempts was not only the inflated self-importance of the princes, though this undoubtedly played a part. The new titles helped to increase their political influence both within the Reich and within Europe. In particular, a foreign crown, that is a kingdom outside the borders of the Reich, provided additional support for a prince's original territory. This was true even if a prince did not have actual possession of that crown, but was only linked by marriage to it. One of the reasons why Württemberg survived Napoleon's reorganisation of Germany while Hessen-Kassel did not is to be found in the former's ties to the Russian royal family.[33] The same is true for the Swabian branch of the Hohenzollerns, who survived thanks to their cousins in Prussia.

Closely associated with these attempts were the efforts of princes such as the Württemberg dukes to revive defunct rights and privileges. This showed their continued interest in the institutions of the Reich, an interest that lasted up to the very end in 1806. Characteristic of the Württemberg attempts are the duke's efforts to revive their Reichstag vote for the duchy of Teck and use their title as 'Imperial Standard Bearer' (*Reichsbannerträger*) as the basis for their claims to be made elector.[34]

One of the consequences of these attempts was a temporary revival in the power and influence of the emperor. As the emperor's agreement was necessary for an

[33] On these ties see H. M. Maurer, 'Das Haus Württemberg und Rußland', *ZWLG*, 48 (1989), 201–22.
[34] G. Richter, 'Die württembergischen Reichstagsstimmen von der Erhebung zum Herzogtum bis zum Ende des alten Reiches. Ein Beitrag zur Frage der Reichsstandschaft von Württemberg, Mömpelgard und Teck', *ZWLG*, 23 (1964), 345–73; W. Burr, 'Die Reichssturmfahne und der Streit um die hannoversche Kurwürde', *ibid.*, 27 (1968), 245–316; E. Schneider, 'Die württembergische Reichssturmfahne', *WVJHLG*, NF30 (1921), 30–5.

increase in status or the recognition of a defunct privilege, the princes were forced to court his favour. Just how the emperor used this to advance Austrian interests will become apparent in the course of the following chapters.

The princes also needed the emperor's co-operation in their desire for territorial increase. Here the second and third ranking were also scarcely less ambitious than aggressive potentates such as the king of Prussia. Chiefly, they were interested in both a 'rounding-off' (*Arrondierung*) of their existing territories at the expense of the imperial knights and cities and in a substantial increase through acquisition of additional regions. Again, in this the dukes of Württemberg were no exception. Although attempts to build a 'land bridge' across the Black Forest between the duchy of Mömpelgard had come to nothing in the confusion of the Thirty Years War, they had not given up hopes of territorial acquisition within Swabia. Eberhard Ludwig tried to gain the Bavarian lordship of Wiesensteig out of the War of the Spanish Succession.[35] His successor Carl Alexander hoped for the cession of Austrian territory in return for his support of the emperor between 1733 and 1735.[36] Prior to the Seven Years War (1756–63), Carl Eugen attempted a rounding-off of his territory at the expense of the imperial knights.[37] Eberhard Ludwig had attempted the same in the 1710s.[38] During the war he wanted the incorporation of imperial cities, including Nuremberg, into his duchy and pressed to be enfiefed with the Reichslehen Ortenau.[39] His contemporaries were no less ambitious.[40]

Just how doggedly the lesser German dynasties pursued these wild ambitions despite continued failure is revealed by the way they seized every chance, no matter how unrealistic, to press them. Even in the twilight of monarchical Germany during the First World War, all the old schemes resurfaced, including a plan for a Bavarian kingdom of Belgium and a Württemberg Polish crown.[41]

---

[35] HSAS, A202: Bü. 2101–4.

[36] HSAS, A74: Bü. 114, 117, reports of Regierungs Räte Zech and Keller 1735–36; E. Schneider, *Württembergische Geschichte* (Stuttgart, 1896), p. 346.

[37] Press, 'Angriff auf die Reichsritterschaft', pp. 336–48. For the completion of his policy under King Friedrich I, see T. Schulz, 'Die Mediatisierung des Kantons Kocher. Ein Beitrag zur Geschichte der Reichsritterschaft am Ende des alten Reiches', *ZWLG*, 47 (1988), 323–57.

[38] Neipperg, *Kaiser und Schwäbischer Kreis*, pp. 53–7.

[39] HSAS, A74, Bü. 145: rescript to Straube, 28 Oct. 1761 and his report 7 Nov.; A. Brabant, *Das heilige römische Reich teutscher Nation im Kampf mit Friedrich dem Großen* (3 vols., Berlin, 1904–31), II, pp. 41–2; A. Schäffer, *Geschichte des siebenjährigen Krieges* (2 vols. in 3, Berlin, 1867–74), I, p. 665.

[40] For example see H. Gerspacher, *Die badische Politik im siebenjährigen Kriege* (*Heidelberger Abhandlungen zur mittleren und neuren Geschichte*, 67, Heidelberg, 1934), pp. 42–76, 98; A. Stoffers, 'Das Hochstift Paderborn zur Zeit des siebenjährigen Krieges', *Zeitschrift für vaterländische Geschichte und Altertumskunde Westfalens*, 69 (1911), 1–90 at p. 30; L. Hüttl, 'Die österreichisch–bayerischen Beziehungen in Zeitalter des Prinzen Eugen', in J. Kunisch (ed.), *Prinz Eugen und seine Zeit* (Freiburg/Würzburg, 1986), pp. 128, 133, 137. In 1607 Bavaria had annexed the imperial city of Donauwörth.

[41] K. H. Janssen, *Macht und Verblendung: Kriegzielpolitik der deutschen Bundesstaaten 1914–1918* (Göttingen, 1963).

That these schemes all came to nothing – Prussia's seizure of Silesia in 1740 is really the only exception – demonstrates just how effective the system of the Reich was in preserving the status quo. This is underlined by what happened when it ceased to function after the impact of the French Revolution and the mounting Austro-Prussian dualism. Once Austrian protection for the traditional imperial clients – the knights, the cities and bishoprics – was removed, these fell prey to the territorial states between 1803 and 1806. Under these circumstances all the traditional Württemberg aims were achieved by Carl Eugen's nephew, Friedrich, but only at the expense of helping to destroy the Reich.[42] In participating in this, the small states such as Württemberg ultimately brought about their own loss of political independence. Although a similar system of checks and balances was attempted in the German Confederation established in 1814, it lacked the unique characteristics that had made that of the old Reich work. Still militarily and politically weak in relative terms, the successors to the old small states were powerless to prevent the growth of Prussian domination in 1866–71.

---

[42] Duke Friedrich (1797–1816) became elector in 1803 and king in 1806. Between 1803 and 1810 he increased his territory by 10,675 km² to 19,513.6 km² at the expense of seventy-eight other political entities and most of the Swabian imperial knights.

2

Strategies and resources

STRATEGIES FOR DYNASTIC ADVANCEMENT

As long as the Reich remained intact, few of the German princes had the power to secure their dynastic goals by force alone. Force achieved significant, permanent territorial adjustment on only two occasions after 1648. The first was in 1715–21 when both Prussia and Hanover profited from Sweden's collapse in the Great Northern War (1700–21) by seizing most of its territory in north Germany. The second was the Prussian annexation of Austrian Silesia in 1740. Both took place under exceptional circumstances and benefited major rather than minor German states. The first example involved the expulsion of a foreign power from Reich territory and occurred in north Germany, far from the centre of imperial influence and at a time when the emperor was in any case distracted in the Balkans and Italy. The second was achieved during the unique period of the imperial interregnum of 1740–2 and at a time of acute Austrian weakness. It also involved vast military and diplomatic effort and nearly led to Prussia's destruction during Austrian attempts to recover Silesia in the Seven Years War (1756–63). Both Bavaria and Saxony were ruined in similar attempts to use force at various times between 1700 and 1745. Smaller states stood no chance whatsoever.

The lack of success is striking testimony to the strength of the old Reich. It is also a legacy of the Thirty Years War which left a deep impression on the German consciousness.[1] The use of violence to achieve political ends was not only costly and invited overwhelming retaliation; it also had unpredictable consequences. Once unleashed in 1618, the conflict rapidly spun out of control. The complex internal structure of the Reich encouraged a chain reaction, sucking ever more states into the fray. While some had made significant gains, it was only at enormous cost. Most took decades to recover from the damage. Moreover, the lesson for the weaker states was clear. Internal conflict rendered the Reich inoperative. Without its protection there was little to defend them from the depredations of foreign armies and acquisitive neighbours. Thus, in the period after 1648 the lesser princes had to develop a strategy that would allow them to achieve their ambitions without

---

[1] Hughes, *Early modern Germany*, pp. 98–100; G. Parker et al., *The Thirty Years War* (London, 1987), pp. 191–226.

destroying the protective framework of the Reich. What was required was an adjustment in their favour that would leave the system intact and deny similar advantages to their rivals. In the conditions after 1648 such adjustments could only be made with the active co-operation of the emperor. Only he retained sufficient influence to alter the system without calling its continued existence into question. Even then, changes could be made only after careful preparation and negotiation with influential parties. Imperial politics encouraged compromise and consensus. The basis for change had to be accepted by at least a significant number of the key players within the system. In particular, the claimant had to appear more worthy than potential rivals in order to take precedence and forestall their appeals for preferment. These calculations can be seen during Hanover's elevation to electoral status, which took sixteen years to complete (1692–1708). The achievement of political ambition thus became a question of image and persuasion, rather than of force and violence.

This took place against a background of the 'internationalisation' of imperial politics.[2] The Peace of Westphalia which ended the Thirty Years War was not just a German settlement, but part of an international system. The presence of two foreign guarantors, France and Sweden, linked the Reich's internal structure to questions of European diplomacy. This tendency was reinforced by the growing number of ties between German dynasties and European crowns. Alterations to the Reich's internal balance could affect these international connections. Thus, the emperor was not the only power the princes had to please, even if he remained the most important.

Compelled to act on both a German and an international stage, the lesser German princes needed an appropriate image in order to be taken seriously. It was vital, otherwise their representatives would be refused admission to the conference table, or left waiting in the ministerial antechamber, and their correspondence would remain unanswered. This explains their obsession with status, prestige and precedence, which has often been the subject of ridicule and indeed was so at the time outside Germany.[3] To achieve the desired image, many princes set about creating what Carl Eugen's chief minister, Count Montmartin, was to term an 'imposing state' (*staatliche Verfassung*). He defined this as a large court, a powerful army and well-ordered finances.[4] The first attracted attention, created the image of an influential and cultured prince and provided a suitable backdrop for princely

---

[2] V. Press, 'The Holy Roman Empire in German history', in E. I. Kouri and T. Scott (eds.), *Politics and society in Reformation Europe* (London, 1987), pp. 51–77 at p. 66; H. Duchhardt, *Altes Reich und europäische Staatenwelt 1648–1806* (Munich, 1990), pp. 6–33.

[3] M. S. Anderson, *Europe in the eighteenth century 1713–1783* (3rd edn, London, 1987), pp. 284–5. For numerous contemporary examples see A. Fauchier-Magnan, *The small German courts in the eighteenth century* (London, 1958).

[4] HSAS, A74: Bü. 143, Montmartin to Legationsrat Straube, 25 July 1759. On his attempts to create it see pp. 215–33.

policy. The second was his chief political bargaining counter and added substance to the image created by the court. Both the army and the court required a sound financial base to sustain them. The next section investigates the elements of the imposing state and assesses their expense.

THE 'IMPOSING STATE' AND ITS COST

The political role of the early modern European court has often been underestimated. Writing in an age imbued with the bourgeois values of thrift and sobriety, nineteenth-century historians were often too quick to dismiss the court as an expensive luxury devoid of significant political purpose. That the court siphoned off the wealth of the state for the benefit of a privileged few is undisputed, even if it did fuel the development of European 'high' culture. However, to ignore the court's political role is to underestimate its importance as an element in the early modern state and in the fabric of European relations.

Recent work has gone a long way to re-evaluating the court in the larger European states. It is now seen as assisting the monarch in domesticating the nobility and boosting his image on the international stage.[5] However, the concept of cultural competition denies the courts of the smaller German territories such a political role. Instead, it is seen as a compensation for an inability to compete politically and militarily with their larger rivals.

This was not the case. On the contrary, its role in image-building was accentuated in the smaller states, given the greater discrepancy between the ruler's aims and his practical ability to achieve them. While self-indulgence and extravagance certainly played a part, the courtly display was nonetheless also a means to an end. It reinforced the image of the prince as a great, almost superhuman ruler, and in more practical terms, tended to make neighbours and rivals believe he was more powerful than he really was. Cultural competition thus formed an adjunct to, not a substitute for, political and military competition.

In this sense, the minor German courts mirrored those of the larger European states in more than just artistic styles. The new residences built by German princes in the later seventeenth century were intended, like the French palace at Versailles, to symbolise the new, more assertive style of rule associated with absolutism. Like Versailles, many of these new palaces were sited apart from the old capitals and so underlined the ruler's intention to govern without the constraints imposed in the past by the estates. This influenced Eberhard Ludwig's decision to build an entire new 'residence town' around his new palace of Ludwigsburg, 10 km north of the

[5] P. Burke, *The fabrication of Louis XIV* (New Haven, 1992); J. Kunisch, *Absolutismus. Europäische Geschichte vom Westfälischen Frieden bis zur Krise des Ancien Regime* (Göttingen, 1986), pp. 63–71; R. G. Asch and A. M. Birke (eds.), *Princes, patronage and the nobility. The court at the beginning of the modern age* (Oxford, 1991).

old capital at Stuttgart, after 1704. His contemporaries in the Palatinate and Baden-Durlach created similar towns at Mannheim (1689) and Karlsruhe (1715) respectively, while the Bavarian elector built the Nymphenburg palace outside the old capital of Munich. The physical distance also served to set the prince apart from other mortals and reinforce the absolutist notion of his higher status. This was repeated in the decorative motifs that adorned the new buildings and the allegorical images employed in the musical and theatrical performances that filled much of court life.[6]

The object of this display extended beyond the desire to reinforce absolutist rule at home: it was also intended to convince potential allies and rivals that the prince was worthy of the lofty titles and additional territory he desired. The court provided the venue for receiving visiting dignitaries and was clearly intended to impress them. They would be met at the frontier by elaborately dressed guard units and escorted to the palace where they would often be entertained on a lavish scale. In an age when access to accurate information was difficult, personal impressions counted for much. The criteria by which contemporaries measured power and efficiency were in any case not always the same as those of subsequent commentators. While Friedrich Wilhelm I of Prussia's mania for giant guardsmen was thought distinctly odd, tall soldiers were generally seen as fitter and better able to load muskets in line of battle than men of average height. The fact that they drilled like automatons was not seen by contemporaries as ridiculous. The British hired two Ansbach-Bayreuth regiments in 1777 on the basis of their representative's report that 'no clockwork could be more regular'.[7] Precision was seen as a sign of discipline and efficiency. The efforts to impress extended to more cultural spheres. Each of the Württemberg dukes in this study, especially Carl Eugen, sought to make his court a cultural capital of European standing. Elector Charles Albert of Bavaria had done the same to support his efforts to secure the imperial title. This had even included an attempt to revive the Bavarian dialect as a standard high language.[8]

Such display was used by the lesser states to mask their lack of genuine power. It could work on occasion. Baron von Pöllnitz, normally a fairly astute observer, was so impressed by the bodyguards of Eberhard Ludwig in 1730 that he estimated the strength of the Württemberg army at 5,000, or twice its real size. The British were induced to take Carl Eugen's offer of a subsidy corps seriously because their representative had been so dazzled by the Ludwigsburg

---

[6] C. Belschner, *Ludwigsburg in Wechsel der Zeiten* (3rd edn, Ludwigsburg, 1969); W. Fleischhauer, *Barock im Herzogtum Württemberg* (2nd edn, Stuttgart, 1981); H. A. Klaiber, *Der württembergische Oberbaudirektor Philippe de la Guêpière* (*VKGLK*, Reihe B, vol. 9, Stuttgart, 1959); G. Kleeman, *Schloß Solitude bei Stuttgart* (Stuttgart, 1966); A. Yorke-Long, *Music at court: Four eighteenth-century studies* (London, 1964).

[7] PRO, SP81/186, Faucitt to Suffolk, 10 Feb. 1777.

[8] Hughes, *Early modern Germany*, p. 140.

court.[9] More usually, it led to the pathetic and the absurd. In order to impress the Russian Grand Duke Paul in 1782, Carl Eugen had men of his garrison regiment dress in uniforms of other units on separate days to inflate their strength. Earlier, in 1759, he had changed the wording in the court calendar announcing the date of his birth from 'was born on' to the preposterous 'has increased the number of the mighty in the world on'.[10]

The court also fulfilled a more practical function as the hub of the patronage network. Though on a proportionally inferior scale, its use in this manner mirrored that in the larger states. Patronage worked through a system of service, protection and reward. Its object was to create an extensive clientele which could be manipulated to further policy objectives. It could be used internally to bind elements of the local elite to the ruler and ease the exercise of his authority. Externally it could be developed to secure friends and placemen in the administration of powerful states and to establish a client network among neighbouring minor states.

The lack of a native nobility rendered the first function less important in Württemberg than elsewhere. Nonetheless, patronage played a vital role in the extension of Württemberg influence throughout Swabia. The dukes had long desired to annex the scattered holdings of the Swabian imperial knights. Offering them employment in the duchy's court and army was a useful preparatory stage, reducing them to dependency. It also helped silence complaints to Vienna where the knights had numerous relations in Austrian service. This practice seems to have begun in earnest in the later years of Eberhard Ludwig's reign when increasing numbers of Swabian knights were appointed as officers in the army. It was continued under Carl Alexander, who extended it to reward members of the Viennese clientele he knew from his Austrian military service (1701–33). The various Austrian regiments of which the dukes were colonels-in-chief provided further openings for this policy of winning friends with influence at the imperial court. Their control over the Kreis military structure provided additional opportunities within Swabia. Carl Alexander also gave commissions to the offspring of a number of minor German ruling houses including Baden-Durlach, Waldeck, Wied, Isenburg and Sayn-Wittgenstein. This policy was continued by his son Carl Eugen. Mirroring Europe's leading monarchs, the dukes also created their own system of honours, regulated by tables of ranks, and complete with an order to St Hubertus to confer on visiting dignitaries.[11]

---

[9] C. Belschner, 'Ludwigsburg ums Jahr 1730. Nach dem Memoiren des Barons von Pöllnitz', *LBGB*, 3 (1903), 81–96 at p. 92.

[10] J. Steininger, *Leben und Abenteuer des Johann Steininger . . .* (Stuttgart, 1841), pp. 47–8; quotation from Vann, *Making of a state*, p. 272.

[11] HSAS, A6: Bü. 15, 19, 24, 50–2; A30c: Bd. 5–8; C14: Bü 185, 192, 217, 489, 490, 713; *Württembergische Hof- und Staats-Handbücher*, 1736–94; W. Pfeilsticker, *Neues württembergisches Dienerbuch* (3 vols., Stuttgart, 1957–74); Lemcke, 'Ein Blick in das herzoglich württembergisch Offizierskorps des vorigen Jahrhunderts', *WVJHLG*, 2 (1879), 111–17.

Image-building such as this was vital if they wished to attract the attention of the European powers. It also explains their obsession with titles. The higher the title, the more likely they would be noticed. In Württemberg's case, the duke desired electoral status. At times of imperial elections, the electors were courted by the major powers who wished to influence the course of German politics. Votes could be traded for valuable concessions. Moreover, several electors managed to use the position as a stepping-stone to a royal title elsewhere. A royal title bought access to the select club of the major decision-makers as indicated by the experience of Brandenburg-Prussia. In 1697 Friedrich III's representative was denied access to the Ryswick peace conference despite the heavy Prussian military involvement in the war. The acquisition of a royal title four years later removed this barrier and gave Prussia a full voice in international relations.[12]

In addition to advancing political ambitions, cultural competition furthered another key dynastic aim, that of defending a prince's existing possessions. The hard-won territorial sovereignty acquired at Westphalia in 1648 had to be maintained. Given the complex web of conflicting jurisdictions and claims to territory within the Reich, no prince could afford giving a rival opportunity to exert influence or establish authority in any part of his domains. Equally, the desire for higher titles stemmed in part from a downgrading of many princes' existing status experienced in the internationalisation of imperial politics after 1648. With the intrusion of European monarchs into German politics and the acquisition of foreign crowns by potential rivals, the lesser princes had to improve their own position or risk losing influence over their own affairs.

The army was the second element of the imposing state. It added substance to the representational role of the court and served as the prince's chief bargaining counter. This role has generally been overlooked in the past. There has been a tendency to see the armies of the smaller German states as devoid of any real purpose. They certainly seem minuscule when compared with the mighty arrays of Prussia and Austria. Their structure and composition also casts doubt on their practical purpose. Regiments were undersized and over-officered, the cavalry generally lacked horses and there was rarely any modern heavy artillery. Altogether, they were insufficient to defend their territory against anything more than a modest threat. Understandably, the conclusion has been that their sole purpose was 'to impart an aura of military grandeur to . . . [the] . . . overblown court'.[13]

Defence was nonetheless important. It was a primary function of a prince and a chief justification for his authority. It was also an obligation towards the emperor, especially after the development of a permanent Reichsarmee after 1681. As such it could hardly be neglected by princes wishing to win the emperor's favour. In

---

[12] Duchhardt, *Altes Reich*, pp. 6–8.
[13] Vann, *Making of a state*, p. 273; F. C. G. Kapp, *Soldatenhandel deutscher Fürsten nach Amerika (1775 bis 1783)* (Berlin, 1874 edn) is full of examples of this view.

Württemberg 's case, as one of the two Swabian *Kreisausschreibenden Fürsten*, or executive princes, the duke needed troops to fulfil their obligations to execute Kreis and Reich's decisions under the various *Exekutionsordnungen* (executive ordinances). While this was essentially a policing function, in the absence of a separate police force, an army was required to carry it out.[14]

The same was true of internal policing. Like many other German states, Württemberg established a squadron of hussars in 1735 as a sort of gendarmerie to patrol the highways and hunt criminals. Other troops were regularly used to round up vagrants, collect tax arrears and exercise crowd control on public occasions.[15] Six hundred infantry with fixed bayonets, backed up by a similar number of militia, were required to hold back the curious hordes who turned up to witness the execution of the financier Süss Oppenheimer in 1738. Other soldiers had to be posted to guard Carl Eugen's much-prized opera house in 1766 after it had become the target of vandals.[16]

The presence of troops in the duchy's towns and villages reinforced the authority of the state and its ruler. State occasions such as weddings and funerals had always been accompanied by martial display. However, increasingly this was restricted to the regular military and the duchy's militia, with its associations with decentralised authority and the estates' liberties, was progressively excluded. Whereas several thousand Stuttgart citizens participated in parades before the duke in 1748–50, the bulk of their civic guard was disbanded in May 1751, and thereafter only regular soldiers were to be seen on important public occasions.[17]

The army was considered such a vital symbol of sovereignty that the dukes refused to allow the estates any say in fixing its strength. Joseph Anton Bandel, an apologist for Carl Eugen's absolutist measures, went so far as to argue:

Should, however, a sovereign have to ask his subjects' permission as to how many troops he should and may maintain, then [his] sovereignty is at an end and we would have a permanent peasants' war [*Bauernkrieg*]. And precisely to prevent this we have a sovereign and it is up to him to maintain as many troops as he likes so that the peasants learn manners and dutiful respect.[18]

For this reason, ever since the question of the maintenance of an army in peacetime first arose in Württemberg in 1698, the dukes refused to permit the estates to

---

[14] HSAS, A28: Bü 99, privy council protocol, 16 Jan. 1720; J. A. von Bandel, *Auf eine Lüge eine Maultasche!* (1766), pp. 52–6. On the *Kreisausschreibenden Fürsten* see Storm, *Feldherr*, pp. 158–9. The other in Swabia was the Catholic prince bishop of Constance.

[15] HSAS, L6.22.7.2, 25 June 1735; A202: Bü. 2278, 17 Nov. 1736. See T. Bolay, *Chronik der Stadt Asperg* (Bietigheim-Bissingen, 1978), pp. 93, 112–13 for examples of the hussars' duties.

[16] C. A. Fischer, *Geschichte der Stuttgarter Stadtgarde zu Pferd* (Stuttgart, 1887), p. 14; R. Krauß, 'Das Theater', *HKE*, I, pp. 481–554 at p. 525.

[17] HSAS, A202: Bü. 863; Fischer, *Stadtgarde*, p. 2; K. Pfaff, *Geschichte der Stadt Stuttgart* (2 vols., Stuttgart, 1845), II, pp. 235–42; A. von Pfister, *Der Milizgedanke in Württemberg und die Versuche zu seiner Verwirklichung* (Stuttgart, 1883).

[18] Bandel, *Auf eine Lüge*, pp. 50–1.

discuss the *quaestio an*, whether the army should be maintained at all and how big it should be. Instead, they were only to discuss the *quaestio quomodo* of how it should be funded.[19] The estates continually contested this and during the court case against Carl Eugen, 1764–70, tried to write into the constitution a fixed limit on the number of troops.[20] That they failed to secure this in the famous Erbvergleich settlement in 1770 proves just how vital the duke considered this question to be.

Possession of a permanent army, however small, was also necessary to demonstrate sovereignty to those outside the territory. Along with the court, an army was a visible demonstration of princely status. Indeed, it was probably the most important, for without it, a prince lost the status of Armierter Stand crucial to sustaining territorial sovereignty. Whatever the cost, he had to be seen to be maintaining this, otherwise he risked giving the impression he was willing to allow his sovereignty to lapse. This representational value of military force was essential to the continued territorial integrity and princely status of rulers of minor states such as Schaumburg-Lippe and Neu-Wied, who were surrounded by predatory neighbours.[21]

It could assume a more active form through a display of force to intimidate a rival, or to reinforce a claim. The first example for Württemberg was in 1704 when ducal troops occupied Wiesensteig after Bavaria's defeat at Blenheim. Between 1735 and 1747 a detachment also occupied Count Fugger's possessions at Stettenfels and Gruppenbach to enforce Württemberg claims to sovereignty. The troops added weight to the duke's arguments by evicting the count's officials and demolishing a Catholic church they had built.[22] When the count of Öttingen disregarded ducal rights in the enclave of Weiltingen, Carl Eugen again sent in the troops in 1742. An entire regiment was stationed at Heidenheim nearby as a reserve; again obviously an attempt at intimidation.[23] In a dispute over forestry rights in 1763 with Hohenzollern-Sigmaringen, a Württemberg dragoon squadron was quartered on the Hohenzollern village of Heiligenzimmern, though it had to be withdrawn after Prussia protested.[24] The dukes were also prepared to take on their more powerful neighbours. In 1742, for example, a strong detachment was sent in when the

[19] W. Grube, *Der Stuttgarter Landtag 1457–1957* (Stuttgart, 1957), p. 367.
[20] On these attempts see K. Pfaff, *Geschichte des Fürstenhauses und Landes Wirtenberg* (4 vols., Stuttgart, 1850), IV, pp. 320–1, 349–50 and his *Geschichte des Militärwesens in Württemberg* (Stuttgart, 1842), pp. 78–9.
[21] J. Arndt, *Das Niederrheinisch-Westfälische Reichsgrafenkollgeium und seine Mitglieder (1653–1806)* (Mainz, 1991), pp. 50–1, 62, 122–5; H. H. Klein, *Wilhelm zu Schaumburg-Lippe* (*Studien zur Militärgeschichte, Militärwissenschaft und Konfliktforschung*, 28, Osnabrück, 1982).
[22] HSAS, A202: Bü. 2196, 2 July 1742, 22 Jan. and 21 May 1743; Bü. 2256, 30 July 1743; Bü. 2266, 1738; L5: Tom. 148, fol. 378; H. Tüchle, *Die Kirchenpolitik des Herzogs Karl Alexander von Württemberg 1733–1737* (Würzburg, 1937), pp. 100–2.
[23] HSAS, A202: Bü. 2256, 30 July 1743; Bü. 2276, 13 Aug. 1742; Bü. 2278, March 1742 to May 1744.
[24] E. Gönner, 'Hohenzollern und Württemberg', in *Bausteine zur geschichtlichen Landeskunde von Baden-Württemberg* (Stuttgart, 1979), pp. 239–59.

Palatinate began levying fines in a Württemberg district.[25] That Württemberg was not alone in using troops in this way is borne out by other cases. For example, the bishop of Würzburg mobilised his entire army in 1750 during a dispute with the elector of Mainz over the unauthorised felling of trees in his forests.[26]

The fact that in virtually none of these cases did the participants actually come to blows is further evidence for the effectiveness of the system of the Old Reich.[27] This further underlines the impracticability of the use of force to advance dynastic aims. Hessen-Kassel twice had to evacuate the county of Schaumburg it claimed from Lippe, even though the latter was incapable of organising an effective defence. Similarly, despite overwhelming military superiority it still took an expensive financial settlement before the duke had his way in the long-running dispute with Count Fugger.[28]

Although the opportunities for achieving objectives by force were very limited, dynastic ambitions still required a sizeable military establishment. A large standing army was considered by contemporaries to raise the reputation, prestige (*Ansehen*), honour (*Ehre*) and sovereignty (*Hoheit*) of a prince and thereby make him a more attractive alliance partner.[29] As the Württemberg pastor Philipp Ludwig Röder wrote in 1786: 'A prince who can lead his 12 to 20,000 men into the field, undertake sieges, fight battles, whose friendship is constantly sought after by the courts of Vienna and Versailles, always plays a considerable role in the theatre of war.'[30] This 'considerable role' was expected to bring results in the form of his status and territory. This was recognised by Eberhard Ludwig in 1698 when he resolved, despite estates' opposition, to retain the army in peacetime to boost his chances of attracting alliance partners. Thereafter, it became consistent ducal policy to maintain as many troops as possible. However, as we shall see, soldiers were expensive and their numbers were always restricted by lack of adequate funding.

In most cases even if they had cut back on court expenditure and devoted all available resources to the army in the manner of the Prussian Hohenzollerns, few of the minor German states would have been able to raise the 12,000–20,000 mentioned by Röder. Of the non-electoral states, only Hessen-Kassel managed

---

25 HSAS, A202: Bü. 2278, 10 Dec. 1742.
26 W. Kopp, *Würzburger Wehr. Eine Chronik zur Wehrgeschichte Würzburgs* (*Mainfränkische Studien*, 22, Würzburg, 1979), p. 88.
27 For an exception see A. von Witzleben, *Der Wasunger Krieg zwischen Sachsen-Gotha-Altenberg und Sachsen-Meiningen 1747 bis 1748* (Gotha, 1855).
28 Carl Eugen was obliged to buy the three properties in question for 213,646fl. 54xr. in 1747: HSAS, A256: Bd. 233, fol. 344. On the dispute see L5: Tom. 155, fols. 129–47, 160–3, 175–9; Tom. 156, fols. 35–9.
29 HSAS, A202: Bü. 2208, privy council to Carl Eugen, 23 Nov. 1752; Bandel, *Auf eine Lüge*, pp. 50–2; Grube, *Landtag*, p. 369.
30 P. L. H. Röder, *Geographie und Statistik Wirtembergs* (2 vols., Laibach in Krain/Ulm, 1787–1804), I, p. 159.

figures approaching this on a long-term basis, and this was at the cost of militarising its entire society. The most Württemberg ever managed in the eighteenth century was 16,000 in 1760. Its strength usually fluctuated between 2,500 and 5,000.[31] In any case, cutting back on court expenditure was not a viable option since this too was a vital element in their bid to further their aims. This compelled princes such as the Württemberg dukes to organise their armies in the form of a cadre around which a larger force could be built up when the opportunity arose. In the meantime the military administration economised by releasing the least essential elements (usually the infantry and cavalry privates) from service. The drawback of this system was that the army could only be raised to effective strength through the infusion of large numbers of untrained recruits. Military effectiveness was seriously impaired until these unseasoned elements had become battle experienced. This is the reason behind the deficiencies in organisation of the smaller armies. It also explains their often poor performance, most notably that of Württemberg, whose raw conscripts mutinied rather than go to the front in 1757. Nonetheless, these cadres could be useful to the major powers, who often found it more expedient to hire foreign forces than add to their own establishments. Thus, by maintaining even a small army, a prince had an important bargaining counter which could be used to attract political support for his dynastic objectives. This worked through the medium of the subsidy treaty which will be explained in Chapter 3.

The third element in the imposing state was a sound financial base. Well-ordered finances were themselves seen as a factor raising princely prestige. 'If a prince wants to be well respected', wrote Friedrich II of Prussia, 'it is necessary that he keeps his finances in proper order, an impoverished government has never won respect.'[32] Substantial funds were also essential to sustain both the court and the army.

Lack of precision in contemporary accounting procedures, together with incomplete survival of the records, make any computation of these costs difficult.[33] The following figures should be treated with caution. Nonetheless, they do indicate the level of expense and will serve to put the statistics in the following chapters into perspective.

Court expenditure under Eberhard Ludwig averaged 391,000fl. a year between

---

[31] HSAS, A5: Bü. 71–2; A6: Bü. 30, 68–9; A8: Bü. 51, 54; A30a: Bü. 57–67, 119, 180; A32 series; A202: Bü. 1871, 2206, 2278; G230: Bü. 48; L5: Tomi Actorum; L6 series; L12 series. For a fuller discussion of the size of German armies see Wilson, 'War, state and society in Württemberg, 1677–1770' (Cambridge Ph.D., 1990), pp. 62–73.

[32] Hartmann, *Geld*, p. 2.

[33] The Württemberg *Kriegskasse Rechnungen* only survive for the years 1753/4–1754/5, 1759/60 onwards. The Kriegskasse kept separate account books for the Kreistruppen for which only the years 1759/60 onwards survive and during the Seven Years War for the separate *Feldkriegskasse* of the field corps for which only the volume 1757/8 survives: HSAS, A32: Bd. 1–39, 80–114, 152. For practical purposes in military accounting the year was taken from 1 May to 30 April and split into two halves (summer and winter). Throughout this work the dates are given in this style, e.g. 1715/16 meaning financial year May 1715 to April 1716. Confusingly, the civil financial year ran from Georgii (St George's Day, 23 April) to Georgii.

1714 and 1733, or about twice what it had been on his accession in 1693.[34] It rose under subsequent regimes to peak at over 516,000fl. between 1757 and 1765. These averages conceal major outlays on individual items, chiefly palace construction. The huge Ludwigsburg palace, built 1704–33, cost up to three million florins. Carl Eugen's Neues Schloss, constructed in Stuttgart 1746–62, cost at least 600,000fl., while his later palaces of Monrepos (1760–5) and Solitude (1763–7) cost 300,000fl. and 1,000,000fl. respectively. Considering that two further residences were built (La Favorite, 1714–23 and Grafeneck, 1760–4), the total must have been over six million florins. Entertainment consumed additional sums. Carl Eugen spent no less than 345,000fl. trying to impress Grand Duke Paul in 1782.[35]

Expenditure on this scale represented a considerable burden for the smaller states. At 2,500,000fl. a year in 1729, the cost of the imperial court in Vienna was over six times that of Eberhard Ludwig. Yet it represented only 8.5 per cent of Austria's total central government expenditure, compared with the Württemberg proportion of nearly 25 per cent. Even in a minor state such as Bamberg, the court consumed 15 to 20 per cent of total expenditure. The financial strain of cultural competition is most graphically revealed by the equivalent figures for Bavaria, the only German state to approach the Habsburg levels of expenditure. The annual cost of the Bavarian court varied between 1,363,700fl. (1701) and 2,307,100fl. (1760). Though still lower than that of Vienna, these figures represent respectively between 55 and 34.4 per cent of total Bavarian expenditure.[36]

The problem for the smaller princes was that they had to compete on the same level as their larger and financially more powerful neighbours. Diplomatic representation was also expensive, not least because of the prestige element involved.[37] A prince whose representatives were shabbily turned out and unable to entertain on the expected scale ran the risk of not being taken seriously. Even greater difficulties were encountered when they were unable to offer the 'presents' and 'gratifications' essential to diplomatic success.

It was not that eighteenth-century German diplomacy was especially corrupt, but rather that bribery was an accepted part of the system and those failing to play and pay by the rules were likely to find their aims frustrated. Payment was roughly in line with the status of the recipient, the nature of the objective and the level of competition. Miscalculation of any of these factors was likely to lead to disappointment, as Carl Alexander discovered in 1734 when he was trying to secure his appointment as Reichsfeldmarschall against Prussian competition. The Württemberg agent at the Reichstag woefully reported that although the elector of

---

[34] See Appendix; Vann, *Making of a state*, p. 205.
[35] Appendix; Belschner, *Ludwigsburg*, pp. 38–9; Pfaff, *Geschichte des Fürstenhauses*, IV, p. 251; J. Walter, *Carl Eugen von Württemberg* (Mühlacker, 1987), p. 210; Kleemann, *Solitude*, p. 23.
[36] Kunisch, *Absolutismus*, p. 70; Caspary, *Bamberg*, esp. p. 379.
[37] Württemberg's modest representation in the Reichstag cost about 14,000fl. annually, while a further 8,000 to 24,000 was spent on other diplomatic missions. HSAS, A256 and L10 series.

Mainz's representative had been given 100 ducats, 'he accepted these coldly and spoke even of 1,200fl.'.[38]

For larger objectives the costs could be enormous. Austria spent one million florins on securing the votes of the Cologne cathedral chapter in Max Franz's election as archbishop in 1780. Hanover's acquisition of the ninth electoral hat in 1692 – 'the most expensive hat in history' – is said to have cost 1,100,000 taler. Five years later, Elector Augustus of Saxony paid 2,000,000 taler in bribes to secure the Polish crown, while his son is supposed to have paid four times that amount to retain it in 1733. Even the realisation of less ambitious aims was expensive. Carl Alexander spent 142,096fl. trying to secure a favourable verdict at the Reichshofrat in a court case over the claims of the former mistress of his predecessor.[39]

However, payment of these sums was no guarantee of success. Money was often poured into the pockets of those already in the pay of a rival, or upon whom superior political influence had been brought to bear. Both the Bavarian Wittelsbachs and the deposed Mecklenburg duke, Carl Leopold, spent large sums in the 1720s in futile efforts to further their respective causes.[40] Even a government's own diplomats could prove unreliable. Johann Georg Daniel von Pfau (1686–1748), the Württemberg envoy at The Hague in 1716–48, creamed off 55,000fl. in pay and expenses without doing anything to further ducal interests. His brother Kaspar (1686–1744) managed to alter a ducal decree in 1720, doubling his salary, without this being discovered for fourteen years. Having lived in high style at the duke's expense, Pfau died a penniless bankrupt, obliging the duke to pay for his funeral.[41]

Though the cost of cultural competition was high, it was dwarfed by military expenditure. Unfortunately, calculating this is also no easy task. The following attempt is intended both as an assessment of these costs and as a guide for those wishing to investigate them in a state other than Württemberg.

In the eighteenth century, military finance in Württemberg, as elsewhere, did not categorise expenditure according to broad definitions such as manpower and provisions, but distributed money via the military formations that made up the army. In the light of this, it is best to consider the army's financial requirements in three categories that correspond to the three main periods in the life of a military unit: mobilisation, maintenance, disbandment.

In putting actual figures against the three categories of military expenditure,

[38] HSAS, A6: Bü. 15 Legationssekretär C. L. L. von Pfeil to Duke Carl Alexander, Jan. 1734. One hundred ducats were worth about 500fl. On Carl Alexander's appointment see pp. 169–70 below.

[39] S. Stern, *The court Jew* (Philadelphia, 1950), pp. 63–70; Pfaff, *Geschichte des Fürstenhauses*, IV, pp. 193 n. 1.

[40] Hartmann, *Geld*, pp. 56–65; Hughes, *Law and politics*, pp. 50–4, 126.

[41] HSAS, A202: Bü. 2462, 2465–7; Pfeilsticker, *Dienerbuch*, 1140, 1151, 1159, 1165, 1198, 1358, 2001.

calculation of the mobilisation costs is fairly straightforward, as these were usually expressed as a round figure covering the cost of recruiting and equipping each soldier. Generally, in the Württemberg calculations an infantryman was reckoned to cost between 34fl. and 40fl. and a cavalryman, together with his horse, about 140fl.–160fl. Grenadiers cost around 4fl.–6fl. more, because of their expensive hats. This was the age of the tall, brass-fronted mitre caps, and when bearskin hats were still made from bears. Recruiting problems could push up these costs owing to the higher bounties demanded, especially by the taller and fitter men required for the grenadiers. However, these costs do appear to have remained roughly constant for the first half of the eighteenth century and are in line with those in other states.[42] The especially high payments offered by the Venetians are explained by their difficulties in recruiting for their service and the fact that the money offered was also intended to cover the transport costs to the Lido.[43]

Based on this information the cost to raise an infantry regiment on the imperial establishment worked out at 78,000fl.–92,000fl. to raise and equip, while a cavalry regiment cost between 153,000fl. and 175,000fl. These figures demonstrate clearly the expensive nature of the mounted arm, especially considering that an imperial cavalry regiment was less than half the size of one of infantry.[44] In addition to these costs, each regiment required a set of field equipment before it could be considered fully combat effective. This added a further 8,648fl. 36xr. to the price of a foot unit and 3,838fl. to one of horse.[45]

Calculation of the maintenance costs is more complex and is beset with pitfalls for the unwary. Any calculation needs to take into consideration not only the levels of pay and rations, but also the organisation of the unit in question, as different ranks received different rates. Thus, although a unit might have a comparatively low overall strength, it could still, owing to a disproportionately large officer corps, be expensive to maintain. Taking these factors into account and considering those units organised on the imperial establishment, it emerges that annual maintenance costs for a 2,300-man infantry regiment were 155,000fl.–185,000fl. while those for a 1,094-strong cavalry regiment were 148,700fl.–170,000fl. This gives average

[42] The figure of 34fl. appears to have been the norm and was based on Kreis regulations: HSAS, A202: Bü. 1157, draft convention 28 Sept. 1735; A202: Bü. 1361; A6: Bü. 57, 11 Dec. 1715; C14: Bü. 334, May 1741. Figures for Bavaria are for Feb. 1738: 36fl. 32xr. for one infantryman and 201fl. 18xr. for one cavalryman with horse (Hartmann, *Geld*, p. 87) and for 1743: 34fl. for one infantryman, 60fl. for a dragoon, 73fl. for a cuirassier – in both cases without horses (K. Staudinger, *Geschichte des bayerischen Heeres* (Munich, 1908), III, p. 243).

[43] In 1695 Venice paid 50tlr. (75fl.) and in 1715 offered 60fl. HSAS, A5: Bü. 66, 20 Apr. 1695, 18 Jan. 1715. The Dutch paid 60rtlr. for each cavalryman supplied by Friedrich Carl in the fateful treaty of 1688: A202: Bü. 2469, 2 Aug. 1688.

[44] An imperial inf rgt numbered 2,300 officers and men while one of cavalry totalled 1,094. The cavalry referred to here are heavy cavalry (dragoons and cuirassier) and not light (hussars). Normally, officers were omitted from calculations as they were expected to pay for their own uniforms and equipment.

[45] HSAS, A6: Bü. 34, 3 Mar. 1734.

per capita costs of around 67fl.–80fl. and 136fl.–155fl. respectively.[46] Again, these figures demonstrate clearly the expense involved in maintaining a fully mounted cavalry unit and explain why most of those in the smaller German states were kept dismounted in peacetime. Compared with other states, these estimates are roughly in the middle of the range.[47] They also appear to show little change on similar figures from the Thirty Years War.[48]

In addition to these expenses, we must remember that even eighteenth-century armies, like those today, did not consist solely of front-line units, but also required various ancillary services such as a general staff and a commissariat as well as military installations such as fortresses and barracks. Often the cost of these additional requirements was proportionately greater in the small states as they did not enjoy the economies of scale of their larger neighbours. For example, to provide a city such as Mainz or Würzburg with fortifications of a 'state of the art' technological standard did not cost any less than fortifying cities such as Lille or Magdeburg. When Prussia spent about 160,000tlr. a year between 1748 and 1752 on strengthening its fortresses in Silesia, this represented only 2 per cent of its military budget.[49] However, it was the equivalent of nearly 70 per cent of that of a state such as Württemberg.[50]

---

[46] The Alt-Württemberg rgt cost 154,896fl. according to the 1716 regulations listed in A. von Pfister, *Denkwürdigkeiten aus der württembergischen Kriegsgeschichte* (Stuttgart, 1868), pp. 17–20. An Austrian foot rgt in 1733 cost 146,692fl. a year in peacetime and 185,044fl. in wartime (81,160fl. for the six summer months and 103,884 in the winter): K. u. K. Kriegs-Archiv, *Feldzüge des Prinzen Eugen von Savoyen* (21 vols., Vienna, 1876–96), XIX, p. 106. The cost of the Würzburg and Mainz foot rgts hired to the emperor in 1733 was 155,352fl. and 170,628fl. respectively: *ibid.*, XIX, pp. 113–19. The Württemberg commissariat calculated the cost of the DR Prinz Louis hired the same year at 169,608.5fl. while the Austrians claimed the costs were only 148,692fl: HSAS, A6: Bü. 34, 3 Mar. 1734.

[47] Examples of per capita maintenance rates are: *Kurköln* 1703, infantry 61.2fl., cavalry 134fl.; P. C. Hartmann, 'Die französischen Subsidienzahlungen an den Kurfürsten von Köln . . . (1701–1714)', *Historische Jahrbücher*, 92 (1972), 358–71 at p. 361). *Paderborn* 1734/5 *Reichskontingent* (foot soldiers), 52fl. (F. Mürmann, 'Das Militärwesen des ehemaligen Hochstiftes Paderborn seit dem Ausgange des dreißigjährigen Krieges', *Westfälische Zeitschrift*, 95 (1939), 64). *Sachsen-Weimar* 1756, *Garde du corps* (elite cavalry), 148fl. (H. Müller, *Das Heerwesen im Herzogtum Sachsen-Weimar* (Jena, 1936), p. 6). *Bavaria* 1726, infantry 120fl., cavalry 360fl.; 1742, 120fl. and 355fl. respectively (Hartmann, *Geld*, p. 220 n. 325).

[48] In 1615 a 3,000-strong German foot rgt was reckoned to cost 324,000fl. annually or 108fl. per man: F. W. Barthold, *Geschichte der Kriegsverfassung und des Kriegswesens der Deutschen* (2 vols., Leipzig, 1864), II, pp. 227–8.

[49] For this and the following comparisons with Prussia and Austria see G. B. Volz and G. Küntzel, *Preußische und österreichische Acten zur Vorgeschichte des siebenjährigen Krieges* (Leipzig, 1899); C. Jany, *Geschichte der königlich-preußischen Armee* (4 vols., Osnabrück, 1967), I–III; D. Stutzer, 'Das preußische Heer und seine Finanzierung in zeitgenössischer Darstellung 1740–1790', *Militärgeschichtliche Mitteilungen*, 24 (1978), 23–47; J. Niemeyer, 'Die preußische Heeresversorgung unter Friedrich dem Großen', in *Die Bewaffnung und Ausrüstung der Armee Friedrichs des Großen* (Rastatt, 1986), pp. 73–88; B. R. Kroener, 'Die materiellen Grundlagen österreichischer und preußischer Kriegsanstrengungen 1756–1763', in Kroener (ed.), *Europa im Zeitalter Friedrich des Großen* (*Beitrage zur Militärgeschichte*, 26, Munich, 1989), pp. 47–78; Dickson, *Finance and government*, II, chs. 4–6.

[50] For an excellent assessment of the burden on a small state produced by construction of fortifications see B. Sicken, 'Residenzstadt und Fortifikation. Politische, soziale und wirtschaftliche Probleme der

If we consider the per capita maintenance costs of an army as a whole, that is not only the units, but also the general staff, fortresses, barracks and so on, we arrive at the following figures for Württemberg. In the period after 1714 the average annual cost for each man on the establishment was at least 120fl.[51] At first sight this compares relatively favourably with the highest estimate of similar costs in Prussia of 117.75fl. (1713/14). However, in reality the costs for Württemberg were probably ten to twenty florins higher as a result of hidden payments for items of military expenditure that came from other sources not appearing in the military accounts.

Expenditure figures from the period after 1750, for which more complete data are available, show per capita costs in Württemberg to be between about 120fl. and 197fl. per annum.[52] Figures from 1792 for Ansbach-Bayreuth, which was approximately the same size as Württemberg, indicate similar costs. Each of the 1,368 Haustruppen cost nearly 176fl. a year, while those of the 1,386-strong Brigade Reitzenstein hired to the Dutch cost about 191fl.[53] Here, the economies of scale enjoyed by the bigger states become more obvious. Annual peacetime maintenance figures for Prussia varied between under 98fl. per man in 1740 to 91fl. in 1756 and 96.25fl. in 1786; those for Austria rose from 130fl. per man in 1749 to about 200fl. during the Seven Years War.

The virtual impossibility of the small states being able to conduct actual military operations without outside financial assistance is demonstrated by the dramatic rise in costs incurred in wartime. Two examples will suffice to illustrate this. The mobilisation of its 28,000-strong army and conduct of operations in 1757 cost the electorate of Hanover no less than 8,446,320tlr. or over 453fl. per man.[54] Friedrich II of Prussia estimated the additional costs of a campaign for a field army of about 160,000 men at 5,000,000 taler (7.5 million florins) over and above the normal maintenance costs. The actual campaign of 1757 cost 11,200,000 taler.

As far as the third category is concerned, the bulk of this in practice consisted of meeting deferred payment of costs which have already been considered under the heading of maintenance. In addition to these were the pensions and allowances due to retired or discharged officers and men. In Württemberg throughout the

barocken Neubefestigung Würzburgs', in H. W. Herrmann and F. Irsigler (eds.), *Beiträge zur Geschichte der frühneuzeitlichen Garnisons- und Festungsstadt* (*Veröffentlichungen der Komission für saarländische Landesgeschichte und Volksforschung*, 13, Saarbrücken, 1983), pp. 124–42; F. P. Kahlenburg, *Kurmainzische Verteidigungseinrichtungen und Baugeschichte der Festung Mainz in 17. und 18. Jahrhundert* (*Beiträge zur Geschichte der Stadt Mainz*, 19, Mainz, 1963).

[51] HSAS, A5: Bü. 72; A6: Bü. 30, 35, 68, 69; A28: Bü. 99; L5: Tom. 125–43; L12: *Kriegsparticulare* 1713/14–1735/6.

[52] HSAS, A8: Bü. 51, 54, 391; A30a: Bü. 58, 59–62, 67; A32: Bd. 1–15; A202: Bü. 2236; L12: *Kriegsparticulare 1750/1–1771/2*.

[53] O. Bezzel, *Die Haustruppen des letzten Markgrafen von Ansbach-Bayreuth unter preußischer Herrschaft* (*Münchener historische Abhandlungen*, 2. Reihe, II, Munich, 1939), pp. 9, 24.

[54] J. Niemeyer and G. Ortenburg, *Die Churbraunschweig-Lüneburgische Armee im Siebenjährigen Kriege* (2 vols., Beckum, 1976), I, p. 12.

eighteenth century the cost of officers' pensions varied between 10,000fl. and 15,000fl. per year.[55] Allowances paid to discharged soldiers, which in the 1730s amounted to less than 1,000fl. per year, had, by the middle of the century, risen to between 6,000fl. and 7,000fl. per year.[56] Even so, by 1770, arrears of such payments amounted to more than 84,000fl.[57]

Collectively, these expenses consumed over a quarter of Württemberg's central government expenditure in peacetime. The proportion rose to over a third during the War of the Polish Succession and to well over half in the Seven Years War. The situation elsewhere was similar. Bavaria spent an average of just over 26 per cent on its army in the eighteenth century, while the figure for Bamberg in the second half of the seventeenth was 39 per cent.[58] However, these figures obscure the true costs, because the smaller states often received outside help in the form of subsidies and free rations. If fully mobilised, Carl Alexander's 12,660-man army would have required at least 1,017,155fl. a year in 1736, or nearly 65 per cent of annual pre-war income. In May 1760, when the army totalled 15,209 men, its annual cost was put at no less than 2,107,547fl. 35xr. or equivalent to over 94 per cent of peacetime revenue.[59]

Not surprisingly, most princes continually overspent. Debt management generally consumed between a quarter and a third of the total Württemberg budget, or roughly the same as in Bavaria.[60] Reckless pursuit of ambition could ruin a state for decades. In his desperate bid after 1758, Carl Eugen abandoned financial propriety. Debts and interest arrears rose to over thirteen million florins as loans were not repaid and all available money diverted to meet current expenses. The duke's virtual bankruptcy was a major factor in the estates' victory over him in the imperial courts after 1765.

Bavaria's experience was worse. Despite considerable financial and military support from France, Max Emanuel was driven from his electorate which was occupied by the Austrians between 1704 and 1714. This fiasco created debts of

---

[55] HSAS, A8: Bü. 51, 391; A30a: Bü. 58, 60, 63, 66, 119; A32: Bd. 1–15; A202: Bü. 2196, 2206, 2207, 2244. The number of recipients varied between thirty and sixty, but always included some who were still fulfilling useful functions, such as fortress commandants.

[56] HSAS, A5: Bü. 64, 69; A32: Bd. 154–215; A202: Bü. 2283, 2284; L6. 22.5.83. The number of recipients rose from 173 in 1715 to 224 by 1727 and then levelled out at 300, before falling to about 180 due to the straitened financial circumstances of the 1770s.

[57] HSAS, A32: Bd. 189. The arrears had built up because the military administration diverted money from the pension fund (*Invalidenkasse*) during the Seven Years War to cover other items of expenditure. In the meantime the local authorities were obliged to pay allowances to the ex-soldiers. Payments were resumed after 1770.

[58] Hartmann, *Geld*, p. 30; Caspary, *Bamberg*, p. 379. Figures for Saxony appear similar, see P. C. Hartmann, *Das Steuersystem der europäischen Staaten am Ende des Ancien Régime (Beiheft Francia*, 7, Munich, 1979), p. 239; K. Biedermann, *Deutschland im achtzehnten Jahrhundert* (5 vols., 2nd edn, Leipzig, 1880), I, pp. 199, 229.

[59] HSAS, L5: Tom. 144, fol. 77–83, 19 Feb. 1736; A8: Bü. 51, *Ohngefahre Berechnung*, 20 May 1760.

[60] Appendix; Hartmann, *Geld*, p. 30.

twenty-two million florins by 1722. Continued attempts to keep up with potential rivals had added a further five to six-and-a-half million by 1726. Interest on these debts alone consumed at least 35 per cent of state revenue, thus adding to the elector's difficulties in raising the money required by the army and court. His successor, Charles Albert, continued the same reckless policies, but with now even less chance of success. Only with a further massive injection of French financial aid was he able to mobilise an army to realise his dream of becoming emperor. However, the ruinous state of electoral finances prevented that army reaching even three-quarters of the size of that of Max Emanuel. This force proved completely inadequate to defend his electorate against the Austrians' counter-attack in 1741–5, especially as French military assistance was, at best, half-hearted. Charles Albert died early in 1745 leaving a massive thirty-four to forty million florins of debts, and so effectively condemning his successor, Max Joseph (1745–77), to playing a purely minor role within the Reich. Naturally, to this already large financial cost must be added the cost in human lives and the suffering caused by the heavy taxation and foreign invasions.[61]

It is now time to put these costs in the context of the resources available to a prince. Here, three factors are of importance: the total resources available, how these were taxed and the proportion of this tax that was actually controlled by the prince.

WÜRTTEMBERG: TERRITORY AND RESOURCES

Turning to Württemberg as an example, we see that the lands of the ducal family in 1700 fell basically into two parts.[62] The main part under the rule of the senior line formed a fairly consolidated block roughly in the middle of the Swabian Kreis. It comprised the actual duchy of Württemberg itself around the capital Stuttgart, the duchy of Teck to the south, the counties of Calw, Tübingen and Urach further to the south and west and, detached from these, the lordship of Heidenheim as an enclave to the east. These territories collectively covered an area of approximately 8,343 km².[63]

---

[61] Hartmann, *Geld*; K. u. K. Kriegs-Archiv. *Oesterreichischer Erbfolgekrieg 1740–48* (9 vols., Vienna, 1896–1914), IV and VI; Staudinger, *Geschichte des bayerischen Heeres*, I–III; F. Wagner, *Kaiser Karl VII und die Grossen Mächte 1740–45* (Stuttgart, 1938); T. Bitterauf, *Die kurbayerische Politik im siebenjährigen Krieg* (Munich, 1901).

[62] K. S. Bader, *Der deutsche Südwesten in seiner territorialstaatlichen Entwicklung* (Sigmaringen, 1978 edn); A. F. Büsching, *Erdbeschreibung* (9 vols., Hamburg, 1788–92), VII; Röder, *Geographie und Statistik*, I; *Das Land Baden-Württemberg. Amtliche Beschreibung nach Kreisen und Gemeinden* (issued by the Staatlichen Archivverwaltung Baden-Württembergs, Stuttgart, 1974), I, pp. 187–229; G. W. Sante (ed.), *Die Territorien bis zum Ende des alten Reiches* (*Territorien Poletz*, Würzburg, 1964), pp. 19–47. See map, p. xviii.

[63] Storm, *Feldherr*, pp. 51–5. The most realistic estimates (Storm, Röder, *Geographie und Statistik*, I, p. 20) place the duchy at 150 to 151 German square miles (*Quadratmeilen*) or 8,250 to 8,305 km². The

They were surrounded on all sides by a string of minor political entities and parcels of Austrian territory forming a kind of buffer zone. Beyond this lay a number of more powerful states: to the north the four electorates of Mainz, Trier, Cologne and the Palatinate, together with the landgraviate of Hessen-Kassel; to the east the electorate of Bavaria; to the south Austrian territory and the Swiss Confederation, and to the west France. Since the loss of Alsace (1648) and Burgundy (1679) to France, Württemberg was separated from this aggressive neighbour only by a narrow strip of Austrian and Baden territory sandwiched between the Rhine and the Black Forest.

The second part of the ducal house's possessions was actually surrounded by French territory. This part was considerably smaller (about 550 km²) than the main area east of the Rhine and until 1723 was ruled by the Mömpelgard branch of the family. It consisted of the county of that name, together with seven dependent lordships, to the south of Belfort and two enclaves (Horburg and Reichenweiher) near Strasbourg in Alsace.[64]

These lands gave the Württemberg duke considerably more territory than any of the three ecclesiastical electors (Mainz, Trier, Cologne), though these were usually able to enlarge their total possessions by their pluralist holding of other bishoprics. Württemberg, even without the territories west of the Rhine, was also larger than any other non-electorate state within the Reich apart from the economically impoverished Mecklenburg-Schwerin.

In terms of population Württemberg was not unimportant either. In 1700 its 340,000 inhabitants represented over a quarter of the total population of Swabia. By about 1790 the duchy's population had grown to over 620,000 despite large numbers of emigrants leaving for America and Hungary. Within the Reich, only Hessen-Kassel matched this growth rate.[65]

However, beyond these human resources, Württemberg's economic potential was relatively small. In particular, it lacked the structure necessary to turn raw produce into the hard currency the duke needed to pursue his aims. Industrial development was inhibited by the almost total lack of mineral deposits, and most ducal attempts to stimulate it failed. The reasons for this are those usually

---

size given by A. von Pfister and T. Schott in *HKE*, I, pp. 20, 314 and accepted by Vann, *Making of a state*, p. 230, of 170 QM is too large. The general view is that the territory grew by 9 QM (495 km²) through land purchases 1737–84.

[64] W. Grube, '400 Jahre Haus Württemberg in Mömpelgard', in Uhland (ed.), *900 Jahre Haus Württemberg*, pp. 438–58; W. Scherb, *Die politischen Beziehungen der Grafschaft Mömpelgard zu Württemberg von 1723 bis zur französischen Revolution* (Tübingen Ph.D., printed 1981).

[65] Storm, *Feldherr*, pp. 51–6; Röder, *Geographie und Statistik*, I, pp. 69–70; Pfaff, *Geschichte des Fürstenhauses*, IV, p. 407 n. 2. In 1719 the Privy council estimated the population at 400,000: HSAS, A28: Bü. 99, 5 April 1719. At least 150,000 people emigrated from the duchy in the course of the eighteenth century; see W. Kress, 'Einwanderungs- oder Auswanderungsland?', *Stuttgarter Illustrierte*, 12 (1986), 20–2; P. Kapff, 'Schwaben in Amerika seit der Entdeckung des Weltteils', *WNJB*, 10 (1893).

associated with the failure of such mercantilist undertakings – an over-eagerness to switch from capital investment to profit-taking at too early a stage in the enterprise's development.[66] This left agriculture as the mainstay of the economy. In contrast to Hessen-Kassel or Mecklenburg, Württemberg was blessed with very fertile soil.[67] While complete data are lacking, it seems that by the 1790s at least, the duchy produced about twice what was necessary to ensure each inhabitant a basic minimum of 2,000 calories a day.[68] At that time it was reckoned that a peasant only had to do a leisurely five-and-a-half days' work a week to guarantee his livelihood, and contemporaries wondered why so many Württembergers were prepared to forsake their fertile land to emigrate to the desolate wastes of West Prussia and Hungary.[69] Conditions at the beginning of the century had been clearly much worse. The wars between 1688 and 1713 badly affected the land 'because it had not even fully recovered from the old Thirty Years War'.[70] However, only in the years 1709, 1770/1 and 1789 did the duchy experience real food shortages, and these were years of generally poor European harvests.

While full information is again not available, it appears that Württemberg also enjoyed a favourable balance of trade. Like the production of foodstuffs, this seems to have improved steadily throughout the century. Whereas commentators in the first half of the century deplored the flow of hard cash out of the duchy, exports in the 1780s appear to have exceeded imports by a million florins.[71] However, the main export articles were raw materials: chiefly wool, cotton, wood, cattle, sheep and

---

[66] H. Schmäh, 'Ludwigsburger Manufakturen im 18. Jahrhundert', *LBGB*, 15 (1963), 29–51; O. Schifferer, 'Die wirtschaftliche Entwicklung Ludwigsburgs von der Grundung der Stadt bis zum Beginn des 2. Weltkrieges', *ibid.*, 20 (1968), 53–81; W. Söll, *Die staatliche Wirtschaftspolitik in Württemberg im 17. und 18. Jahrhundert* (Tübingen Ph.D., printed 1934), pp. 13–123; G. Krauter, 'Die Manufakturen des Herzogtums Wirtemberg in der zweiten Hälfte des 18. Jahrhunderts', *WJSL*, 1 (1954/55), 260–77; A. Schott, 'Wirtschaftliches Leben', *HKE*, 1, pp. 313–60.

[67] On the productivity of the duchy's soil see H. Jänichen, 'Zur Landwirtschaftlichen Ertragsbewertung vor 200 Jahren. Erläutert am Beispiel vom Dömuch, Kr. Tübingen', *ZWLG*, 26 (1967), 113–20; W. A. Boelcke, *Handbuch Baden-Württemberg. Politik, Wirtschaft, Kultur von der Urgeschichte bis zur Gegenwart* (Stuttgart, 1982), p. 122.

[68] A basic calorific intake of 2,000 calories requires an annual consumption of 200kg of grain. Thus for 620,000 inhabitants 124,000t would be required. In 1790 the duchy produced 2,498,800 *Scheffel* (a measurement of volume) of corn or roughly 265,000t. Production of rye, German wheat and barley alone stood at 119,187t. Production figures from Pfaff, *Geschichte des Fürstenhauses*, IV, p. 408 n.1; Schott, 'Wirtschaftliches Leben', p. 317.

[69] *Ibid*, pp. 318–19.

[70] HSAS, A28: Bü. 99, 5 Apr. 1719; H. Musall and A. Scheuerbrandt, 'Die Kriege im Zeitalter Ludwigs XIV und ihre Auswirkungen auf die Siedlungs-, Bevölkerungs- und Wirtschaftsstruktur der Oberrheinlande', in *Hans Graul-Festschrift (Heidelberger geographischer Arbeiten*, 40, Heidelberg, 1974), pp. 357–78.

[71] HSAS, A28: Bü. 99, 5 Apr. 1719; A. E. Adam, 'Württemberg vor dem siebenjährigen Krieg geschildert in einem Gutachten Johann Jakob Mosers von 9. November 1752', *WVJHLG*, NF12 (1903), 205–26; Söll, *Wirtschaftspolitik*, pp. 102, 126; Schott, 'Wirtschaftliches Leben', I, p. 358.

horses. Wine and low-grade cotton and canvas goods were the only finished products exported. This brought problems of the kind associated with chiefly agricultural economies: if the duchy had a poor harvest there was not enough produce to sell, if it had a good one there was a glut and prices fell.[72] Wine, which was the chief export article around 1700, was also subject to fierce competition and changes in taste. It was also generally exchanged directly for Bavarian salt rather than hard cash. Nonetheless, in 1700 this trade produced a net surplus of about 235,000fl., though this had dropped to only 60,000fl. by the 1780s.[73] Textiles, the only native industry of any note, took over as the mainstay of exports. This was almost exclusively in the hands of three cartels based in Calw, Urach and Heidenheim which sold about 70 per cent of their produce abroad. In the 1780s, this trade was valued at over a million florins a year and accounted for one-third of all exports. In addition, the Calw cloth-dyeing industry made about 100,000fl. a year. The export of cattle and sheep, which suffered a decline after 1714, appears to have picked up again in the second half of the century, while after about 1750 the export of horses also became important.[74]

Unfortunately, Württemberg's ability to profit from this boom was impaired by the fact that its trade was largely in the hands of its neighbours. The duchy lacked any significant towns to provide a suitable market centre, while its only important river, the Neckar, was not navigable for the stretch that lay within its borders. The city of Heilbronn, where the navigable section began, managed to frustrate ducal attempts to open up the Württemberg part and so, together with Esslingen, controlled a large part of the duchy's north–south trade. As Württemberg territory did not extend far enough southwards to enclose the River Danube, most of its east–west trade was in the hands of the Ulm boatmen and merchants.[75] Finally, the turmoil of the Thirty Years War had halted Württemberg's territorial expansion westwards and so ended dreams of a land link to Mömpelgard and a port on the Rhine. This prevented the duke of Württemberg from enjoying the same lucrative source of revenue through river tolls as the Rhenish electors.

The lack of an industrial base and the fact that most of the duchy's trade was in the hands of others prevented the development of a native merchant and banking class. The few merchants who did live in Württemberg were held by the mercantilist bureaucrats to be chiefly responsible for the flow of currency out of the duchy through their import of luxury goods such as coffee and tobacco.[76] The absence of

---

[72] HSAS, A28: Bü. 99, 5 Apr. 1719. This document gives a good summary of the duchy's economy.
[73] Söll, *Wirtschaftspolitik*, pp. 75, 120; E. Schremmer (ed.), *Handelstrategie und betriebswirtschaftliche Kalkulation im ausgehenden 18. Jahrhundert. Der süddeutsche Salzmarkt. Zeitgenössische qualitive Untersuchungen* (Wiesbaden, 1971).
[74] Söll, *Wirtschaftspolitik*, pp. 81–2, 112–13, 120; Schott, 'Wirtschaftliches Leben', pp. 332, 342–50.
[75] Söll, *Wirtschaftspolitik*, pp. 11–12, 72–4, 98; Hessen-Kassel faced similar problems, see Ingrao, *Hessian mercenary state*, p. 55.
[76] HSAS, A28: Bü. 99, 5 Apr. 1719; Adam, 'Württemberg vor dem siebenjährigen Krieg', 210.

a native merchant class also made it difficult for the duke to borrow money. He was forced either to approach foreigners or go cap-in-hand to his estates.

THE WÜRTTEMBERG ESTATES AND 'THE GOLD OLD LAW'

The estates represented a major brake on a prince's ability to exploit the resources of his territory.[77] They were nominally the representatives of the entire population and met with varying frequency at an assembly known as a *Landtag*. In practice, the delegates represented only a narrow section of society, usually the nobility and most of the towns. The peasantry, who made up the bulk of the population in virtually all the German territories, were excluded entirely, or at best, underrepresented.[78] Estates had come into being as a result of the growth of the money economy and the increasing inability of princes to live off the resources of their own private domains. In return for granting taxes and taking over princely debts, the estates of the various territories had secured an important say in government. This, in turn, was guaranteed in charters and declarations of rights which the prince was forced to acknowledge and which were often recognised in imperial law.

In Württemberg the most important of such charters was the Tübingen Treaty which the duke had been compelled to sign on 8 July 1514 in return for the estates taking over his debts.[79] Over the next two centuries, the estates extracted confirmation of this and other agreements in return for further debt take-overs.[80] The sum of these agreements was known as 'the good old law' (*'das gute alte Recht'*) and effectively formed the duchy's constitution.

The real safeguard for these rights, however, was the degree to which a particular prince was financially dependent on his estates. Where a prince was able to increase his own private income or persuade his estates to vote a regular tax grant, he no longer needed to make political concessions or respect their liberties. It is thus

---

[77] For a new survey of the development of estates in Germany and particularly the conflicts between them and the princes, Haug-Moritz, *Württembergischer Ständekonflikt*, pp. 5–42. The Württemberg jurist Johann Jakob Moser defined an estate as 'the body of those subjects who, by force of the freedoms or traditions of a land, must be consulted in certain concerns affecting the welfare of the land', quoted in M. Walker, *Johann Jakob Moser and the Holy Roman Empire of the German Nation* (Chapel Hill, 1981), p. 93.

[78] Of Württemberg's population, 75 per cent lived in 1,200 villages, the rest in 72 'towns', many of which were also hardly more than villages: Röder, *Geographie und Statistik*, I, pp. 73, 177–539.

[79] Printed in W. Grube (ed.), *Der Tübinger Vertrag vom 8. Juli 1514. Faksimile Ausgabe mit Transkription und geschichtlicher Würdigung* (Stuttgart, 1964). On the Württemberg estates see Grube, *Landtag*; Carsten, *Princes and parliaments*, pp. 1–148; F. Wintterlin, 'Die Anfänge der landständischen Verfassung in Württemberg', *WVJHLG*, NF23 (1914), 327–36 and his 'Die altwürttembergische Verfassung am Ende des 18. Jahrhunderts', *ibid.*, 195–209; V. Press, 'Der württembergische Landtag im Zeitalter des Umbruchs 1770–1830', *ZWLG*, 42 (1983), 255–81.

[80] Between 1514 and 1652 the estates took over at least 8.6 million fl. of ducal debts, 1514 900,000fl.; 1553 1,700,000fl.; 1583 600,000fl.; 1607 1,000,000fl.; 1618 1,100,000fl.; 1620 200,000fl.; 1652 3,000,000fl. In 1697 they were still responsible for 5.4 million fl. debts including 300,000fl. arrears of interest. Carsten, *Princes and parliaments*, pp. 12, 34–5, 40–1, 47, 50, 54, 75–6, 103.

not surprising that those princes who were best able to shake off the restraints imposed by their estates were those whose private incomes accounted for a substantial part of state revenue. This was true of the electors of the Palatinate (50 per cent), Saxony (54 per cent), Bavaria (55 per cent) and Hanover (56 per cent), all of whom had greatly reduced the power of their estates during the seventeenth century.[81] On the other hand, the estates remained the most powerful – and the princes correspondingly the most dependent – in those states where princely income was lowest. This was especially true for the ecclesiastical territories where the cathedral chapter generally took the place of the territorial estates. Here, the development of princely authority was further inhibited by the fact that the prince abbot or prince bishop was not hereditary, but chosen each time by the chapter. In these territories the prince controlled only a very small percentage of the total revenue: Freising (25–43 per cent), Regensburg (17–36 per cent), Paderborn and Bamberg (both 25 per cent), Hildesheim and Cologne (both 12 per cent), Liege (8 per cent) and Mainz (1 per cent).[82] The same was also true of Württemberg where the duke controlled little more than one-third of the total revenue. This was the result of the tripartite structure of the duchy which created separate church, estates and ducal revenues. Though the duke remained undisputed overlord of all Württemberg and possessed important rights and privileges right across the duchy, his ability to interfere in both church and estates was seriously curtailed by the terms of the 'gold old law'. This was particularly true regarding the crucial issue of taxation.

The duke's private income derived from his own property, the *Kammergut*. This was administered by a government department known as the *Rentkammer*.[83] The Kammergut basically consisted of farms, mills, fish ponds and small economic undertakings scattered throughout the sixty or so secular districts (*Ämter*) which made up most of the duchy. Only the most important assets, the 246 forests, were grouped together in fifteen separate administrative districts known as *Forstämter*.[84] The handful of villages that remained part of the Kammergut contributed a meagre 1,200fl. a year in direct taxes.[85] The other ducal villages had either been alienated entirely or hived off to the *Kammerschreibereigut* created by Eberhard III as a special fund to maintain various members of the family.[86] Although details of its

[81] Hartmann, *Geld*, pp. 15, 21–7; and *Steuersystem*, pp. 239–41, 260–1, 284–303.

[82] Hartmann, *Steuersystem*, p. 131; and his *Geld*, pp. 23–4, 58, 61, 64; Caspary, *Bamberg*, p. 378.

[83] F. Wintterlin, *Geschichte der Behördenorganisation in Württemberg* (2 vols., Stuttgart, 1904–6), I, pp. 31–41, 81–6.

[84] J. Hartmann, 'Württemberg im Jahr 1800', *WNJB*, NF5 (1900), 23–4. The duchy had 852,449 *Morgen* (± acre) of forest of which 128,005 belonged to the church and the rest to the duke. After 1762 the Forstämter were titled *Oberforstämter*.

[85] HSAS, A256: Bd. 197–252; *Landschreiberei Rechnungen* 1713/14–1766/7. With the establishment of the *Generalkasse* in 1767 accounting procedures were changed, making the figures after this date not entirely comparable with those before.

[86] Wintterlin, *Behördenorganisation*, I, pp. 81–6; Vann, *Making of a state*, pp. 111–15.

revenues are now lost, a reliable contemporary estimate places them at 120,000fl. annually.[87] Altogether these properties contained less than 4 per cent of the population.[88]

The Württemberg Kammergut revenues were similar to those of other princes and consisted of the usual customs duties (*Zölle*), prerogatives (*Regalien*) such as the right to mint coins (*Münzregal*), and the returns from the forests, farms and other undertakings.[89] Most of these were leased out rather than administered directly by ducal servants. The money was collected by a ducal official known as the *Keller* who was present in each Amt. As the Keller were allowed to deduct both the running costs and their salaries before remitting the returns to the ducal treasury (*Landschreiberei*), the actual amount flowing into the hands of the duke was very low.[90] Under Duke Eberhard Ludwig in the years following 1714, the Keller remitted on average about 108,000fl. to which the Forstämter added about 22,550fl. and the Zölle around 59,400fl. Thus, together with various other small sources of income, the duke had a regular Kammeral income of only 292,000fl.[91]

This corresponds to a total per head of population of less than 45xr. compared with about 1fl. 20xr. in Bavaria, 2fl. in Hanover, 2fl. 50xr. in the Palatinate and 4fl. in Saxony.[92] This placed the duke of Württemberg on the same disadvantageous level as a prince bishop, and considerably behind his secular rivals. His main competitor, the landgrave of Hessen-Kassel, for example, directly controlled two-thirds of the territory, and five-sixths of the population, and so was largely free from financial dependence on his estates. In fact, the roles were reversed, as his profits from the foreign subsidies put him in a position to lend his estates money and so

---

[87] Zentrales Staatsarchiv Merseburg, Rep. XI, Nr. 298, Fasz. 30, vol. 7, fol. 392: a Prussian estimate from 1767.

[88] By 1786 the *Kammerschreibereigut* comprised 19 districts inhabited by over 22,000 people or 3.8 per cent of the total population: Röder, *Geographie und Statistik*, I, pp. 488–509.

[89] For a breakdown of these revenues see K. O. Müller, 'Die Finanzwirtschaft in Württemberg unter Herzog Karl Alexander (1733–1737)', *WVJHLG*, NF38 (1932), 276–317.

[90] The Keller deducted the revenues received in kind which only appeared in the central accounts with the establishment of the *Generalkasse* in 1767. Then such payments totalled about 330,000fl., of which perhaps 100,000fl. was a result of Carl Eugen's reckless exploitation of the forests. HSAS, A257: Bd. 1–3. As the *Kammerplan* of 1777 (Pfaff, *Geschichte des Fürstenhauses*, IV, pp. 392–3) states the level of revenue destined for the pay and expenses of local officials at 266,824fl. (out of 1,212,000fl. total revenue), it seems fair to assume that running costs at the beginning of the century were 200,000 to 250,000fl. annually.

[91] HSAS, A256: Bd. 197–216. Note: this figure excludes the contributions from the estates and from Kirchengut as well as the Kammerschreiberei. The other main sources of revenue were the various economic undertakings which under Eberhard Ludwig were still listed separately, but thereafter were included under the Keller remittances: iron works (45,000fl.), saw mills (5,000fl.) etc. In addition came the tobacco monopoly (4,000fl.), fines (4,500fl.), the so-called *Tax Gelder* collected from civil servants after 1709 (9,000fl. rising to 25,000fl.), deductions from inheritances (1,000fl.), direct taxes from the remaining Kammergut villages (1,200fl.), etc.

[92] Hartmann, *Steuersystem*, pp. 284–303, and *Geld*, pp. 15, 21–7; Carsten, *Princes and parliaments*, pp. 333–40.

make them dependent on him. This goes a long way towards explaining the relatively harmonious relationship between ruler and estates there.[93]

The church lands formed the second part of the tripartite structure. Whereas Duke Ulrich had confiscated church property in the manner of the Saxon and Hessian rulers when he introduced the Reformation into Württemberg in 1534, his pious son and successor, Duke Christoph, had formed it into a separate trust known as the *Kirchengut*.[94] Right until the end of the old order in 1806, the exact status of the church property was a matter of dispute. Technically, it remained part of the ducal property as the duke was simultaneously head of the church (*Landesbischof*). The 2,400 or so ecclesiastics, school teachers and church administrators also remained salaried ducal servants, subordinated to two government departments: the *Kirchenrat* for financial and economic affairs and the *Konsistorium* for religious matters. However, the fourteen prelates, representing the fourteen monastical districts (*Klosterämter*) into which the church property was divided, each had a seat on the Landtag and so were simultaneously part of the estates. Officially, the prelates had no say in the financial administration which remained in the hands of ducal officials called *geistliche Verwalter*.[95] Nevertheless, their presence in the Landtag weakened ducal control over the church property as a whole, especially with the *Reversalien* document of 1733 by which the Catholic Carl Alexander was forced to renounce his rights as head of the church.[96] A more significant weakness derived from Duke Christoph's church ordinances of the 1550s, which were confirmed by all his successors.[97] These specified that the revenue of this property, after deduction of the church's considerable running costs, was to be paid into a separate treasury (the *Kirchenkasten*), and only to be used for pious purposes. By these decrees, the dukes signed away their ability to exploit the resources of about a quarter of the duchy's cultivable land, worth 32,759,000fl. and inhabited by around 11 per cent of the total population.[98] This land generated revenues of up to

---

[93] Ingrao, *Hessian mercenary state*, pp. 37–44.

[94] LBS, Cod. hist. fol. 636, *Kurtzer actenmäßiger Bericht von dem württembergischen geistlichen Gut* (1765); H. Hermelink, 'Geschichte des allgemeinen Kirchenguts in Württemberg', *WJSL* (1903), 78–101, and *ibid.*, part II, pp. 1–81; M. Leube, 'Die fremden Ausgaben des altwürttembergischen Kirchenguts des vormaligen Herzogthums Württemberg', *BWKG*, NF29 (1925), 168–99; K. V. Riecke, 'Das evangelische Kirchengut des vormaligen Herzogthums Württemberg', *BBSAW* (1876), 129–35, 167–74.

[95] Wintterlin, *Behördenorganisation*, I, pp. 40–3; Dehlinger, *Württembergs Staatswesen*, I, pp. 87–94.

[96] On the *Reversalien*, see pp.159–60 and 166–8 below.

[97] The *Große Kirchenordnung* of 15 May 1559 is printed in A. L. Reyscher (ed.), *Vollständige, historisch und kritisch bearbeitete Sammlung der württembergischen Gesetze* (29 vols., Stuttgart/Tübingen, 1828–51), pp. 106–284.

[98] Dehlinger, *Württembergs Staatswesen*, I, p. 93 and Riecke, 'Kirchengut', 168 put the value at 32,759,931fl. 6xr. In addition the 833 pious institutions (*Fromme Stiftungen*) had property worth 3.5 million fl.: Pfaff, *Geschichte des Fürstenhauses*, IV, p. 425. The Kirchengut encompassed 52,582ha of directly owned land and 122,282ha of partly owned and feudal holdings. The population of the Klosterämter totalled 68,412 in 1790 (including 7,000–8,000 serfs).

two million florins a year.[99] Though the average surplus between 1714 and 1733 after deduction of the running costs was only around 191,000fl. the church remained an enormously rich institution, especially because of its low level of indebtedness.[100] If the dukes could regain control of it, they would not only gain access to new sources of revenue, but would greatly enlarge their capital base upon which they could attract foreign loans. This would go a long way to freeing them from their financial dependence on the estates.

The third part of the structure comprised the rest of the population. While these were just as much the duke's subjects as the inhabitants of the other two parts, the right to tax them rested solely with the estates. Under the legislation of the 'good old law' the estates were obliged to raise taxes to pay off those ducal debts they had agreed to amortise. To do this they levied a direct tax known as the *Ordinari Ablösungshilfe*, which in the eighteenth century was worth about 184,000fl.[101] In the course of the Thirty Years War even the estates realised that the duke could not finance his role in the tripartite structure solely from his own resources and so in 1638 they agreed to the introduction of a new indirect tax called the *Accise*. Here, Württemberg was acting in accordance with other German states which also introduced similar taxes in the course of the seventeenth century. The only difference was that in Württemberg the Accise remained firmly under the estates' control and was paid into their treasury, the *Landschaftliche Einnehmerei*.[102] They not only controlled its collection, but also specified how it would be spent. By the early eighteenth century the Accise brought in around 100,000fl. Of this, they generally made a voluntary contribution called the *Kammerbeitrag* of 40,000fl. to the duke while the rest went to pay their running expenses (about 15,000fl.), the cost of the duchy's representative at the Reichstag (about 7,000fl.), and the interest and debt repayments. Additional payments or 'gifts' were made annually to the duke and members of his family on the occasion of marriages or birth of children. In the early eighteenth century, these averaged 10,000fl.–25,000fl. a year and were, like the Kammerbeitrag, voluntary and could be withheld or cancelled.[103] Finally, as the result of the almost constant warfare produced by Louis XIV's wars of aggression

---

[99] C. Belschner, *Ludwigsburg*, p. 38. The average was 836,208fl. Revenue increased dramatically in the last third of the century and stood at 2,370,415fl. including 649,298fl. surplus carried over from the previous year. The pious institutions were said to have an annual income of 1 million fl.: Pfaff, *Geschichte des Fürstenhauses*, IV, pp. 408, 474 n.1.

[100] HSAS, A282: Bd. 1449x–1468x. According to Hermelink, 'Kirchengut', pp. 33–4 the church's capital borrowing stood at only half of the value of the money it had lent out to others between 1743 and 1793.

[101] Introduced in 1554 and also known as the *Catherinae* as it was collected from Catharinae (25 Nov.) to Catharinae until this was changed 1739/40 to Georgii (23 Apr.) like other civil taxes. HSAS, L5: Tom. 147, fol. 700–8. As the estates regularly 'moderated' the tax quotas by at least 3,000fl. per year as a result of crop failures, adverse weather etc., the full 184,000fl. was never actually collected. For the totals actually collected see HSAS, L10: *Einnehmerei Rechnungen*.

[102] Grube, *Landtag*, pp. 315–16; Söll, *Wirtschaftspolitik*, pp. 62–5.

[103] HSAS, L10: *Einnehmerei Rechnungen* 1713/14–1770/1.

and the resultant obligation of the duchy to provide its contingent to the Reichsarmee, the estates agreed to an additional tax. This was the *Extraordinari* introduced in 1681 as a direct tax collected using the same tax books as the Ordinari. As a result the Extraordinari was always expressed as a proportion, such as seven-eighths or one-and-a-half times, of the Ordinari. Like the Ordinari, its precise level was determined by the estates whose officials then collected it and paid it through the Einnehmerei to the ducal war treasury (*Kriegskasse*).[104]

Compared with other states, this system of taxation not only produced very low returns, but was also very favourable to the estates. Collection of the direct taxes (Ordinari and Extraordinari) was carried out in the sixty or so secular Ämter according to a property register which had remained unchanged since 1628/51. Considering that over 80 per cent of the population lived in these Ämter and that these covered the bulk of the duchy, the tax register's valuation of the property at less than thirty-four million florins represented a gross undervaluation.[105] The church lands, which were inhabited by only 11 per cent of the population, were worth almost as much, while the fire insurance value of the buildings alone was worth over forty-two million florins in 1773.[106] Moreover, as the register remained virtually unchanged throughout the century despite ducal efforts to revise it, the assessment fell from about 85fl. of taxable capital per head in the 1720s to 65fl. by 1780. Although this still remained higher than some other territories,[107] tax was levied at the very low rate of about half a per cent of total value.

As the estates rarely granted an annual Extraordinari of more than two times the value of the Ordinari during the eighteenth century, the total value of direct taxes in Württemberg was around 540,000fl. (3 × 180,000). With a total population conservatively estimated at 400,000 for the first half of the century, this gives a per capita burden of about 1fl. 20xr.[108] This is over 20 per cent lower than that in Prussia, about half that in France and not much more than a third of that in Saxony.[109]

This tripartite structure worked to the advantage of the estates and especially the group which came to dominate them. This group was already known by

[104] HSAS, L5: Tom. 160, fol. 391–2; Grube, *Landtag*, p. 351. A full Extraordinari was nominally worth one 'annual tax' (*Jahressteuer*) of 184,000fl. but like the Ordinari was subject to deductions for bad weather etc. (see note 101 above). On the amounts actually collected see L10: *Einnehmerei Rechnungen*, 1713/14–1770/1.

[105] Schott, 'Wirtschaftliches Leben', p. 356. Population from Röder, *Geographie und Statistik*, I, pp. 177–539.

[106] Pfaff, *Geschichte des Fürstenhauses*, IV, pp. 427–9. Thirteen years later the buildings were valued at over 54 million fl.

[107] According to Büsching, *Erdbeschreibung*, VII, pp. 790–1 taxable capital per head of population in Pfalz-Sulzbach was about 40fl. in 1780.

[108] HSAS, A38: Bü. 99, 5 Apr. 1719, privy council estimate. Storm, *Feldherr*, pp. 51–5 estimates the population in 1700 at 340,000. In 1733 it totalled 428,000 and 1750 467,000.

[109] Hartmann, *Steuersystem*, p. 321.

contemporaries as the *Ehrbarkeit* or worthies and, in the absence of a native nobility, was the most important social group in the duchy.[110]

Having undergone a number of changes since their origins in the fifteenth century, the worthies had become a closed elite of families by the late seventeenth century. After the 1680s it was almost impossible for any individual to join them either from lower social orders within the duchy, or from other groups outside it. By 1790 they still numbered only 4,000 out of the duchy's total population of 630,000.[111] Although economically differentiated, they all had a stake in the duchy's traditional economy of small-scale trade and agriculture. However, it was their monopoly of the positions of power within the duchy's administrative structure that provided the real basis of their influence.

The key to this monopoly was their control of the administration of the district towns (*Amtsstädte*). Each Amtsstädt was governed by a magistracy which, in addition to general civic administrative duties, was charged with exercising a wide range of important governmental and judicial functions for the whole district. These included both the appointment of local officials and the distribution of the tax quota assigned to the district by the estates, as well as assisting the central authorities in arranging military quarters and transport, and selecting militiamen. Any group that could monopolise the office of magistrate would be in a position to control local affairs. The worthies were able to establish such a monopoly by influencing the elections. Though still nominally chosen by the citizens, most magistrates had in fact become, by the eighteenth century, life appointees who chose their own replacements. The small size of most Württemberg towns, many of which were little more than large villages, undoubtedly helped by limiting the number of potential challengers. The franchise was restricted to those possessing full citizenship (*Bürgerrecht*), applications for which were judged by the magistrates. Through their dominance of civic high office, the worthies could consolidate their hold over the entire region through manipulation and favouritism to create extensive networks of patronage.[112] Politically, their position was secured by the ruling of 1515 that only the magistrates could choose who was to represent the entire district at the Landtag, and by the practice, developed in the sixteenth century, of always choosing at least one magistrate as a delegate. Thus, by about 1650, the Württemberg Landtag was firmly in their hands.[113]

By successfully infiltrating the state church after the introduction of Lutheranism in 1534, the worthies gained another area for patronage in ecclesiastical appointments. This was reinforced through their domination of the

[110] H. M. Decker-Hauff, 'Die geistige Führungsschicht Württembergs', in G. Franz (ed.), *Beamtentum und Pfarrerstand 1400–1800. Büdinger Vorträge 1967* (Limburg, 1972), pp. 51–80.

[111] Haug-Moritz, *Württembergischer Ständekonflikt*, p. 76.

[112] For good examples of how patronage functioned in Württemberg see M. N. Wessling, 'Medicine and government in early modern Württemberg' (University of Michigan Ph.D., 1988), pp. 28–52, 70–5.

[113] Wilson, 'Power to defend', 39–40.

University of Tübingen which was largely funded by the church and served as the main training establishment for the duchy's priests and lawyers. The fact that the prelates generally came from worthy families strengthened their hold still further.[114] It also produced a close spirit of co-operation between the secular and ecclesiastical elements of the estates and shut out any possibility of the duke's playing one off against the other, despite the latent antagonisms that existed.[115]

Such local elites existed elsewhere in the German states, but the absence of a native nobility meant that the worthies were relatively unique. For example, similar groups of families controlled village and district affairs in Hessen-Kassel by dominating local office and limiting the franchise. However, these Hessian provincial elites were themselves the clients of the local nobility, who in turn represented the countryside in the estates, held important positions in the princely administration and judiciary, and were often local landlords as well. The secession of the Württemberg nobility in the early sixteenth century had removed this key level in the duchy's hierarchy of patronage and gave the worthies considerable autonomy. The Hessian nobility's special relationship to the landgrave obliged them to enforce his decrees, even when this adversely affected the operation of their patronage system. This proved the case with the conscription laws introduced in 1762. The nobility were no longer able to protect their clients from the draft, compelling them to develop other strategies to preserve their local position. The Württemberg worthies were not obliged to follow the dictates of the duchy's civil bureaucracy in the same way, as they were neither their tenants nor their clients.[116]

The tripartite structure described above fully conformed with the worthies' view of the world in which each component in Württemberg society was accorded its place and share of the burdens. In their eyes, the Kirchengut supported the church and its system of schools and poor relief. This was anchored in Duke Christoph's church ordinances which both imposed Lutheran orthodoxy, and with it the worthies' lucrative monopoly of church posts, and kept the duke financially weak. The duke was supported by the revenue of his own property and was responsible for defence and the maintenance of an administrative and legal system that ensured the continuation of the worthies' network of patronage. The third part of this structure, the general population, was to pay for the amortisation of ducal debts and provide the manpower, but not the money, for the defence of the duchy. This was

---

[114] Decker-Hauff, 'Führungsschicht', p. 68; M. Fulbrook, *Piety and politics. Religion and the rise of absolutism in England, Württemberg and Prussia* (Cambridge, 1983), pp. 77–80; M. Hasselhorn, *Der altwürttembergische Pfarrstand im 18. Jahrhundert* (Stuttgart, 1958); R. Po-Chia Hsia, *Social discipline in the Reformation: central Europe 1550–1750* (London, 1989), pp. 14–20.

[115] These antagonisms have been played down in the traditional Württemberg literature and centred on a dispute over how much the church was to contribute to the estates' taxes. By 1719/20 the church had arrears of over 1.7 million fl. in their contribution: HSAS, L10: *Einnehmerei Rechnung 1719/20*.

[116] P. K. Taylor, 'The household's most expendable people: The draft and peasant society in 18th century Hessen-Kassel' (Univ. of Iowa, Ph.D., 1987), pp. 190–211.

enshrined in the Tübingen Treaty and the structure of the Landtag. Through its power to vote and collect taxes, the Landtag was entrusted with the role of regulator ensuring that the duke received just enough money to enable him to fulfil his role, but not so much that he was able to break out of the structure altogether. In effect, the 'good old law' in Württemberg was a miniature version of the system of checks and balances of the Reich as a whole that we met in the preceding chapter.

The worthies remained remarkably consistent in their defence of this structure. In 1622 the Tübingen law professor Christoph Besold (1577–1638) published a treatise which effectively summarised the attitude they were to hold for the next 170 years.[117] Like virtually every other German political theorist, Besold considered estates an essential component of any state. Their function was 'to defend the laws and liberties of the people' from acts of tyranny by serving as the custodians of the territory's constitution. All subjects were to be permitted to appeal to them for protection against unlawful arrest, arbitrary judgment and unconstitutional taxation. Such safeguards were denied individuals under absolutism, which Besold termed 'the ruin of the Reich'. The estates thus formed a crucial link between ruler and subject, acting as an intermediary 'so that neither princely government degenerates into tyranny, nor the people into anarchy through unlimited freedom'.

However, the estates considered themselves as more than merely a constitutional watchdog. Their presence contributed positively to the efficiency of the state, making a monarchy with estates superior to absolute rule. People were more likely to obey laws to which their representatives, the estates, had agreed, than arbitrary princely decrees. Harmony between prince and estates would encourage subjects to support princely policy. Thus, in the eyes of the estates, it was in the duke's own interest to co-operate with them as his power and military potential would be enhanced. Moreover, the estates were better placed to provide impartial advice than paid, mercenary advisers. Only a bad prince believed the flattery of his courtiers that co-operation with the estates lowered his prestige and status. An examination of ruler–estate relations in Württemberg show that the duke increasingly did not share the estates' opinion.

THE NATURE OF RULER–ESTATE RELATIONS

Interpretations of ruler–estate relations have been shaped by the overall view of estates and the question of their link to modern parliamentary institutions. This has produced three schools of thought which are of relevance here. The first is the older German interpretation which is closely linked to Borussian concepts of state-building. The estates are dismissed as reactionary oligarchies which had nothing to

---

[117] *De consilio politico axiomata aliquam multa* (2nd edn, Tübingen, 1622). This work is summarised in H. Dreitzel, *Absolutismus und ständische Verfassung in Deutschland* (Mainz, 1992), pp. 36–41.

contribute to the process of state-formation and merely obstructed the 'progressive' policies of their ruler out of a desire to defend their own material position and influence. Most were crushed within a few decades of 1648 as a necessary part of the development of absolutism. The Western liberal or 'whiggish' school offers a more positive interpretation. Though ruler–estate relations were still characterised by conflict, the estates contributed constructively to state development through limiting the excesses of absolute rule. There is a strong tendency to trace a linear development from the late medieval estates, through the early modern period, into nineteenth-century constitutional monarchy, and in some cases, even into the re-establishment of parliamentary democracy in West Germany after 1945.[118] This is contested by the Marxist model which emphasises consensus rather than conflict between rulers and estates. Both are seen as part of the same social elite which resolved its differences through various compromises in order to maintain a common hold on power. The estates' decline was due to the nobles' preference for absolute monarchy which made retention of such institutions unnecessary.[119]

Apart from the Marxist model, these interpretations emphasise dualism and conflict. The implication is that ruler and estates were mutually hostile, their differences irreconcilable and, consequently, conflict between them inevitable. The lengthy lists of complaints, or *Gravamina*, which estates across the Reich regularly presented to their rulers, do appear to confirm this.[120] However, emphasis on dualism has distorted the picture of early modern ruler–estate relations. There was common ground, though not as much as the Marxists have suggested. Relations were characterised as much by co-operation as conflict. The German princes, like their contemporaries elsewhere, did not intend to remove or crush the estates and other intermediary bodies at all costs. Internal consolidation was not an end in itself but a means to achieve dynastic and political goals. Estates could play a vital part in this because they carried out useful functions. Princes generally recognised the validity of Besold's arguments that harmony between ruler and estates increased state efficiency. Most were consequently at pains to minimise conflict and, above all, avoid an open confrontation. A certain level of friction was unavoidable, hence the lengthy Gravamina. However, serious conflict only arose when the sides could no longer compromise.[121]

---

[118] Both Grube and Carsten are examples of this school. The most recent and extreme exponent is P. Blickle, 'Communalism, parliamentarism, republicanism', *Parliaments, Estates and Representation*, 8 (1986), 1–13. The older nineteenth-century literature is summarised in G. Birtsch, 'Die landständische Verfassung als Gegenstand der Forschung', in D. Gerhard (ed.), *Ständische Vertretungen in Europa im 17 und 18. Jahrhundert* (Göttingen, 1969), pp. 32–71.

[119] Anderson, *Lineages*; Dorpalen, *German history*, pp. 138–67.

[120] The Württemberg Gravamina are in HSAS, L5: Tomi Actorum. The first was presented in 1459, or two years after the first known Landtag.

[121] Haug-Moritz, *Württembergischer Ständekonflikt*, pp. 5–14; Gagliardo, *Germany under the old regime*, pp. 99–104; R. G. Asch, 'Estates and princes after 1648: The consequences of the Thirty Years' War', *German History*, 6 (1988), 113–32.

Demands for war finance provided the trigger for ruler–estate conflict in Württemberg, as they did generally throughout the Reich. The amount of money threatened to shift decisively the internal balance of power to the duke's favour and so undermine the means by which the worthies maintained their social and political influence. The new standing army required high levels of continuous taxation. If the estates voted money on a regular basis, it was very difficult to compel the duke to observe whatever promises he had made.[122]

A compromise proved impossible in Württemberg because the views of duke and estates diverged so sharply. Differences in opinion were endemic to ruler–estates relations throughout Europe, given their different priorities. Rulers' preoccupation with war and dynastic advancement inclined them to take a broader view than their estates, whose concern for local privileges gave them narrow horizons.[123] The crucial issue was the relative balance between common ground and divergent priorities. The development of a new style of kingship associated with baroque absolutism tipped the balance towards the latter in many of the German states. Compromises remained possible provided at least part of the estates saw sufficient advantage in co-operating with a ruler's new policies. This proved not to be the case in Württemberg, where the common ground was steadily eroded after 1677.

As the outlook of the worthies was essentially non-noble, it was already at odds with that of the duke, which was essentially aristocratic. The lack of any noble membership of the estates, despite periodic ducal attempts to re-establish control over the local imperial knights, denied the duke potential allies within the Landtag. Further differences appeared with the introduction of French culture into Württemberg by Regent Friedrich Carl in the 1680s. The worthies remained firmly rooted in their German-speaking closed cultural environment with its parochial world view, and so were increasingly out of step with the French-speaking cosmopolitan court.[124]

The importation of foreign styles and tastes aroused the worthies' xenophobia. Typical of this is the outburst by the estates' legal adviser, Johann Dietrich Hörner (1652–1724) in 1724, that a large army would allow into the duchy an influx of foreigners who would destroy true Württemberg values. Particular criticism was levelled at foreigners in the bureaucracy whose numbers were greatly exaggerated and whose influence was believed to be behind sinister ducal designs.[125]

---

[122] Wilson, 'The power to defend', pp. 36–7.

[123] F. Tallett, *War and society in early modern Europe 1495–1715* (London/New York, 1992), pp. 193–8; C. Russell, 'Monarchies, war and estates in England, France and Spain c. 1580 to c. 1640', *Legislative Studies Quarterly*, 7 (1982), 205–20.

[124] For examples see Vann, *Making of a state*, pp. 152–3, 159–61. On this 'small town' mentality generally, see M. Walker, *German home towns. Community, state and general estate 1648–1871* (Ithaca, 1971).

[125] Pfaff, *Geschichte des Militärwesens*, p. 45. On foreigners in the bureaucracy, see pp. 130–5, 163–5 and 219–21.

Religious prejudice deepened these suspicions. Lutheran orthodoxy and the development of pietism in the late seventeenth century strengthened the worthies' common outlook and gave it moral overtones. To leading figures such as Dr Johann Heinrich Sturm (1651–1709), defence of their power base became inextricably mixed with defence of their version of Christianity.[126] In their eyes the duke was failing in his duty as head of the state church by encouraging the immigration of Catholics, Calvinists and Jews to assist in his schemes. The lavish baroque court and his often scandalous personal behaviour only further antagonised them. The gap widened with the accession of a Catholic branch of the ducal family in 1733.

This atmosphere bred mistrust which further fuelled the conflict. The estates were unable to comprehend the magnitude of war costs. They were convinced the duke was squandering the money on other, less essential areas. Their view was groundless as the investigation of ducal finances will show (pp. 126–30, 203–9, 228–9). However, regardless of whether they were justified or not, such fears made the worthies immediately suspicious of the duke's ultimate intentions. Equally, their prevarication encouraged the duke to see their hand behind every obstacle in his path.

The worthies could only see disadvantages in the duke's alien culture and absolutist policies. Particularly menacing was the way they threatened to change the existing structure of the duchy. Change was considered both contrary to their interests and unnecessary. This attitude made them very inflexible and led them to oppose virtually any innovation even if it was beneficial to the rest of the population. For example, their desire to preserve patronage caused them to hinder improvement in the duchy's medical service. Local doctors were generally graduates of Tübingen and integrated into their network of families. The practice of doctors holding responsibility for more than one district to improve their remuneration was defended on the grounds that they were still satisfactorily performing their duties. Evidence to the contrary was concealed by minimising the problems of health care in the localities. The medical community was pressurised to limit both therapeutic and administrative innovation. Carl Eugen was compelled to abandon a reform of the duchy's antiquated medical code as politically too controversial.[127]

Equally, tax reforms were opposed as they threatened both to place the worthies in a higher tax bracket and provide the duke with more money. Ducal attempts to stimulate the economy and boost revenue by establishing new industries and government monopolies threatened their stake in the duchy's existing economy. As they were neither merchants nor bankers, they had nothing to gain from agreeing to a standing army. Indeed, it is significant that they sought to prevent the few

---

[126] For examples of Sturm's speeches, see Vann, *Making of a state*, pp. 159–61, 166–7.
[127] Wessling, 'Medicine and government', pp. 21, 76–158.

Württemberg merchants engaged in supplying the army and court from supporting the duke during the court case of 1764–70.[128] Very few of their relations served as army officers and the proportion declined as the century wore on and the number of noble-born officers increased. Only after the worthies had themselves undergone a change did certain disadvantaged sections request entry to the officer corps at the end of the century.[129] The traditional core, however, persisted in the belief that the army was disreputable and alien to true Württemberg values. As late as 1818, the Tübingen bookseller Hauff refused to allow his daughters to consider marrying a military man: 'An officer can be as good or as bad as he likes, but his estate is always beneath ours and even the best of them is a starving wretch, not to speak of his morals.'[130] This attitude contrasted strongly with that of elite groups elsewhere. The Prussian, Saxon and Hessian nobility were reconciled to a standing army through the career opportunities it offered. The sons of two-thirds of all Hessian nobles along with one-third of civil servants found employment in the Hessian army.[131]

By excluding ducal officials from the Landtag in 1628, the worthies 'drew a rigid distinction between themselves and the central government' and in doing so abdicated participation in the central bureaucracy.[132] While they continued to have close links with the bureaucrats themselves, many of whom married into worthy families, the worthies did not share in the process of ducal policy-making. Although they did send delegates to sit on the various government committees (*Deputationen*) which developed during the eighteenth century, they boycotted those such as the *Commerzien Deputation* which the duke had established as 'think tanks' for new ideas.[133] Therefore, they did not have a stake in the success or failure of key areas of ducal policy. The lack of common ground paradoxically encouraged the estates' survival. The worthies needed to keep the old institutions alive because absolutism had nothing to offer them.

Innovations threatened to undermine rather than improve existing arrangements which they in any case regarded as the best available. For example, they viewed the duchy's high infant mortality as simply a fact of life and not something that could be altered through better health care.[134] Moreover, their continued procrastination and obstruction was not purely an instance of a hopeless and reactionary resistance

---

[128] HSAS, A202: Bü. 2776; A203: Bü. 162; L6.4.13.3; L6.4.13.10 (Apr. 1767).
[129] Wunder, *Privilegierung und Disziplinierung*, pp. 82–97; and the sources cited in note 11 above.
[130] Hasselhorn, *Pfarrstand*, pp. 31–2.
[131] Carsten, *Princes and parliaments*, pp. 240–1; C. W. Ingrao, 'Kameralismus und Militarismus im deutschen Polizeistaat: Der hessische Söldnerstaat', in G. Schmidt (ed.), *Stände und Gesellschaft im Alten Reich* (Stuttgart, 1989), pp. 171–86 at p. 174.
[132] Vann, *Making of a state*, pp. 98–100, 103.
[133] Söll, *Wirtschaftspolitik*, pp. 86, 98–100, 115–20; Dehlinger, *Württembergs Staatswesen*, I, pp. 104–5, II, p. 659; Wintterlin, *Behördenorganisation*, I, pp. 78–102. Carsten, *Princes and parliaments*, pp. 132–3 overestimates the estates' co-operativeness.
[134] Wessling, 'Medicine and government', p. 21.

to the inevitable. It was also the product of a timeless view of life. Like other groups within the Reich, the worthies' world picture remained fixed within a seemingly unchanging agrarian social order.[135]

However, this should not lead us to characterise ruler–estate conflict as a simple struggle between a 'reactionary' estate and a 'progressive' and 'modernising' duke. This was the general tendency, but neither party was entirely consistent in its attitude and policies. Though the duke wanted change, he also had no desire to destroy the old order. His standpoint was also contradictory. Within his territory he followed what contemporaries termed Machiavellian or Hobbesian absolutist concepts. Towards the Reich he pursued the 'king-maker' (*Monarchomacher*) estates' principle of limiting princely power, in this case that of the emperor, through the representation of the princes in the Reichstag.[136]

Equally, though the worthies generally remained a closed group with narrow horizons, this did not prevent them developing personal contacts across Europe to defend their interests. They had a representative in Vienna and secured Saxon mediation in their efforts to induce the Catholic Dowager Duchess Maria Augusta to relinquish the regency in 1737. An extensive network was built up after 1758 to secure support against Carl Eugen's arbitrary rule by using the contacts of Christian Dietrich Keller (1699–1766). Keller came from an established worthy family with close ties to the bureaucracy. He himself became a privy councillor before entering Sachsen-Gotha service in 1751. However, his career was exceptional among the worthies. He played a double game during the negotiations over the regency in 1737 for which he was rewarded with elevation to the nobility by the emperor. Ostensibly he continued to represent the interests of the worthies and their friends in the privy council throughout the subsequent Protestant regency. Behind the scenes he furthered his own career by advancing Prussian interests and making useful contacts in foreign governments.[137]

In contrast, most of the worthies had little desire to mix with the movers and shakers of imperial politics. Their contacts outside the duchy were a defence mechanism to protect the Württemberg status quo, not to alter it. Within the duchy they remained to the end incapable of generating significant reforms.[138] This was perceived as contrary to their functions which, as defined by Besold, were primarily to limit princely transgressions and prevent the duke becoming a despot. Altogether, their attitude is best summed up by the exclamation of one of the prelates: 'Your grace! *nuh nex nuis!* – just nothing new!'[139]

---

[135] Arndt identifies the same for the imperial counts, *Reichsgrafenkollegium*, p. 333.

[136] For discussion of these concepts, see Dreitzel, *Absolutismus und ständische Verfassung*, pp. 17–32.

[137] Haug-Moritz, *Württembergischer Ständekonflikt*, pp. 299–308; Pfeilsticker, *Dienerbuch*, pp. 1153, 1209, 1235, 1367, 1369, 1381.

[138] E. Grothe, 'Der württembergische Reformlandtag 1797–1799', *ZWLG*, 48 (1989), 159–200.

[139] Quoted in Walker, *Moser*, p. 201.

DUCAL FINANCIAL POLICIES: CONFLICTS AND CONSTRAINTS

If Württemberg dukes were to achieve their aims, they had to secure more money than the existing structure of the duchy would allow. There were few possibilities to do this without involving the estates. One was to exploit ducal prerogatives and grant monopoly rights to economic undertakings, in return for a share in the profits. Public office could also be sold. Neither of these expedients brought in good returns.[140] Borrowing offered a traditional solution to cash-flow problems and was extensively used by Eberhard Ludwig. Under his rule the Rentkammer borrowed an average of 130,000fl. a year between 1714 and 1733.[141] However, this was only a short-term solution and was fraught with difficulties. First, the absence of a native banking class forced the dukes to borrow outside the duchy. This could be dangerous when these outsiders were other princes, as was the case with a Prussian loan negotiated by the regency government (1737–44).[142] Second, the policy over-burdened the Kammergut with debt and in the long run reduced its revenues as the more profitable parts had to be pawned to creditors as security. As we have seen above, up to a third of expenditure was devoted to managing these debts, diverting valuable resources away from other areas of policy. Altogether, borrowing threatened to make the dukes still more dependent on their estates as they would be compelled to grant further political concessions to secure the amortisation of these additional debts. Their only real hope lay in inducing the estates to grant new taxes, by either force, persuasion, or a slow process of attrition, whereby the existing fiscal controls were circumvented or rendered ineffective.

The possibilities for using force were limited by the structure of the Reich. Its use had to be legitimised, at best by open rebellion on the part of the estates. This had allowed the Habsburgs to considerably curtail the powers of the Austrian and Bohemian estates in 1620, though, significantly, they did not abolish them entirely.[143] Subsequent caution by the estates prevented such opportunities occurring again. Some rulers resorted to force without such excuse. Recalcitrant estates could be crushed by the arrest of their leaders, or the prolonged occupation of their property by disorderly soldiers. The Great Elector of Brandenburg

---

[140] LBS; cod. hist. fol. 74; Wunder, *Privilegierung*, pp. 71–80.

[141] HSAS, A256: Bd. 197–216.

[142] See pp. 196–8 below. Eberhard Ludwig borrowed from the estates (e.g. in 1728 HSAS L5: Tomi 136–7), courtiers, high government officials, General von Phull, and the merchant Eisenbach. His foreign creditors included the Jewish financiers Gabriel Fränkel and Levin (e.g. a large loan in 1721 A256: Bd. 205, fols. 10–13), Count Christian von Bar (100,000fl. in 1724/25: A256: Bd. 208, fol. 19b), and the *Ritterkanton* Kocher (100,000fl. in 1724/25: *ibid.*, fol. 18b). A few months before his death he began negotiating 300,000fl. in foreign loans (A202: Bü. 1996, 12 Aug. and 14 Sept. 1733).

[143] R. J. W. Evans, *The making of the Habsburg monarchy 1550–1700* (Oxford, 1979), pp. 71, 198–213; Asch, 'Estates and princes', 117–19; C. Kampmann, *Reichsrebellion und kaiserliche Acht. Politische Strafjustiz im dreißigjähren Krieg und das Verfahren gegen Wallenstein 1634* (Münster, 1993), pp. 19–74.

successfully used these methods against the Prussian estates (1661–3), and also subdued those of Cleves and Mark by threatening an invasion (1661). The rulers of Münster, Mainz and Wolfenbüttel used their armies to curtail the autonomy of the cities of Münster (1661), Erfurt (1664) and Brunswick (1671) respectively. However, these successes were achieved under relatively exceptional circumstances. The emperor had not yet restored his authority after the damage of the Thirty Years War. Civil unrest provided an excuse for Mainz's intervention in Erfurt. This was sanctioned by an imperial mandate to restore order. The privileges of Münster and Brunswick lacked solid legal foundation. Prussia lay outside the Reich and so beyond the emperor's jurisdiction. The failure of Württemberg dukes to use force successfully against their estates indicates just how rare these opportunities were.[144]

Emergencies, such as the threat of foreign invasion, could enable a prince to introduce additional taxes on the grounds of necessity. However, this was at best a temporary measure. Consequently, princes made use of imperial legislation to justify such taxation on a permanent basis. In particular they cited Paragraph 180 of the Reichstag's last recess, the *Jüngster Reichsabschied* (JRA) of 1654, which bound all subjects to contribute towards the cost of maintaining fortresses and garrisons.[145] Although intended as a measure to finance defensive installations, the princes interpreted the word 'garrisons' to include other troops as well. This explains their preoccupation with maintaining and developing castles such as Freudenstadt, Hohentwiel, Asperg, Neuffen and Urach in Württemberg, and Bützow, Dömitz and Schwerin in Mecklenburg, despite these being both obsolete and indefensible. Their arguments were reinforced by the legislation of 1681 which established a permanent Reichsarmee to which every state was obliged to contribute. Princes such as the dukes of Württemberg and Mecklenburg argued that such imperial legislation took precedence over local agreements between ruler and estates.[146] In addition Württemberg dukes pointed to their obligations as Swabian executive princes which required troops to implement Kreis and Reichs decisions. Mention was also made of the duke's traditional title as Reichsbannerträger which was said to require an appropriately martial establishment.[147] Haustruppen as well as Kreistruppen should be paid for as they were also helping to defend both the territory and the Reich. Moreover, the princes constantly reminded their estates

---

[144] Carsten, *Princes and parliaments*, pp. 301–9; G. Benecke, *Society and politics in Germany 1500–1750* (London, 1974), pp. 58–64; Hughes, *Early modern Germany*, pp. 99–100.

[145] The text of the relevant section reads 'jedes Churfürsten und Standes Landsassen. Unterthanen und Bürger zu Besetz und Erhaltung der einem oder anderem Reichs-Stand zugehörigen nöthigen Vestungen, Plätzen und Guarnisonen ihren Landes-Früsten, Herrschaften und Obern mit hülflichen Beytrag gehorsamlich an Hand zu gehen . . . ': K. Zeumer (ed.), *Quellensammlung zur Geschichte der deutschen Reichsverfassung in Mittelalter und Neuzeit* (Tübingen, 1913 edn), p. 460.

[146] Grube, *Landtag*, pp. 353–75; P. Wick, *Versuche zur Errichtung des Absolutismus in Mecklenburg in der ersten Hälfte des 18. Jahrhunderts* (Berlin, DDR, 1964), pp. 125–7; Hughes, *Law and politics*, pp. 91–5.

[147] Bandel, *Auf eine Lüge*, p. 50. See p. 23 above.

that they were living in troubled times[148] and that other states were increasing their forces.[149] By referring to the armies of their predecessors and the current establishments of their neighbours, they sought to demonstrate that the size of army they wanted was genuinely 'in proportion to the ability of their land to sustain it' ('nach Proportion der Kräften ihres Landes').[150] Naturally in doing so they interpreted the facts to suit their arguments. In the case of Württemberg, the dukes usually cited the fact that Duke Ulrich had maintained large numbers of troops, while the estates had agreed in 1622 to fund a force of 12,000 men. They passed over the fact that Ulrich's military adventurism had cost him his duchy, while the force the estates had agreed to pay for consisted of militiamen, not regular soldiers.[151]

The estates continually refuted these arguments. They maintained that imperial law did not supersede local arrangements, especially where these were confirmed by the emperor. Here the Mecklenburg estates were in a stronger position than those of Württemberg because the key agreements of 1572, 1621 and 1701 had all been approved by the emperor. The Württemberg estates rectified this by securing imperial recognition of the important 1739 recess (see pp. 188–9). Both refused to acknowledge that their territories had any fortresses in order to undermine their rulers' interpretation of the 1654 JRA. Princely references to the troubled international situation were countered by the argument that larger armies aroused suspicion and jealousy of neighbours and made invasion more, not less, likely.[152]

Continued opposition to their interpretation of the JRA prompted a number of princes to combine in an effort to compel their estates to agree. Though directed primarily against a resurgence of Habsburg power, the Rhenish Alliance of 1658–68 also included provision for mutual military assistance to suppress the members' estates. This was invoked in 1664 against Erfurt. Simultaneously in 1658, the princes obliged the new emperor, Leopold I, to agree to a limit on the subjects' right

---

[148] HSAS, A6: Bü. 35: Eberhard Ludwig to the privy council 13 Sept. 1721; L5: Tom. 126, fols. 6b–10b: Eberhard Ludwig to the estates, 28 Nov. 1714; Tom. 129, fol. 38–61b; A202: Bü. 1992: protocol 16 Jan. 1720; Bü. 2207: Carl Eugen to the estates 15 Dec. 1752; L5: Tom. 132, fol. 263; Tom. 160, fol. 386.

[149] HSAS, A6: Bü. 35 13 Sept. 1721; A28: Bü. 99 privy council protocol Dec. 1735; A202: Bü. 1992 protocol 16 Jan. 1720; Bü. 2207 Carl Eugen to the estates 15 Dec. 1752; L5: Tom. 132 fol. 263; Tom. 160 fol. 386.

[150] HSAS, A28: Bü. 99; A202: Bü. 2207, 15 Dec. 1752; L5: Tom. 129 fol. 43b–44 30 June 1718; Tom. 144 fol. 173b 29 Mar. 1736; Tom. 146 fols. 981–96b 11 Nov. 1738. K. F. Dizinger, *Beiträge zur Geschichte Würtembergs und seines Regentenhauses zur Zeit der Regierung Herzogs Karl Alexanders . . .* (2 vols., Tübingen, 1834), I, pp. 21–2; Bandel, *Auf eine Lüge*, pp. 52–3. Röder, *Geographie und Statistik*, p. 158 estimated in 1787 on the basis of a comparison of Württemberg with Prussia that the duchy ought to be able to maintain 20,000 soldiers. This phrase recurs in documents of both dukes and estates, e.g. HSAS, A28: Bü. 99 31 Dec. 1735.

[151] After Duke Ulrich besieged and annexed the imperial city of Reutlingen in 1519, the duchy was invaded by the Swabian League, who sold it to the Habsburgs a year later.

[152] HSAS, L5: Tomi Actorum esp. estates' response to the duke's half-yearly demands for money; Wilson, 'The power to defend', pp. 34–5; Wick, *Mecklenburg*, pp. 125–7; Tessin, *Mecklenburgisches Militär*, pp. 49–59.

of appeal to the imperial courts and to further restrictions on the estates. They went a step further in 1670 by voting at the Reichstag to extend the provisions of JRA Paragraph 180 to permit rulers to set fiscal obligations without references to their estates.

This represented the high-water mark of the princes' efforts. Thereafter the emperor progressively intervened to prevent any prince from becoming too powerful by ensuring the survival of internal restraints on his power. By refusing in 1671 to confirm the Reichstag's decision, he denied the princes the legitimacy needed to act without their estates' consent. Meanwhile, the estates increasingly found their objections overruled by individual imperial decisions obliging them to contribute to the Kreistruppen. This happened in Württemberg in March 1690 and in most other small states by 1700. However, the questions *quo modo*, or how much they were to contribute, and whether they had to pay for Haustruppen as well, were left undecided. This was a clever tactic. Imperial authority was strengthened by compelling the estates to pay for the defence of the Reich, while by withholding final judgment the emperor retained possibilities for renewed intervention into the domestic affairs of individual states. As the subsequent fate of the dukes of Württemberg and Mecklenburg shows, attempts to use force after 1671 merely played into the hands of the emperor by providing additional excuses for intervention.[153]

Peaceful persuasion was a highly problematic method of obtaining additional taxation. Invariably, the estates made their consent to a new financial package conditional upon further ducal guarantees for their privileges. This threatened to bind the duke further to an already unsatisfactory constitutional arrangement.

The unsatisfactory nature of both force and persuasion compelled the duke to embark on the slow process of circumventing the existing controls and, where possible, rendering them ineffective. In particular, he tried to gain access to the rich resources of the Kirchengut and weaken the worthies' hold over tax assessment and collection. He had a chance if he could loosen their grip on the Landtag and secure the support of part of the estates. Besold had predicted this in 1622 when he listed the ways princes sought to divide their estates. Rulers would seek to remove popular support by portraying the estates as an oligarchy solely concerned with protecting its own interests. All the dukes in this study pursued this policy with some success, as did their contemporaries elsewhere. Besold also warned that rulers would try to split estates by negotiating with individual groups and offering titles and positions to win support.[154]

The worthies had forced the exclusion of ducal officials from the Landtag in 1628

---

[153] Grube, *Landtag*, pp. 359–60; Haug-Moritz, *Württembergischer Ständekonflikt*, pp. 27–8; Carsten, *Princes and parliaments*, p. 318; C. Dipper, *Deutsche Geschichte 1648–1789* (Frankfurt am Main, 1991), pp. 247–8, 291–2.
[154] Dreitzel, *Absolutismus und ständische Verfassung*, p. 40; Grube, *Landtag*, pp. 373–4; Carsten, *Princes and parliaments*, p. 302.

precisely to prevent such a move. Moreover, by extending the dominance of the estates' standing committee (*engere Ausschuß*) they consolidated their hold of the Landtag's affairs. The engere Ausschuß was a permanent body which could be reinforced as a large committee (*größere Ausschuß*). The committee members were nominally elected by the Landtag from among the ranks of the delegates. In practice, the committee, especially the 'smaller' part, was firmly in the hands of the worthies and nominated its own successors. The committee's power derived from the fact that it continued to meet regularly two to three times a year even when the Landtag was not in session. It dealt with all correspondence between duke and estates and took a major hand in drafting all documents and fixing the tax quotas.[155]

The relative social homogeneity of the Württemberg estates further hindered ducal efforts at divide and rule. The lack of affinity with the world of the court disinclined the worthies to seek preferment. Apart from Carl Alexander, only Carl Eugen seriously attempted to win over any of the committee members, and then only in the 1780s.[156]

Nonetheless, as a result of the Thirty Years War, there developed an opportunity for the dukes to undermine the worthies' dominance. This opportunity was presented by the increasing power of the villages and the corresponding decline in importance of the towns both in the economy and in the terms of proportion of the population. As the worthies were solely urban based, this development worked to their disadvantage. The dukes were not slow in appreciating this and sought to encourage the growth of the district assemblies (*Amtsversammlungen*).[157] Their development had been retarded by a ruling of 1515 restricting the powers to choose Landtag delegates to the town magistracy. However, they had never entirely disappeared from the Württemberg political landscape, especially as there were a few Ämter that lacked a district town. Thus, of the eighty-six mandates in the Landtag, ten were already in the hands of these exclusively rural areas.[158] The dukes tried to encourage the development of such assemblies in the remaining Ämter and to further their demands that the Landtag delegate of their Amt should vote as they desired. In this process, the senior ducal district official, the bailiff (*Vogt* or *Amtmann*), played a leading role as he acted as president of the assembly.[159] The

---

[155] Grube, *Landtag*, pp. 197–223. The committee, especially the 'smaller', almost invariably contained the delegates of Stuttgart, Tübingen and the other strongholds of the higher echelons of the worthies, i.e. those with the biggest stake in the status quo.

[156] Haug-Moritz, *Württembergischer Ständekonflikt*, pp. 69–71.

[157] Grube, *Landtag*, pp. 399–408, and 'Dorfgemeinde und Amtsversammlungen in Altwürttemberg', *ZWLG*, 13 (1954), 194–219; Vann, *Making of a state*, pp. 103–7.

[158] Vann, *Making of a state*, p. 196. Although there were eighty-six mandates there were only eighty-three votes, as seventy-two towns and villages together shared sixty-nine votes. The other fourteen votes were held by the fourteen prelates.

[159] It had been the Vögte whom the estates had excluded from the Landtag in 1628. The post of senior bailiff (*Obervogt*) was abolished in 1755 and from 1759 the junior bailiff (*Untervogt*) was retitled *Oberamtmann*. Dehlinger, *Württembergs Staatswesen*, I, pp. 97–8.

dukes particularly tried to encourage the growth of such assemblies in the Klosterämter, where the peasants had never had the right of mandate and the prelates were only obliged to vote as their consciences dictated.

It is important to note here, however, that in encouraging these assemblies, the dukes were not furthering the cause of democracy in any liberal sense. Apart from representatives from the district town's magistracy, the Amtsversammlung generally only contained members of the rural elite, who exercised the same kind of control in the villages as the worthies did in the towns.[160] They were thus not forums for the free expression of the true views of the population. Moreover, the dukes did not intend that the Amtsversammlung should vote as the peasants wanted, but rather as they themselves wanted. The less-educated peasants were unable to develop as consolidated a political and social solidarity as the worthies. They were thus more easily overawed by the local officials into agreeing to the ducal demands, particularly when these were presented in the positive language of lightening their burden and fairer taxation. Both Eberhard Ludwig and Carl Alexander ensured that their Amtmann was present at the Amtsversammlung to swing the votes and Carl Alexander made it clear that the Amtmann would also report those who voted against the motion. While this development could be slowed by the worthies during the regency (1737–44), it could not be reversed and was again encouraged by Carl Eugen, particularly with reference to his new tax system of 1764.

By 1700, therefore, the worthies were already under threat and they began to look around for added security for their position. As their power rested on the sum of all agreements between them and the duke since 1514, they sought guarantees for these. The guarantors they chose were the emperor and the association of Protestant states at the Reichstag (*Corpus Evangelicorum*). The drawback was that these powers were usually slow in reacting to a call for help and could – and frequently did – use their guarantees as a means of extracting advantage for themselves. Therefore, in addition to outside guarantees, the worthies needed some method of internal sanction should the duke break the agreements.

The imperial 'public peace' of 1495 (*Landfrieden*) deprived the estates of the *ius belli* (which the princes retained) and so made armed resistance illegal. The Tübingen Treaty did allow some potential for popular resistance to arbitrary ducal policy by making the subject's obedience conditional on the duke himself observing the agreements. However, this potential was removed in the sixteenth century when the oath of allegiance was changed. In any case, popular resistance was hardly a desirable sanction for the worthies, especially as it threatened to place them in the wrong in the eyes of the emperor. Moreover, the two incidents of popular revolt in

---

[160] L. Baur, *Der städtische Haushalt Tübingens vom Jahre 1750 bis auf unsere Zeit* (Tübingen, 1863), pp. 13–14; Wintterlin, *Behördenorganisation*, I, pp. 61–2.

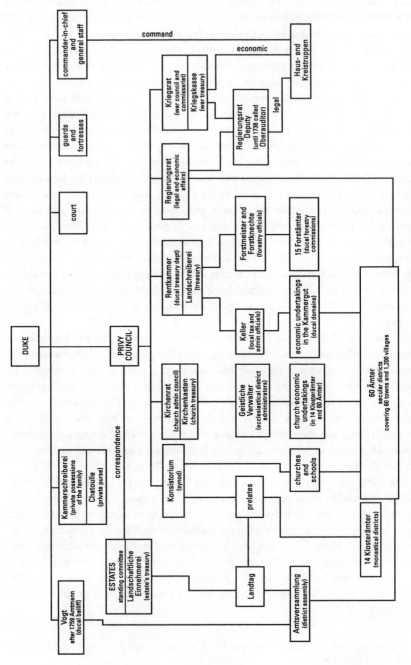

Fig. 2: The bureaucratic structure as set out in the 1660 Kanzleiordnung

Württemberg's history (1514, 1525) had shown a dangerous undercurrent directed at the destruction of their oligarchy.[161]

The best sanction lay in infiltrating or controlling the bureaucracy, as this was the instrument for carrying out ducal orders. If the bureaucracy could be persuaded to honour the agreements, the duke alone would be in a poor position to break them. Therefore, this is precisely the policy the worthies followed.[162]

In practice this generally meant institutionalising the bureaucracy, that is defining the extent and power of each office, and binding those in office to observe the agreements by an oath of allegiance to the constitution. Added security was sought by trying to secure protection against unfair dismissal, as this would prevent the duke simply sacking those civil servants who opposed his will. The key move in this policy was made in 1660 when Duke Eberhard III was persuaded to issue the ninth chancellery ordinance (*Kanzleiordnung*).[163] What appears, at first sight, to be purely a guideline for administrative procedure became a central pillar in the structure maintaining the 'good old law'.

The Kanzleiordnung elevated the privy council, formed in 1629, to the head of the civil bureaucracy[164] (see fig. 2). All other government departments had to report through it to the duke, who was obliged to act only after the council had given its advice. As the council was sworn on the agreements and instructed to object to any measure it believed unconstitutional, the worthies achieved a built-in check on arbitrary ducal policy.

Just how effective that check was depended of course on who the privy councillors were.[165] A council packed with ducal favourites was hardly likely to consider a ducal instruction unconstitutional. On the other hand, the senior bureaucrats often had much in common with the worthies. Lutheran orthodoxy helped to reinforce this. In particular they often shared a common view of the world outside Württemberg. They were distrustful of the overtures of the bigger princes and preferred alliances with the smaller ones. Above all, they wanted to avoid all agreements that threatened to involve the duchy in additional expenses or, worst of all, war. Such an attitude was shared by the rest of the Swabian Kreis, but was contrary to the achievement of princely aims which required risks to be taken.[166]

Thus, the central bureaucracy and particularly the council developed as a kind of

[161] Grube, *Landtag*, pp. 74–82; H. Ühler, 'Der Aufstand des Armen Konrad im Jahr 1514', *WVJHLG*, NF38 (1932), 401–86.

[162] Wunder, *Privilegierung und Disziplinierung*, pp. 36–91.

[163] Printed in Reyscher (ed.), *Gesetze*, XIII, No. 450.

[164] On the privy council see Wintterlin, *Behördenorganisation*, I, pp. 63–5; and his 'Landeshoheit', *HKE*, I, pp. 170–1; Vann, *Making of a state*, pp. 135, 150–1.

[165] Whereas Raeff, *Well-ordered police state* tends to see bureaucratic change as due to an impersonal 'internal dynamism', Vann, *Making of a state*, ably demonstrates the effect of the personal motives of the bureaucrats on policy-making.

[166] Vann, *Making of a state*, pp. 121–7, 178. The 1660 Kanzleiordnung stipulated that only Lutherans could be employed as civil servants.

third force between duke and estates which swung from one to the other depending on the motives of the preponderant group within it at any given time. The same appears to have been true for those in the lower echelons, although this is an area that still requires research. Certainly in times of tension between duke and estates, the lower officials such as those at district level experienced inner conflicts of loyalty.[167]

RULER–ESTATE RELATIONS IN THE REICH

The Thirty Years War is often seen as a critical turning-point in the history of the German estates. Most are described as having been crushed by the introduction of standing armies and militaristic absolutism. Apart from Württemberg, only those of Mecklenburg are regarded as having retained important functions into the eighteenth century.[168] This section intends to challenge this by providing a brief survey of ruler–estate relations between 1648 and 1806. In doing so it will also provide the general context for the more specialised discussion of Württemberg in the following chapters.

The period after 1648 was certainly a critical one for the German estates. The war had ruined their creditworthiness, upon which much of their political power had previously depended. Some, such as those in Austria and Bohemia, had already had their privileges severely curtailed during the conflict. The peace settlement considerably strengthened the territorial princes, whose power was further extended by the imperial legislation of 1654 and 1658. However, the war by no means meant the end for all estates, many of which retained considerable influence into the early nineteenth century. How well they survived depended on how well they had coped with the problems of the past. Those that had developed institutions and procedures which kept pace with those of their rulers generally fared better. Permanent committees, such as those created in Württemberg and Mecklenburg, enabled estates to maintain a presence even when rulers refused to call full assemblies. Furthermore, estates that remained united as a single institution could challenge their ruler's claim to be the sole representative of the common good. This unity needed to be extended across the entire territory. The estates of Hanover, Brandenburg and the Habsburg possessions failed to keep pace with the territorial consolidation of their rulers and still represented the old historic provinces into which the area was formerly divided. They failed to act together to confront rulers who could divert resources from one area to subdue estates in another. The Great Elector of Brandenburg was particularly successful in this. In contrast, the ruling

---

[167] This was certainly the experience of Amtmann Johann Ludwig Huber (1723–1800); see Walter, *Carl Eugen*, pp. 228–30.
[168] Anderson, *Europe in the eighteenth century*, pp. 283–4. For useful overviews of this topic see in addition to Carsten and Asch, Haug-Moritz, *Württembergischer Ständekonflikt*, pp. 15–42, and the literature cited there.

house of Mecklenburg fragmented into rival branches, reversing the usual situation. This also happened in the Rhineland duchies of Jülich, Berg, Cleves and Mark whose estates remained united when the territory was divided between Brandenburg and the Palatinate. Despite mutual rivalry, the two electors managed to split the estates by 1660 and consequently could reduce their powers. This proved impossible in Mecklenburg where the estates preserved their union and defeated attempts to introduce absolutism in the early eighteenth century.

Estates without a chamber (*Kurie*) of noblemen proved particularly vulnerable in the decades immediately after 1648. Such was the case in Fulda, Würzburg, Baden and the Palatinate where the estates consisted entirely of commoners or ecclesiastics. Towns had been especially badly hit by the war and many never fully recovered. Their decline adversely affected their voice in territorial affairs. Rulers in any case now preferred to consult privy councils which had been established in many territories by the early seventeenth century. Delegates from provincial towns proved no match for the noble-born councillors who were increasingly well educated and professional.

The Württemberg estates avoided this fate because the worthies already enjoyed a position in many ways similar to that of the nobility elsewhere. Their close ties to the bureaucracy also helped. Further, by retaining the administration of the Accise they prevented this important new form of indirect taxation falling into ducal hands. They defeated an attempt by Eberhard Ludwig in 1694 to wrest control of their treasury by appointing a ducal receiver. Subsequent efforts also proved unsuccessful. Their survival in this difficult period is mirrored by that of the East Frisian estates. These were made up almost entirely of representatives of the provincial towns and wealthy peasants. They too had suffered in the course of the early seventeenth century, but retained their political influence through the weakness of the ruling Cirksena dynasty. This weakness was preserved by constant intervention in Frisian affairs by Münster, Hanover, Brandenburg and the Dutch Republic.[169]

Where the nobility was the predominant group in the estates, relations with the prince were normally characterised by some form of compromise. The most famous is the Brandenburg Recess of 1653 whereby the elector confirmed the nobles' control over their serfs in return for money for his army. Though conceded out of weakness, this arrangement strengthened the elector's position in the long run. However, this was only possible because the elector had extensive crown domains and so already controlled a considerable part of the country directly. The same was true in Hessen-Kassel and to a lesser extent in Bavaria, the rulers of which successfully restricted their estates to financial management boards in 1655 and 1669

---

[169] HSAS, L5: Tom. 102, fols. 56–7, 108–9, 227–31; Carsten, *Princes and parliaments*, pp. 100–2; B. Kappelhoff, *Absolutistisches Regiment oder Ständeherrschaft? Landesherr und Landstände in Ostfriesland im ersten Drittel des 18. Jahrhunderts* (Hildesheim, 1982).

respectively. This was not possible in Mecklenburg-Schwerin where the duke only had direct access to 38 per cent of the territory. The nobility owned 47 per cent and controlled a further 3 per cent through the church lands which had been pawned to them in 1572. The remaining 12 per cent was in the hands of the duchy's towns. Rostock, the most important of these, consistently sided with the nobles because it depended on the export of their agricultural produce for its livelihood. The other towns proved too weak to provide the duke with significant assistance.[170] Paradoxically, because he was weak, the duke had very little to offer the nobility, unlike his contemporaries in Brandenburg, Saxony and Hessen-Kassel, whose expanding armies and administrations created new career prospects.

The period after 1670 opened up a new phase in ruler–estate relations which was characterised by a stabilisation of the various positions reached in the different territories. Changes became less dramatic and although many estates continued to decline, others survived and some even assumed new importance.

The prolonged warfare after 1672 put pressure on princes and estates to co-operate in the face of common threats posed by French and Turkish aggression. The establishment of a permanent Reichsarmee in 1681, followed by the declaration of official imperial declarations of war (*Reichskriege*) in 1689 and 1702, encouraged the estates to accept responsibility for maintenance of at least part of the new standing armies. Württemberg's exposed position near the frontier with France induced its estates to accept responsibility for maintaining the Kreistruppen a little earlier in December 1675.[171] This obligation was confirmed by the emperor in 1690. For their part, princes were prepared to be conciliatory, for they appreciated the increased fiscal and administrative efficiency that co-operation could bring.

Recently it has been suggested that such a convergence of interest was behind Britain's phenomenal success in sustaining a large military machine and colonial expansion after 1688. Parliament was prepared to co-operate with royal foreign wars to avoid a Jacobite restoration and further the colonial and commercial interests of its members. Though few MPs desired an extension of state power, their success in limiting its expansion paradoxically strengthened it: 'Public scrutiny reduced speculation, parliamentary consent lent greater legitimacy to government action.'[172] Though Britain's experience did bear out the validity of Besold's arguments for ruler–estate co-operation, such extensive co-operation did not materialise in the German states. The estates were only prepared to fund troops for common imperial defence, whereas princes required their own independent forces. Serious disagreements developed when rulers attempted to retain large armies after peace had been concluded in 1697 and again in 1714.

Nonetheless, the possibilities of princes using force to settle these disputes was

[170] Wick, *Mecklenburg*, pp. 13–34.
[171] Pfaff, *Militärwesen*, p. 33.
[172] J. Brewer, *The sinews of power. War, money and the English state, 1688–1783* (New York, 1989), p. xix.

now limited by the revived influence of the emperor. As stated in the preceding section, after 1671 the emperor intervened to prevent either side achieving a decisive victory. It is noteworthy that the instances of the successful use of force against estates all occurred between 1648 and 1671. Princes who persisted in such policies after 1671 suffered serious reverses. This is best illustrated by the fate of Mecklenburg.

Like those of Württemberg, the dukes of Mecklenburg wished to enhance their voice in the Reich and lessen their dependence on the emperor and neighbouring princes. The methods they adopted were also similar. They tried to create an 'imposing state' complete with a large army, a palace at Schwerin and a full treasury. They too saw the estates as an obstacle, primarily because the nobility refused to grant the necessary taxes. To induce them, Duke Christian I Louis (1658–92) joined Bavaria, Cologne, Brandenburg and Pfalz-Neuburg in a league known as the Extensionists (*Extendisten*) in 1671. They wanted the emperor to confirm the Reichstag's decision of the previous year extending the provisions of JRA Paragraph 180. They were prepared to use force against their estates and agreed to lend each other troops if required. Significantly nothing came of their intentions, though Regent Friedrich Carl contemplated similar ideas in Württemberg in the 1680s. Duke Friedrich Wilhelm (1692–1713) continued his predecessor's efforts to introduce more absolute rule. He suffered a serious setback between 1695 and 1701 when the emperor intervened in both his dispute with the estates and the quarrel over the Güstrow inheritance with his relations. Similar intervention in Württemberg after Friedrich Carl's capture by the French (1693) also reversed a trend towards absolutism. After 1701 Friedrich Wilhelm revived the methods of the Extensionists by seeking foreign alliances, first with Sweden, then with Prussia in 1708. Simultaneously he tried to expand his army and win over further political support through foreign subsidies. Eberhard Ludwig pursued similar policies in Württemberg after 1698. Like his cousin in Stuttgart, Friedrich Wilhelm found that such foreign assistance could prove double edged. Though Prussian military assistance temporarily subdued the estate's opposition, Friedrich Wilhelm was obliged to acknowledge Prussian claims to Mecklenburg. After 1708 Prussia progressively extended a protectorate over the southern part of the duchy. Four districts were occupied continuously 1733–87 and the territory was ruthlessly exploited for money and recruits.

However, it was under Friedrich Wilhelm's successor that ducal policy came seriously off the rails. Like Carl Alexander of Württemberg, Carl Leopold (1713–28/47) is normally portrayed as a despot with little interest in co-operating with the estates. In fact, both made great efforts to reach a consensus and to win support from at least part of their estates. However, continued rebuffs prompted Carl Leopold to seek a military solution. By 1716 he had allied with the tsar, who loaned him two regiments to reinforce his army. Troops were quartered on the property of those nobles who opposed him, while those who co-operated were spared or given a reduced burden. Rostock, which refused to renounce its alliance with the nobility, was also occupied and its council arrested. The estates refused to be intimidated. The withdrawal of the main Russian army from the area late in 1718 cleared the way for the emperor to act. In a desperate attempt to stave off the inevitable, the duke appealed to his fellow princes to join him in reviving the Extensionist league. No one responded. Hanover and Wolfenbüttel finally executed the emperor's order to restore order by invading in 1719. Respect for imperial authority was sufficient for Carl Leopold to order his still sizeable army not to resist. Left with two tiny garrisons shut in Dömitz and Schwerin, he spent the rest of his life devising ever-more fanciful plots to recover his lost lands. His brother Christian II Louis was appointed administrator in 1728, and formally duke in 1747. Effectively his territory was controlled by Hanover, Wolfenbüttel and, from 1733, Prussia. Large parts of the ducal domains were pawned to them to cover their alleged expenses. Without resources, he was compelled to sign a hereditary agreement in 1755 with the estates, obliging all his successors (in fact until 1918) to respect their privileges. This was subsequently confirmed by the emperor who had done much in the meantime to restore his authority, damaged by his failure to intervene successfully between 1701 and 1719. Even though imperial retribution for the duke's actions was painfully slow, the structure of the Reich had still prevented force being used to effect lasting change to domestic political arrangements.[173]

The same occurred in East Frisia, where the prince attempted to use force against the estates after efforts to contest the legal basis for their privileges had failed. Both sides took up arms and rival miniature armies fought an inconclusive struggle between 1725 and 1727. As in the Mecklenburg case, the Reich's structure provided numerous opportunities for external intervention; in this instance by Prussia, Denmark and the Dutch Republic. Though imperial authority was seriously compromised by the failure to find a settlement, a prince's use of force again proved abortive. The estates survived, and indeed continued to do so even after East Frisia fell to Prussia on the extinction of the Cirksena in 1744.[174]

Imperial intervention in Württemberg was considerably more successful. Both East Frisia and Mecklenburg were on the periphery of Habsburg influence, whereas Württemberg lay close to their heartlands. The emperor's authority was contested in north Germany by external powers such as Britain, Denmark, Russia, Sweden and the Dutch Republic, as well as the rising German power of Prussia. The resultant tensions had rendered the imperial system of checks and balances significantly less effective than in the south and south-west of the Reich.

[173] Wick, *Mecklenburg*; Hughes, *Law and politics*, pp. 60–7, 91–112, 156–240; Tessin, *Mecklenburgisches Militär*, pp. 36–143; W. Schulz, *Die preussischen Werbungen unter Friedrich Wilhelm I und Friedrich dem Grossen bis zum Beginn des Siebenjährigen Krieges, mit besonderer Berücksichtigung Mecklenburg-Schwerin* (Schwerin, 1887).

[174] Kappelhoff, *Ostfriesland*; Hughes, *Law and politics*, pp. 67–76, 123–55, 240–58.

Religion proved to be a further factor in the estates' survival after 1670. Though the constitutional settlement of 1648/54 had generally strengthened the princes, it did give the estates one significant advantage by making them the guardians of the territory's religion should the ruler convert to a different faith. A wave of princely conversions swept the Reich in the late seventeenth century. Christian I Louis converted to Catholicism in 1663, followed by Augustus of Saxony-Poland in 1697, Anton Ulrich of Brunswick-Wolfenbüttel in 1710, Carl Alexander of Württemberg in 1712, Crown Prince Friedrich of Hessen-Kassel in 1749 and a number of lesser princes. All were obliged to sign Reversalien, committing them to preserving the existing religious and administrative arrangements within their territories. These documents were frequently guaranteed by the emperor and other German rulers. What made them so significant was the still-controversial nature of religion within imperial politics. Estates threatened by a prince of a different faith immediately enjoyed the support of their co-religionists. Religion provided a further excuse for the emperor and other interested parties to intervene to preserve the internal balance of power.[175]

The dukes of Württemberg were thus not alone in being constrained by their estates. Nor were they unique in being restricted by the checks and balances built into the Reich. To increase their resource base and find political support for their objectives, they joined their contemporaries in the soldier trade which forms the subject of the next chapter.

---

[175] The best discussion of Reversalien and their role in imperial politics is Haug-Moritz, *Württembergischer Ständekonflikt*, pp. 172–214.

3

The German soldier trade

The preceding two chapters have established that if a prince were to achieve his dynastic and political aims, he required a large army and a full treasury. To secure these he needed large revenues. If his existing revenues were inadequate, or he was unable to exercise full control over them, he was forced to look for outside assistance. The most important and politically significant form of such assistance was the subsidy treaty.

Subsidy treaties originated in the 'pensions' paid by the king of France in the late fifteenth century to the leaders of the Swiss cantons in return for mercenaries for his army. From then on, the treaties developed a number of different forms, but always retained the same basic characteristic – one party provided military assistance in return for financial or political advantage from the other.

This has been one of the most misunderstood areas of early modern international relations. Traditionally, the subsidy treaties of these princes have been regarded as a Soldatenhandel, whereby the princes sold their subjects to foreign powers to 'increase their revenues and satisfy their [desire for] luxury'.[1] This interpretation has profoundly influenced the historical view of the lesser German princes and their role within the Reich and the European states system. Only recently has it begun to be revised. So far these revisionist attempts have failed to escape from a particularist standpoint which re-evaluates the treaties of a particular state but leaves intact the traditional interpretation of those of other states. This chapter aims to reassess the role of subsidy treaties for German princely politics as a whole and so provide the context for the more detailed examination of the Württemberg treaties in the following chapters.

The root of the misunderstanding lies in a failure to distinguish between the recruitment of foreigners directly into an army and their temporary hire under a subsidy. The former was always illegal within the Reich and the subject of frequent condemnation by publicists. Later writers have often mistaken these for attacks on subsidy treaties. However, during the first half of the eighteenth century the

---

[1] Kapp, *Soldatenhandel*, p. 20. For a useful bibliography of the pre-1930 literature on this subject see P. Losch, *Soldatenhandel* (Kassel, 1974 edn), pp. 61–110.

treaties were regarded in a largely positive light. Some even welcomed them, believing that they led to a decline in the direct recruiting of soldiers by foreign powers in the Reich. The jurists agreed that the treaties conformed to the Peace of Westphalia of 1648 which gave the princes the right to make foreign treaties as long as these permitted the prince to provide his contingent to the Reichsarmee and were not directed against the emperor or the Reich. These rights had been confirmed in subsequent election promises (*Wahlkapitulationen*) by the emperor. The leading German philosopher, Christian Wolff, maintained that such treaties were also compatible with natural law. The Württemberg jurist Johann Jakob Moser argued that the estates were bound by paragraph 180 of the 1654 JRA to support their prince in the fulfilment of treaty obligations. Prior to the Seven Years War the Württemberg estates themselves held that such agreements were not unconstitutional as long as the recruits were all volunteers.[2]

However, from the 1760s the opinions became increasingly negative, and by the 1780s the treaties were seen as a prime example of the evils of absolutism and contrary to the Enlightenment ideas of freedom and human rights. It was not that the treaties themselves had changed, but rather the attitudes towards them. Instrumental in this were the subsidy arrangements of Hessen-Kassel and other princes in 1776 to supply George III with troops to crush the rebellious American colonists. In practical terms these agreements were no different from the despatch of Hessian and Hanoverian troops in 1746 to suppress the Jacobite Rebellion in Scotland. However, whereas the Scots Highlanders had been of little interest to Enlightenment thinkers, the American colonists were regarded as striving to create a nation free of the flaws that marred European society. To these thinkers the princes, in their greed, were conniving with a tyrant to destroy the kind of social experiment they wanted to see in Europe. Their criticism was quickly seized upon by the colonists and their allies for propaganda purposes and was taken up again in the nineteenth century by German liberal nationalists.[3]

The most influential of these was Friedrich Kapp, whose work first appeared in 1864. In order to make their case for a unified Germany more attractive, Kapp and other nationalist writers painted the Germany of the eighteenth century in as bad a light as possible. Their chief victims were the smaller states which still existed in the nineteenth century and which they saw as the main hindrance to unification under Prussian leadership. As America was seen as the forerunner of the nation

---

[2] HSAS, L5: Tom. 160, fol. 388–996. C. Presser, *Der Soldatenhandel in Hessen* (Marburg, 1900), pp. 13–23; R. Atwood, *The Hessians. Mercenaries from Hessen-Kassel in the American Revolution* (Cambridge, 1980), pp. 23, 30–1; G. Brauer, *Die hannoversch-englischen Subsidienverträge 1701–1748* (Aalen, 1962), p. 97; R. Frhr von Rosenberg, *Soldatenwerbung und militärisches Durchzugsrecht im Zeitalter des Absolutismus. Eine rechtsgeschichtliche Untersuchung* (Berlin, 1973); Walker, *Johann Jakob Moser*, pp. 220–2. Moser later (1757) retracted his arguments.

[3] Atwood, *Hessians*, pp. 228–31.

state he wanted, Kapp used the emotive case of German mercenaries crushing American freedom fighters to condemn this Kleinstaaterei. In a highly moralistic tone, he argued that the princes' sole motive for the treaties was their own greed and love of luxury, implying that their nineteenth-century descendants were no better.[4] The sole exception to this was, of course, Prussia, whose receipt of subsidies was justified as necessary to its development as the motive force for Germany's unification: 'Every Prussian soldier died for Germany.'[5] To conform to this argument, all the clauses in the other princes' treaties concerning mutual assistance and alliances naturally had to be dismissed as merely an attempt to disguise their commercial character. To have credited the subsidy treaties of these princes with political motives would have compelled the nationalists to acknowledge that the small states were acting in the same manner as Prussia. This led to the paradox of Hessen-Kassel being condemned for its treaty of 1776, but praised for that of 1757, as this put it on Prussia's side in the Seven Years War.

Kapp's work struck a popular chord, and was followed by a string of works which have carried this interpretation to the present. All use the same emotive language, describing the treaties as little better than a sort of slave trade (Soldatenhandel, *Soldatenverkauf, Menschenhandel*).[6] In the late nineteenth century the attempt was made to distinguish between subsidy treaties dictated by political reasons and true 'soldier trade' purely for profit.[7] However, these attempts still followed the earlier nationalists in recognising political motives only in the treaties of the larger powers such as Austria and Prussia. Moreover, even the best product of these attempts[8] is still marred by an obsessive concern for 'German interests', in which the constitutional reality of the old Reich is confused with the nationalist concept of Germany. The dividing-line between a political subsidy treaty and the 'soldier trade' is whether the prince provided his contingent for the imperial army or not. Whereas Württemberg and Würzburg 'cannot be reproached' for their treaties during the Spanish succession conflict, because they fielded their full contingent, Saxony, the Palatinate, Hessen-Kassel and others are criticised for having 'used their forces in the interests of foreign powers and not for their own fatherland'.[9] Here again, the motive behind this is given as the princes' love of luxury.[10] It is

---

[4] Kapp, *Soldatenhandel* (1864 edn), p. xiii. The dates of the editions of Kapp's book (1864–74) span the unification of Germany 1866–71.
[5] Kapp's review of the anonymous pamphlet 'Friedrich II von Hessen und die neuere Geschichtsschreibung', in *Historische Zeitschrift*, 42 (1879), 304–30 at p. 314.
[6] For example Biedermann, *Deutschland*, I, p. 203, and recently A. Hochheimer, *Verraten und Verkauft. Die Geschichte der europäischen Söldner* (Stuttgart, 1967).
[7] M. Jähns, *Heeresverfassung und Völkerleben* (Berlin, 1885), p. 285; A. von Boguslawski, 'Soldatenhandel und Subsidienverträge', *BMWB*, 7 (1885), 297ff.; J. N., 'Über Soldtruppen. Vortrag, dem Offiziercorps gehalten den 18. März 1881', *BMWB*, 4 (1884), 330–52.
[8] M. Braubuch, *Die Bedeutung der Subsidien für die Politik im spanischen Erbfolgekrieg* (Bonn, 1923).
[9] *Ibid.*, pp. 86–7, 159–60.
[10] *Ibid.*, pp. 104–26, 136–7, 148–9.

supposed to have been largely immaterial to these princes whom they made an agreement with so long as it filled their treasury, and the heavy losses of the hired regiments is taken as proof of their callous profit-making: of the 18,500 Germans hired to Venice in the 1680s, 14,000 failed to return, while of the 3,200 Württembergers supplied to the Dutch East India Company a hundred years later, fewer than 200 saw the duchy again.[11]

Recently this view has been revised with regard to individual states: Hessen-Kassel, Hanover and the Wittelsbach territories including Bavaria. Those writing on Hessen-Kassel emphasise the beneficial role subsidy income played in keeping taxation low, promoting cultural achievement and funding enlightened social and educational reforms. Hanoverian subsidies are seen in the light of strengthening the electorate's defences. The Wittelsbach treaties are depicted as the chief vehicle for advancing their numerous dynastic ambitions.[12]

Thus fiscal, domestic reform, defence and dynastic ambition have been variously emphasised without any clear reinterpretation of the soldier trade emerging. Such a picture does emerge when all factors are taken together. While the emphasis obviously varied according to local circumstances, subsidy treaties played an identical role in all German states: they represented the main – often the only – method for a prince to achieve grandiose plans on limited resources. Furthermore, when political content of the treaties and princely dynastic ambition is taken seriously, the place of both in contemporary international relations becomes clear. Only by capitalising on the military potential of their territory could the lesser princes hope to escape from their subordinate role in the grand drama of European politics.

Of course this approach does view the soldier trade primarily in terms of a balance sheet of princely gains and losses. While in keeping with the cameralist attitudes of princes and their ministers, it is not helpful in assessing the wider social and domestic political impact. It is appropriate to examine these points in the next section, before exploring more fully the fiscal and military aspects of the treaties and their role in international relations.

---

[11] R. von Andler, 'Die württembergischen Regimenter in Griechenland, 1687–89', *WVJHLG*, NF31 (1922–4), 217–79 at p. 266 n. 80.

[12] Revision of the Hessian treaties began with the works of the local patriots: Presser, *Soldatenhandel in Hessen*, and Losch, *Soldatenhandel*. Two recent works have completed the task: Atwood, *Hessians*, and Ingrao, *Hessian mercenary state*. For Hanover see Brauer, *Subsienverträge*; for the Wittelsbachs see Hartmann, *Geld*. The traditional view of the numerous other treaties has not been challenged. H. M. Maurer, 'Das Württembergische Kapregiment. Söldner im Dienste früher Kolonialpolitik (1787–1808)', *ZWLG*, 47 (1988), 291–308 gives the old view of both Württemberg and Hessian treaties. The same view was expressed in the 1987 exhibition at the HSAS, see C. Bührlen-Grabinger, *Verkauft und Verloren. Das württembergische 'Kapregiment' in Südafrika, Ceylon und Java 1787–1808. Ausstellung des Hauptstaatsarchivs Stuttgart* (Stuttgart, 1987). For similar comments see H. J. Harder, *Militärgeschichtliches Handbuch Baden-Württemberg* (Stuttgart, 1987), pp. 42–4.

IMPACT ON SOCIETY AND DOMESTIC POLITICS

Previous explanations of the domestic impact of the soldier trade are unsatisfactory. The older view is coloured by the same mix of moral indignation and nationalist prejudice that distorts its interpretation of the subject as a whole. The domestic impact is seen as essentially negative. Subsidies encouraged rulers to recruit larger armies than their populations and economies could sustain. Recruitment met with opposition and took men away from productive activity in trade and agriculture. Soldiers had little interest in the conflicts and responded by deserting in large numbers. In contrast, the revisionists see the impact as largely positive. Subsidies provided rulers with additional income which enabled them to lower domestic taxation and fund beneficial reforms. Recruitment opened up economic opportunities for impoverished sons of peasants and nobles alike. War was a trade like any other and accepted as such by the bulk of the community.

Neither view is particularly helpful. The former rarely goes beyond the prejudices of the writers, while the latter has been rightly accused of perpetuating the 'Swiss myth'.[13] This denies the element of compulsion in military service and relativises Soldatenhandel into *Kriegshandwerk* (the trade of war). We can better understand the impact if we know more about the forces that shaped it and can identify areas of society and domestic politics most affected. The impact was determined by the interrelationship of three factors: the number of troops required, the method of recruiting them and the socio-economic structure of the state concerned. The areas most affected were the local social and political arrangements at village or parish level and the way these related to the central political duality of court and estates.

At the most basic level the nature of the impact was a question of numbers. Obviously, a populous territory with a plentiful supply of volunteers would be able to absorb the requirements of treaties for modest numbers of troops with little dislocation of domestic social and political arrangements. The impact would be more pronounced in territories where princely policy required the maintenance of a high level of military preparedness on a permanent basis. Thus, the ratio of the army as a proportion of a territory's population will give some indication of the overall level of impact. Most German states maintained peacetime armies equivalent to 0.5–2 per cent of their population in the mid-eighteenth century. Both Prussia (3.9 per cent) and Hessen-Kassel (4.4 per cent) stood out from the rest, while the most extreme case was the tiny state of Schaumburg-Lippe which had 8.8 per cent of its 18,000 inhabitants under arms by 1760. Taken at face value, these figures indicate a burden comparable to or greater than that during any time

---

[13] Taylor, 'The draft and peasant society', pp. 3–16.

before 1914 when German mobilisation of 2,100,000 men represented just over 3 per cent of the total population.[14]

However, these figures only tell us part of the story. As the discussion of military costs (pp. 37–42) showed, the smaller states did not enjoy the economies of scale of their larger neighbours and thus could find it difficult to sustain even a relatively small force. This becomes clearer when we place the army's size against the other two factors shaping its impact: recruiting methods and the socio-economic context.

The latter determined the number of potential recruits and the level of compulsion required to enlist them. Throughout the period under review, military service was rarely an attractive option for most inhabitants of the various German territories. Financial stringency generally kept soldiers' wages and conditions to a bare minimum. Although recruitment bounties might provide an initial incentive, it normally took adverse socio-economic conditions to induce large numbers of volunteers to come forward. The most common examples include recession in a local industry, subdivision by inheritance custom of farms into uneconomic units and a discrepancy between population growth and economic activity. Though these economic problems were fairly common throughout the Reich, they rarely produced sufficient volunteers, forcing most states to resort to some form of compulsory enlistment.[15] The level of disruption to local social and political arrangements was roughly proportional to the extent and duration of conscription.

All forms of conscription in the German states, including Prussia, were derivatives of a militia system. This in turn derived from the feudal obligations of subjects to serve in the defence of the territory. These obligations were revived in many areas in the early seventeenth century and reinforced by subsequent legislation. Although there were numerous local variations, the basic militia structure was the same throughout the Reich.[16] Officials in each district of a state were obliged to keep lists of men eligible for duty. Theoretically the entire male population was generally liable, but in practice social and economic criteria

---

[14] See Wilson, 'War, state and society', pp. 62–73 for a fuller discussion of the size of German armies; Klein, *Schaumburg-Lippe*, pp. 35–41.

[15] A. Corvisier, *Armies and societies in Europe 1494–1789* (London, 1976); Redlich, *German military enterpriser*, II; W. Thum, *Die Rekrutierung der sächsischen Armee unter August dem Starken (1694–1733)* (Leipzig, 1912); P. H. Wilson, 'Violence and the rejection of authority in 18th-century Germany: the case of the Swabian mutinies in 1757', *German History*, 12 (1994), 1–26.

[16] For Württemberg see HSAS, A6: Bü. 34, 40–2, 44; A28: Bü. 99; L6.22.6.34; L6.22.7.5a; E. Pflichthofer, *Das Württembergische Heerwesen am Ausgang des Mittelalters* (Tübingen Ph.D., printed 1938), pp. 33–43; Pfister, *Milizgedanke*. For other states see: Staudinger, *Bayerischen Heeres*, III, pp. 215–38; Tessin, *Mecklenburgisches Militär*, pp. 154–6; Thum, *Rekrutierung*, pp. 19–72, 83–5; R. Harms, 'Landmiliz und stehendes Heer in Kurmainz namentlich im 18. Jahrhundert', *Archiv für hessische Geschichte und Altertumskunde*, NF6 (1909), 359–430; B. Sicken, 'Die Streitkräfte des Hochstifts Würzburg gegen Ende des Ancien Regime', *Zeitschrift für bayerische Landesgeschichte*, 47 (1984), 691–744; Taylor, 'The draft and peasant society', pp. 15–125; H. Schnitter, *Volk und Landesdefension* (Berlin DDR, 1977).

excluded all but a select portion or *Auswahl*. These were supposed to exercise at regular intervals under the supervision of professional officers. Often the estates were heavily involved in the administration of this system and had various constitutional safeguards designed to prevent rulers from placing the militia under their direct control. The most common device was the proviso that the militia could not be made to serve outside the frontiers. However, many princes manipulated the weakness of their estates during the emergency of the prolonged warfare in the later seventeenth century to reduce the militia to a recruitment pool for the politically more useful regular army.

This transformation of the militia system into conscription took three forms. In the first two the militia remained formally in being, but was used to provide recruits for the regular regiments in emergencies. In Bavaria and Mecklenburg men were drafted from militia formations into regular units. This method was also used in Württemberg by Regent Freidrich Carl, who converted the duchy's entire militia into permanent formations in 1691 (see pp. 115–17). More usually the militia was bypassed altogether and men were drafted directly into the army. This took place in Saxony, Mainz and Würzburg, and was used in Württemberg to meet the treaty requirements of 1733–5 and 1757–60 (pp. 169–76 and 213–22). The third method extended the system of emergency direct drafts to provide a regular annual intake to keep the army permanently up to strength. Each regiment was assigned a district as its recruitment area (*Kanton*). The militia was formally abolished, but the system of lists and selection procedures was continued, with the men now going to their local regiments. This was not universal conscription due to the numerous exceptions and virtually unlimited period of service; rather, the entire army now became a hybrid combining characteristics of both a regular force and a militia. This was enhanced by the practice of giving 30–40 per cent of the soldiers unpaid leave for up to ten or eleven months a year in order to ease the burden on the population and economise on the wage bill. The Kanton system was adopted most notably in Prussia by 1733, copied in Schaumburg-Lippe in 1749, Hessen-Kassel in 1762 and Austria between 1771 and 1780. It was introduced briefly into Württemberg in 1736 by Carl Alexander, but abandoned after his death.[17]

The adoption of the Kanton system had the most profound effect because it was invariably used to sustain an inflated establishment and because it represented a permanent intrusion into local communities. The impact of the other two methods of conscription was sharp, sudden but seldom prolonged. Financial stringency forced most princes to maintain small armies. Political ambition drove them to conclude treaties obliging them to provide more men than they currently had under

[17] Büsch, *Militärsystem*; C. Jany, 'Die Kantonsverfassung Friedrich Wilhelms I', *Forschungen zur brandenburgisch–preußischen Geschichte*, 38 (1926), 225–72; Klein, *Schaumberg-Lippe*, pp. 35–41; M. Lehmann, 'Werbung, Wehrpflicht und Beurlaubung im Heere Friedrich Wilhelm I', *Historische Zeitschrift*, 67 (1891), 254–89; Taylor, 'The draft and peasant society', pp. 38–125, 340–3. See also pp. 176–82 below.

arms. The reluctance of volunteers to come forward made it difficult to cover even peacetime attrition. As subsidy treaties could require two or three times the entire actual strength, and as they always specified tight deadlines, resort to conscription was unavoidable. Regardless of whether they were drafted from mobilised militia units or directly from the militia register, large numbers of men would be taken from settled civilian life. This caused considerable disruption in their communities. The duration of this disruption was determined by the level of losses suffered by the subsidy corps and the time it was hired. While losses could be high, treaties were often terminated before casualties needed to be replaced. Most major powers preferred to keep freedom of action by avoiding long-term contracts. Treaties for over five years were relatively rare. In any case, the major powers frequently defaulted on their payments, forcing princes to reduce their armies prematurely. The local impact was, therefore, likely to be unpredictable, but less severe in the long term than the steady annual intake through the Kanton system.

Families whose husbands and sons were threatened with conscription were likely to take evasive action. Most commonly this is thought to be behind the allegedly high desertion rates suffered by eighteenth-century German armies. In fact these were far lower than previously believed. Recently, the accepted figure of a 20 per cent annual desertion and death rate for the Prussian army between 1713 and 1740 has been convincingly disproved. The actual desertion rate was about 1.9 per cent, while the death rate was even lower at under 1.4 per cent.[18] Data on the contemporary Württemberg and Saxon armies reveal comparable rates of 2–5 per cent for desertions and 0.7 to 2.3 per cent for deaths.[19] The reason why desertions were considered so serious was that, with limited funds at their disposal, it was difficult and time consuming for military administrations to replace even the small numbers involved.

Moreover, desertion was motivated by practical considerations and should not be taken as evidence of popular criticism of the soldier trade. It is noteworthy that Johann Gottfried Seume, the most celebrated and oft-quoted example of a critical serviceman, published his attack on Hessen-Kassel in 1802, long after it had become fashionable to condemn the subsidy treaties. Most soldiers who kept diaries of their service in America expressed unthinking loyalty to the prince who had allegedly 'sold' them into foreign service. Even Seume, who later claimed he had been abducted against his will, voiced his disappointment in 1783 that the American war had not been more bloody and exciting.[20]

Desertion was in any case a highly unsatisfactory way to escape involuntary

---

[18] W. R. Fann, 'Peacetime attrition in the army of Frederick William I 1713–1740', *Central European History*, 11 (1978), 323–34.

[19] HSAS, A6: Bü. 27, 28, 68, 69; Thum, *Rekrutierung*, pp. 76–7. Foreigners were more prone to desertion than natives. For this in Prussia, Jany, *Königlich preußischen Armee*, II, p. 665.

[20] Atwood, *Hessians*, p. 228; Ingrao, *Hessian mercenary state*, p. 154; B. E. Burgoyne (ed.), *A Hessian diary of the American Revolution by Johann Conrad Döhla* (Norman/London, 1990).

military service for those aiming to return to settled civilian life. The authorities generally responded by confiscating deserters' property and returning those recaptured to their regiments. Not surprisingly, mass desertion occurred in extreme circumstances. The most common case was where the soldiers suspected, rightly or wrongly, that they were not merely being temporarily hired but permanently transferred into another army. This occurred in Württemberg prior to the march of the subsidy corps in 1757, when the recruits mistakenly believed they had been 'sold', rather than hired, to France. Under the influence of alcohol and – very likely Prussian – agitators, discipline collapsed and mutineers terrorised Stuttgart for a day and a night. As with mutinies elsewhere, such action brought only temporary respite. Within five weeks the vast majority of deserters were obliged to return and the corps began its march to the front.[21]

A more satisfactory way to escape military service was to avoid being called in the first place. An examination of these strategies to avoid the draft opens up the true nature of the impact of subsidy recruitment. The best strategy was to gain an official exemption. These were numerous and, although they varied from place to place, were basically the same throughout the Reich. Blanket exemptions were generally extended to the residents of privileged regions such as capital cities and industrial centres. Individual exemptions were made on the basis of occupation, age, health, property and marital status. Local officials were instructed only to grant exemptions to those who could provide proof of eligibility. This was to be verified by checking parish registers and land surveys. Marriage and inheritance laws were revised to prevent early marriages and premature devolution of property in order to gain exemption.[22] However, as with many other areas of legislation in early modern Europe, the very volume of official decrees indicates how poorly they were enforced.

Enforcement largely depended on the officials on the spot. These were ideally placed to extend their influence by providing patronage and protection to those wishing to avoid the draft. In this sense, princely recruitment requirements tended to reinforce the existing pattern of patronage that existed in the localities. However, if those requirements increased beyond a minimum level, or were put on a permanent basis through the adoption of the Kanton system, traditional forms of patronage broke down. The numbers were simply too large for local protection brokers to meet them from their usual pool of victims: the poor and marginal families on the fringe of the community. As recruitment legislation was tightened up and the officials made more accountable, they were less able to avoid drafting their own clients. Denied protection, potential recruits were forced to devise their

---

[21] Wilson, 'Violence and the rejection of authority'.
[22] HSAS, A6; Bü. 59; A30a: Bü. 105; A202: Bü. 2005–7, 2278; L6.22.7.4a; L6.22.8.1; Reyscher (ed.), *Württembergische Gesetze*, XIX, Nos. 168, 187, 188, 193, 196, 211, 248, 258, 269, 279, 444; and sources in notes 16 and 17 above. Numerous recruiting regulations, especially Prussian, are printed in E. von Frauenholz, *Entwicklungsgeschichte des deutschen Heerwesens* (Munich, 1940), IV.

own strategies, often in conflict with those of their former patrons. Tensions in local communities increased.[23]

These local tensions fed into the political conflict at the centre. For example, the Württemberg estates' committee was compelled to intercede with the duke to release conscripts in order to maintain its credibility in the localities. For the same reason, the committee also took up a whole range of other complaints including the quartering of troops, labour services and the depredations of the ducal hunt. In this sense, the estates were obliged to act in a genuinely representative fashion.[24] Conversely, those in the princely administration were often forced to compromise in order to preserve their local positions. Ducal officials were noticeably reluctant to carry out confiscation of deserters' property after the 1757 mutiny. Overzealous adherence to the law was bound to provoke hostility and make the exercise of their other functions nearly impossible.[25] Sustained recruitment was only possible in Prussia because the crown adapted the Kanton system to suit the needs of the local nobility. Conflict was deliberately avoided by allowing the nobles to use the recruitment legislation to reinforce their control over their peasant labour force.[26] The opposite appears to have happened in Hessen-Kassel, where the nobility found their client network eroded by their inability to protect influential members of village communities. As the traditional system disintegrated, ordinary villagers adapted their marriage strategies and inheritance practices to gain exemption. It has been argued recently that this fuelled population growth and created the dramatic increase in the number of marginal families that characterised Hessian society in the last quarter of the eighteenth century.[27]

Württemberg's population expanded at a similarly dramatic rate. This is unlikely to be linked to the duke's military policy, as the duchy never experienced sustained high levels of conscription. However, ducal policy did have a similar impact on local patronage through fiscal demands. As the following chapters will show, attempts to revise outdated tax registers and to induce local assemblies to agree to new fiscal demands threatened to disrupt the way the worthies managed local affairs.

Thus, the domestic impact of the soldier trade varied according to local circumstances. The results were neither overwhelmingly negative nor entirely positive, nor indeed obvious to contemporaries. One reason for the absence of serious opposition from the Hessian estates to their ruler's subsidy policy was that the local nobility were unaware of its true social consequences. In spite of mounting evidence

---

[23] Taylor, 'The draft and peasant society', pp. 81–379; P. K. Taylor and H. Rebel, 'Hessian peasant women, their families and the draft: A social–historical interpretation of four tales from the Grimm collection', *Journal of Family History*, 6 (1981), 347–78.

[24] HSAS, L5: Tom. 125–67 for numerous *Gravamina*.

[25] Wilson, 'Violence and the rejection of authority', pp. 22–5 and the sources cited there.

[26] Büsch, *Militärsystem*, pp. 21–48, 100–43.

[27] Taylor, 'The draft and peasant society', pp. 176–211.

to the contrary, they remained convinced that the country's population was actually declining. Moreover, military service did bring tangible benefits. The value of foreign subsidies, which between 1702 and 1784 brought in about forty-five million taler or more than half the state's revenue, was widely appreciated. All sections of society felt the benefit of the resultant reduced tax burden, while both the estates and civil bureaucrats looked to the army as a lucrative source of employment. Subsidy income enabled the landgrave to extend loans to both the estates and individual nobles which compensated for their declining local influence. Finally, while conscription may have encouraged the growth of marginal families, military service did provide a means for their survival. Many soldiers had sufficient savings to build small cottages upon their discharge. Unmarried daughters of impoverished families were able to escape parental control through illicit liaisons with furloughed soldiers.[28]

In many respects, however, Hessen-Kassel was an exceptional case. Indeed, 'social militarisation' was as far advanced there as in Prussia and contemporaries referred to the state as resembling an armed camp. Other states were not so militarised, but neither was there the 'cosy symbiosis between the crown, bureaucracy, and privileged estates' that characterised the political impact in Hessen-Kassel.[29] In this sense Württemberg is far more typical. The duke's inability to accommodate the worthies' opposition to his plans prevented him from militarising Württemberg society through a system of permanent conscription. This in turn lessened his ability to compete with his rivals in the soldier trade.

Hessen-Kassel was relatively alone in being able to avoid such problems. The high military reputation of its army generally enabled it to command a high price for its services. This permitted higher pay for its conscripts plus better bounties to attract genuine volunteers to make up any shortfall in numbers. Moreover, Hessen-Kassel's reputation was established early on, giving it a distinct advantage over potential rivals. British experts in the 1720s rated the Hessians superior to the Prussians.[30] Without such an established reputation, it was difficult to attract adequate subsidies, but without these it was difficult to provide first-rate troops. As the discussion of Württemberg's search for subsidies will show, except in moments of international crisis, few states were able to break out of this vicious circle.

---

[28] *Ibid.*, pp. 218–31, 255; Ingrao, *Hessian mercenary state*, pp. 22–44 and Ingrao, 'Kameralismus und Militärismus im deutschen Polizeistaat: Der hessische Söldnersstaat', in G. Schmidt (ed.), *Stände und Gesellschaft im Alten Reich* (Stuttgart, 1989), pp. 171–86.

[29] Ingrao, *Hessian mercenary state*, p. 42.

[30] J. Black, 'Parliament and foreign policy in the age of Walpole: The case of the Hessians', in J. Black (ed.), *Knights errant and true Englishmen: British foreign policy 1600–1800* (Edinburgh, 1989), pp. 41–54.

SUBSIDY TREATIES

The subsidy treaties of the late seventeenth and eighteenth centuries were a by-product of the inability of early modern governments to raise the size of army they wanted. If unable or unwilling to raise troops within his own territories, a prince had to recruit elsewhere. Four possibilities were open to him which, collectively, form the four main variants of the soldier trade. First he could recruit directly on a foreign territory through his own agents, either with or without permission of the relevant authorities. Second, he could approach these authorities or some other middleman to do the recruiting for him. Third, he could arrange for the transfer of existing units from another army directly into his own. Finally, he could hire foreign formations for a limited period of time. It is this fourth method that primarily interests us here, as this involved the subsidy treaties proper.

A subsidy treaty was a written agreement between two (occasionally three) states concerning troop-hire terms, and usually included political co-operation.[31] The element of troop hire was contained in a military convention which was either written into the treaty itself, or attached in a separate document. Under such conventions, one of the treaty partners agreed to raise and maintain a fixed number of troops which were placed at the disposal of the other. In return, it received a fee known as a subsidy.

The military convention meant that a subsidy treaty was a special kind of alliance. Although the treaties often contained clauses covering mutual assistance and promises of aid should one partner be attacked as a result of hiring out its troops, they were nonetheless almost invariably agreements between unequals. On the one side stood the politically and financially more powerful partner who paid the subsidy, and on the other the correspondingly weaker signatory who provided the troops.

The reasons why the stronger partner signed such agreements are relatively simple to explain. Irrespective of which state was involved, it often proved faster and simpler to pay for regiments to be raised elsewhere than to recruit locally.[32] This was especially true of Venice, Spain and England where the native army was of low social standing, making recruitment very difficult.[33] English cabinets could also avoid awkward debates on the legality of a standing army in the kingdom by simply hiring foreigners on the continent. Hiring foreigners was frequently

---

[31] More than two states were involved in those treaties where two (usually England and the United Provinces) shared responsibility for paying the subsidies.

[32] This is evident during 1733–5 when the Austrians were able to hire over 55,000 auxiliaries, but add only 26,794 men to their own army of 146,000. Kriegs-Archiv, *Feldzüge*, XIX, pp. 106–40 and pp. 169–76 below.

[33] C. W. Eldon, *England's subsidy policy towards the continent during the Seven Years War* (Philadelphia, 1938), pp. 41, 54, 65–70; W. Kohlhaas, *Candia. Die Tragödie einer abendländischen Verteidigung und ihr Nachspiel in Morea 1645–1714* (Osnabrück, 1978), pp. 29–38.

considered less expensive and less damaging to the economy, as it left the native workforce free to continue their productive labour and add to the national wealth.[34] By hiring troops, governments also obtained 'no recruits, but disciplined soldiers',[35] and the foreign professionals were often considered superior to local units.[36] This inclined such states to make agreements in peace as well as wartime, so as to be sure that the regiments were up to strength and on call whenever needed. Subsidy treaties had the added advantage for the hirer that he need only pay for troops when he required them. At the end of a war they could be conveniently returned to their supplier, thus sparing the hirer their peacetime upkeep and eventual expensive reduction.

Finally, there were important political advantages to be considered. These have often been overlooked, but were a significant factor, especially for France and Austria. These advantages included the use of strategic fortresses, land for winter quarters and the right of passage. Simultaneously, these were denied to a potential opponent.

Indeed, a territory's strategic position was sometimes more important than the troops it could offer. This was true of Trier, which rarely had an army of more than 1,200 men, but controlled key points on the Moselle and the Rhine. Through Trier, France could circumvent the Barrier fortresses in Belgium – the eighteenth-century equivalent of the Maginot line – and invade either the United Provinces or the north German states. The German princes could also offer a prospective client their vote at the Reichstag, which was of interest to powers such as Austria, France and England when matters such as the Pragmatic Sanction or the election of a new emperor were at stake.[37]

However, perhaps the greatest advantage a treaty offered the big powers was the possibility to use the subsidies as a way of extending their influence over their weaker neighbours. By making these dependent on subsidies they could compel them to do their bidding by threatening to withdraw financial support. As will become apparent over the course of the following five chapters, France was constantly searching for an opportunity to breach the imperial defences along the Rhine by luring over one or more of the smaller German princes with a tempting subsidy offer. To prevent this, the Austrians were no less interested in establishing a client relationship with the strategically sited princes. Though their weaker financial position made it more difficult to match the French offer in monetary

---

[34] Brauer, *Subsidienverträge*, p. 101 n. 80; Eldon, *Subsidy policy*, pp. 65–70.
[35] The British Library, Add. Mss. 23680, fol. 3.
[36] For example, during the army reorganisation in Spain in the 1760s. See the reports of the Austrian Ambassador Count Orsini-Rosenberg to Kaunitz, 27 Dec. 1762 and 5 Apr. 1763 in H. Jüretschke (ed.), *Berichte der diplomatischen Vertreter des Wiener Hofes aus Spanien in der Regierungszeit Karl III. (1759–1788)* (14 vols., Madrid, 1970–87), II, pp. 262–4, 314–16.
[37] Austria secured Württemberg recognition of the Pragmatic Sanction by its treaty with Carl Alexander (see pp. 172–3 below), while France obtained Carl Eugen's co-operation at the Reichstag in its treaties of 1752 and 1759 (pp. 203–7 and 222–3).

terms, they did have the advantage of being able to offer other rewards through their influence in the imperial church, army and legal system.

The reasons why the smaller princes signed subsidy treaties are more complex. While the Württemberg treaties will be discussed in the following chapters, it is worth making some general points here. As already noted, the traditional explanation has been that their main motive was the financial reward that these treaties offered. Such writers have therefore stressed their 'commercial character' and have argued 'that the troops were hired to the highest bidder'. In other words, according to those who took this view, it was irrelevant who the hirer was as long as he paid well. A few writers, usually with military backgrounds, have sought to justify this as being the only way such princes could have raised an army at all.[38] The majority, however, claim that 'the subsidies were mostly squandered on the court' rather than spent on raising the men required. Carl Eugen's treaty of 1752 is often cited as evidence for this.[39] Recently, this idea has been developed further with the theory of cultural competition which maintains that the money was necessary if the princes were going to rival their neighbours with a dazzling display.[40]

Neither of these arguments really grasps the point. Of course, the princes were very keen to obtain as much money as possible from the arrangement. It is true that the money was essential if they were to be able to raise an army and also that some of the subsidies were spent on palace construction and patronage of the arts, although not nearly to the extent previously assumed. However, both the army and the cultural competition were not ends in themselves, but means to an end. The final goal was the realisation of the kind of dynastic and political ambitions outlined in Chapter 1. The reason why the smaller princes engaged so heavily in the 'soldier trade' was that the disparity between their aims and the resources available to achieve them was so much greater than for the larger states such as France or Austria.

Most princes certainly did not hire to 'the highest bidder'. Instead, they selected their treaty partner not so much on his ability to pay well, but on how useful he would be in helping them secure their dynastic and political ambitions. This goes a long way towards explaining why so many of the princes preferred to sign with the emperor rather than with 'big spenders' such as France, despite the fact that the emperor offered less money and was usually unable even to pay what he had promised.[41] Where they did sign treaties with other powers it was often because the

---

[38] Harder, *Militärgeschichtliches Handbuch*, p. 42. See also Pfister, *Denkwürdigkeiten*, pp. 204–5 in similar vein.

[39] Harder, *Militärgeschichtliches Handbuch*, p. 42. The treaty of 1752 is discussed on pp. 203–7 below.

[40] Vann, *Making of a state*, esp. pp. 264–5.

[41] The emperor often had to 'pay' his subsidy partners by allowing them to retain the Römer Monat payments they owed to the imperial treasury. For examples involving Württemberg see HSAS, L5: Tom. 125, fols. 110–14; A202: Bü. 1159, 2111, 7 Feb. 1737. For further examples of the emperor's inability to make his payments in full see pp. 172–4 and 190–5.

emperor was simply unable to pay any money at all. Even then, many of the princes preferred to make agreements with powers in a position to influence the emperor on their behalf, such as the Dutch and English, who in turn were frequently payers of subsidies to Austria.[42]

Both parties to a subsidy treaty regarded the monetary element as necessary principally to put the hired prince in a position to provide the troops required. While the smaller princes naturally tried to make a profit from the payments, they also hoped their services would be rewarded with political concessions. Often they failed to have these included in the treaty terms. Where they did manage this, the promised concessions were usually framed in vague terms as a set of secret articles attached to the main body of the treaty. This, and the fact that the promised concessions almost invariably failed to materialise, has resulted in their being ignored by later writers. Thus, many of the treaties discussed in the secondary literature as purely financial arrangements in fact contained important political clauses. This is true of many of the treaties signed by Hessen-Kassel as well as those made by Württemberg.[43] In any case, as the following chapters will prove, the negotiations leading up to the treaties often give a better indication of what the princes were trying to achieve than the actual terms.

The relative importance of the political clauses becomes clearer when we examine how poor the actual financial rewards proved to be. Not only were there frequently no profits to be made, but some princes even entered into agreements in the certain knowledge of a loss, gambling that the promised political concessions would make it worthwhile.[44] At best, most subsidies literally just 'subsidised' the costs incurred in raising and maintaining the troops. The gap between the subsidy and the true cost had to be covered by the prince's own treasury. That subsidy payments almost invariably fell into arrears, and were frequently never paid in full, only widened the gap. This affected not only Württemberg, but virtually all the princes who were party to such arrangements. Even the normally efficient Hessians had trouble obtaining payment in full.[45] As these princes were really in a 'buyers' market' and as they had little hope of realising their aims from their own resources, they had to accept the terms offered.

It is perhaps helpful, however, at this stage to indicate the level of profits the princes were hoping to make. During Eberhard Ludwig's unsuccessful attempt

---

[42] For examples see Brauer, *Subsidienverträge*, pp. 16–20, 74–90, 96; Presser, *Soldatenhandel in Hessen*, pp. 38–9.

[43] For Hessen-Kassel see Losch, *Soldatenhandel*, pp. 7–14; von Dalwigk, 'Der Anteil der hessischen Truppen am österreichischen Erbfolgekriege (1740–48)', *Zeitschrift für hessische Geschichte und Landeskunde*, 42 (1908), 72–139. For another non-Württemberg example see Brabant, *Heilige römische Reich*, I, p. 10.

[44] This is true of Carl Alexander and especially Carl Eugen in 1760. See pp. 169–76 and 213–25.

[45] Ingrao, *Hessian mercenary state*, p. 128. See also the complaints from German princes in PRO, SP100/14; SP100/15; SP100/17; SP102/25, Eberhard Ludwig to Queen Anne, 27 Feb. 1709.

to negotiate English subsidies in 1721, the actual cost of raising the troops was calculated at 36fl. for an infantryman and 120fl. for a mounted cavalryman. The negotiator was instructed to ask for 40fl. and 150fl. respectively, which would have brought a very modest profit of only 17,700fl.[46] Carl Eugen was more ambitious. During his negotiations with Colonel Frederick in 1771 over the hiring of 2,000 NCOs and men to the English East India Company, he optimistically expected to make no less than 42,711fl. 40xr. from the raising and maintenance costs for one year. It was hoped more money could be made as the army still had a large stock of surplus weapons and equipment left over from the Seven Years War and so could practically equip the corps for next to nothing. Further savings could be achieved by employing the soldiers to build the Solitude palace until the company called for them, enabling the duke to dispense with paying the normal construction workers. Finally, he looked forward to receiving a cash-down payment four to five months in advance, which in view of his straitened financial circumstances following the Erbvergleich settlement the previous year 'would be a great coup' ('Welches bey gegenwärtige Umständen ein großer Coup wäre').[47]

Occasionally, a prince did land 'a great coup' that lived up to such optimistic expectations. Ansbach-Bayreuth, for example, made 93,671fl., or 67fl. per man, in 1791 on its brigade hired to the Dutch.[48] Another example of such a windfall is that enjoyed by Duke Friedrich II of Sachsen-Gotha in 1703 when he received payment from the Dutch and English to raise troops the French had already paid for the previous year.[49] However, such cases were the exception rather than the rule.

A characteristic of Württemberg subsidy treaties is that the dukes were singularly unable to make agreements that brought them a financial profit. More often than not, they failed even to ensure that their costs were covered, and generally ended up with a huge deficit as in the case of Carl Eugen after 1763. That they were not alone is demonstrated by the case of Bavaria. This indicates the relative exceptionality of Hessen-Kassel and to a lesser extent Hanover in that they were both lucky enough to make substantial gains.

It is enlightening to see how they spent these surpluses. Far from squandering

[46] HSAS, A6: Bü. 59; L6.22.6.27, 28 May 1721, 29 May 1721. An individual horse was estimated at 90fl., but Osiander was to ask for 100fl. On these negotiations see pp. 146–7.

[47] L6.22.6.27, 23 Jan 1771. The Württembergers estimated the company would pay 264,484fl., whereas they hoped to keep costs down to 221,772fl. 20xr. The plan fell through because the company, reacting to a rising tide of popular xenophobia in England, decided to limit the number of foreign troops in its army. Frederick therefore only took 300 men as a 'sample', who were later shipped to Bombay where they were impressed into other company regiments. Frederick made a considerable loss on the enterprise as neither the company nor the duke could be persuaded to pay his expenses: HSAS, A6: Bü. 59, Nos. 25–39; A32: Bd. 14 (expenses listed under *Werb- und Recroutenkosten*); The British Library, Add. Mss. 23680.

[48] Bezzel, *Haustruppen*, p. 24. See pp. 60–5 for text of the treaty.

[49] Braubach, *Subsidien*, p. 11.

the money on mistresses and palaces as they are normally depicted, the princes generally spent the profits to further their aims. In the case of Friedrich II of Hessen-Kassel this meant 'enlightened' reforms, such as reductions in taxation to mitigate the side effects of the militarisation of the population.[50] The Hanoverian electors chose to reinvest their profits in their military system in an effort to reduce their dependence on such financial assistance in future. Like their neighbours in Hessen-Kassel they also funded a number of mercantilist economic enterprises designed to boost state revenue to the same ends. The level of military taxes was also temporarily reduced. The landgrave's Darmstadt cousin, Ludwig X, used his subsidy surplus to bribe the French into assigning him an extra 200,000 inhabitants in the reorganisation of the Reich in 1803.[51]

That there were occasionally profits to be made explains the existence of treaties devoid of any political content. Examples of these include Carl Eugen's negotiations with the English East India Company in 1771 and his agreement with that company's Dutch counterpart in 1786 as well as the treaties signed by Landgrave Friedrich II von Hessen-Kassel and other princes with England in 1775–6. Such treaties were thought to be low-risk arrangements with politically neutral partners which promised good returns. This is evident in the genuine surprise shown by the landgrave at the public outcry occasioned by the news of his treaty in 1775.[52]

While their limited resources prevented many princes from participating in full subsidy treaties, the recruitment of soldiers still offered attractive rewards. By acting as 'military enterprisers' or recruiting agents, to raise an entire regiment for a foreign power, such princes could advance themselves or their offspring directly into the senior position of colonel.[53] They would thereby not only profit from the fee for raising the unit, but secure employment considered appropriate to their noble birth and accompanied by a regular income. This was particularly attractive for those princes from junior branches of princely families who had no prospect of inheriting the throne.

It is therefore not surprising that it was precisely these princes who, from the 1680s, began to take a leading role in the provision of regiments for foreign powers. Among the numerous examples of this are the counts of Öttingen who raised two infantry regiments for the Venetian Republic in 1716. A third was raised by the prince of Waldeck, who also provided one for the emperor in 1733 and others for the Dutch. The motives were almost invariably those outlined above. Thus, the prince of Waldeck provided his regiment in 1733 on the condition that he was made

---

[50] Presser, *Soldatenhandel in Hessen*, pp. 76–88; Ingrao, *Hessian mercenary state*, pp. 145–53, 165–87.

[51] Brauer, *Subsidienverträge*, pp. 98–101, 186–90; Losch, *Soldatenhandel*, p. 58.

[52] Ingrao, *Hessian mercenary state*, pp. 122–34.

[53] Redlich, *Military enterpriser*; T. Barker, 'Military entrepreneurship and absolutism. Habsburg models', *Journal of European Studies*, 4 (1974), 19–42. See also pp. 16–17 above.

an Austrian general and his brother a colonel.[54] Elector Max Emanuel of Bavaria formed the Royal Bavière Regiment for France in 1706 to give respectable employment to his illegitimate son, who eventually became a French lieutenant general.[55] Just how difficult it was to be successful in this field will be illustrated by the discussion of Regent Friedrich Carl in Chapter 4.

The emergence of such princes as intermediaries forced out most of the traditional 'military enterprisers', who were either imperial knights or commoners.[56] These were now forced to become subcontractors to the princes. The only possibility that remained open to them as independent contractors was the formation of the 'free corps' (*Freikorps*). These were so called because they were originally small units not attached to any regiment. Initially they were employed as garrisons for fortresses, but soon took on other roles as 'light troops'.[57] They were never regarded as an integral part of an army and tended to be the first units to be disbanded as an economy measure. They therefore provided a poor field for the realisation of princely dynastic aims, but remained attractive for lesser mortals further down the social scale, for motives which, although more modest, were essentially the same.

Thus, the men who raised such units wanted an elevation in status or at least promotion to a higher rank than that which they already held. In addition, they tried to secure the appointment of relations as officers and to accumulate wealth through pay and booty; hence the name sometimes also given to such men – freebooters. Realising that theirs was a risky business, they also sought security should things go wrong or their unit be disbanded. For example, when the famous free corps commander, Johann Michael Gschray (1701–c. 70), approached Carl Eugen in 1760 with a proposal to raise an 800-strong *corps cheveauleger*, he requested that, should the duke later disband the unit, he and his other officers were to be retained on full pay. He also tried to arrange for his son to be appointed captain.[58] Gschray was unsuccessful, but his competitor, Baron Joachim Reinhold von Glasenapp, managed to persuade the duke to promote him from captain to major in return for

---

[54] Kriegs-Archiv, *Feldzüge*, XIX, pp. 113–19. Waldeck also provided an infantry regiment to Venice in 1688. On this and other German regiments recruited for Venice see Andler, 'Regimenter in Griechenland'.

[55] K. Frhr von Reitzenstein, 'Kurze Lebensabrisse der bayerischen Generale und Obristen', *DBKH* 13 (1904), 1–59 at pp. 36–8.

[56] Redlich, *Military enterpriser*, II, pp. 88–102.

[57] On the 'free corps' and 'light troops' see E. Schnackenburg, 'Die Freicorps Friedrichs des Grossen. Ein Beitrag zur Preußens Heeresgeschichte', *BMWB* 4 (1883), and J. Kunisch, *Der kleine Krieg. Studien zum Heerwesen* (Wiesbaden, 1973) which also has copies of documents covering the raising of the Austrian free corps 'Grün-Loudon'.

[58] HSAS, A8: Bü. 250. His son had been rendered unemployed when the French disbanded the free corps in which he had been serving. After his rejection in Württemberg, Gschray raised a formation for the Prussians. On this unit see Schnackenberg, 'Freicorps', pp. 328–9. For a somewhat jaundiced account of Gschray's extraordinary career see J. C. von Thürriegel, *Merckwürdige Lebensgeschichte des Generalmajors Herrn von Gschray* (1766, reprint Osnabrück, 1974).

raising a 150-man hussar unit. His wife was guaranteed half his pay as a life pension should he be killed in action.[59] In the style of the old military enterprisers, Glasenapp subcontracted the formation of the three companies of his *Freihusaren* to other entrepreneurs, one of whom was appointed on the basis of his claim to know where Frederick the Great's buried treasure was![60]

The few officers who still acted as intermediaries in raising regular regiments were motivated by similar concerns. Colonel Felix Frederick, the illegitimate son of the self-crowned 'King of Corsica', attempted in 1771 to recruit a regiment in Württemberg on behalf of the English East India Company on the condition that he would be made its commander. Owing to the astronomical cost of commissions in the English army, this was often the only way for men without connections to secure high rank.[61]

The problem encountered at all levels of such arrangements was the difficulty in compelling the other party to adhere to its side of the bargain. This problem was less serious for the power that commissioned the recruiting. It could, of course, find that it had paid good money for soldiers who deserted almost immediately, or failed to materialise at all. However, these dangers were kept to a minimum by obliging the recruiter to bear all losses up to the point when the troops officially entered service.[62] Furthermore, payment was normally divided into two parts with the recruiter receiving a lump sum as mobilisation costs (*Aufstellungskosten* or *Werbegeld*) to cover his expenses until the time when the regiments were complete. Only then did he receive the second part of the payment, which was intended to cover the costs of maintaining the regiments and keeping them up to strength (*Verpflegungskosten*).[63] In agreements that were unfavourable to the recruiter, these payments were made directly to the troops themselves, thus preventing any

---

[59] HSAS, A8: Bü. 251, esp. the letter of Frau von Glasenapp to Carl Eugen, 29 Mar. 1761. The actual unit totalled 234 officers and men and was the only free corps in the history of the Württemberg army.

[60] HSAS, G230: Bü. 52, Glasenapp to Carl Eugen 7 Oct. 1760. The man in question was *Rittmeister* Franz von Prangen who claimed his brother-in-law was guarding the treasury. After Glasenapp himself had used his unit to kidnap the 82-year-old Johann Peter Vryheer van Rosenfeld, chancellor of Cleve, to extract a debt owed him, and after the 'free hussars' had plundered their way across Saxony, Carl Eugen disbanded the unit and had Glasenapp arrested. Glasenapp later raised a regiment of 'free dragoons' for Prussia. Needless to say, all attempts by Prangen to find the buried treasure during the 1760 campaign proved fruitless.

[61] The British Library, Add. Mss. 23680, 'The case of Col. F. Frederick with the E.I. Company 1773': 'After this I declared that my sole view by such an undertaking was to merit the honour to enter into their service with my son'. Frederick had already served as a Württemberg agent in Carl Eugen's attempt to counter the estates' propaganda during the court case of 1764–70, see PRO, SP100/17, 26 Sept. and 7 Oct. 1765. On his case and another example, see also A. N. Gilbert, 'Military recruitment and career advancement in the 18th century. Two case studies', *Journal of the Society for Army Historical Research*, 57 (1979), 34–44.

[62] Thum, *Rekrutierung*, p. 10.

[63] Traditionally the hirer paid the cost of recruiting replacements for battle, fire, plague and siege casualties while the contractor replaced deserters at his own expense. Tessin, *Mecklenburgischer Militär*, p. 154; Storm, *Feldherr*, p. 277.

profiteering by the recruiter through keeping wages below the credited amount.[64] Only in the most favourable treaties did the recruiter receive an additional payment, officially called a 'subsidy', over and above the mobilisation and maintenance money. Often this subsidy was intended merely to'subsidise' the maintenance of troops which the recruiter had been paid to raise and hold in readiness in peacetime. Usually the subsidy stopped when the troops were called for and passed fully into the pay of the hirer's commissariat, as was the case with Eberhard Ludwig's Dutch subsidy of 1704–13.[65] Occasionally, the hirer continued to pay the subsidy as well as now meeting the maintenance costs in full. This occurred in Carl Alexander's agreement with the emperor in 1733–5. However, in his case any chance of profiting from this bonus was lost as the amount paid in mobilisation costs was considerably below the true cost, while the regiments were returned with large arrears owing.[66]

The recruiters were well aware of these dangers and made every effort to limit the risks involved. Before beginning negotiations they consulted previous treaties they had signed and, if possible, those of their competitors.[67] Armed with such information, they were less likely to be hoodwinked into accepting poor terms when they could, as did the Ansbach negotiator in 1777, in the middle of discussions, flourish a copy of the terms offered to their competitors.[68] In 1687 Regent Friedrich Carl bribed a Venetian official to give him details of a treaty signed by that republic with Hanover enabling him to negotiate better terms for himself.[69] The singular failure of his successor ninety years later to take such precautions contributed to the hopelessness of the attempt to hire troops to George III to fight the American colonists.

The smaller partner tried to limit his liability by writing into the treaty that he could remain neutral and was not to be considered a participant in any conflict in which the other partner was involved. This practice was accepted in contemporary legal theory and was widely used.[70] As added security they tried to oblige their treaty partner to come to their aid should they be attacked as a consequence of having supplied him with troops. This was important for states such as Württemberg which lay close to the front line between France and Austria. Such guarantees could fail as the French invasions of Hessen-Kassel in 1757 and Württemberg in 1688 show. In both cases France used the fact that these states had made a subsidy treaty with its enemies as grounds for attack. However, it was not

---

[64] For examples of such profiteering see Brauer, *Subsidienverträge*, pp. 51–2, 187–8; Ingrao, *Hessian mercenary state*, pp. 141–2; Braubach, *Subsidien*, pp. 90–2, 131.
[65] HSAS, A6: Bü. 59; A202: Bü. 2469; L6.22.5.85. See also p. 140.
[66] See pp. 172–6.
[67] For examples of this HSAS, A6: Bü. 56, 57, 59.
[68] PRO, SP81/186, Col. Faucitt to the earl of Suffolk 7 and 10 Feb. 1777.
[69] Andler, 'Regimenter in Griechenland', 235.
[70] Brauer, *Subsidienverträge*, pp. 91–3. It was for example written into Carl Eugen's treaty with France of 4 Feb. 1752: HSAS, A202: Bü. 2219 (Articles 2 and 3).

the treaties that were the real cause, but rather that the geographical position of these states made them strategically important to the invader. In other words, they would have been invaded whether they had made a treaty or not.

As their troops represented their most important instrument of power, the princes were very keen to ensure that they were exposed to as little danger as possible. Far from the traditional picture of the greedy despots willingly selling their soldiers as cannon fodder, they took precautions to limit the absolute control of the hirer.[71] The permitted radius of action was carefully outlined. Normally service in dangerous places, such as plague-ridden Hungary, or in areas far from home, such as overseas, was specifically forbidden. In addition, most treaties ruled that the units being hired should be kept intact and not separated, put into garrisons, or made to serve as marines. This all safeguarded a level of control over the hired troops, something which was usually reinforced by the proviso that they were to be commanded by their own general who was to be given a full voice in all councils of war.

Another limitation was provided by the right of recall which permitted the prince to withdraw his corps if he himself should be attacked or no longer wished to continue the treaty. Obviously, this right was gravely restricted by such princes' financial dependence on their larger partners. The most tragic case is the Württemberg *Kapregiment* hired to the Dutch East India Company to garrison the company's holdings in South Africa. Not only did the Württemberg negotiator fail to insert a right to recall into the treaty, but even if he had done, there was no way the duke could fetch his soldiers back as he was totally dependent on the company's ships to collect them. Thus he had to stand by helpless when the company, contrary to the other terms of the treaty, split the unit up and sent it to garrison its unhealthy posts in Java, Ceylon (Sri Lanka) and the Moluccan Island of Amboina. Twelve men were even sent as far as Peking.[72] That the hirer resented such limitations not merely out of greed, or disregard for the lives of the troops he hired, is demonstrated by the case of the Anglo-Hanoverian subsidy. When the elector suddenly refused to co-operate with the English generals in 1712, and withdrew his subsidy corps, the English feared that their own troops would become isolated and be overwhelmed by the French.[73]

In addition to the difficulty of trying to secure full payment for their services, the smaller princes were faced with the problem of how to compel their more powerful partners to make the political concessions they desired. Their limited resources usually prevented them from withdrawing their troops as retaliation for not being given what they wanted. Few were as fortunate as the landgrave of Hessen-Kassel in amassing such a large surplus as to be able to absorb losses and hold out for

---

[71] On these, see Brauer, *Subsidienverträge*, pp. 55–60.
[72] J. Prinz, *Das württembergische Kapregiment 1786–1808* (Stuttgart, 1932 edn), pp. 195–293.
[73] Brauer, *Subsidienverträge*, pp. 74–90.

better terms. Most were forced to become even more heavily committed through further agreements in the hope that they would eventually be rewarded. The fate of Carl Alexander and especially that of his son, Carl Eugen, illustrates this very clearly.

The troop transfers often cited as further evidence for the commercial nature of the soldier trade were, in fact, the way princes tried to solve the problems created by such over-commitment. As the term implies, this was the transfer of whole or part units raised by one prince to the army of another, rather in the manner of football players transferred from one team to another. This differed from the hire of troops in that the men transferred were permanently incorporated into the other army either in their original unit or distributed among other regiments. The commercial aspect was the transfer fee, usually approximately equivalent to the cost of raising the unit, though on one occasion Friedrich Wilhelm I of Prussia exchanged his porcelain collection for one of the Saxon elector's cavalry regiments.[74] Such an exchange was unusual. Generally, the transfers were a desperate measure to prevent a budget deficit and avoid having to cope with a mass of demobilised soldiers.[75] The existing welfare and policing systems were inadequate to deal with such a sudden influx of unemployed and potentially violent men and their dependants, most of whom were without either a home or another profession and whose only future appeared to be as beggars or brigands. It could also be politically sensitive to discharge the officers, many of whom were nobles who might have influential friends. This was particularly true at the time of a disputed regency when the army might assume a political role and declare its support for the faction that guaranteed its continued employment.[76]

The threat of withdrawal of financial support was thus a powerful weapon in the hands of the larger states.[77] They were not slow in exploiting the opportunity to reduce their subsidy partners to little more than satellites which, as noted above, was one of their objectives in signing such treaties. Frequently, it would have harmed their own interests to have made the requested concessions, which in any case were often beyond their power to grant. This was especially true of the emperor. To have met one prince's demands for an increase in status and territory would have almost invariably provoked a disagreeable reaction from the others, as was the case when Emperor Leopold I elevated the duke of Calenberg to elector of

---

[74] Jany, *Geschichte der königlich-preussischen Armee*, I, pp. 651–2. The unit was thereafter known as 'The Porcelain Dragoons'.

[75] As evidenced by the transfer of three Bavarian rgts to Austria in 1749 when the elector received only 24fl. per man whereas it had cost him 10fl. a head more to recruit them: Staudinger, *Geschichte des bayerischen Heeres*, III, pp. 243, 955–61. For Württemberg examples see pp. 190–5.

[76] See pp. 184–9. In 1748 the new regent in Sachsen-Weimar transferred 211 guardsmen to Prussia in return for confirmation of his uncertain position and co-operation to end the Wasungen conflict with Altenburg: Losch, *Soldatenhandel*, p. 22: H. Müller, *Das Heerwesen im Herzogtum Sachsen-Weimar von 1702–1775* (Jena, 1936), p. 3.

[77] For an example of when it failed to work see Brauer, *Subsidienverträge*, pp. 74–90, 96.

Hanover in 1692.[78] Furthermore, the sort of territorial increase envisaged by most princes was bound to be at the expense of those who were the emperor's chief supporters: the bishops, imperial knights and cities. To allow a prince to annex these would be to allow him to cut into the emperor's own power base in the Reich.

This, of course, did not prevent the emperor hinting at the possibility of such concessions to induce the princes to overreach themselves and so become dependent on his continued good will. As there were precedents for both territorial increase and elevation in status, the princes were encouraged to believe that their requests would also one day be granted.[79] There was also the fear that if they did not continue to press their own claims, a rival might succeed before them and put them at a disadvantage.[80] The emperor's success at manipulating these desires in order to extend his own influence will be a recurring theme throughout the following chapters.

The findings of this and the previous two chapters will become clearer in the discussion of the career of the Württemberg regent Friedrich Carl (1677–93). His aims correspond to those that were identified in the first chapter as common to the princes of the smaller states in general. In his attempts to realise these he ran up against the problems of inadequate resources and uncooperative estates outlined in the second chapter. The form which the resultant conflict took was to characterise relations between duke and estates until the end of the old Reich. Finally, the methods to which Friedrich Carl resorted to solve his difficulties were those discussed in this chapter. Not only did he create the first standing army in Württemberg, he also used all four forms of the 'soldier trade' outlined here to advance his aims.

---

[78] V. Press, 'Kurhannover im System des alten Reiches 1692–1806', in *Prinz-Albert-Studien*, 4 (Munich, 1986), 53–79.

[79] For examples, see pp. 22–5.

[80] This is particularly evident in Württemberg and Hessen-Kassel rivalry over the electoral title and the possibility of becoming king of Poland. HSAS, G230: Bü. 54.

4

Regent Friedrich Carl, 1677–1693

CHARACTER AND AIMS

Friedrich Carl (1652–98) came to power as regent of Württemberg as a result of the unexpected death of his elder brother, Duke Wilhelm Ludwig, after a reign of a mere three years (1674–7). His dual role as 'Duke Administrator' and prince of the junior Winnenthal line of the family was to impart special characteristics to his regency. On the one hand, he realised that his nephew Eberhard Ludwig would one day become reigning duke and he would once again he reduced to the relative obscurity of prince of a junior line. He therefore tried to extract maximum advantage for himself and his own sons while his power lasted. On the other hand, owing to the length of his rule – Eberhard Ludwig was scarcely a year old when Friedrich Carl became regent on 27 November 1677 and under Württemberg law could not become duke before his eighteenth birthday in 1694 – he developed attributes of a reigning duke. He therefore interfered in the internal structure of the duchy to a far greater extent than the indecisive regents of the period 1737–44, from whom he differed radically in both youth and character.

Although nominally obliged to share power with the privy council and with Eberhard Ludwig's mother, the pious Magdalene Sibylle (1652–1712), he soon seized the reins of government for himself.[1] His ruthless determination to establish himself as absolute ruler overshadowed all previous attempts by Württemberg dukes in that direction, so that, by the time of his death, the estates looked back to the spirit of co-operation and good-natured compromise of the reign of his father Eberhard III (1628–74) as a golden age. In fact, Eberhard III had held a view of sovereignty quite different from that implied by his later image, and his reign too had been filled with disputes with the estates over the establishment of a modest ducal bodyguard, the attempt to fortify Freudenstadt, his disorderly personal life and his various mercantilist schemes.[2] However, 'in tone and style' he had remained a

---

[1] The regency settlement of 27 Nov. 1677 gave him the title of *Obervormünder* and sole control of affairs, though he was obliged to inform Magdalene Sibylle of all business. She was granted the title *Obermitvormünderin* and sole control over Eberhard Ludwig's education.

[2] J. Fischer, 'Herzog Eberhard III (1628–1674)', in Uhland (ed.), *900 Jahre Haus Württemberg*, pp. 195–209; Vann, *Making of a State*, pp. 115–16; Grube, *Stuttgarter Landtag*, pp. 313–41; Söll, *Wirtschaftspolitik*, pp. 46–68.

traditional Württemberg duke.[3] Friedrich Carl, in contrast, was very much a man of the baroque age.[4] Through his introduction of new forms of court etiquette and his importation of foreign fashions and styles,[5] he created a wide cultural gap between duke and estates which only reinforced the existing gap in political outlook. The lines for the future conflict were thus drawn, and when the accession of the Catholic Carl Alexander (1733) removed the last area of common ground, this gap became unbridgeable.

To the estates, one of the most alarming things about Friedrich Carl was his attempt to change the course of traditional Württemberg policy. The reasons behind this attempt were, in part, an effort by the regent to find more efficient means to achieve his aims and, in part, a reaction to the new balance of power in Europe following the rise of Louis XIV of France. An examination of these attempts shows how the duke, the emperor and the king of France all, to a greater or lesser extent, sought to profit from the system of the Reich outlined in Chapter 1.

WÜRTTEMBERG, FRANCE AND THE EMPEROR

The traditional policy of Württemberg dukes had been to support the emperor in his capacity as head of the Reich (*Reichsoberhaupt*), while at the same time trying to avoid falling too much under his influence as head of the House of Habsburg.[6] This was a precarious balance to hold and it was made all the more unsteady by the duchy's geographical proximity to the Austrian heartlands. The Austrian occupation of 1634–8 had shown the dangers of attempting too independent a policy – in this case a defensive neutrality between 1608 and 1628 and then open hostility to the emperor between 1632 and 1634.[7] After 1634, the privy council had chosen to follow the policy of the least risk, which meant accepting the decision of the majority in the Reichstag. Thus, like the other weak states, Württemberg displayed the Reichspatriotismus discussed above in Chapter 1: a concept of loyalty to the Reich, defined in such terms as to leave no room for Habsburg aggrandisement.[8]

In practice, however, this tended to work to the emperor's advantage as it provided him with numerous opportunities to put pressure on the weaker states to conform to his will. These opportunities were exploited during the long reign of

---

[3] Vann, *Making of a state*, p. 128.

[4] Fleischhauer, *Barock im Herzogtum Württemberg*, pp. 127–8, calls him the duchy's first baroque prince. On the regent see *ADB*, VIII (1878), pp. 50–2, Wunder, 'Der Administrator'.

[5] Wunder, 'Der Administrator', p. 158; Vann, *Making of a state*, pp. 135–6.

[6] V. Press, 'Die Herzöge von Württemberg, der Kaiser und das Reich', in Uhland (ed.), *900 Jahre Haus Württemberg*, pp. 412–33.

[7] R. Uhland, 'Herzog Johann Friedrich (1608–1628)', in *ibid.*, pp. 183–94; T. Schott, 'Württemberg und Gustav Adolf 1631 und 1632', *WVJHLG*, NF4 (1895), 343–402.

[8] Vann, *Making of a state*, pp. 125–6; Gebauer, *Außenpolitik*, p. 73.

Emperor Leopold I (1658–1705) in a development which has now come to be known as the 'imperial reaction'.[9]

The internal politics of the Reich had long been characterised by a struggle for predominance between the emperor and the princes. The lines of this struggle were never clearly drawn during the early modern period. From the late fifteenth century the princes had been divided among themselves whether to assert control through an elitist electoral oligarchy or through participation of all princes at the Reichstag. Simultaneously, the emperor had been distracted by his dynastic interests elsewhere and had only intermittently sought to strengthen his authority within the Reich. Two major challenges to imperial authority had been mounted during the Reformation and the Thirty Years War. These only complicated matters further by inextricably mixing the political dispute with the growing confessional strife. Neither challenge was successful. Instead, they pushed the Reich through two prolonged and painful stages (1495–1555 and 1618–48/54) towards an ever-more refined balance between princes, the electors and the emperor. This process strengthened the Reich's system of checks and balances which prevented any of its major components achieving a preponderance.

However, the emperor had only fought off these challenges at considerable cost to his authority. His prestige as impartial supreme judge, upon which much of his authority rested, had been severely undermined by his misuse of the imperial office to further his dynastic aims and by his partisan association with the Catholic cause, especially during the Thirty Years War. The imperial reaction was an attempt to rebuild this lost authority and influence after the setbacks of the war years. It also represented a change in direction for imperial politics. Attempts to establish any form of imperial absolutism were abandoned. Instead, the emperor now sought to work within the post-1648 structure and exploit what opportunities it offered.

Defeat in the Thirty Years War forced the emperor to fall back on his own resources: the possessions of the Habsburg family. These were already considerable and expanded greatly during the course of the seventeenth century. Although most of the new territory lay outside the Reich, its acquisition greatly enhanced the emperor's position. Greater resources permitted more independent and ambitious policies. The spectacular victories over the Turks at the end of the century did much to restore imperial prestige. The facade of Christian unity created by these *Türkenkriege* lessened the inter-German confessional disputes which had

---

[9] See esp. the articles by V. Press, 'Das Römisch–Deutsche Reich – ein politisches System in verfassungs- und sozialgeschichtlicher Fragestellung', in G. Klingenstein and H. Lutz (eds.), *Spezialforschung und Gesamtgeschichte* (Vienna, 1981), pp. 221–42; 'The Holy Roman Empire in German history', in Kouri and Scott (eds.), *Politics and society in Reformation Europe*, pp. 51–77; 'Die kaiserliche Stellung im Reich zwischen 1648 und 1740 – Versuch einer Neubewertung', in G. Schmidt (ed.), *Stände und Gesellschaft im alten Reich* (Stuttgart, 1989), pp. 51–80. For a useful overview see A. Schindling and W. Ziegler (eds.), *Die Kaiser der Neuzeit 1519–1918* (Munich, 1990), pp. 169–277.

undermined the imperial position in the past. Influence within the Reich was extended by rewarding loyal followers with estates and appointments in the captured territory. This continued the practice of the 1620s when the property of the Bohemian rebel nobility had been redistributed to the emperor's German followers.

The imperial court at Vienna now became the hub of an extensive patronage network and a worthy rival to that of Versailles as a model for the princes' cultural competition. Despite the development of these separate princely courts, that of the Habsburgs remained ahead in magnificence and lucrative opportunities. The expanding Habsburg administration and army offered numerous career openings which proved highly attractive for the imperial knights, lesser nobility and the younger sons of ruling families.[10] Furthermore, only the Habsburgs enjoyed the position of supreme feudal overlord, enabling them to exercise influence through the Reich's system of honours, status and feudal jurisdictions. Though their powers were limited by the Reichstag in 1654, it was still possible to manipulate the system to elevate followers to princely status and so swell the ranks of the pro-imperial lobby.

The Habsburgs' role within the imperial church (*Reichskirche*) opened up further possibilities. Through their extensive network of client families, they controlled many of the cathedral chapters and could influence elections in ecclesiastical territories throughout the Reich. This was used both as a further means of rewarding loyal followers, and of increasing imperial influence at the Reichstag through the representation of many bishops and prelates in the college of princes.

The restoration of the emperor's prestige helped rehabilitate his position as supreme judge. This proved a highly significant element in the imperial reaction. The horrors of the Thirty Years War produced a revulsion at the use of force to settle disputes and encouraged a return to the late medieval practice of judicial settlement through the imperial courts. The later middle ages had seen a phenomenon known as the Landfrieden movement, whereby estates of the Reich agreed to put disputes to arbitration at a mutually recognised tribunal. This culminated in the establishment in 1495 of a supreme court, the *Reichskammergericht*, for the entire Reich. This court had been opposed by the emperor who saw it as a vehicle for princely infringement of his authority. Its effectiveness was in any case undermined by its inability to process cases quickly and by the growing confessionalisation within the Reich. Unlike this earlier attempt, the post-1648 'juridification of the empire' worked to the emperor's advantage.[11]

This was due to the pre-eminence of a second imperial court, the *Reichshofrat*,

---

[10] For examples see Arndt, *Reichsgrafenkollegium*, pp. 265–86 and pp. 15–17 above.
[11] Press, 'Holy Roman Empire', p. 66; F. R. H. Du Boulay, *Germany in the later middle ages* (London, 1983), pp. 76–8.

over the ineffective Reichskammergericht. The Reichshofrat was based in Vienna and had been virtually dependent on the emperor since the mid-sixteenth century. It only took action after consultation with the Habsburg administration and its verdicts were dependent on the emperor's confirmation. An attempt by the princes to detach it from Austrian control had failed in 1648. Thereafter, it won increasing influence because of the relative speed and efficiency with which it processed cases and, most importantly, because it was perceived by the majority of litigants to be impartial. Its reputation derived in part from the emperor's increased prestige. This had gone a fair way to allaying fears of partiality raised during the Thirty Years War.[12] The reliance on Roman law, which was supposedly impartial and implied a direct continuity between the present and the glories of ancient imperial Rome, also helped. However, the most significant factor was that the Reichshofrat did not appear to consistently favour any one element of the Reich's structure. Thus peasants of small principalities such as Hohenzollern-Hechingen felt able to appeal in the confidence that the court would not automatically support their prince. Similarly, the citizens of Frankfurt could appeal for justice against their oligarchical city council, just as the estates of Mecklenburg, East Frisia and Württemberg could against the alleged tyranny of their princes. On the other hand, rulers could look to the emperor to back their measures against public disorder or unreasonable opposition within their territories.[13] As the needs of Habsburg policy varied from place to place, and indeed over time, the emperor was not compelled to continually back any one element. To observers unaware of the Habsburgs' true agenda, this inconsistency could appear as impartiality.

Finally, the imperial reaction was also assisted by the weakness of many of the princes. The war had left many of them heavily in debt and in no position to participate in the policy of administrative reform, military expansion and cultural competition begun by their larger and richer neighbours. As the seventeenth century progressed, fewer and fewer princes could keep up. The gap widened between the larger electorates, especially Brandenburg, and the mass of small and minor principalities. The latter were forced back into dependence on the emperor, who appeared to offer protection not only against the acquisitiveness of their more powerful cousins, but also against the growing threat from France. The same tendency was even more pronounced among the lesser political entities of the Reich. The imperial cities, counts, knights and prelates had even less chance of maintaining parity with the electorates than the minor princes. They looked to the

---

12 Hughes, *Law and politics*, pp. 27–59; Kampmann, *Reichsrebellion*.
13 J. Q. Whitman, *The legacy of Roman law in the German Romantic era* (Princeton, 1990), pp. 3–91; Hughes, *Law and politics*; Wick, *Mecklenburg*; G. L. Soliday, *A community in conflict: Frankfurt society in the 17th and 18th century* (Hanover, NH, 1974); V. Press, 'Von den Bauernrevolten des 16. zur konstitutionellen Verfassung des 19. Jahrhunderts. Die Unterkonflikte in Hohenzollern-Hechingen und ihre Lösungen', in H. Weber (ed.), *Politische Ordnungen und soziale Kräfte im alten Reich* (Wiesbaden, 1980), pp. 85–112.

emperor to preserve their integrity by maintaining the system of checks and balances of the Reich.

Herein lay the chief limitation on the extent of the imperial reaction. The emperor could only further his influence if he worked within the structure established by 1648. The imperial courts could not be reduced to vehicles for the arbitrary advancement of Habsburg objectives without placing their judicial function in question. In order not to destroy the very instrument upon which the restoration of his influence depended, the emperor had to refrain from obvious manipulation. In any case, even the Reichshofrat maintained a degree of independence and on occasion refused to follow Habsburg policy.

The same was true in his use of honours and titles to extend his client network. While members of a particular stratum of the Reich's hierarchy almost invariably desired elevation into the next, they were determined to prevent infiltration from below. For example, while the majority of counts were aspiring to princely status, they were equally intent on preserving the exclusivity of their own estate from parvenu counts elevated from the imperial knights.[14] The emperor's use of his feudal powers in this manner could provoke widespread opposition, as Leopold I discovered when he elevated the duke of Calenberg to electoral status in 1692. It took until 1708 before he could secure formal recognition from the Reichstag. There were also limits to the use of the Austrian court, army and bureaucracy to extend patronage within the Reich. Positions in all three had to be kept open to pacify the nobility of the Habsburgs' own territories. Furthermore, the possibilities of extending influence through the Reichskirche declined with the secularisation of many ecclesiastical territories in 1648 and the growth of competition for the remaining places from the Wittelsbach and Schönborn dynasties. Finally, much as they needed his protection, the minor political entities of the Reich had no desire to be reduced to pawns in the Habsburg designs. Even the prelates, who could normally be counted among the emperor's most loyal supporters, could refuse to co-operate.[15]

By generally following cautious policies that remained within the limits, Leopold I had done much to restore imperial fortunes by 1705. The length of his reign helped by denying the electors the opportunity of redefining the emperor's position by a new electoral agreement (Wahlkapitulation). The wave of Reichspatriotismus generated by the conflicts with France and the Turks continued the momentum of the imperial reaction into the beginning of Charles VI's reign (1711–40). Then it began to falter. Continued Austrian successes against the Turks (1716–18), combined with the new emperor's obsession with dynastic claims to parts of Italy, increased the profile of Habsburg Hauspolitik and called into

---

[14] Arndt, *Reichsgrafenkollgeium*, pp. 36–111, 208–64.
[15] A. von Reden-Dohna, 'Problems of small estates of the empire. The example of the Swabian imperial prelates', *Journal of Modern History*, 58 (1986), Supplement, 76–87.

question the impartiality of the imperial office. This was further placed in doubt by the emperor's apparent partisan support for Catholic princes during a period of heightened religious sensibilities immediately after the War of the Spanish Succession (1701–14). These problems coincided with a fundamental weakness within the Habsburg family. Charles' inability to produce a male heir led to his obsession with gaining international recognition of the Pragmatic Sanction, a document revising Habsburg inheritance law to allow his daughter, Maria Theresia, to inherit. This desire compelled Charles to pursue conciliatory policies within the Reich designed to secure the agreement of influential princes.[16]

Several of these princes were becoming considerably more aggressive following a period of territorial consolidation and military expansion between 1672 and 1714. This process significantly altered the balance within the Reich and increasingly distorted its system of constitutional restraints. It began what has become known as Austro-Prussian dualism, though Hanover, Saxony and Bavaria continued to play important subordinate roles for a long time after 1714.

By 1740 Prussia had become a serious rival to Habsburg influence. Over the preceding decade it had effectively usurped the leadership of the Protestant faction within the Reichstag (Corpus Evangelicorum), left vacant since the Saxon elector's conversion to Catholicism in 1697. Though Hanover continued to contest leadership into the 1760s, Prussia consolidated an important weapon to counter the policies of the imperial reaction. Prussia was quick to play on latent Protestant fears of Catholic and imperial absolutism to mobilise resistance to Habsburg designs. Prussian influence was further extended by creating a rival client system within the Reich. Though Friedrich Wilhelm I (1713–40) abandoned any attempt to rival the Viennese court, he copied the Habsburg methods of patronage and marriage alliances. The latter was used in an attempt to tie Württemberg to the Prussian orbit (see pp. 141–2). Similar motives dictated Friedrich Wilhelm's tour of the smaller German courts in 1731. While still smaller than that of the emperor, Prussia's client system outdid those of its Protestant rivals. The only serious contender was the network of the Bavarian Wittelsbachs which extended into North Germany through the ecclesiastical holdings of their numerous relations.[17]

Both Bavaria and Prussia were well poised to take advantage of the unique opportunity of the interregnum following Charles VI's death in 1740. However, only Prussia had the military might to preserve its gains from the unexpectedly fierce Habsburg retaliation. In contrast, the Bavarian position crumbled as the

---

[16] PRO, SP102/25, esp. Eberhard Ludwig to George I 9 Jan. 1722 and pp. 144–54 below; M. Braubach, *Prinz Eugen von Savoyen* (5 vols., Munich, 1963–5), III and IV. For the role of religion in eighteenth-century imperial politics, see Haug-Moritz, *Württembergischer Ständekonflikt*, pp. 138–63.

[17] Examples of Prussian policy can be obtained from Kappelhoff, *Ostfriesland*, pp. 77–87, 242–6, 294–8; Wick, *Mecklenburg*, pp. 110, 127–35, 234–51; Hughes, *Law and politics*, pp. 60–271; Arndt, *Reichsgrafenkollegium*, pp. 309–13. For Bavaria, see Hartmann, *Geld*.

Wittelsbach relations failed to rally round and French military assistance proved ineffective.[18]

The period 1740–5 was a crucial turning-point. The Habsburgs' loss of the imperial title, together with the annexation of Silesia by Prussia, severely dented their prestige. After 1745, as in 1648, their policy was primarily aimed at restoring their position within the Reich. However, the next two Habsburg emperors, Francis I (1745–65) and Joseph II (1765–90), no longer adhered so strictly to the limits imposed by the structure of the Reich. The imperial office and institutions, which had already suffered a serious loss in prestige during the weak Wittelsbach emperorship (1742–5), were further endangered by more open manipulation in the interests of Habsburg Hauspolitik. This was most extreme during the Seven Years War (1756–63) which saw Austrian attempts to mobilise the Reich for a recovery of Silesia.[19]

Such manipulation merely heightened Austro-Prussian dualism by playing into the hands of Prussian policy. Prussian *Reichspolitik* was directed not at securing an alternative Prussian-led Reich, but at exploiting the existing structure to block Austrian designs. Through personal contact and correspondence, Prussian officials sought to establish good relations at all levels of the Reich's structure, not merely the Reichstag and Kreis assemblies, but to the princes' advisers and bureaucrats as well. These contacts were mobilised to block any measure perceived as contrary to Prussian interests. The system of checks and balances already encouraged inertia. Under Prussian influence it could be paralysed to obstruct Austrian designs. These measures were facilitated by judicious manipulation of religious sensibilities and by playing on the theme of imperial constitutional 'liberties' under threat from Habsburg 'tyranny'. Thus, gradually, though never completely, Prussia began to usurp the traditional role of the emperor as defender of the lesser entities of the Reich.[20]

The development of this dualism lessened rather than increased the opportunities for the minor princes. This was partly due to the practical disparity in resources. Austria, and to a lesser extent Prussia, were already considerably more powerful than any other German territory by 1700. By the 1770s this gap had grown even wider through the acquisition by both states of vast tracts of land outside the Reich. However, the distortion wrought by their antagonism within the Reich was probably even more serious. The system of patronage and protection that had

---

[18] P. C. Hartmann, *Karl Albrecht – Karl VII: Glücklicher Kurfürst, unglücklicher Kaiser* (Regensburg, 1985); H. Weber, *Die Politik des Kurfürsten Karl Theodor von der Pfalz während des österreichischen Erbfolgekrieges (1742–1748)* (Bonn, 1956).

[19] Haut-Moritz, *Württembergischer Ständekonflikt*, pp. 125–38, 163–9, 272–92; Gagliardo, *Reich and nation*. For Joseph's views see H. Conrad (ed.), 'Verfassung und politische Lage des Reiches in einer Denkschrift Josephs II von 1767–1768', in L. Carlen and F. Steinegger (eds.), *Festschrift für Nikolaus Grass* (2 vols., Innsbrück, 1974), I, pp. 161–85, and D. Beales, *Joseph II: In the shadow of Maria Theresa 1741–1780* (Cambridge, 1987), pp. 110–33.

[20] Haug-Moritz, *Württembergischer Ständekonflikt*, pp. 127–31, 215–19; pp. 195–8 below.

existed in the era of the imperial reaction and from which several princes, notably those of Hanover, had profited, was transformed into one of manipulation and exploitation. Simultaneously, the range of potential rewards was considerably reduced. The decline in the emperor's influence lessened his ability to make worthwhile concessions. Meanwhile, Prussia had no alternatives to offer since it was merely subverting the existing system for its own purposes. When the challenge of the French Revolutionary Wars after 1792 threw both powers on the defensive, the system collapsed altogether. As it became obvious that Austria was sacrificing its traditional clients in the interests of its own defence, the smaller princely states joined the larger electorates in destroying a system in which they perceived only disadvantages. Not only had the Reich long thwarted their dynastic ambitions, but it was now denying them protection when they needed it most.

These developments can be examined through our case study of Württemberg. The reigns of Regent Friedrich Carl and Duke Eberhard Ludwig spanned the era of imperial reaction. That of Carl Alexander coincided with the period of Habsburg weakness in the last years of Charles VI's reign before the development of open Austro-Prussian rivalry. The critical years of the interregnum, Wittelsbach emperorship and open Austro-Prussian conflict occurred during the regency in Carl Eugen's minority. They represented perhaps the best, certainly the last, genuine opportunity for any Württemberg ruler to achieve major political objectives. The weakness of the regency government robbed the ruling house of this opportunity. Even the Austrian *Anwartschaft*, which was placed in doubt by Charles VI's death, was not formally annulled, allowing the Habsburgs to revive their claims in 1770.[21] The long reign of Carl Eugen took place against the background of Austro-Prussian dualism which helped push Württemberg into its disastrous involvement in the Seven Years War and provoke the open conflict between duke and estates in 1758–70.

Württemberg's geographical position meant that its relations with the emperor had to be worked out within the context of its ties to the Swabian Kreis and, increasingly, also its attitude towards France. An examination of these will further illustrate the elements of the imperial reaction.

In addition to acquiring more territory wherever possible,[22] the emperor exploited the institutions of the Reich for his own ends. In the south-west, this meant the Swabian Kreis. Here he was represented by his Kreis representative (*Kreisgesandte*), through whom he tried to influence the discussions at the Kreis Konvent.[23] The fact that the Swabian Kreis only covered about two-thirds of Swabia also gave him numerous opportunities for intervention. His own territorial holdings there were segregated from the other states and incorporated into the

---

[21] Haug-Moritz, *Württembergischer Ständekonflikt*, pp. 96, 223–5; Chapter 7 and p. 233 below.
[22] Kallenberg, 'Spätzeit', 61–93 at p. 72.
[23] Borck, *Schwäbische Reichskreis*, p. 46.

Austrian Kreis instead. This created many areas for confusion through Austrian enclaves within the Swabian Kreis over which the Kreis Konvent had no control. The emperor exploited this confusion by trying to bring disputes between Austria and Swabian states before the courts situated in his own Swabian holdings rather than the more independently minded central imperial courts. He was assisted in these attempts by the fact that certain other imperial institutions of the area, such as the imperial provincial administration (*Kaiserliche Landvogtei*) and the district court (*Landgericht*), had been pawned to Austria.[24] He was also aided by the presence of numerous imperial knights,[25] who, as we have seen, counted among his most ardent followers. The knights were excluded from the Kreis organisation altogether and subordinated directly to the emperor himself. As their holdings were nonetheless scattered throughout the territories of the Kreis members, disputes remained unavoidable. In his dual capacity as head of the Reich and feudal overlord of the knights, the emperor had many opportunities to intervene in such disputes and so put pressure on individual Kreis members.[26]

Such a policy was naturally not without its disadvantages for the structure of the Reich, particularly in the area of common defence. Fear of external aggression did occasionally cause a closing of ranks between the Austrian authorities, the knights and the Swabian Kreis, as the combined militias of 1734 and 1794 prove.[27] However, the long-term effect of the emperor's tactics was to prevent such co-operation and encourage the most powerful princes to view the knights and the scattered Austrian holdings as thorns in their sides and obstacles to territorial expansion.

The emperor also kept alive the idea of the medieval 'duchy of Swabia' (*Herzogtum Schwaben*) as an Austrian possession. In 1699 a rumour that he was trying to re-establish this greatly alarmed the Swabian princes.[28]

The emperor's position as head of the Reich also entitled him to intervene as supreme judge in any conflict within one of the princely states. As far as Württemberg was concerned, this possibility was reinforced by his claims to the succession through the Anwartschaft. The increased imperial activity in this area was clearly demonstrated by the emperor's intervention in the regency dispute

---

[24] Vann, *Swabian Kreis*, pp. 284–7; Gebauer, *Außenpolitik*, pp. 73–8, 81–4. According to Storm, *Feldherr*, pp. 54–6, Austrian territory in Swabia totalled 8,260km² with 360,000 inhabitants.

[25] Storm, *Feldherr* puts the knights' territory at 3,855km² with 180,000 inhabitants.

[26] Press, 'Württembergische Angriff', pp. 329–48.

[27] HSAS, A28: Bü. 99; C14: Bü. 306 and 307; O. Heinl, *Heereswesen und Volksbewaffnung in Vorderösterreich im Zeitalter Josefs II. und der Revolutionskriege* (Freiburg i.Br., Ph.D., printed 1941). The knights were invited to co-operate, but generally chose not to; see Vann, *Swabian Kreis*, pp. 165–6, 284–93.

[28] H. G. Hofacker, 'Die schwäbische Herzogswürde. Untersuchungen zur Landfürstlichen und kaiserlichen Politik im deutschen Südwesten im Spätmittelalter und in der frühen Neuzeit, *ZWLG*, 47 (1988), 71–148; Gebauer, *Außenpolitik*, pp. 75–6.

following Wilhelm Ludwig's death. The last time there had been a regency dispute (1457), the Württembergers had solved it without reference to the emperor.

By the appointment of Friedrich Carl, who was already serving in the Austrian army, the emperor hoped to have a man at Stuttgart through whom he could control Württemberg policy. However, to be doubly sure of this control and to prevent Friedrich Carl from becoming too independent, the emperor confirmed the rights of two of the other claimants to the regency, namely Magdalene Sibylle and the privy council.[29] This was a wise move. As we have seen in pp. 66–8, through its position at the head of the bureaucracy given it by the 1660 Kanzleiordnung, the privy council was in an excellent position to block ducal policy. Although a series of opportune deaths among the councillors enabled Friedrich Carl to appoint his supporters to it, the remainder generally enjoyed the backing of Magdalene Sibylle. Thus, a delicate balance in government was created, which the emperor could influence in whichever way seemed most opportune.

This policy of divide and rule was to prove its worth, as Friedrich Carl did precisely what had been feared and attempted to free Württemberg from imperial domination. He tried to do this by profiting from the rise of France. Ever since the collapse of Burgundy in 1477 as an independent buffer between the Reich and France, the latter had represented a potential counter-weight to the emperor within imperial politics. This fact had not been lost on the princes, especially the Protestant ones, who during the Reformation and the Thirty Years War repeatedly called upon the king of France when they needed help against the emperor. Duke Ulrich of Württemberg (1498–1519/1534–50) had done this early in the 1520s during his attempts to recover his duchy from the Austrians.[30] While the resurgence of Austrian influence in south Germany after 1634 had brought home the dangers of appealing to outsiders against the emperor, Württemberg edged cautiously back towards such a policy when Eberhard III joined the French-sponsored Rhenish Alliance in 1660.

However, in the case of Württemberg an appeal to France was not always entirely voluntary. France's eastward expansion represented a grave threat to the ducal family. With the French annexation of Alsace (1648) and Burgundy (1678), the family's holdings in Mömpelgard and Reichenweiher became completely surrounded by French territory. France, which already had a legal pretext for intervention as one of the two guarantors of the Peace of Westphalia, was now directly in a position to do so. For reasons of geography, the French could not directly attack the emperor's Austrian heartlands in central Europe, and so they

---

[29] Wunder, 'Der Administrator', pp. 123–6.
[30] T. A. Brady Jr, 'Princes Reformation versus urban liberty: Strasbourg and the Restoration in Württemberg 1534', in I. Batori (ed.), *Städtische Gesellschaft und Reformation* (*Spätmittelalter und frühe Neuzeit, Tübinger Beiträge zur Geschichtsforschung*, 12, Stuttgart, 1980), pp. 225–91; V. Press, 'Ein Epochenjahr der württembergischen Geschichte. Restitution und Reformation 1534', *ZWLG*, 47 (1988), 203–34.

sought to weaken him by winning over the west German princes by a mixture of threats and rewards. Now that Mömpelgard and Reichenweiher were firmly in their grip, they were in an excellent position to prise open imperial defences along the Rhine by winning over Württemberg. Not only was the duchy the most important state within the Swabian Kreis, which would be paralysed without it, it also lay as a convenient stepping-stone on the way to Bavaria. This became particularly important after 1700 with the development of the Franco-Bavarian alliance.

However, if the duke bowed to pressure to co-operate with France, he ran the risk of provoking Austrian retribution. Through his claims to the duchy and his position as head of the Reich, the emperor was in a good position to sequestrate Württemberg as punishment for such 'treacherous' collaboration. The duke had, therefore, to tread carefully when entering into an agreement with either France or the emperor.

INITIAL SUCCESS AND FIRST SETBACK, 1677–83

Friedrich Carl was determined to turn the tables and profit from the fact that both France and the emperor needed his help, and might therefore each be induced to provide protection against retaliation from the other. This was nonetheless a dangerous policy as, quite apart from the possibility of retaliation, the duke ran the risk of merely exchanging dependence on one power for dependence on the other. However, given the duchy's geographical position and limited resources, such a policy represented the only hope if he was to achieve his political and dynastic ambitions. The same was true of his successors and the policy of all of them is characterised by their attempts to make political capital out of the strategic position of their possessions.

Such an opportunity appeared in 1680 with the development of renewed tension between the emperor and France. The former was still smarting from his defeat between 1672 and 1678, and hoped to mobilise the Reich for a new war against France. The latter hoped to consolidate its new gains on the eastern frontier by reactivating old – and indeed inventing new – claims to other pieces of territory.[31] To win support for this policy and prevent the emperor intervening, the French launched a diplomatic offensive. Friedrich Carl hoped to profit from this situation by seeking on the one hand a closer co-operation with France, while on the other keeping the back door open should things go wrong and the need arise to call upon the emperor for support.

In moving towards France, Friedrich Carl was really recognising the new balance

---

[31] This was the so-called *Reunion* policy. On this see F. L. Ford, *Strasbourg in transition 1648–1789* (Cambridge, 1958), pp. 28–54. On the Württemberg reaction to it see B. Wunder, *Frankreich, Württemberg und der schwäbische Kreis während der Auseinandersetzungen über die Reunionen (1679–97). Ein Beitrag zur Deutschlandpolitik Ludwigs XIV.* (Stuttgart, 1971).

of power on the Upper Rhine. In 1680 the Parliament of Besançon proclaimed Mömpelgard and its dependent territories to be a Burgundian fief and therefore now under French sovereignty. French troops moved in to make good these claims, causing the Mömpelgard family to flee to their relations in Oels where they remained until 1698.[32] Friedrich Carl realised he had to act quickly or the possessions would be lost to the family for good. Despite protests from his Mömpelgard relations, he recognised French overlordship on 18 February 1681 on their behalf in order to recover actual possession for Leopold Eberhard (1670–1723), who succeeded as count in 1699. Although he had by now also aroused the hostility of the privy council, Friedrich Carl continued his pro-French course and was one of the few German princes to recognise the French annexation of the imperial city of Strasbourg later that year.[33]

Meanwhile, he tried to profit from the emperor's preparations against the French. In March 1681 the emperor had finally persuaded the Reichstag to pass the legislation necessary to form the Reichsarmee. As has already been indicated on pp. 17–22 above, the formation of the Reichsarmee gave considerable impetus to the development of standing armies within the Reich. This was as true of Württemberg as elsewhere.

Up till then the duchy had never maintained more than a few ducal bodyguards. In 1681 the entire regular 'army' consisted of only two companies totalling 300 men. Basing their arguments on the Tübingen Treaty of 1514, the estates had steadfastly refused to agree that they were obliged to provide financial support to enable the duke to maintain troops. During the emergencies of 1664, 1668 and 1672–8 they did make contributions, but each time only on a temporary basis.[34] In addition, they made a fundamental statement of policy on 22 December 1675 which summarised their stance on the matter altogether. Any regular soldiers maintained by the duke were to be used in wartime as the Kreistruppen needed to meet the duchy's obligations towards the common defence of the Reich. In other words, there was to be no force for carrying out an independent ducal policy.[35] Naturally such a view was totally unacceptable to the regent and to the later dukes as well, as without troops they would be condemned to political insignificance. So long as the estates held this view, conflict with them was unavoidable.

From the end of the Dutch War (1679) until 1681 Friedrich Carl used the delaying tactics, developed by Eberhard III, of persuading the estates each time to

[32] W. Grube, '400 Jahre Haus Württemberg in Mömpelgard', in Uhland (ed.), *900 Jahre Haus Württemberg*, pp. 438–58 at p. 450; H. Schukraft, 'Die Linie Württemberg-Oels', in *ibid.*, pp. 379–89 at pp. 385–6.

[33] Wunder, 'Der Administrator', pp. 127–30; Vann, *Making of a state*, pp. 146–50.

[34] Reyscher (ed.), *Gesetze*, XIX/1, 219–20, 222–3, 234–7, 246–9; Grube, *Landtag*, pp. 342–51; Carsten, *Princes and parliaments*, pp. 78–93; Pfaff, *Militärwesens*, pp. 28–33; A. von Schempp, *Der Feldzug 1664 in Ungarn unter besonderer Berücksichtigung der herzoglichen württembergischen Allianz- und schwäbischen Kreistruppen* (Stuttgart, 1909).

[35] Reyscher, *Gesetze*, XIX/1, 246; Pfaff, *Militärwesens*, pp. 28–9, 33.

make one last grant towards the upkeep of the troops, promising they would then be disbanded. Then in 1681, he used the decision of the Reichstag to form the Reichsarmee as a pretext to compel the estates to finance a modest increase to the Württemberg regular forces.[36] The money came from a new tax called the *Notpfennig*.[37] He then exploited the general emergency following the Turkish attack on Vienna in 1683 to compel the estates to extend the Notpfennig into what in effect became a permanent tax known as the Extraordinari. The almost continuous warfare following 1683 prevented the estates from finding a reason to disband the regent's troops.[38]

Friedrich Carl clearly intended to use these new forces to improve his position within the duchy. In 1683 he wanted to shake off imperial domination by openly allying with France. With French protection, he planned to expand his army by confiscating the church property (Kirchengut) and then to intimidate the estates. The plan fell through, as most of the privy councillors simply refused to co-operate with the regent to break the constitution, while the despatch of the troops to relieve the siege of Vienna deprived him of his instrument of power.[39] For the moment, the regent had to bide his time, but he returned to his project again in the late 1680s. That he was planning such a military putsch is clear from the comments to the French envoy in 1687. He made it plain that he intended to use the troops he had just raised for Venice, once they returned, to overthrow the estates and make his nephew Eberhard Ludwig absolute ruler. He also claimed that he would have done this if he had been born sovereign duke himself. It appears that he was hoping thereby to make himself indispensable so that he could continue to direct affairs once Eberhard Ludwig had achieved his majority.[40]

INVOLVEMENT IN THE 'SOLDIER TRADE', 1677–88

The setback he received in 1683 caused him to look more closely to his own future. As Eberhard III's second son, Friedrich Carl had had from birth virtually no chance of inheriting the duchy. Although granted a regular income from the ducal treasury under the terms of Eberhard's will, he was at the mercy of the good will of the reigning duke to continue to pay this. His own property was restricted to the castle of Winnenthal, over which he did not even have full sovereignty.[41]

As we have seen on pp. 16–17 and 90–2, a military career offered an attractive

---

[36] HSAS, L6.22.3.3; Grube, *Landtag*, p. 351.
[37] Reyscher, *Gesetze*, XIX/1, 255. The tax was intended to maintain 200 cavalry and 639 infantry. For actual strengths at this period see HSAS, L6.22.3.10.
[38] HSAS, L6.22.3.4–11. For the size and method of collection of the Extraordinari see pp. 50–1 above.
[39] Vann, *Making of a state*, pp. 146–50; Wunder, 'Der Administrator', pp. 129–30.
[40] Wunder, 'Der Administrator', pp. 129, 146, 149.
[41] *Ibid.*, pp. 131–2.

method of advancement to junior princes such as Friedrich Carl. In the early 1670s he had considered entering French service, but the outbreak of war between France and the emperor put an end to these plans. Once it was safe to do so, his brother Duke Wilhelm Ludwig had arranged for him to take command of one of the two Kreis cavalry regiments in 1674.[42] When the Kreis disbanded its troops in the spring of 1677 in protest at the quartering of imperial troops in its territory, Friedrich Carl bought his way into the Austrian army by recruiting a cavalry regiment from the discharged soldiers. His brother permitted him to do this, because Württemberg now had nothing to lose from being seen to be supporting the emperor; after 1676 France had no longer regarded the duchy as a neutral party to the conflict. However, once Friedrich Carl became regent later that year, the privy council regarded the continuation of his Austrian service as a political liability and enlisted the support of the estates to force him to resign his command. Once the estates agreed to pay compensation for the cost of raising his regiment Friedrich Carl reluctantly complied with their request in February 1678.[43] The same happened when he tried in the winter of 1683/4 to get himself appointed commanding general of the Swabian Kreis corps sent to fight the Turks. Again the privy council combined with the estates to oppose this and again Friedrich Carl agreed to back down in return for financial compensation for his missed opportunity.

It is significant that two years later he traded this compensation for an extension of his sovereignty over Winnenthal for himself and his sons.[44] This improvement in status was more important to him than mere financial gain. To further enhance this, he spent 35,000fl. in 1685 to acquire the property of Freudenthal which lay outside Württemberg jurisdiction entirely. This purchase demonstrates how important it was to such junior family members to shore up their princely status, but also just how expensive and difficult this was: Freudenthal comprised a mere seventeen peasants.[45]

From 1682 the need to find a secure future became even more pressing. In that year Friedrich Carl married the margrave of Ansbach's younger sister who, from 1684, with unnerving regularity bore him seven children, five of them sons. The need to provide for his growing family prompted Friedrich Carl to enter the 'soldier trade'.

In 1683 he had already helped his brother Georg Friedrich (1657–85) to recruit

---

[42] *Ibid.*, pp. 121–3; L. I. von Stadlinger, *Geschichte des württembergischen Kriegswesens von der frühesten bis zur neuesten Zeit* (Stuttgart, 1856), pp. 69–70.

[43] HSAS, L6.22.2.27; L6.22.2.32; L6.22.2.49. Friedrich Carl used the two Württemberg Kreis cavalry companies Hallweil and Truchseß as the core of the unit. When he resigned command on 6 Feb. 1678, the rgt. passed to Col. von Hallweil.

[44] Wunder, 'Der Administrator', pp. 132–4; Vann, *Making of a state*, pp. 151–2.

[45] Wunder, 'Der Administrator', pp. 134–5. According to Röder, *Geographie und Statistik*, I, p. 497 the population in 1787 was somewhat larger, numbering 275 Christians and 230 Jews.

an imperial regiment and three years later took over the contract from the estates to recruit reinforcements for the duchy's Kreistruppen.[46] However, his major breakthrough on to the market came in January 1687 when he subcontracted to provide an infantry regiment required by Duke Ernst August of Hanover (1629–98) to meet his contract to Venice. Ten months later he worked his way up to direct contractor by negotiating to provide a further two regiments, followed early in 1688 by another one-and-a-half.[47] These activities fall into the fourth method of recruitment discussed in the previous chapter, namely a subsidy treaty, as Friedrich Carl did not recruit the regiments directly for the Venetian army, but leased them to it for a limited period instead. While he received no actual 'subsidy' for this, he was paid a lump sum for the recruitment, while the Republic took over the cost of the actual maintenance.[48] The regiments were in effect his private army, though his position as regent enabled him to make use of Württemberg government officials to help him with the recruiting. Financial affairs were handled by War Councillor (*Kriegsrat*) Tobias Heller who was also responsible for the duchy's Kreistruppen and so was both government official and the regent's private agent.[49] The importance of this distinction has previously been missed in the Württemberg literature which regards the regent's agreement with Venice as responsible for the duchy being deprived of troops to resist the French invasion in 1688.[50] Not only were the soldiers not the duchy's army, but that of the regent, they would not have been there in 1688 anyway as the estates alone were hardly likely to have raised such a force.

While Friedrich Carl made every effort to extract financial gain from the enterprise,[51] the primary motive was to provide an income and career considered appropriate for his sons. He himself stated that 'he was not looking for profit, but honour and reputation'[52] and said the formation of the first regiment was 'out of fatherly care for our eldest [son] Prince Carl Alexander and to lay the foundation of his future fortune'.[53] Not only was Hanover obliged by the terms of its agreement with the regent to use its good offices with the Venetians to secure an annual pension for the three-year-old 'colonel' Carl Alexander, but Friedrich Carl also continually tried to persuade the Republic to hire a regiment of the more prestigious cavalry. This attempt failed, but in his second treaty with Venice in November 1687

[46] Wunder, 'Der Administrator', pp. 136, 138, 162.
[47] HSAS, A28: Bü. 92–93; L6.22.3.14–17; Andler, 'Regimenter in Griechenland'. In all, the four-and-a-half regiments totalled 4,544 officers and men.
[48] The terms of the agreements are printed in Andler, 'Regimenter in Griechenland', 219, 235; Stadlinger, *Kriegswesens*, pp. 326–8.
[49] HSAS, L6.22.3.1.
[50] For example the article by Müller-Loebnitz, in K. Linnebach (ed.), *Deutsche Heeresgeschichte* (Hamburg, 1935 edn), pp. 261–77 at p. 264.
[51] On these attempts, Andler, 'Regimenter in Griechenland', 220, 222, 224, 229–30, 232.
[52] Quoted in Wunder, 'Der Administrator', p. 142: 'in diesen ganzen werk kein profit, sondern Ehr und Reputation suche'.
[53] Quoted in Andler, 'Regimenter in Griechenland', 218–19: 'aus fürstväterlicher vorsorge für unseren ältesten Prinz Karl Alexander und zu Anpflanzung dero künftiger Fortune'.

he did manage to secure an annual pension for seven years of 1,000 ducats for the young prince.[54]

It is also significant that the regent's main helpers in the Venetian enterprise were individuals in a similar position to his. His right-hand man in the raising of the first regiment was his cousin Prince Carl Rudolph of Württemberg-Neuenstadt (1667–1742). Like Friedrich Carl, Carl Rudolph also came from a junior branch of the family with little territory and virtually no prospect of acquiring more. He had already assisted Friedrich Carl in 1677, by loaning him 8,000fl. to help raise the imperial cavalry regiment. In 1687 he recruited one of the companies of the Venetian regiment and later in the year took command of one of the two directly raised by the regent for the Republic.[55] This close co-operation between the Winnenthal and Neuenstadt branches continued after Carl Alexander became duke in 1733. During 1734–5 he used his influence with the Austrians in an attempt to secure vacant colonelcies of imperial regiments for Carl Rudolph's sons.[56] He also pressed the estates to increase Carl Rudolph's allowance.[57] Carl Rudolph's two younger brothers also followed him into military careers. One of them, Ferdinand Wilhelm, was with him in command of the Danish auxiliaries at the Battle of the Boyne in 1690. Friedrich Carl's own brothers, who had even less chance of succeeding to the duchy, also took up military careers.[58] Similarly his other main assistant, Prince Georg von Hessen-Darmstadt (1669–1705), as brother of the reigning landgrave, was also a man with no prospect of becoming a sovereign ruler.[59]

The regent's next project was also directed towards similar aims. This was a contract signed on 25 July 1688 to provide three cavalry regiments totalling 1,296 men for the Dutch, who feared French intervention as a result of William III's accession to the English crown. In contrast to his Venetian enterprise, this agreement was an example of the second form of recruitment encountered in the previous chapter, whereby the contractor raised entire units which then passed directly into the service of the client. Here the regent secured both a generous fee for the recruitment and the appointment of his second son, Heinrich Friedrich (1687–1734), as one of the colonels.[60]

---

[54] *Ibid.*, pp. 219, 235; Wunder, 'Der Administrator', pp. 136–7. The young prince was only titular colonel; the actual command was entrusted to the Danish-born Baron Christer von Horn (died 1729), the future Württemberg Major General. In 1687 a Venetian ducat was worth 3.5fl.

[55] Andler, 'Regimenter in Griechenland', 220–1, 235; Wunder, 'Der Administrator', p. 131. Carl Rudolph was Württemberg regent between 1737 and 1738.

[56] HSAS, A6: Bü. 52.

[57] HSAS, L5: Tom. 143, fols. 333–7b.

[58] On their careers see Stadlinger, *Kriegswesens*, pp. 333–7.

[59] Andler, 'Regimenter in Griechenland', 235. Prince Georg subcontracted the second IR required by Friedrich Carl to fulfil his agreement with Venice of Nov. 1687.

[60] HSAS, A202: Bü. 2469–70, with copies of the agreement in Dutch.

RETURN TO POWER, 1688–90

The unforeseen consequences of this agreement were to catapult Friedrich Carl back into the Württemberg political arena. The French used the fact that the regent was aiding their Dutch enemies as an excuse to invade the duchy in December 1688. The real object of the invasion was to intimidate the duchy into siding with them against the emperor. As the estates had rejected the regent's plans in October to reorganise the duchy's traditional militia into an effective force and as the Kreistruppen were still in Hungary, there were no troops left to oppose the French. The arrival of a small French invading party to levy contributions by force threw both the privy council and the estates into a complete panic. Magdalene Sibylle quickly gave in to French threats and surrendered the duchy's fortresses. This capitulation naturally discredited the Württemberg elite in the eyes of the emperor, who now gave his full support to the regent instead, as he was still prepared to fight.[61] On 24 December the emperor issued a decree instructing all Württemberg military personnel to obey only the regent and no longer to accept orders from the privy council. Three days later Friedrich Carl was appointed imperial lieutenant general.[62]

Friedrich Carl could now resume his plan of 1683 of creating an army to overturn the duchy's constitution. He had already tried to avoid negotiating with a full Landtag and where possible only called meetings of the estates' committee. This policy was continued by his successors who all hoped that the less numerous committee members could be more easily browbeaten. To strengthen his hand against the estates, Friedrich Carl now did his best to please the emperor by offering both him and his English and Dutch allies troops for the new war against France.

Twelve days after his appointment as imperial general, Friedrich Carl agreed to hand over his first regiment which had just returned from Venice.[63] Despite a lucrative offer from that republic for a renewal of the lease of the remaining regiments, Friedrich Carl recalled these once the contract expired late in 1689 and used them to bring the new imperial regiment up to the required strength of 2,100

---

[61] Grube, *Landtag*, pp. 354–6; Wunder, *Frankreich, Württemberg und der schwäbische Kreis*, pp. 81–92, and 'Der Administrator', 139–42; Stadlinger, *Kriegswesens*, pp. 337–8. On the invasion itself see T. Schott, 'Württemberg und die Franzosen im Jahr 1688', *WNJB*, 5 (1888), 1–52; A. Siben, 'Der Kontributionszug des französischen Generals Marquis de Feuquière durch Franken und Schwaben im Herbst 1688', *ZGO*, NF54 (1941), 108–91; K. von Martens, *Geschichte der innerhalb der gegenwärtigen Gränzen des Königreichs Württemberg vorgefallene kriegerischen Ereignisse...* (Stuttgart, 1847), pp. 500–22; C. du Jarrys de La Roche, *Der deutsche Oberrhein während der Kriege seit dem westphälischen Frieden bis 1801* (Stuttgart/Tübingen, 1842), pp. 48–58.
[62] HSAS, L6.22.4.4.
[63] HSAS, A202: Bü. 2242; L6.22.3.19. The regiment served on the Upper Rhine 1689–91 and in Piedmont 1691–96.

men.[64] Then, having rejected a Spanish request for troops at the beginning of 1690, he agreed to a second request and provided a further three regiments totalling 2,364 men for the defence of Milan. He overcame his initial hesitation, because the Spanish had now requested that two of the regiments be of the more prestigious cavalry and because the emperor urged him to agree.[65]

These efforts were rewarded by considerable imperial support for his plans within the duchy. The emperor supported him, because between 1688 and 1690 he desperately needed troops to hold off the French offensive. Accordingly, he sent three threatening letters to the estates reminding them of their obligations under paragraph 180 of the 1654 Reichsabschied to provide financial assistance.[66] After steadfastly refusing throughout 1689 to co-operate, the estates finally bowed to this pressure in March 1690.[67] This was partly because Friedrich Carl had dropped his demand for 5,100 regular soldiers in addition to a strong militia, and partly because in 1690 Swabia was virtually defenceless after the departure of all four Kreis regiments for Flanders.[68]

This new co-operation with the emperor was significant as it was the first time since 1514 that a Württemberg duke had called for imperial support against the estates. The imperial backing that Friedrich Carl received was to enable him to come closer than any previous duke to overturning the duchy's constitution. But for a single accident he might have succeeded in realising his plans completely. However, the circumstances of his downfall demonstrate that it was not yet possible for a prince to free himself from the system of checks and balances that made up the structure of the Reich.

THE MILITARY SYSTEM, 1690–2

The military system that Friedrich Carl established between 1690 and 1691 is interesting both as a typical example of the time and because it set a precedent for his successors, notably Eberhard Ludwig. He began by exploiting the duchy's traditional militia system to provide the necessary manpower which he then 'transformed' into the sort of army that best suited his purposes.

The transformation, or *Transmutation* as it was termed, began on 15 March 1690

---

[64] Andler, 'Regimenter in Griechenland', 253 n. 58, 263–4. Prior to his new understanding with the emperor, Friedrich Carl tried unsuccessfully Sept.–Dec. 1688 to hire two of the rgts to the English and Dutch for service in Piedmont.

[65] HSAS, A202: Bü. 2224; L6.22.3.18; Andler, 'Regimenter in Griechenland', 263, 267 n.83; Wunder, 'Der Administrator', 138–9, 147. The regiments served in the Spanish Duchy of Milan until 1696 when they were apparently disbanded.

[66] Reyscher, *Gesetze*, XXIV, Nos. 359–60; Vann, *Making of a state*, pp. 156–8.

[67] HSAS, A202: Bü. 1984; Bü. 1990.

[68] Plans drawn up in September 1689 in HSAS, C14: Bü. 336 indicate that the regent was considering a force of three IRs (each 1,200 men) and three cavalry rgts (each 500) in addition to 2,000 militia cavalry and 6,000 militia infantry. See also A202: Bü. 2228 and C14: Bü. 740.

with a general muster of all young men. A total of 5,940 were chosen to form five militia regiments. Under the command of Colonel Christian Friedrich von Eyb these were then despatched to the western border between Freudenstadt and Knittlingen to prevent further invasion.[69] This new force was termed a 'regulated militia' (*reguliert Miliz*) as it was subject to the same organisation and discipline as regular soldiers. During the course of 1690 a number of instructions were issued to combat the initially chaotic methods of supply, culminating in a comprehensive set of regulations on 23 December 1690.[70]

To fund this force, the like of which the duchy had not maintained for sixty years, the estates voted an increase to the purchase tax (Accise) on 8 March 1690 and an Extraordinari on 13 May. Two other emergency taxes were introduced that winter.[71] While all of these were essential to the militia's maintenance, none improved the ducal financial position as they were all controlled by the estates. Stage two of the regent's plan was intended to rectify this; however, he was still prepared to seek their consent first before implementing his plan, and so tried on 14 January 1691 to justify it to them.[72]

He argued that the traditional method of recruitment through the Auswahl was harmful to the duchy, as it took economically useful subjects away from their work. To prevent this he proposed either discharging the men and recruiting volunteers in their place, or transforming the units into paid regular formations. In either case, he argued, the military effectiveness of the force would be enhanced and it would become more useful as it could serve outside Württemberg, whereas the present militia was bound by the constitution to remain within the duchy. Thus, Württemberg would finally take its place among the Armierter Stände and so avoid the expense of having imperial and allied troops quartered on its territory. This had cost the duchy 950,000fl. between 1672 and 1675, and no less than 1,374,000fl. during the winter of 1689/90.[73] Avoidance of these expenses would be of considerable benefit to all and outweigh the cost of the upkeep of the troops.[74] In any case, the new regulars would enhance the *Splendour* of the ducal house and so attract foreign subsidies which would enable maintenance costs to be reduced.

The estates voiced their traditional fears that a large force of regular soldiers would both provoke foreign invasion and yet be too small to provide adequate

[69] HSAS, A202: Bü. 2246; L6.22.4.8; Pfaff, *Militärwesens*, p. 36.
[70] The regulations of 23 Dec. 1690 are printed in Reyscher, *Gesetze*, XIX/I, No. 176. They included a set of drill instructions originally issued for the militia in 1669. These are printed in K. Mayer, 'Württembergisches Militärwesen im 17. Jahrhundert', *Der Schwabenspiegel*, 6 (1912/13), 140–2. The various ordinances are discussed in Stadlinger, *Kriegswesens*, pp. 344–5.
[71] HSAS, A202: Bü. 2202; L6.22.4.9; Reyscher, *Gesetze*, XIX/I, pp. 271, 289. A poll tax on 24 Nov. 1690 and a tax on wine and the wages of messengers, 24 Feb. 1691.
[72] Quoted in Pfister, *Milizgedanke*, pp. 17–19.
[73] Carsten, *Princes and parliaments*, pp. 90–7; Vann, *Swabian Kreis*, pp. 271–7.
[74] The annual maintenance costs of both the 5,100 regulars and 8,000 militia originally planned by Friedrich Carl was estimated at 406,800fl.: HSAS, C14: Bü. 336.

defence. They were also doubtful that sufficient volunteers would be forth-coming.[75] The regent ignored these protests and went ahead with his plans. On 14 May the long-projected Transmutation of the militia into regular soldiers was enacted[76] and on 25 June a fifth emergency tax was introduced to cover the increased expense. This was the *Tricesimation* which was the ducal answer to the estates' Accise. For the first time the duke had a tax that both approximated to the level of economic production and above all was under his control.[77] The regent had thus gone a long way towards realising his aims and in 1692 felt confident enough to dismiss the Tübingen Treaty as *alte Historie* that no longer conformed to the times.[78] However, things had already begun to go wrong.

WÜRTTEMBERG AND THE SWABIAN KREIS

First, and perhaps most important, the regent had failed to secure adequate means to preserve his freedom of action should the emperor for some reason choose to withdraw his support. Although he did find encouragement from William III, he failed to secure Württemberg's entry into the Grand Alliance as an equal partner. He also failed to widen his power base by exploiting the duchy's leadership role within the Swabian Kreis.

Württemberg had long striven for this by seeking to control the key posts in the Kreis organisation and to develop these as a directorship of affairs (*Kreisdirektorium*).[79] Religion was a powerful weapon which the dukes were not slow to use in these attempts. Although the Protestant states covered one-third of Kreis territory containing about 45 per cent of the total population, they were under-represented at the Kreis Konvent where they had only one-fifth of the votes.[80] This was because each prince, bishop, count or imperial city of the Kreis had a single vote, regardless of the size of population of the territory. Württemberg as the undisputed leader of the Protestants was quick to play on their fears of being over-whelmed by the myriad of petty Catholic prelates and counts. Memories of the 1629 Restitution Edict, whereby the secularised church property of the Protestants had been confiscated by the Catholics, were still very much alive. These fears ensured

---

[75] Pfaff, *Militärwesen*, p. 38.
[76] HSAS, A202: Bü. 1982, 1986, 1989; L6.22.4.11. Organisational details of the new force which totalled 6,015 men are printed in Stadlinger, *Kriegswesens*, p. 347. In addition, the duchy had 1,127 Kreistruppen, or together 7,142 soldiers. As a point of comparison, the much larger electorate of Saxony maintained proportionately fewer troops: in 1693 its army numbered 11,809 effectives: Thum, *Rekrutierung*, p. 88.
[77] HSAS, A202: Bü. 2201; Reyscher, *Gesetze*, XIX/I, p. 295. The Tricesimation was a one-thirtieth purchase and produce tax collected by ducal officials and paid via the local *Vogteikassen* to a central *Tricesimationskasse* administered by the Kriegsrat. No records of the level collected survive, but around 1700 the Tricesimation brought in about 100,000fl. annually.
[78] Quoted in Grube, *Landtag*, p. 363.
[79] On these efforts see Storm, *Feldherr*, pp. 156–68; Borck, *Schwäbische Reichskreis*, pp. 47–56.
[80] Storm, *Feldherr*, pp. 54–6, 134–5.

the duke a reserve of supporters at the Kreis Konvent, although these supporters were not always faithful followers. The margrave of Baden-Durlach, in particular, was always waiting to exploit any weakness shown by Württemberg to make good his claims to leadership of the Protestants.

While the possibilities of extending influence through Kreis policy on coinage, the economy and road building are not to be underestimated,[81] by far the most important was the area of common defence. Unlike the division of voting rights, the distribution of military burdens did attempt to reflect the economic potential of the members. Württemberg, as the largest member, therefore had to provide by far the biggest military contingent.[82] While this represented a strain on the duchy's resources, it did provide the duke with another powerful weapon to extend his influence within the Kreis. Through threatening to withdraw his contingent, the duke could put pressure on the other Kreis members, who would be seriously exposed without it. The dukes sought to make this threat still more effective by making the weaker Kreis members even more dependent upon them for military protection. This was done through taking over the provision of their contingents for money,[83] and by signing treaties of protection (*Schirmverträge*) with them.[84]

However, we should be careful not to overemphasise this, or see ducal efforts to extend Württemberg influence within the Kreis as an outright attempt to subordinate it to the duchy entirely, or even destroy it altogether. Precisely because it was useful to them, they were interested in its preservation.[85] They therefore generally tried to allay fears of the smaller Kreis members that they were planning to withdraw their contingent.[86] Furthermore, right to its collapse in 1806 the structure of the Kreis Konvent proved an effective brake on attempts by Württemberg or any other member to reduce it to a rubber stamp for its own policy.

Regent Friedrich Carl was also hindered in these attempts in that he was not himself sovereign duke, but only represented the duchy until Eberhard Ludwig achieved his majority. This weakened his presence in the Kreis institutions and, together with the opposition of the privy council and the estates, was responsible for

---

[81] J. A. Vann, 'The economic policies of the Swabian Kreis, 1664–1715', in Vann and Rowan (eds.), *The old Reich*, pp. 105–27; Kallenberg, 'Spätzeit und Ende', pp. 70–80.

[82] The Württemberg Kreis contingent as a proportion of the total between 1664 and 1793 was as follows: 1664: 400 men out of 3,530 (11.3 per cent); 1674–7: 754 out of 5,081 (14.8 per cent); 1683–90: 836 out of 4,941 (16.9 per cent); 1691–8 1,127 out of 6,143 (18.3 per cent); 1701–14 1,996 out of 10,718 (18.6 per cent); 1714–32: 1,018 out of 5,852 (17.4 per cent); 1732–34: 1,725 out of 7,894 (21.8 per cent); 1734–93: 1,728 out of 7,944 (21.8 per cent); HSAS, C14: Bü. 332, 334, 338; Storm, *Feldherr*, pp. 303–41; Stadlinger, *Kreigswesens*, pp. 524–32.

[83] HSAS, L6.22.4.13. See also pp. 20–1 above on the *Relutionen*.

[84] Such treaties were signed with Esslingen (1674) and Reutlingen (1698). Details printed in Stadlinger, *Kriegswesens*, p. 147 n.1.

[85] However, Vann in *Swabian Kreis*, p. 155 goes too far when he claims that Eberhard Ludwig was prepared to forgo territorial expansion in order to preserve the Kreis as a vibrant institution, as will be demonstrated in Chapter 5 below.

[86] Gebauer, *Außenpolitik*, pp. 28–9.

the failure of his attempt in 1683/4 to be appointed commander of the Kreis corps. He therefore had to be content to have the post given to someone he preferred. This failure led to the exclusion of Württemberg from the post of commanding Kreis general until 1707, as from the late 1680s the appearance of the exceptional Margrave Ludwig Wilhelm von Baden-Baden (the famous 'Türkenlouis') removed any chance of either Friedrich Carl or Eberhard Ludwig being appointed.[87]

The relatively weak position of Friedrich Carl also led to his failure to develop the Kreis as a buffer against the effects of the emperor withdrawing his support. He tried to do this in a manner resembling his efforts to make himself indispensable to the continued administration of Württemberg. Using arguments similar to those he put before the estates, Friedrich Carl persuaded the Kreis Konvent to establish a militia like that he had just formed in the duchy. In view of the fact that the four regular Kreis regiments were in Flanders, the Konvent decreed the establishment of a 6,000-strong militia on 11 August 1690. Two weeks later Friedrich Carl ordered its mobilisation, but the orders were never carried out.[88] Despite having obtained support from William III for the project, Friedrich Carl ran up against imperial opposition as the emperor feared his own influence within the Kreis might be curtailed. The return of the four regular regiments was sufficient excuse for the other Kreis members to save themselves the expense of providing additional militiamen. Working through Margrave Ludwig Wilhelm, who was firmly in the imperial camp, the emperor persuaded the Kreis to raise additional regular soldiers instead.[89] On 29 November 1690 the Konvent decided to add a further 2,480 regulars, bringing its forces up to 9,000. In March 1692 another 3,000 were raised and co-operation with the Franconian Kreis through the Kreis Association was strengthened.[90] Thus Swabia's armaments remained firmly within the framework of the existing organisation of the common defence, and so under the control of the emperor.

THE IMPERIAL ASCENDANCY, 1692–3

Friedrich Carl's failure at Kreis level was only confirmed by his failure within the duchy itself. The regent's conversion of the Württemberg militia to regulars in

[87] Storm, *Feldherr*, pp. 184–214. Margarve Ludwig Wilhelm (1655–1707) was appointed commander-in-chief of the Swabian troops in 1693 and Kreisfeldmarschall in 1696. On his career see A. Schulte, *Markgraf Ludwig Wilhelm von Baden und der Reichskrieg gegen Frankreich 1693–1697* (2 vols., Heidelberg, 1901).

[88] HSAS, C14: Bü. 307; Stadlinger, *Kriegswesens*, pp. 72–3.

[89] HSAS, C14: Bü. 334; L6.22.4.11, L6.22.4.32; Storm, *Feldherr*, pp. 320–2. Another 135 infantry and 81 dragoons were added to the duchy's Kreistruppen, bringing the total up to 777 foot and 350 horse. For the decree regulating their recruitment, see Reyscher, *Gesetze*, XIX/1, No. 178.

[90] HSAS, C14: Bü. 334; Stadlinger, *Kriegswesens*, pp. 73–6; Sicken, *Wehrwesen*, I, pp. 88–9. Although Türkenlouis was not altogether against the idea of a militia himself, he needed imperial co-operation to help defend his own exposed territories.

1691 had proved an expensive business. The authorities had difficulty in finding volunteers to keep the units up to strength, which necessitated an increase in the recruiting bounties.[91] In addition, it was now not so easy to offload the burden of maintenance onto the Ämter as had been the case with the militia.[92] The regent was able to salvage something from his failure over the Kreis militia by persuading the Kreis Konvent to hire three of his new regular regiments to make up the quota required by the Association with Franconia. However, this still left two foot regiments totalling 3,000 men which had to be maintained by the duchy in addition to 1,127 Kreistruppen.[93]

In order to guarantee the maintenance of these forces, Friedrich Carl had to call a Landtag in 1692 and seek legitimisation of the taxes he had introduced the previous year. As the estates only partly agreed to these, the army remained chronically underfunded, thus sowing the seeds for future trouble. Moreover, the estates used the opportunity of the Landtag to deliver a massive protest to the regent and to appeal to the emperor. The latter seized on this as an opportunity to bring his ambitious protégé to heel. On 22 May he appointed Reichshofrat vice president Count Sebastian Wunibald von Zeil to investigate the estates' complaints.[94]

Although the emperor was still free to pass a favourable verdict for Friedrich Carl, there were signs he was unlikely to do this. Already jealous of the regent's attempts to establish Württemberg supremacy within the Kreis, the emperor acted swiftly to prevent him extending the duchy's influence over the imperial knights. Many of these knights had feudal obligations to the duke, who had traditionally called upon them to provide part of the duchy's cavalry.[95] As elsewhere, Friedrich Carl now tried to reactivate these obligations.[96] The thinking behind this was not primarily to obtain additional cavalrymen – the numbers involved were insignificant – but to strengthen Württemberg's claims to levy taxes and recruits from the knights' territories. Friedrich Carl's attempts were thus part of traditional ducal policy and his efforts were taken up again by his son between 1733 and 1734.[97]

---

91 Reyscher, *Gesetze*, XIX/I, Nos. 180–2; Pfaff, *Militärwesen*, p. 38. For these problems at a local level see H. Weisert, *Geschichte der Stadt Sindelfingen 1500–1807* (Sindelfingen, 1963), pp. 217–18.

92 HSAS, L6.22.4.14–16A, L6.22.4.17–19, L6.22.4.21–22, L6.22.4.24–26A.

93 HSAS, A202: Bü. 1987; C14: Bü. 307; Bü. 512. Under an agreement of 15 July 1691 the Kreis hired Reiter Rgt von Freudenberg (600 men), DR Carlin von Somaripa (600) and IR Horn (1600) to bring its forces up to the 12,000 men required by its association with Franconia. In return Württemberg received 155,000fl. annually. The two remaining rgts – IRs Sauerbrey and Eyb – were each 1,500 strong.

94 HSAS, L6.22.4.5–6. On the Landtag, see Grube, *Landtag*, pp. 362–4; Vann, *Making of a state*, pp. 159–61.

95 Reyscher, *Getetze*, XIX/I, Nos. 8, 9, 37, 71, 77, p. 113; Pflichthofer, *Heerwesen*, pp. 3–10.

96 Reyscher, *Gesetze*, XIX/I, No. 179 (13 Jan. 1691), No. 183 (Apr. 1691). An example of a state where such a policy was forced through successfully – in this case against native nobility – is Prussia: see Schnitter, *Landesdefension*, pp. 152–3.

97 Reyscher, *Gesetze*, XIX/I, No. 377 (10 Nov. 1734), No. 386 (24 May 1735).

As it threatened the interests of some of his most loyal supporters, the emperor warned the regent on 4 September 1692 to desist. As a result, the knights took the opportunity not to turn up.[98]

Faced with such opposition at the Landtag, Friedrich Carl made the mistake of leaving Magdalene Sibylle to continue negotiations and left for the front. On 17 September his forces were surprised by the French at Oetisheim and he himself was captured and taken to Paris.[99] There, the French returned to their plan of 1688 of trying to intimidate Württemberg into abandoning the emperor so as to breach imperial defences along the Rhine. Louis XIV made it plain that he intended to launch a major offensive on the Upper Rhine in the spring of 1693. Württemberg could avoid the destruction that this would inevitably bring if it and the rest of the Swabian Kreis agreed to armed neutrality under French protection. Friedrich Carl refused to agree to this and instead warned Magdalene Sibylle of the impending danger and told her to arrange neutrality under guarantee of the Swiss Confederation. This would have permitted Württemberg to avoid falling under either French or imperial domination. In spite of his refusal, Louis XIV set him free on 1 January 1693 but he did not reach Stuttgart until 1 February, as settlement of the debts he had incurred in Paris prevented his leaving immediately.

This delay proved fatal. As in December 1688, the emperor feared Württemberg might go over to the French and so intervened on the behalf of those in the duchy who were prepared to prevent this. In this case it was the losers of 1688: Magdalene Sibylle, the privy councillors and the estates. Acting quickly and contrary to Württemberg law, the emperor declared the young Eberhard Ludwig already of age as from 20 January 1693. Magdalene Sibylle and the privy council had to agree in writing not abandon the emperor for the rest of the war and all councillors not to his liking were to be dismissed.[100] This coup secured imperial domination of Württemberg for an entire decade and represents a considerable achievement for imperial politics. The way in which it was achieved also illustrates the numerous possibilities with which the Reich's structure provided the emperor to advance his aims.

Although Friedrich Carl was compensated by promotion to imperial field-marshal on 16 May 1694,[101] he can be considered essentially to have failed to achieve his aims. This is not only true of his wider political ambitions, but also of his attempts to provide security for himself and his family. This is nowhere

---

[98] Stadlinger, *Kriegswesens*, pp. 345–6.

[99] For a description of the battle, see *ibid.*, pp. 348–9; Röder, *Geographie und Statistik*, I, pp. 426–7. Martens, *Kriegerischen Ereignisse*, pp. 525–7; La Roche, *Der deutsche Oberrhein*, pp. 63–7. Friedrich Carl's troops (6,000–8,000 Württembergers and Bavarians) were let down by poor discipline, causing them to leave a favourable position, and to be routed by 7,800 French. Friedrich Carl personally killed twelve Frenchmen before being taken prisoner by Villars, the future field marshal.

[100] Wunder, 'Der Administrator', pp. 132–3.

[101] Stadlinger, *Kriegswesens*, p. 349.

clearer than in his activities in the 'soldier trade', and this bears out the point made in the previous chapter of just how risky a method this was to advance dynastic and political aims and how little financial profit there was to be made in it.

THE REGENT'S 'SOLDIER TRADE' – A BALANCE SHEET

When he was forced to resign command of his first regiment, Friedrich Carl made a net loss of 10,000fl. as the unit had cost him 30,000fl. to form, while he received only 20,000fl. in compensation from the estates between 1678 and 1682.[102] In this case, his salary as regimental commander probably made good most of this, but on no reckoning did he make any significant gain from the enterprise. His recruitment of Kreistruppen, Württemberg garrisons and the regiments for Venice, William III and the emperor between 1686 and 1690 brought in a mere 1,279fl. more than the total cost of 682,028fl.[103] Although individual contracts did produce a respectable profit, this was wiped out by losses incurred on others. For example, he made perhaps as much as 50,000fl. on the Venetian recruiting.[104] Further, as the four-and-a-half regiments were virtually destroyed through sickness and hard campaigning in Greece, he would have been spared the expense of disbanding them had he wanted to.[105] However, the political controversy surrounding the Dutch recruiting in 1688 enabled the Dutch to retain 65,432fl. owed on the mobilisation costs.[106] All attempts by his successors to obtain this proved fruitless, while the loss was scarcely made good by the 17,000fl. compensation the regent managed to extract from the estates.[107] In addition, the provision of the imperial infantry regiment in 1689 cost him another 40,000fl. Worse still, not only did he have to use up his wife's dowry to keep his operations going, but he was also forced to sell Freudenthal at a loss of 4,650fl. in 1696.[108] This wrote off his success in obtaining sovereign territory for his family. The political controversy stirred up by the Dutch recruiting also prevented his second son receiving his promised colonelcy until 1703.

The regent could, however, find some small consolation in his relative success in providing for his first son, Carl Alexander. With the return of the first regiment from Venice and its conversion to an imperial unit, Carl Alexander had lost his titular colonelcy as Friedrich Carl himself became commander. In order to restart

[102] Wunder, 'Der Administrator', 132–3.
[103] HSAS, L6.22.3.12–13; Wunder, 'Der Administrator', 142–6.
[104] Andler, 'Regimenter in Griechenland', 268. Wunder, 'Der Administrator', 142–3 makes it only 12,780fl.
[105] According to figures in Andler, 'Regimenter in Griechenland', 224, 266, at the most 798 out of 4,544 officers and men survived to return to the duchy.
[106] HSAS, A202: Bü. 2469–72.
[107] HSAS, A7: Bü. 56; A202: Bü. 2465–72; Wunder, 'Der Administrator', 142.
[108] *Ibid.*, 145.

his son's career, Friedrich Carl signed another agreement with Venice on 20 April 1695 to provide a 1,000-strong infantry regiment for further service against the Turks. Prince Carl Alexander was made titular colonel and given an annual pension of 1,000 ducats by the Republic.[109] It is possible that the agreement of 4 May 1695 between 'Württemberg' and the duke of Mecklenburg for the transfer of 100 Mecklenburg soldiers was to help raise this regiment.[110] A year prior to his death on 20 December 1698, Friedrich Carl managed to obtain an imperial commission for his son and so put him on the first rung of the ladder to success.[111] Having distinguished himself in the campaigns of 1697–8, the fifteen-year-old prince went to Vienna to try and raise a regiment himself.[112] However, the conclusion of hostilities in 1699 put an end to these plans and led to the disbandment of his father's infantry regiment in 1700.[113] Carl Alexander's career could have ended there and then, but for the (for him) opportune outbreak of the War of the Spanish Succession, which gave him a fresh chance to distinguish himself and led to his appointment in 1703 as colonel-in-chief of an Austrian infantry regiment.[114] His personal bravery[115] and his conversion to Catholicism in 1712, combined with the prolonged warfare of 1701–18 and the need for experienced commanders, led to his meteoric rise in the Austrian military hierarchy. By 1721 he was an Austrian field marshal, governor and commander-in-chief in Serbia, imperial privy councillor and Knight of the Golden Fleece. In 1702 he had an annual income of 49,600fl. which by the 1720s had risen to the equivalent of many of the smaller ruling princes of the Reich.[116] His alliance with the Habsburgs was further consolidated in 1727 by his marriage to Maria Augusta (1706–56), daughter of the emperor's close supporter, Prince Anselm von Thurn und Taxis.

Carl Alexander's career is an example of a successful prince of a junior line, although his success was due more to his own ability and good fortune than his

---

[109] A copy of the agreement is in HSAS, A6: Bü. 55. Andler, 'Regimenter in Griechenland', 269 n.71 is incorrect in believing this unit did not exist.

[110] Tessin, *Mecklenburgisches Militär*, p. 33. Tessin does not specify which 'duke of Württemberg' made the agreement, but it seems unlikely that it was Eberhard Ludwig. Württemberg paid 2,500tlr. for the transfer as the receiver and not the supplier of soldiers. The rgt was probably disbanded in 1698.

[111] HSAS, G196: Bü. 11. Carl Alexander was appointed colonel on 18 July 1697, but without a rgt. On his military career see, Stadlinger, *Kriegswesens*, pp. 389–90.

[112] Tüchle, *Kirchenpolitik*, p. 21.

[113] Wunder, 'Der Administrator', 160. On the rgt see note 63 above.

[114] K.u.K. IR No. 17, raised 1674, disbanded 1918.

[115] During his distinguished service in Hungary, Germany, Belgium and Italy, he was wounded three times: in the thigh at the Schellenberg (2 July 1704), in the foot at Cassano (16 Aug. 1705), and in the head at the siege of Temesvar (Oct. 1716). It was his foot injury that most probably precipitated his early death in March 1737.

[116] HSAS, A19a: Bd. 41–4; H. Schnee, *Die Hoffinanz und der moderne Staat. Geschichte und System der Hoffaktoren und deutschen Fürstenhöfen im Zeitalter des Absolutismus* (6 vols., Berlin, 1953–67), IV, pp. 103–5. The fact that he had debts of 147,400fl. by 1727 was due to personal extravagance rather than lack of income.

father's efforts on his behalf.[117] When, by a twist of fate, Carl Alexander inherited the duchy in 1733, he returned to his father's policy of making Württemberg the dominant power in the south-west corner of the Reich. Unlike his father, as reigning duke Carl Alexander could dispense with activities as 'military enterpriser' on his own account, and make subsidy treaties directly to further his political aims. However, as in addition he had a large family, this was also coupled with an attempt to provide careers for his younger sons. Like his father, Carl Alexander also ran up against strong opposition to his plans from within the duchy – an opposition which was all the more difficult to overcome as a result of the Reversalien document he had been obliged to sign to secure his accession and because of the weakness of his predecessor Eberhard Ludwig in the last years of his reign. Like his father, Carl Alexander also came close to overcoming this opposition, and like him was prevented only by a sudden twist of fate – in his case his premature death in March 1737. The ability of the estates to exploit the weakness of the two regents that followed his death effectively put an end to any chances of the dukes succeeding in their aims so long as the system of the old Reich remained effective. Friedrich Carl's grandson, Carl Eugen, was to make one last attempt, but the extent of his failure only demonstrated just how effective this system was.

---

[117] His success also had a positive effect on the careers of his brothers. Heinrich Friedrich (1687–1734) became an imperial GFML and col. of an IR (1715–16) and then a KR (1716–34: raised 1682, disbanded 1775). Friedrich Ludwig (1690–1734) entered Saxon and then imperial service, becoming a GFML in 1716 and col. of his brother's IR. In 1723 he was promoted GFZM and on 19 Sept. 1734 was killed at Guastella. Maximilian Emanuel (1689–1709) entered Swedish service and died of fever after the Battle of Poltava.

5

Eberhard Ludwig, 1693–1733

CHARACTER AND AIMS

Traditionally, Eberhard Ludwig has been regarded as a somewhat superficial dilettante, who was more concerned with his own enjoyment than the day-to-day running of affairs.[1] In particular, he is supposed to have been heavily influenced by those around him, leading to the rise of a court clique composed of the Grävenitz and Schütz families centred around the duke's mistress, Christiane Wilhelmine von Grävenitz (1686–1744).[2] His policy is said to have lacked firm orientation until about 1708, when this group established its influence and became the determining factor behind his actions. Though his foreign adventures met with no success, his domestic policy is seen as the introduction of absolute rule in Württemberg. His agreement with the estates in 1724, which secured funding for the army, is regarded as the key stage in this process. This view has been put most strongly by Walter Grube, who sees the estates as virtually eclipsed by the time of Eberhard Ludwig's death in 1733. Taken up by Bernd Wunder, this has become something of an orthodoxy in Württemberg historiography and has now found its way into the English-language textbooks.[3]

As will become apparent in the course of this chapter, my interpretation of Eberhard Ludwig differs in a number of respects from the previous assessments. These differences centre on the nature of his aims, policies and level of success. The duke will emerge as far more determined and consistent, but also less successful, than previously thought. Rather than seeing the introduction of absolutism into

---

[1] The best assessment is the brief survey by B. Wunder, 'Herzog Eberhard Ludwig (1677–1733)', in Uhland (ed.), *900 Jahre Haus Württemberg*, pp. 210–26. See also the two articles by W. Grube, 'Württemberg's erster Barockfürst. Im Zeichen des Absolutismus – Politische Aspekte der Regierung Eberhard Ludwigs', *Beiträge für Landeskunde*, 6 (1976), 1–4; 'Herzog Eberhard Ludwig. Betrachtungen zum 300. Geburtstag des Stadtgründers', *Hie gut Württemberg*, 27 (1978), 33–5. Older interpretations are to be found in Schneider, *Württembergische Geschichte*, pp. 313–43; K. Pfaff, *Württembergs geliebte Herren. Biographie der Regenten von Herzog Eberhard im Bart bis zum König Friedrich* (Stuttgart, 1965), pp. 57–60.
[2] On Christiane Wilhelmine see O. von Alberti, *Württembergisches Adels- und Wappenbuch* (Neustadt an der Aisch, 1975 edn), p. 1089; Pfeilsticker, *Dienerbuch*, Nos. 5, 209, 369. She was not the adventuress commonly portrayed, but a member of an old and distinguished Mecklenburg family.
[3] Gagliardo, *Germany under the old regime*, pp. 288–9.

Württemberg, his reign exemplifies the limits placed on princely power by both the duchy's internal structure and the system of the Reich. In this way Württemberg illustrates the difficulties faced by Eberhard Ludwig's contemporaries in most other small German states.

While acknowledging that the role of the Grävenitz–Schütz clique was important, this chapter will argue that its influence on policy-making has been exaggerated. The root of the exaggeration probably lies in the cliché of the 'evil advisers' which runs through Württemberg historiography and is still expressed in more recent works.[4] Blame for the failings of each duke has often been offloaded onto shadowy figures behind the throne, who are consequently credited with considerable influence: the Grävenitz–Schütz clique in the case of Eberhard Ludwig; Süss Oppenheimer and General Remchingen in the reign of Carl Alexander, Minister Montmartin and a host of others (Wittleder, Gegel, Rieger, Wimpffen) under Carl Eugen. Part of the reason for this is that it was easier for the estates to criticise ducal policy by referring darkly to the evil influence of such 'verfassungsunkundiger und um des Landes Wohlfahrt unbekümmerter Ratgeber' than openly to attack the duke himself.[5]

While the influence of such advisers on princely policy-making is not to be underestimated, it was nonetheless the princes themselves who determined the overall goals. Eberhard Ludwig was no exception to this and was far more single-minded than has previously been believed. He was no less determined to achieve his aims than the other Württemberg dukes under discussion here. He also shared their ambitions for an increase in status and territory and, like them, considered a large army and a full treasury as the best way of obtaining this. Moreover, he had begun to pursue these objectives well before his liaison with Christiane Wilhelmine, though her influence certainly contributed to his more overambitious projects. Where there is a difference between him and the other dukes in this study it is mostly a question of style. Eberhard Ludwig was readier to leave the details to his advisers once he had determined the overall policy to be followed.

This view differs from the interpretation put forward by the late Professor Vann. Vann denied Eberhard Ludwig any foreign policy objectives, and saw in him a prime example for his theory of cultural competition. In addition to the duke's supposed lack of interest in foreign policy. Vann cites Eberhard Ludwig's poor financial condition as evidence for his arguments. He believed that this has been caused by the duke's numerous artistic and building projects, in particular the construction of the huge Ludwigsburg palace north of Stuttgart. In contrast to the older interpretation of F. L. Carsten, Vann maintains that it was these financial difficulties and not the problem of military funding that caused the conflict between

---

[4] For example, Grube, *Landtag*, pp. 429–30; Walter, *Carl Eugen*, pp. 150–1.
[5] HSAS, L6.22.8.1, estates complaint of 27 May 1758. The *Ratgeber* in the quotation is Carl Eugen's minister Montmartin.

duke and estates and encouraged Eberhard Ludwig's desire to establish absolute control within the duchy.[6]

It is true that court expenditure was very high under Eberhard Ludwig. Between 1714 and 1733, he regularly spent 40,000–50,000fl. a year on luxury goods, especially silverware, on which he spent 300,000fl. between 1706 and 1733.[7] All told, in the last twenty years of his life the court consumed an annual average of 391,600fl., or only 19,000fl. less than what was spent on the army.[8] It is also true that Eberhard Ludwig devoted much time and energy on activities which might fall within the category of 'cultural competition'. He was a passionate huntsman and, to raise the prestige of the Württemberg hunt, created the Order of St Hubertus in 1702.[9] The La Favorite palace, built 1713–23 within walking distance of the Ludwigsburg complex, was even fitted with a special flat roof from which the duke and distinguished guests could mow down game animals driven within range by his lackeys. On a somewhat more artistic note, he revitalised the long-neglected court orchestra, and it was during his reign that opera performances became a permanent feature of court life. He also introduced French comedy theatre to Württemberg (1711), and had a special palace theatre constructed in 1728.[10]

However, there was nothing extraordinary about this activity, nor was it peculiar to Württemberg. Almost without exception, all German princes, regardless of political status and resources, were competing in this manner. Eberhard Ludwig, therefore, was not alone in spending large sums on building Ludwigsburg at a time when he was also heavily involved in military adventures. The Saxon and Bavarian electors, for example, also built expensive palaces, while simultaneously competing politically and militarily with one another. The palaces, art patronage and elaborate court ceremony were not a compensation for these princes' inability to play a major role on the political stage, but were to help them to do this. The allegorical themes used in the architecture and music, for example, were not only entertainment, but were also intended to boost the image of their patron as a great prince.[11] Such princes tried to disguise their lack of real resources with dazzling show and display.

In the case of Eberhard Ludwig, this 'cultural competition' expenditure was not

---

[6] Vann, *Making of a state*, pp. 171–214: 'He entertained no ambitions for independent aggressive foreign policy nor did he consider expanding his holdings' (p. 172). See also his *Swabian Kreis*, p. 155 in similar vein; Carsten, *Princes and parliaments*, pp. 100–23.

[7] HSAS, A256: Bd. 197–216; Fleischhauer, *Barock*, pp. 256–9.

[8] HSAS, A256: Bd. 197–216; A282: Bd. 1449x–1468x; L5: Tom. 139, fols. 388–93; L12: *Kriegsparticulare* 1713/14–1732/3. See Appendix.

[9] Pfaff, *Geschichte des Fürstenhauses*, IV, pp. 143–4.

[10] R. Krauß, *Das Stuttgarter Hoftheater von den ältesten Zeiten bis zur Gegenwart* (Stuttgart, 1908), pp. 1–38; N. Stein, 'Das Haus Württemberg, sein Musik – und Theaterwesen', in Uhland (ed.), *900 Jahre Haus Württemberg*, pp. 554–73, at p. 557.

[11] This is obvious from the musical performances held under Carl Eugen: see Yorke-Long, *Music at court*, pp. 56, 59. See also K. Czok, *Am Hofe Augusts des Starkens* (Stuttgart, 1990).

the main cause of his poor financial condition, nor was it the root of the conflict with the estates. Apart from the expenditure on Ludwigsburg, the actual cost of the artistic projects was relatively modest. The court orchestra cost just over 11,250fl. a year in 1719/20,[12] while the theatre averaged 7,000–8,500fl.[13] Combined, they cost not much more than it would take to pay and feed a single infantry battalion for six months.[14]

One could, of course, argue that had the duke not built the Ludwigsburg palace he could have substantially increased his army.[15] However, such a hypothesis ignores the fact that it was largely beyond his ability to use the resources that went towards its construction for the army instead. Apart from the fact that a good deal of these resources were in the form of wood and other building materials provided by the Ämter, most of the actual money came from the Kirchenkasten and not the ducal Landschreiberei.[16] While, as head of the church, he could divert church funds towards the building work on the grounds that the palace was built on church land, he could not have redirected money to the army without openly flouting the church ordinances. This would have been sure to have provoked a strong response from the estates, to whom, after their experience under Regent Friedrich Carl, the army represented a far greater threat than the palace. While they did complain loudly about its construction, in practical terms it did not harm them beyond a loss of trade for their Stuttgart colleagues when the court left for Ludwigsburg. The removal of the central government there in 1718 was only a symbolic break, as the estates had long since abdicated responsibility for policy-making. It did not affect their right to be consulted on taxation and their committee continued to meet just as regularly as before. Neither did the move to Ludwigsburg represent a break between the duke and his opponents in the central bureaucracy as Vann believes, as all government departments had transferred there by 1730. The delay in moving there was not due to any reluctance on Eberhard Ludwig's part, but rather to the sheer lack of adequate accommodation in the makeshift new town built around the palace.[17]

---

[12] Belschner, *Ludwigsburg*, p. 154. The Kirchenkasten contributed 8,000–9,600fl. a year to this: HSAS, A282: Bd. 1449x–1468x.

[13] Krauß, *Hoftheater*, p. 32.

[14] HSAS, A28: Bü. 99, *Berechnung*, 11 Apr. 1719 estimated the costs for a 470-man battalion at 16,590 to 17,340fl.

[15] Belschner, *Ludwigsburg*, pp. 38–9 provides the most reliable estimate of the cost of construction, which he puts at 2.5 million fl. plus half a million's worth of wood and iron provided by the *Bauverwaltung* and the *Forstämter*. This works out at an annual average of 86,200fl. in cash for the period of construction 1704–33. According to the calculation quoted in note 14 above, an additional 1,165 infantrymen could have been maintained for this money.

[16] HSAS, A19a: Bd. 970–5, *Ludwigsburg Rentkammer Bauverwaltungsrechnungen 1709/10–1729/30* (the annual budget averaged 33,000fl. in cash); A256: Bd. 197–216, *Landschreibereirechnungen* (detail cash transfers to LB Bauverwaltung); A282: Bd. 1449x–1468x, *Kirchenkastenrechnungen* (in the last years of his life, the duke took an annual average of 60,000fl. from this source for the palace).

[17] Belschner, *Ludwigsburg*, pp. 75–6.

The duke's other cultural activities were also not a cause of his dispute with the estates. On no occasion did he approach their committee for a major grant towards any one of these projects.[18] The few additional taxes he introduced to help pay for them did represent a real burden to the common folk and so featured regularly in the estates' complaints. However, their returns were so low as never to raise the possibility of his becoming independent of the estates' taxes.[19] Hence such cultural expenditure did not directly cause the conflict, though it undoubtedly contributed to it by preventing the Landschreiberei from helping out the Kriegskasse. Furthermore, the reason for the poor state of the Landschreiberei was not rising court expenditure as Vann believes, but falling revenue. While the level of court expenditure (including palace construction) remained roughly constant in the period 1714–33, the returns of the three main sources of Landschreiberei revenue fell by nearly 45 per cent between 1714 and 1721.[20] Over the same period, Kirchenkasten revenue declined by virtually 75 per cent. Although revenue levels had been restored by the time Eberhard Ludwig died, the Landschreiberei could only be kept afloat by a massive borrowing programme.[21]

What alarmed the estates far more than Eberhard Ludwig's extravagance and the poor state of his finances were his incessant demands for money for the army, and the ambitious policies for which he intended to use it. The army was recognised by contemporaries to be his *dominante passion* which it was 'difficult to persuade him to give up'.[22] The duke himself always placed it at the top of his spending priorities as illustrated by his comments in 1721:

---

[18] See the ducal proposals presented every six months to the estates committee which are listed in the *Tomi Actorum*, HSAS, L5: Tom. 125–41.

[19] The most onerous of these was the so-called 'sparrow money' (*Spazengelder*), introduced 1 Dec. 1719, which obliged each subject to kill twenty-four sparrows and present them to the authorities or otherwise pay a fine of 6xr. In 1724/5, for example, this tax brought in only 2,319fl. 18.5xr. (A19a: Bd. 974, fol. 35b). Another measure, introduced in 1707, was the so-called *Concurrenzgelder*, which was technically a voluntary contribution from each Amt. This brought in only 7,489fl. 32xr. in 1724/5 (*ibid.*, fol. 36b), and was discontinued in 1737. On these measures see also Weisert, *Sindelfingen*, pp. 237–8; Müller, 'Finanzwirtschaft', at pp. 302–3. The other taxes introduced for the civil budget were also insignificant. The stamped paper duty existed only 1719–21, while the *Kapitalsteuer* (1717) and *Bürgersteuer* (1713) were both given to the communities in 1728. Only the *Taxgelder* (1709) was of lasting importance. On these see Dehlinger, *Württembergs Staatswesen*, II, pp. 827, 839, 844; Wintterlin, *Behördenorganisation in Württemberg*, I, pp. 82–3.

[20] Remittances from the Ämter, Forstämter and Zölle totalled 276,161fl. in 1713/14 as opposed to only 153,929fl. in 1721/22: HSAS, A256: Bd. 197, 205. For an explanation of the Württemberg financial system see pp. 47–51.

[21] Remittances from the monasteries, nunneries and ecclesiastical foundations declined from 290,050fl. in 1713/14 to 73,770fl. in 1720/1; HSAS, A282: Bd. 1449x, 1456x. On the borrowing see p. 60.

[22] HSAS, L5: Tom. 132, fol. 250b: 'es seye eben die Miliz die dominante passion von derselben, die sich schwerlich abstellen Laße' (1721). Premier minister Grävenitz commented in similar vein to the Austrian ambassador ten years later: see Neipperg, *Kaiser und schwäbischer Kreis*, p. 30 n. 17.

We are not at all inclined to undertake a reduction in either one or the other regiments, but rather make it a *point d'Honneur* to maintain our troops at their present level, and if this should mean our other pleasures [*plaisirs*] suffer, then we prefer to accept this than reduce the army.[23]

As this chapter will show, it was Eberhard Ludwig's determination to fund a large army that provoked the conflict with the estates. The outcome was far from the establishment of ducal absolutism commonly maintained. By the time of his death, Eberhard Ludwig's position had deteriorated dramatically, while the influence of the Grävenitz–Schütz clique was seriously curtailed. Given that the group played a key role in Eberhard Ludwig's reign, it is appropriate that we begin by an investigation of its rise to power and the extent of its influence.[24]

THE GRÄVENITZ–SCHÜTZ CLIQUE

The Grävenitz–Schütz clique is a singular phenomenon in Württemberg history, and indeed it is difficult to find parallels elsewhere either. There were court factions both before and after it, but none was so successful at integrating all family members into the court, army and senior bureaucracy. This clique is commonly portrayed as running the duchy into the ground to line their own pockets.[25] They were certainly very adept at accumulating not only government posts, but also the salaries and privileges that went with them. It is also perhaps more than a coincidence that ducal revenue declined dramatically during their regime. However, more research is required at local level before this can really be attributed to their mismanagement. The fact that only two families monopolised the presents and privileges merely makes their profiteering more obvious than that at courts where this was divided among a number of competing groups.

Ironically, the clique rose to power through the attempt of another faction to gain control over the duke. Baron Johann Friedrich Staffhorst (1653–1730), the head of the privy council, had hoped to make the young Eberhard Ludwig dependent upon him through the charms of an attractive mistress.[26] To find a suitable candidate, Staffhorst persuaded the Mecklenburg officer Friedrich Wilhelm von Grävenitz (1679–1754) to bring his younger sister, Christiane

---

[23] HSAS, A6: Bü. 35, Eberhard Ludwig to General von Phull, 14 Mar. 1721. The fact that military spending was always placed at the top of the duke's half-yearly budget proposals is another indication of this.

[24] For traditional surveys of the clique see Pfaff, *Geschichte des Fürstenhauses*, IV, pp. 121–47; F. Cast, *Historisches und genealogisches Adelsbuch des Königreichs Württemberg* (Stuttgart, 1839), pp. 421–2; A. Kaufmann, *Geschichte von Stetten im Remstal* (Stetten, 1962), pp. 324–33.

[25] Typical of this view is the unfounded claim made by the estates in 1734 that the clique had done more damage than the three French invasions of 1688, 1693 and 1707: HSAS, L5: Tom. 142, fol. 1032.

[26] Staffhorst had been Eberhard Ludwig's *Hofmeister* 1684–93, and thereafter *Hofmarschall* and a privy councillor. See Pfeilsticker, *Dienerbuch*, Nos. 7, 201, 400, 1123, 2345; Alberti, *Wappenbuch*, p. 753.

Wilhelmine, to Württemberg.[27] The plan failed, as the infatuated duke married her in July 1707, causing international scandal as he was already married to the margrave of Baden-Durlach's daughter, who naturally was not pleased. As he was unable to cope with the storm of protest, Staffhorst was dismissed on 18 December.

His dismissal opened the way for the clique to gain control of Württemberg government posts, especially after 1710, when the problems caused by the duke's bigamy were ingeniously solved by a sham marriage between Christiane Wilhelmine and the aged and bankrupt Baron Würben (died 1720). In the marriage agreement, negotiated by Johann Heinrich von Schütz (1669–1732), Würben was given a downpayment of 20,000fl., together with an annual salary of 8,000fl. and lifetime appointment as *Landhofmeister* and Kriegsrat president. In return, he had to promise never to consummate the marriage, set foot in Württemberg again or take up his appointments.[28] As the nominal wife of the Landhofmeister, the highest court and government official in the land, Christiane Wilhelmine not only had a pretext to reside in the duchy, but was also able to advance the interests of her family. The clique's influence at court was further consolidated by its monopoly of the other key positions.[29]

However, the family's real power derived from its infiltration of the privy council. The structure of Württemberg bureaucracy worked to their advantage by permitting them to control the other government departments, as the department chiefs were almost invariably also councillors. The way was opened up by a series of dismissals and opportune deaths from 1708 onwards which thinned the ranks of the existing councillors. By 1717 the entire council was staffed by family members and their supporters.[30]

---

27 Pfeilsticker, *Dienerbuch*, Nos. 30, 1163; *ADB*, IX, pp. 616–17; K. von Priesdorff, *Soldatisches Führertum* (10 vols., Hamburg, 1936–41), I, pp. 169–70. Grävenitz was already a captain in the Mecklenburg army by 1700 and in 1701 commanded a company in IR Schwerin, one of the two rgts hired to the Dutch. Two years later his rgt was part of the Dutch corps sent to reinforce the imperialists in Swabia. In 1704 it was assigned to Marlborough's forces and was present at Schellenberg and Blenheim. Grävenitz had left Mecklenburg service by 1 Sept. 1704 as he is no longer listed in the company lists for that month, and had entered Württemberg service by 27 Feb. 1705 at the latest, when he is listed as a chamberlain. Tessin, *Mecklenburgisches Militar*, pp. 94–103.
28 On the problems arising from the bigamous marriage and their settlement, see Vann, *Making of a state*, pp. 190–3; Grube, *Landtag*, pp. 380–2; Schneider, *Württembergische Geschichte*, pp. 323–7. On J. H. von Schütz see Cast, *Adelsbuch*, p. 323; Belschner, *Ludwigsburg*, p. 90. Würben never participated in any way in the military administration and his salary as Kriegsrat president was already stopped by order 14 Apr. 1714: HSAS, L13: *Tricesimations Rappiate* 1714/15, fol. 61.
29 F. W. von Grävenitz was lord chamberlain (*Hofmarschall*) from 1708, while his younger brother Johann Friedrich was chief equerry (*Oberstallmeister*).
30 In 1717 the privy council consisted of F. W. von Grävenitz, J. H. von Schütz, his brother-in-law Johann Nathanael Schunk (dates unknown), David Nathanael Sittmann (dates unknown, brother-in-law to Grävenitz), and their supporters Johann Rudolf Seubert (1653–1721, the duke's former teacher), Dr Johann Andreas Frommann (1672–1730, who gave legal advice during the marriage dispute), and Baron Adam Hermann Heinrich von Thüngen (died 1723).

The influence extended down to the level of local administration through their accumulation of posts as regional bailiffs (*Obervögte*). In the 1720s family members and their allies controlled at least nineteen out of the sixty or so Ämter of the duchy.[31] The title of Obervogt meant more than just a supplementary income. As Obervögte they could play a key role in ducal efforts to influence the Amtsversammlungen.

Their control over the lower echelons of the bureaucracy was further strengthened by the establishment of the *Landesvisitation* in 1713, headed by Christiane Wilhelmine's brother-in-law, the self-styled Baron David Nathaniel von Sittmann (dates unknown). This body was empowered to supervise civil service efficiency and local government finance and to deal with public complaints. These powers gave those in charge ample opportunity to dismiss opponents in the bureaucracy on trumped-up charges. Indeed, the evidence seems to suggest that the Landesvisitation used the same methods of extortion as its successor agency, the *Fiscalamt*, under Carl Alexander.[32]

The clique also gained considerable influence within the army. Here the emphasis was more on obtaining lucrative officer posts for sons and relations than on building up a political power basis. That this was so is demonstrated by Friedrich Wilhelm von Grävenitz's career choice in 1712. Four years previously he had become nominal commander of Infantry Regiment Hermenn, then serving in Flanders. By right of the strictly regulated promotion based on seniority, he would have become colonel-in-chief when General Hermenn resigned in June 1712. This would almost certainly have brought him general's rank and the chance of later becoming commander-in-chief. Instead he chose to relinquish his rights in favour of Brigadier Count Leiningen-Westerburg in return for financial compensation and the freedom to pursue a political career in Württemberg.[33]

Only later, when the clique's control over the duchy's political institutions was more secure, did they extend their influence to the army command. In October 1715 another of Christiane Wilhelmine's brothers-in-law, Josua Albrecht von Boldevin (1670–1740), was appointed Kriegsrat vice president and thereby head of the military administration.[34] The following year, his brother Carl Christoph (died 1732) was made commander-in-chief on the colossal salary of 8,000fl., making him

---

[31] F. W. von Grävenitz (Urach, Neuffen, Nürtingen, Pfullingen), his eldest son Friedrich Wilhelm (Brackenheim), his younger son Victor Sigismund (Stuttgart), his brother Carl Ludwig (Lauffen, then Heidenheim), his brother-in-law Josua Albrecht von Boldevin (Hornberg, then Kirchheim/Teck), J. H. von Schütz (Blaubeuren, Münsingen), G. T. von Pöllnitz (Ludwigsberg, Markgröningen, Waiblingen, Cannstatt); J. A. von Phull (Göppingen, Lorch), J. N. von Schunk (Schorndorf), General von Wittgenstein (Leonberg).

[32] Pfaff, *Geschichte des Fürstenhauses*, IV, p. 141. On the Fiscalamt see p. 181.

[33] HSAS, L5: Tom. 143, fols. 25b–6.

[34] HSAS, A202: Bü. 2185, 11 Oct. 1715. Boldevin had been assistant to the former Kriegsrat chief since July. On his career see A30c: Bd. 5, fol. 33b; Pfeilsticker, *Dienerbuch*, Nos. 2468, 2482.

the highest-paid Württemberg general that century.[35] Both quickly proved unequal to the task of coping with the administrative problems of the duchy's underfunded army and were replaced by a third brother-in-law, the experienced professional soldier Baron Johann August von Phull (1669–1746). While politically allied to the clique, Phull appears to have remained aloof from the various intrigues at court.[36] Apart from General Wittgenstein the elder, all other Württemberg generals remained unattached to any political faction and did not participate in policy-making.[37]

This situation was quite different from that under Eberhard Ludwig's two successors. Whereas under Carl Alexander and Carl Eugen, officers such as Remchingen, Holle, Laubsky, Rieger and Wimpffen were eager to suggest radical schemes to enable the duke to maintain a larger army, the military members of the Grävenitz–Schütz clique hung back from dangerous policies. Far from seeking a confrontation with the estates over the question of military finance, the clique appears to have been prepared to let Württemberg politics take their traditional course.

The exact reason for this is not clear, but it seems likely that they feared an open confrontation as too dangerous until their own position was more secure. On several occasions in the past, over-zealous advisers had lost their posts or even their lives in the reaction following a duke's death. Above all, they appear to have thought in practical terms. While a bigger army would certainly have given them more officer posts for friends and relations, there was little point in having such positions if the duke was unable to pay the salaries. Judging by the advice they gave him on military finance, they appear genuinely to have believed that the duchy was incapable of paying for a larger force, or at least while no foreign subsidies were available. In a document of 5 April 1719 they painted a sorry picture of a Württemberg stricken by economic decline, devastated by three decades of almost continuous warfare and heavily in debt. From its phraseology it could have been penned by the estates' standing committee, but in fact was signed solely by

---

[35] HSAS, A202: Bü. 2275, 4 Dec. 1716. C. C. von Boldevin had been colonel-in-chief of Hanoverian IR8B between 1709 and 1717, prior to his entering Württemberg service.

[36] On his career see HSAS, A30c: Bd. 5, fol. 214; A6: Bü. 19; A202: Bü. 2275, 2185; C14: Bü. 217; Pfeilsticker, *Dienerbuch*, Nos. 35, 184, 2344; Cast, *Adelsbuch*, pp. 293–5. Phull's association with the clique appears to be confirmed by the fact that after the breakdown of negotiations with the estates in 1730, he retired to Stetten, the residence of Christiane Wilhelmine (L5: Tom. 138, fol. 320).

[37] Wittgenstein's membership of the clique is alleged by Belschner, *Ludwigsburg*, p. 88, and it is significant that his children were buried in Stetten. On his career see A6: Bü. 27; A30c: Bd. 5, fol. 315b. The other generals during Eberhard Ludwig's reign were: Sigmund Christian von Mitscheval (1677–1740); Baron Christer Horn (died 1729), left service 1713; Heinrich Friedrich Kechler von Schwandorf (died 1733); Georg Friedrich von Sternenfels (died 1728); Johann Nicolaus von Hermenn (dates unknown), resigned 1712; Johann Wilhelm Friedrich von Leiningen-Westerburg (dates unknown), left service 1714; Prince Heinrich Friedrich von Württemberg-Winnenthal (1687–1734) brother of Carl Alexander, resigned 1714; Baron von Montigny (dates unknown).

Grävenitz supporters. Particularly significant is their comment that even if there were no estates and 'everything was at the uninhibited disposal of the duke' it would be impossible to continue to maintain the army at its present strength.[38] General Phull also constantly advised against expanding the army so long as secure funds could not be guaranteed.[39] Both he and Friedrich Wilhelm von Grävenitz were even prepared to co-operate with the estates' committee to persuade Eberhard Ludwig to reduce the army in order to ensure that at least the remaining soldiers were properly paid.[40]

The criticism of ducal plans by the clique has been previously undiscovered and means that their position within the duchy needs to be reassessed. The accepted view is that the duke allowed – or even encouraged – them to monopolise the central bureaucratic posts in order to stifle opposition to his plans from the other bureaucrats. This is the reason advanced by Vann for the creation of a cabinet (*Geheime Konferenz Rat*) on 8 April 1717, based in Ludwigsburg and placed between duke and privy council. The cabinet was then firmly embedded in the bureaucracy by a new Kanzleiordnung in 1724 which renamed it a cabinet ministry (*Geheime Konferenz Ministerium*) and reduced the Stuttgart-based privy council to a clearing-house for ducal orders.[41] However, the creation of the cabinet can no longer be seen as an attempt to circumvent the privy council because by 1717 that body was already entirely made up of clique members. Neither can the cabinet be seen as an attempt to limit the clique's influence as it monopolised that institution also.[42]

What Eberhard Ludwig had achieved by allowing them to gain so much power was the removal of those in the bureaucracy who had criticised the new arrangements in his private life on moral grounds and those like Staffhorst who had been unable to resolve their political consequences. He also brought in a group who were prepared to abandon the traditional hesitancy of the council in matters of foreign policy and generally support his ambitious plans. The clique co-operated because it

---

[38] The document was signed by F. W. von Grävenitz, Sittmann, Thüngen, Schunck, Seubert and Frommann. Sittmann and Seubert were unable to attend the meeting on 16 Jan. 1720 when this paper was read out to the duke but all the others were present. HSAS, A202: Bü. 1992.

[39] HSAS, L5: Tom. 137, fol. 119b (1728).

[40] In 1721 Phull, Grävenitz and J. H. von Schütz 'nach ausgestandener großen Mühe, auch fast erfolgter Ungnade' managed to persuade the duke to agree to a troop reduction. For their efforts they were each given 100 ducats by the estates. HSAS, L5: Tom. 132, fols. 250b, 262, 666–7b.

[41] Vann, *Making of a state*, pp. 208–10. On the reorganization see Wintterlin, *Behördenorganisation*, I, pp. 65–73.

[42] The cabinet consisted of F. W. von Grävenitz, J. H. von Schütz, N. J. von Schunk, A. H. H. von Thüngen, assisted by private secretary Kaspar von Pfau. All were also nominally members of the privy council which also included D. N. von Sittmann, J. R. Seubert and J. A. Frommann. After the departure of the latter two in 1721 the vacancies were filled by Schütz's brother, Johann Philipp, and the apparently neutral Wilhelm Ulrich Smalcalder (died 1739). The new appointments to the cabinet ministry were also clique members: Andreas Heinrich von Schütz (1696–1765, son of J. H.) and Gottlob Friedemann von Pöllnitz (1681–1757).

gave them the opportunity to secure foreign guarantees for their own position within the duchy. In virtually all the negotiations with foreign powers after 1707 they tried to extract advantages for themselves in the form of letters of protection or financial reward.[43] Where possible they also sought to acquire property with *Reichsunmittelbar* status, that is property outside Württemberg jurisdiction, to prevent it being confiscated in the event of a possible reaction after Eberhard Ludwig's death. Both Christiane Wilhelmine and J. H. von Schütz traded in properties given them by the duke for others with this status. It was also rumoured that they sent considerable sums of money to foreign banks.[44]

Their policy within the duchy was directed to similar ends. In addition to obtaining tax exemption for their various houses and economic undertakings,[45] they requested guarantees from the estates for their properties and positions. In a considerable feat of negotiating skill, Friedrich Wilhelm managed to obtain a written guarantee on 16 June 1729 not only from the estates but also from Carl Alexander and his brothers. (Events after 1733, however, were to prove that this was not worth the paper it was written on.)[46] Altogether, the politics of the Grävenitz–Schütz clique mirror those of the princes themselves. They too tried to find security and careers for family members and to advance the status of their house. In their search for sovereign territory they also paralleled the attempts of the junior princes such as Regent Friedrich Carl, in this case even down to purchasing the same property of Freudenthal.

DUCAL FOREIGN POLICY 1693–8

Particularly relevant to the delay in Eberhard Ludwig's pursuit of ambitious aims are the circumstances surrounding his accession in 1693. As we have seen in the preceding chapter, he only came to power in return for promising not to abandon the emperor for the duration of the hostilities with France. He was also obliged to purge the privy council of all those not to the emperor's liking, effectively removing advisers who might have encouraged a more independent policy. Loyalty to the emperor was further ensured by the new council chief, Dr Johann Georg von Kulpis (1652–98), who was a close friend of the emperor's main ally in the region. Margrave Ludwig Wilhelm von Baden-Baden.[47] The latter's undisputed military

[43] See Wunder, 'Herzog Eberhard Ludwig', pp. 215–20 for details.
[44] Kaufmann, *Stetten*, pp. 326–8; Pfaff, *Geschichte des Fürstenhauses*, IV, p. 140.
[45] General Phull and F. W. von Grävenitz both received tax exemption for their palatial residences in Ludwigsburg and Stuttgart. Phull in addition received exemption from dues of any kind for all his remaining properties within the duchy for both himself and his descendants. J. A. von Boldevin was also exempted from paying Accise on his pub in Kirchheim/Teck: HSAS, A7: Bü. 54, Mar. 1737; L5: Tom. 135, fols. 305b–6, 316b–18, 444; Tom. 136, fols. 10, 32, 66; H. Gaese, 'Zur Gründung der Stadt Ludwigsburg', *LBGB*, 20 (1968), 7–30 at 26–7.
[46] Pfaff, *Geschichte des Fürstenhauses*, iv, p. 140.
[47] Vann, *Making of a state*, pp. 188–9; Marquardt, *Geschichte Württembergs*, pp. 173–5.

ability also prevented Eberhard Ludwig from applying for his post of Kreis commander-in-chief until his death in 1707. Moreover, Regent Friedrich Carl's warning of an imminent French invasion became a reality in May 1693. As Eberhard Ludwig had disbanded the Haustruppen three months previously in response to pressure from Magdalene Sibylle and the estates, the duchy was defenceless.[48] This made him still more dependent on the emperor to help him evict the French who occupied Stuttgart in July. Thus, he was in a poor position to press his claims to the next electoral title against those of the emperor's main ally Hanover.

The cessation of hostilities in 1697 lessened this dependence, and there were already signs by then that the duke was trying to free himself from being Austria's satellite. Like Regent Friedrich Carl, he tried to enlarge his freedom of action by striving for the status of Armierter Stand. For this it was important to retain the duchy's remaining regular soldiers after the Peace of Ryswick (1697). At that time these consisted of around 1,100 Kreistruppen plus the 2,800 former Haustruppen hired to the Kreis in 1691. Like the regent, Eberhard Ludwig was also faced with massive opposition from the estates, who saw no reason to maintain the troops now that the war was over. To overcome the problems of their funding, Eberhard Ludwig followed the precedent set by the regent and tried to offload the burden of their maintenance onto the Kreis. Through his representatives at the Kreis Konvent, he sought between 1697 and 1699 to persuade the Kreis to fix the peace-time level of the Kreis army as high as possible, calculating that the Kreis would be obliged to continue to hire his troops to make up the required number. Similarly, as the Kreis was an institution firmly embedded in the imperial constitution, it would be difficult for the estates to dodge their obligation to fund the duchy's ordinary Kreis contingent. This attempt failed, because the structure of the Kreis Konvent meant that Eberhard Ludwig was easily outvoted. Led by Constance, which feared that Württemberg would use its influence in the military structure to increase its political power, the majority of Kreis members voted to reduce the Kreistruppen. This made the return of the hired troops in April 1699 unavoidable. As the duke had been unable to persuade the estates to vote increased taxes, he was now compelled to start disbanding them.

However, within the duchy there were also signs that the duke was adopting a tougher and more independent policy. Again this is most apparent in the crucial question of army finance. In March 1698 he was still prepared to trade a partial reduction in strength for secure funding from the estates. The estates still held fast to their traditional demand that all the troops be disbanded, and insisted that the Tricesimation be stopped. In return for this and the granting of a Landtag, they

---

[48] Martens, *Gränzen*, pp. 528–43. The disbandment of the remaining two Haustruppen rgts (IRs Saurbrey and Eyb) left the 2,800 former Haustruppen hired to the Kreis in 1691 unaffected. HSAS, L6.22.4.15–22.

did vote money for one year. However, their unwillingness to make further compromises incensed the duke, who proceeded to dissolve the Landtag in January 1699. Another Landtag was not held until 1737. Although his failure at the Kreis Konvent forced him to disband 1,000 of the hired troops on their return, from June 1699 Eberhard Ludwig began levying the Extraordinari by decree to pay for the remainder. Thus at the outbreak of the War of the Spanish Succession late in 1701, he still had the not inconsiderable force of over 2,100 regular soldiers, or more than seven times the number the duchy had maintained two decades before.[49]

DUCAL INITIATIVES WITHIN THE DUCHY, 1698–1733

Perhaps even more significant was the way in which he stifled the estates' protest at these new arrangements. In January 1699 he dismissed the most vocal of his critics, the estates' legal adviser, Dr Johann Heinrich Sturm, from government service. This highlights the point made in Chapter 2 of just how important it was to the estates to obtain security against arbitrary dismissal for civil servants. Without this, there was little to prevent the duke purging the bureaucracy of those who opposed him. Not surprisingly, throughout the century the institutionalisation of the civil service remained a constant objective of the estates. This helps to explain their growing alliance with the professional bureaucrats and their continual protests at Eberhard Ludwig's sale of government posts (*Diensthandel*), practised from at least 1718.[50]

Later in 1699, Eberhard Ludwig again acted decisively to silence criticism – this time an official complaint to the emperor. This highlights just how dependent the system of checks and balances of the Reich was on the ability of outsiders to interfere in the internal affairs of their neighbours. If a particular body within a territory was inhibited from lodging an appeal, the system often broke down as no one could come to its rescue. It was obviously easier for those princes who enjoyed the privilege of *non appellando* to infringe their subjects' liberties without fear of external intervention. For those such as the duke of Württemberg, who were without this privilege, other methods had to be found.

In 1699 Eberhard Ludwig used his powers as head of the state church to press the prelates into withdrawing their support of the estates' complaint. This effective weapon was denied his successor, Carl Alexander, who was forced in the Reversalien document to transfer these powers to the privy council. However, Eberhard Ludwig had already begun developing another, potentially more effective method. This was the attempt to apply pressure on the estates from below by circumventing the committee and the Landtag and approaching the

---

[49] HSAS, A202: Bü. 1983; L6.22.5.2–10; Grube, *Landtag*, pp. 366–74; Carsten, *Princes and parliaments*, pp. 105–9; Gebauer, *Außenpolitik*, pp. 16–25, 40–4, 64–7; Pfaff, *Militärwesens*, pp. 39–42.
[50] HSAS, L6.10.2.1–2. On the estates' attempts, see Wunder, *Privilegierung*, pp. 36–97.

Amtsversammlungen directly. In this case, he tried in 1699 to induce the Amtsversammlungen to abrogate their powers of authorisation which had been used to instruct the committee to draw up the complaint.[51] As the discussion of the worthies (Ehrbarkeit) in Chapter 2 showed, the Amtsversammlungen represented a weak spot in their influence in the duchy's political system. The *Kommunordnung* of 1702 was a continuation of this policy. By clarifying the organisational and legal structure of the village administration, the Amtsversammlungen became firmly fixed in the constitution and impossible for the worthies to ignore.

At about the same time, Eberhard Ludwig tried another policy which also threatened their position. This was a reform of the duchy's tax system which he pushed for from 1698 onwards. As we have seen, the outdated tax books were largely responsible for the static returns of the estates' taxes and prevented the duke from tapping the duchy's resources. Under the existing system, even if the duke had managed to persuade the estates to vote more taxes, returns would not have risen by much, as the bulk of the burden fell on those least able to pay. From comments he made in 1703 it is clear that he intended that a reform should shift the burden from the poorer rural areas on to the richer urban-based worthies.[52] Their opposition, together with the confusion brought by the War of the Spanish Succession, prevented any practical steps being taken until 1713. Even then the revision of the tax books quickly became bogged down through lack of direction from the centre and the inability of the local officials to cope with the complex technical problems. The work was still only half finished when it was abandoned in 1744, and the new books produced returns that hardly differed from those of the old ones.[53] As a consequence, by 1765 a ducal official calculated that a householder whose property was actually worth 1,000fl.–1,200fl. was assessed at only 300fl. and paid a mere 3.5fl. in annual taxation. On that basis, the burden was only one-twelfth of that in Prussia.[54] The importance of this failure has previously been underestimated and it was a significant factor in the success of the estates' resistance to ducal absolutism.

A second attempt to boost tax returns was begun in 1709 with the establishment of a Chamber of Commerce (*Commerzienrat*). This was intended to suggest and administer various mercantilist economic undertakings designed to improve ducal revenue. The worthies, whose economic interests lay in the existing agricultural

---

[51] Grube, *Landtag*, pp. 369–72.
[52] Vann, *Making of a state*, p. 181.
[53] Pfaff, *Geschichte des Fürstenhauses*, IV, pp. 152–3; W. Schempp, *Der Finanzhaushalt der Stadt- und Amtspflege Tübingen unter Herzog Karl Alexander, Rechnungsjahre 1732 bis 1737* (Würzburg, 1938), p. 18. For an example of the work in the localities see Weisert, *Sindelfingen*, pp. 239–41. The creation of a new ducal official in 1697, called *Amtspfleger*, in each Amt to replace the estates' Bürgermeister as tax collector can also be interpreted as part of this policy. However, it remained without consequence as the *Amtspfleger* was probably too weak a link to enable the duke to divert payment directly through him to the ducal treasury.
[54] Haug-Moritz, *Württembergischer Ständekonflikt*, p. 399 n. 50.

structure, did their best to oppose the Chamber's suggestions. Most of the projects were in any case chronically underfunded and failed miserably, as did those of Eberhard Ludwig's successors who continually returned to the idea.[55]

DUCAL FOREIGN POLICY 1698–1714

In the conflict with the estates over the army the duke received the full backing of the privy council.[56] After Kulpis' death (1698) the new council leader, Staffhorst, led the council in supporting the duke in a slightly more independent foreign policy. While still professing loyalty to the emperor as head of the Reich, Staffhorst and Eberhard Ludwig tried to loosen Austrian control over Württemberg. Between 1698 and 1702 they continually sought to restrain the other Kreis members, who were generally numbered among the emperor's clients, from over-eagerly expanding the Kreis Association. While Eberhard Ludwig wished to continue the Association with Franconia, he feared that a wider alliance including other Kreise might be interpreted by France as offensive rather than defensive. France might then launch the kind of pre-emptive strike Württemberg had suffered in 1688 and 1693. This seemed particularly likely as it was fairly obvious that the emperor was only interested in the Association as security for his own lands, while he competed with France over the Spanish succession. Württemberg therefore resisted the entry of the Kreis into the Grand Alliance against France until late 1702.[57]

Considering the circumstances, this was a sensible policy. Just as at the outbreak of the previous Franco-Austrian conflict in 1688, there was little prospect of Württemberg, or indeed Swabia, being permitted by the various combatants to remain neutral. This was patently clear at the latest by 8 September 1702 when the Bavarians seized Ulm. Eberhard Ludwig kept the duchy out of the new war for as long as was feasible and only entered it after English and Dutch membership of the Grand Alliance guaranteed a degree of security. In the meantime the Kreis was also able to start mobilising its forces ready for the almost inevitable hostile action now that France was allied to Bavaria.[58]

Once involved in the conflict, Eberhard Ludwig tried to extract the maximum possible advantage out of it. First and foremost he sought to consolidate his position as Armierter Fürst by expanding his army. The methods he employed were identical to those of Regent Friedrich Carl: manipulation of the militia system, new taxes and foreign subsidies. Between December 1702 and December 1703 the remaining depleted Haustruppen units were brought back to strength and two new

---

[55] Reyscher (ed.), *Gesetze*, XIII, No. 870; Pfaff, *Geschichte des Fürstenhauses*, IV, pp. 165–71; Söll, *Wirtschaftspolitik*, pp. 87–90, 98–100.
[56] Vann, *Making of a state*, pp. 164–70.
[57] Gebauer, *Außenpolitik*, pp. 39–180.
[58] HSAS, L6.22.5.5, L6.22.5.11.

infantry regiments were formed.[59] Although recruited through the Auswahl, the new formations were all regular soldiers like the regent's 'Transmuted Militia'. The Tricesimation was reintroduced in 1703 to pay for the increased establishment, though for the time being it was administered by the estates and not the ducal Kriegsrat as under the regency.[60] In September that year, Eberhard Ludwig began negotiating with the Dutch for a subsidy treaty.[61] Thanks to the strong support from the allied commander-in-chief, the duke of Marlborough, a treaty for 4,000 men was signed on 31 March 1704.[62] The treaty cannot be interpreted as Soldaten-spielerei, or as an attempt to finance the construction of Ludwigsburg which the duke had just started.[63] Instead, it was clearly an effort to pay for the expanded army considered necessary to pay a major role in affairs. All the money the Dutch actually paid went via the estates' treasury to the army.[64]

Although he was inhibited by the two Franco-Bavarian invasions of 1702–4 and 1707, Eberhard Ludwig now set about pressing his dynastic and political aims. In 1704 he began pushing the traditional Württemberg claim for an extra Reichstag vote for his duchy of Teck.[65] Following Bavaria's defeat at Blenheim in August that year, he reactivated old claims to the elector's Swabian lordship of Wiesensteig. This had been assigned along with five other pieces of Bavarian territory to the interim administrator of the Kreis Konvent. Württemberg possession of it would not only bring an additional vote at the Kreistag, but would finally end troublesome Bavarian competition for Kreis posts.[66] To acquire both this and a vote for Teck, the duke needed the agreement of the emperor. Unfortunately, he made the mistake of using his powers as Kreis director to annex the lordship before he had full imperial approval. Although he made continued efforts to please the emperor, he received nothing more than empty promises and was powerless to prevent

---

[59] HSAS, A202: Bü. 2250–1, 2253; L6.22.5.11–14, L6.22.5.19–20. The two new rgts were IRs Sternenfels and Hermenn. Details of the new army organisation are printed in Stadlinger, *Kriegswesens*, pp. 351, 656–7.

[60] HSAS, A202: Bü. 2201.

[61] HSAS, A202: Bü. 2463. The negotiations were conducted by Privy Councillor Johann Wolfgang von Rathsamhausen (died 1711), and Anton Günther von Heepsen.

[62] H. L. Snyder (ed.), *The Marlborough–Godolphin correspondence* (Oxford, 1975), Nos. 263, 265, 269, 295. This work incorrectly names the duke 'Frederick Karl'. A copy of the treaty is in HSAS, A6: Bü. 59. The subsidy payment was specified as 375,000fl. (Dutch) annually which was worth 300,000fl. (Rhenish).

[63] Wunder, 'Herzog Eberhard Ludwig', pp. 212–13 terms it *Soldatenspielerei*. The discussion of the treaty by Max Braubach also incorrectly implies that the duke signed the agreement purely to fund his court: *Subsidien*, pp. 162–3.

[64] HSAS, A202: Bü. 2469; L5: Tom. 128, fols. 90–108. The total value of the subsidy from 25 May 1704 to 1 Apr. 1709 was 1,911,358fl. (Dutch) or 1,529,166fl. (Rhenish). In 1709 the subsidy was stopped altogether as the corps passed directly into Dutch pay until it was returned in 1713. Of this the Dutch paid only 1,023,208fl. 52.5xr. (Rhenish), leaving some 505,958fl. of arrears.

[65] Pfaff, *Geschichte des Fürstenhauses*, IV, p. 107.

[66] On the basis of his Swabian holdings, the elector had competed with Württemberg in the 1670s for the post of *Kreisoberst*, see Stadlinger, *Kriegswesens*, pp. 68–9.

Wiesensteig being returned to the rehabilitated elector when peace was finally signed in 1714.[67] The incident demonstrates again just how dependent the smaller princes were upon imperial good will to achieve their aims. Eberhard Ludwig was further reminded of this during the uproar caused by his bigamous marriage. As this was illegal he was dependent on the emperor for protection, just as between 1692 and 1698 he was in a poor position to press his claim for electoral status, and had to pass over the opportunity presented in 1708 when Emperor Joseph I approached the Reichstag for confirmation of Hanover's title.[68] In any case, the widespread public disapproval of his private life deprived Eberhard Ludwig of potential allies within the Reich.[69]

The imperial annulment of his marriage on 22 June 1708 showed up the dangers of his dependence and prompted Eberhard Ludwig to look elsewhere for support. As Grävenitz came from Mecklenburg, it was natural that he should turn north to the new rising power of Prussia. In a treaty signed on 9 September 1709 he received impressive-sounding promises of Prussian support for his dynastic ambitions. In addition to Prussian agreement to his retention of Wiesensteig, Eberhard Ludwig gained promises of co-operation to obtain further territory in the French Sundgau, together with the governorship of Strasbourg should that city be recaptured. This presaged a revival of traditional Württemberg policy of expansion towards the Rhine.[70]

Eberhard Ludwig continued to pin his hopes on his new Prussian connection, despite the fact that it brought him nothing at the peace conferences of 1713–14. To ingratiate himself with the new Prussian king, Friedrich Wilhelm I, he sent numerous tall recruits for the prized Potsdam Guard Regiment, though he stopped short of meeting the king's demand for unrestricted Prussian recruitment in Swabia.[71] Under Prussian pressure, he also agreed in 1731 to deserter-exchange cartels with Friedrich Wilhelm and the king's relation, the margrave of Ansbach,

---

[67] HSAS, A202: Bü. 2102–4; Vann, *Swabian Kreis*, pp. 157–9. The attempts to please the emperor include the participation of Württemberg troops in the crushing of the Bavarian insurrections against the Austrians in 1705–6.

[68] Burr, 'Reichssturmfahne', 245–316.

[69] See for example the letter of the elector of Hanover to his resident in Berlin 9 Jan. 1709: PRO, SP100/14.

[70] Wunder, 'Herzog Eberhard Ludwig', p. 218. Knowledge of this early Württemberg–Prussian connection (other than the marriage in 1716) is missing from the discussion of relations between the two states in E. Boepple, *Friedrichs des Grossen Verhältnis zu Württemberg* (Strasbourg Ph.D., printed Munich, 1915).

[71] HSAS, A5: Bü. 64; A6: Bü. 54, 55; A202: Bü. 2226. Between 1719 and 1721 Eberhard Ludwig supplied 150–200 tall recruits to Prussia. Members of the Grävenitz–Schütz clique also recruited tall men for Prussia to further their own aims: A5: Bü. 64, 1721 (Christiane Wilhelmine von G.); A202: Bü. 2299, 6 Nov. 1739 (V. S. von G.). It is also apparent that the Prussian high command chose the recruiting officers sent to Württemberg with considerable care to ensure those sent had influential contacts: e.g. a Lieutenant (later Captain) Ernst Wilhelm von Grävenitz was frequently sent in the 1720s.

even though Württemberg desertion to Prussia was minimal and as he correctly suspected, the cartels were cover for illegal Prussian recruitment in Swabia.[72]

In return he was rewarded with the signing of a mutual defence pact in Berlin on 18 December 1716, sealed by the marriage of his only son, Friedrich Ludwig (1698–1731) to Friedrich Wilhelm's cousin, Henriette Maria von Brandenburg-Schwedt. Prussia offered its support for the duke's claims to Mömpelgard and for the long-desired annulment of Austrian claims to Württemberg.[73] Although renewed in 1731, the pact brought Eberhard Ludwig as little practical gain as that of 1709. The political aims were not realised, and the vague promise that Prussia would hire Württembergers in preference to others did not solve the pressing problems of paying for the army. Eberhard Ludwig also had to suffer Friedrich Wilhelm's moralising on his continued affair with Christiane Wilhelmine. Worse still, the king simply failed to answer his letters when he called on him to help at the eve of the War of the Polish Succession (1733–5).[74]

A similar attempt to find a new partner through an alliance with the Elector Palatine (21 November 1711) proved equally of no practical consequence beyond a series of agreements to exchange army deserters.[75] A more ambitious attempt was made the same year when Eberhard Ludwig used the confusion following Joseph I's death to respond to French overtures. From 1692 Louis XIV had been trying to entice Württemberg into co-operating with France. During the invasions of 1693 and 1707 he had levied heavy contributions in an effort to compel the duke to agree, while during that of 1702–4 he had offered co-operation. In 1711 he hoped to secure the duchy's neutrality as a stepping-stone towards liberating Bavaria. In return, Eberhard Ludwig insisted on a huge French subsidy of 150,000fl. a month, together with co-operation to annex the Swabian imperial cities and crown himself 'king of Franconia'. Louis XIV was prepared to agree to a more limited elevation to electoral status as well as more modest subsidies and territorial increase. However, the negotiations broke down, because the French were unable to gain the upper hand on the Rhine front and so were not in a position to grant Württemberg anything.[76] To win the fickle duke back to the imperial cause, the leading Austrian general, Prince Eugene, arranged for him to be given command of the Reichsarmee in May 1711. This was followed by his appointment on 9 September 1712 as Protestant Reichs-General-Feld-Marschall, the second-highest military rank in the Reich.[77] These appointments remained the duke's only concrete gain for his involvement in the war.

---

[72] HSAS, A6: Bü. 60; A202: Bü. 2196, 2226, 2235.
[73] HSAS, A202: Bü. 1206.
[74] HSAS, A202: Bü. 1996.
[75] HSAS, A6: Bü. 60; A202: Bü. 2226; C14: Bü. 68, 70; Pfaff, *Geschichte des Fürstenhauses*, IV, p. 112.
[76] Wunder, 'Geheimverhandlungen', 363–90.
[77] HSAS, C14: Bü. 194; G184: Bü. 18–23.

THE ACQUISITION OF MÖMPELGARD, 1715–23

This disappointment was followed by his botched solution to the Mömpelgard question. The last of the ruling Mömpelgard line, Leopold Eberhard (1670–1723), whose private life was even more disorderly than Eberhard Ludwig's, had no legitimate heirs.[78] To secure inheritance for his own house, Eberhard Ludwig signed the Treaty of Wildbad (18 May 1715), whereby Mömpelgard and its nine dependent lordships were to pass to Württemberg upon Leopold Eberhard's death. In return, the duke promised his good offices in acquiring recognised titles of nobility for Leopold Eberhard's numerous illegitimate offspring (the so-called 'Mömpelgard bastards'). This arrangement fell through on Leopold Eberhard's death, because his children disputed the Württemberg succession. In return for recognising French sovereignty over all the dependent lordships, they received the backing of France. They were driven out of Mömpelgard itself by the quick action of Friedrich Wilhelm von Grävenitz, who stormed the town with armed peasants. This was possible because Mömpelgard itself was indisputably part of the Reich. Where the other territories were concerned Württemberg could do little, as these were already occupied by French troops.[79]

In practical terms, Eberhard Ludwig had gained little out of the affair apart from the title of count and an additional vote at the Reichstag. He was compelled to leave his new subjects' medieval privileges untouched so as to avoid giving France an excuse for further intervention. This prevented him from exploiting his new territory's resources. The 400-strong Mömpelgard militia therefore had to remain separate from the ducal army and so did not contribute to Württemberg military strength beyond the occasional despatch of recruits.[80] Although the new territory had an annual revenue of 300,000fl., remittances of the surplus to the Landschreiberei in Stuttgart were rarely above 5,000fl. This hardly compensated for the large sums spent on the negotiations 1715–23, which consumed the useful windfall of the Dutch subsidy arrear payments the duke had just received.[81] The political consequences were even worse. France had increased its ability to apply pressure on Württemberg – an ability it retained until it finally annexed all Mömpelgard in 1793. This limited the duke's freedom of action still further. First, he became more dependent on France. Just how serious this had become is shown

---

[78] Fauchier-Magnan, *Small German courts*, pp. 251–64. Leopold Eberhard had been given an eccentric education which included reading the Koran and learning Arabic. To try to circumvent the terms of the Treaty of Wildbad he arranged incestuous marriages between his various children.

[79] Grube, '400 Jahre Haus Württemberg', pp. 438–58; Scherb, *Beziehungen*. The nine lordships were Horburg, Reichenweier, Clermont, Granges, Passavant, Blamont, Clémont, Héricourt, Châtelot.

[80] Characteristic of Württemberg recruiting in Mömpelgard is that it was generally conducted for units that were being transferred into foreign service. See HSAS, A202: Bü. 2255.

[81] HSAS, A256: Bd. 207–52. Between 1719 and 1723 the duke received 156,000fl. from the Dutch as part payment for the arrears owed on the 1704 treaty (see note 64 above). A19a: Bd. 1382, A202: Bü. 2468–70.

by the fact that the only time in the century when Württemberg was able to extract substantial financial support from Mömpelgard was at the time when it was allied to France (1752–65).[82] On other occasions, just a hint of displeasure from Versailles was all that was needed to make the duke abandon a project not to the French king's liking: for example, the attempt to secure the electoral title by hiring troops to Austria during the Scheldt crisis of 1784/85.[83] Second, his dependence on the emperor also increased as alone he was neither able to defend Mömpelgard, nor recover it if it was overrun as in 1734–6. Württemberg's helplessness is graphically illustrated by Eberhard Ludwig's orders to the military commandant in Mömpelgard on the eve of the War of the Polish Succession. The commandant was not even to contemplate a defence, but at the first sign of a French advance was to surrender immediately to save the garrison and spare the population any hardship.[84]

After 1723, Eberhard Ludwig's policy was directed at freeing himself from these constraints. As before, during the War of the Spanish Succession, the methods he chose were the same. On the one hand he tried to find as many powerful foreign sponsors as possible who were prepared to offer the help he needed. On the other hand, he tried to avoid falling too heavily under the sway of one of them by promising too much in return. Here he did not differ from his contemporaries among the smaller princes, or from his successors. Like them he only had his territory's strategic position and limited military potential to offer, and like them he could only develop this with outside help. As before his aims remained hopelessly overambitious, only now the problems he faced were even greater. The precarious balancing act required to succeed in such policies was beyond Eberhard Ludwig's capabilities. Behind his bombastic posturing was a hesitancy which led him to take fright easily under external pressure and he often missed good opportunities by acting too late.[85]

THE SEARCH FOR SUBSIDIES, 1714–33

This was already evident during his search for a foreign subsidy in 1715–16, which led to negotiations with the Venetian Republic. These negotiations are interesting because they highlight the points made in Chapter 3 as to just how difficult such arrangements could be. In October 1714 an approach had been received from Baron von Cornberg on behalf of the Republic for between 5,000 and 8,000

---

[82] See Table 8.5 in Chapter 8 below.
[83] HSAS, A8: Bü. 60, Nos. 103–23; A74: Bü. 189–90, 197, 199; A202: Bü. 2290; Boepple, *Verhältnis zu Württemberg*, pp. 86–9. This was the background to the formation of the Garde Legion. See also p. 235 below.
[84] HSAS, A7: Bü. 55, 21 Sept. 1733.
[85] Eberhard Ludwig's hesitancy is, for example, clear from his constant fears of a religious war in the Reich and his alarm at French troop movements in 1730 and 1733. See his letters in HSAS, A6: Bü. 59 (1721); A202: Bü. 1996; PRO, SP102/25, 9 Jan. 1722.

men[86] and, following the outbreak of hostilities in December between Venice and the Turks, negotiations began in January 1715. As Württemberg had been a major supplier of troops in the previous Turkish War it was natural that the Republic should again turn to the duchy for troops. The negotiations were conducted in Vienna by Privy Councillor Johann Heinrich von Schütz and the Venetian ambassador Count Tadini and were co-ordinated from Stuttgart by Kriegsrat vice president Johann von Wessem.[87] To ensure that Schütz was as fully informed as possible, Wessem researched the old treaties of Friedrich Carl and compared pay rates between the emperor, Venice and Sweden. Despite this, Eberhard Ludwig struck a decidedly bad bargain.

First of all, his army was too small to meet the original Venetian request and he was forced to negotiate on the basis of hiring only 3,000 men. Second, and more critically, he made the mistake of opening negotiations with Prince Eugene on 22 August although Schütz and Tadini had already concluded a draft treaty at the beginning of the month.[88] Having enticed Eberhard Ludwig with the prospect of a long-term agreement, the Austrians then delayed the negotiations, leaving Schütz completely in the dark as to whether they would sign or not. The duke was afraid to begin recruiting in the emperor's name before he had a firm commitment in case the regiments were not taken on, as this would lead to desertion.[89] On 27 October he wrote to Schütz outlining his predicament and fears 'that we shall fall between two stools, especially as it is becoming apparent that the imperial court is only waiting for a break with the Republic, so as to secure greater control over our troops'.[90]

The Austrian tactics worked perfectly. Eberhard Ludwig had already gone too far to be able to pull out without losing face. In addition, a large number of his officers refused to risk their lives in disease-ridden Greece for the ageing Lion of Venice. Some were even prepared to resign to avoid being sent. In contrast there

---

[86] GFML Otto Sigismund Frhr von Cornberg to Eberhard Ludwig, 19 Oct., 21 Nov. and 28 Nov. 1714, HSAS, A6: Bü. 56. As early as January 1714 it was reported that the Venetians were looking for troops. Prior to these negotiations, the duke had hired his troops to the Austrians, 1713–14, upon the termination of his treaty with the Dutch: L5: Tom. 125, fols. 110–14. In 1711 he had transferred a few hundred guardsmen to Savoy, where they became part of the new Rehbinder Rgt: A5: Bü. 62–3; A202: Bü. 2282.

[87] HSAS, A5: Bü. 66; A6: Bü. 56–8; L5: Tom. 126, fols. 386–91, 406–7, 428–35; L6.22.6.3, 20 June 1715. Schütz was appointed to negotiate on 9 Jan. 1715. Wessem himself had served in one of Regent Friedrich Carl's rgts in Greece, 1689–90.

[88] The original (in French) draft treaty of 1 Aug. 1715 for two IRs each 1,500 men is in HSAS, A6: Bü. 57. Since spring 1715 Austria had been preparing to enter the war on the side of the Republic. On 21 June 1715 Prince Heinrich Friedrich von Württemberg-Winnenthal had told Eberhard Ludwig that Prince Eugene was interested in hiring two Württemberg regiments.

[89] Eberhard Ludwig to Schütz, 19 Sept. 1715: HSAS, A6: Bü. 57. This had been suggested by Schütz. However, it is clear from the supply lists that the two Haus IRs began recruiting in Oct.: L6.22.6.10–19.

[90] HSAS, A6: Bü. 57.

was no shortage of volunteers for the command posts for an Austrian regiment.[91] Despite having to suffer the indignity of being presented with the same terms for his battle-seasoned veterans as had been given to the raw recruits of the margrave of Baden-Durlach,[92] Eberhard Ludwig was forced to ratify the treaty with Austria signed by Schütz on Christmas Eve.

Under this treaty, Eberhard Ludwig was to provide one infantry regiment for the emperor's service for five years. It was to be raised on the imperial establishment of 2,300 officers and men and called Alt-Württemberg. All he received in return was the title of colonel-in-chief and the right to appoint the officers. The emperor supplied both food and pay for the duration of service, but made a downpayment for men and equipment of only 8fl. a head.[93] In contrast the Venetians had offered 60fl. in addition to pay and provisions.[94] As the estates later rebuked the duke, the emperor paid nothing, 'aber man von der Republic Venedig viele Tausend Gulden darfür hätte haben können'.[95]

Eberhard Ludwig was also to be disappointed in his hope that by providing the regiment he was no longer obliged to pay his share of the money voted by the Reich in 1716 for the Austrian war effort. Despite three requests, the emperor insisted on payment, arguing that the duke had to set a good example.[96] In the end Württemberg not only paid the 70,000fl. owed, but spent over twice as much again on recruiting and equipping the regiment.[97] Further negotiations continued up to 1718 in an effort to hire out the duke's dragoon regiment, but proved equally fruitless as neither the Austrians nor the Venetians wanted any cavalry.[98]

Equally typical of Eberhard Ludwig's bad timing was his next attempt to find foreign subsidies to solve the financial problems caused by the return of the Alt-Württemberg Regiment in December 1720. The leader of the estates' committee, Prelate Johann Osiander (1657–1724), was sent the following June to London to try to hire the army to George I. He could not have chosen a more inopportune time, the English having just ended their war with Spain, while the Russians were on the

---

[91] HSAS, A6: Bü. 57, 5 July 1715, Stadlinger, *Kriegswesens*, pp. 374–5; A. von Schempp, *Geschichte des 3. württembergischen Infanterie-Regiments Nr. 121, 1716–1891* (Stuttgart, 1891), pp. 5–6.

[92] Eberhard Ludwig to Schütz, 8 Nov. 1715, HSAS, A6: Bü. 57.

[93] A copy of the treaty is in HSAS, A202: Bü. 1157. The text is also printed in full in A. Pfister, 'Das Regiment zu Fuß Alt-Württemberg im kaiserlichen Dienst auf Sicilien in den Jahren 1719 bis 1720', *BMWB*, 5/6 (1885), 157–268 at pp. 160–2, and Schempp, *Geschichte des 3. württ. Inf. Rgts*, pp. 6–8. The regiment served the Austrians against the Turks in Hungary 1716–18 and against the Spanish in Sicily 1719–20.

[94] Cornberg to Wessem, 18 Jan. 1715, HSAS, A5: Bü. 66.

[95] HSAS, L5: Tom. 129, fol. 24.

[96] *Ibid.*, fols. 89b–102.

[97] Of the 70,000fl., 15,225fl. was paid direct to Vienna between 1718 and 1721 while the rest together with an additional 18,945fl. 53xr. was spent on recruiting for the regiment, which had already cost the duchy 150,000fl. by winter 1717/18: HSAS, L5: Tom. 129, fol. 24; Tom. 137, fols. 395b–411. The 72,425fl. 50xr. recorded as paid out from the Tricesimationskasse 1716–19 is possibly additional to that figure. L5: Tom. 139, fols. 388–93.

[98] See especially the letter of Schütz to Eberhard Ludwig of 5 Feb. 1716 in HSAS, A6: Bü. 57.

point of ending theirs with Sweden. The collapse of the South Sea Company still troubled English finances. In short, no one in London wanted troops from far-off Württemberg.[99] The failure of Osiander's mission demonstrates again just how dependent the smaller princes were on circumstances beyond their control in their search for a powerful sponsor.

To widen his freedom of action, Eberhard Ludwig worked hard to make political capital out of Württemberg's position in the Swabian Kreis. As the negotiations with France in 1702 and 1711 showed, Württemberg's ability to attract potential partners could be improved if these powers believed that the duchy could bring the rest of Swabia with it into any alliance. Both France and Austria retained interest in Swabia after 1714. Following the peace settlements of 1713–14 and the establishment of a permanent French Rhine frontier, Swabia became the first line of defence, not only for the Reich, but for the Habsburgs' German possessions. Its strategic value was further enhanced by the French alliance with Bavaria which was renewed for nine years in February 1714. The military experience of 1702–14 proved that Franco-Bavarian co-operation against the Habsburgs would only be successful with the active support, or at least neutrality, of Swabia.

The same events also indicated that Swabian political and military commitment was vital to the effective functioning of the Nördlinger Kreis Association. This alliance of the five western Kreise, including the Austrian, had provided the backbone of the Reichsarmee 1702–14 and played a major role in defending the Rhine frontier against France. Although the peace of 1714 had removed the immediate threat of French attack, it was in Austria's interests to keep the Association alive. Continued Habsburg commitments in Hungary and Italy (1716–20) tied down Austrian troops and further depleted its near-exhausted financial reserves. Little was left to defend the now-exposed Austrian possessions in the German southwest, or the lines of communication to the newly acquired Austrian Netherlands. It was in Austria's interests to offload the burden of guarding these areas onto the Association members in the guise of common imperial defence responsibilities. Austria was keen that the Kreise maintain as many troops in peacetime as possible, and in particular take over responsibility for the upkeep and garrisoning of the two imperial fortresses (*Reichsfeste*), Kehl and Philippsburg, which guarded both the Rhine frontier and the route to the Netherlands.[100]

---

[99] HSAS, A6: Bü. 59; L6.22.6.27.

[100] O. Regele, 'Zur Militärgeschichte Vorderösterreichs', in F. Metz (ed.), *Vorderösterreich* (2nd edn, Freiburg, 1967), pp. 123–37; H. Schmidt, 'Der Verteidigung des Oberrheins und die Sicherung Süddeutschlands im Zeitalter des Absolutismus und der französischen Revolution', *Historisches Jahrbuch*, 104 (1984), 46–62; K. Lang, *Die Ettlinger Linien und ihre Geschichte* (Ettlingen, 1965); H. Nopp, *Geschichte der Stadt und ehemaligen Reichsfestung Philippsburg* (Speyer, 1881), and the three articles by A. von Schempp: 'Die Beziehungen des schwäbischen Kreises und Herzogtums Württemberg zu der Reichsfeste Kehl während der ersten Hälfte des 18. Jahrhunderts', *WVJHLG*, NF8 (1909), 295–334; 'Kehls Ende als Reichsfeste', *ibid.*, NF22 (1913), 336–50; 'Kehl und der schwäbische Kreis gegen Schluß des 18. Jahrhunderts', *ibid.*, NF28 (1919), 167–264.

Württemberg could only make its position in Swabia a potential bargaining counter if it could secure firm control over the other Swabian states. Following Friedrich Carl's example (see pp. 117–19), Eberhard Ludwig tried to consolidate his existing influence by monopolising key Kreis appointments. Meanwhile, he attempted to maintain a precarious balancing-act of posing as Swabian champion against Austrian encroachments on the rights of the lesser territories, while simultaneously trying to win the emperor's favour by compelling the Kreis to fall into line with imperial wishes. Although pursued with some skill, this path ultimately proved too difficult to follow and brought only mediocre rewards for the great effort involved.

Eberhard Ludwig had to wait until 1707 when the death of Margrave Ludwig Wilhelm finally freed the post of Kreis commander-in-chief. As he already held high imperial and Austrian military ranks he had better credentials than the other candidates. However, the decisive factor was his threat to withdraw his Kreistruppen and merge them with the Haustruppen.[101] On 24 March the Kreis Konvent duly elected him Kreis-Feld-Marschall, a post he held until his death on 31 October 1733. Although the Kreis was careful not to give him the same unlimited control over its forces as it had Ludwig Wilhelm, nevertheless, as the duke was simultaneously both Kreis director and co-executive prince, he was in effect his own superior. This near monopoly of the important posts was consolidated by obtaining high Kreis rank for other Württemberg officers, beginning with General von Phull on 29 March.[102]

These were more than empty titles. Through his control over actual military operations, the duke could direct affairs to Württemberg's advantage, such as by ensuring that the duchy was spared the heaviest quartering of Kreis and allied troops. Nonetheless, the Kreis was still too vigorous an institution to fall totally under Württemberg sway. This is demonstrated by the fact that the duke was forced to trade off his support for the promotion of other Kreis members in order to advance the military careers of his son and of Carl Ludwig von Grävenitz.[103] In the case of the passage of the Austrian Alcandetti Infantry Regiment through Swabia in 1730, he was even overruled by the Kreis Konvent and much to his chagrin had to permit the unit to march through the duchy.[104]

The Kreis displayed a similar reluctance to bow to Württemberg wishes in 1714 when it opposed ducal demands to retain a high peacetime military establishment.

---

[101] HSAS, C14: Bü. 194; G184: Bü. 18–23. Vann, *Swabian Kreis*, p. 156; Storm, *Feldherr*, p. 215.
[102] HSAS, C14: Bü. 217. Phull was promoted Kreis major general. Subsequent dukes also furthered his promotion at Kreis level, see C14: Bü. 185, 192.
[103] HSAS, A6: Bü. 19; C14: Bü. 190. Such trade-offs of support became common practice, see A6: Bü. 15, 24; C14: Bü. 217, 217a, 488–90, 499.
[104] HSAS, A6: Bü. 53; C14: Bü. 84; L5: Tom. 139, 140. Neipperg, *Kaiser und schwäbischer Kreis*, pp. 51–3. On this rgt see A. von Wrede, *Geschichte der kaiserlichen und königlichen Wehrmacht von 1618 bis zum Ende des XIX. Jahrhunderts* (5 vols., Vienna, 1898–1905), II, p. 222.

As in 1697, Eberhard Ludwig hoped that this would help overcome his own domestic problems by obliging the estates to pay for large numbers of Württemberg soldiers as Kreistruppen. It would also boost his own international prestige, because the Swabian forces were seen as an extension of those of the duchy. Finally, it would please the emperor, who wished to offload responsibility for the defence of the area. Again, as in 1697, the duke was opposed by Constance and the majority of smaller territories which objected to a large establishment as an unnecessary expense. They forced a reduction from 9,000 to 5,850 soldiers in November 1714 and, despite determined Württemberg opposition, eventually to 4,000 by 1732.[105]

Eberhard Ludwig was initially more successful with his policy towards the two Reichsfeste. Although there was little likelihood of either the emperor or the Reichstag ever refunding the expenses, he managed to persuade Swabia to pay for the upkeep and garrison of Kehl, while Franconia did the same for Philippsburg. He also persuaded the Swabians to renew the Kreis Association. In return he was rewarded by being appointed supreme commander over both fortresses by the emperor in October 1714.[106]

The emperor also supported him against Constance's bid for the Kreis directorate after 1716. With the onset of religious tension in the Reich in 1719, the emperor's initial support for Constance became untenable owing to the bishops' misguided policy of playing on Catholic fears of Protestant Württemberg predominance. By avoiding all references to religion Eberhard Ludwig won over the emperor, who was conscious of the need to scotch rumours of an impending religious war.[107] Austro-Württemberg co-operation peaked in 1721 when the duke secured Swabian agreement to financial assistance for the repair of Breisach, even though this was an Austrian, not an imperial, fortress. In return, the emperor passed a favourable first verdict in the duke's case against the Mömpelgard bastards.[108]

However, Eberhard Ludwig quickly discovered that this imperial support was double-edged. The emperor had given very little away and each time the duke had been compelled to pay a high price for it. His appointment as commander of the two fortresses, like that as Reichs-Feld-Marschall in 1712, was a means to bind him more closely to the imperial system. Though it gave him a prestigious title, it lumbered him with the odious task of persuading the reluctant Swabians

---

[105] HSAS, A5: Bü. 70–1; C14: Bü. 332; L6.22.6.1; Neipperg, *Kaiser und schwäbischer Kreis*, pp. 15–31; Storm, *Feldherr*, pp. 110–11, 258–63, 268, 330–46. The official size of the Württemberg contingent declined from 1,996 men in 1714 to 869 by 1732. Its actual strength remained roughly constant at about 1,065 men. In addition, the duchy maintained between 1,850 and 2,500 Haustruppen throughout this period.

[106] Neipperg, *Kaiser und schwäbischer Kreis*, pp. 7–15.

[107] *Ibid.*, pp. 32–40, 79–105; Hughes, *Early modern Germany*, pp. 134–6.

[108] HSAS, A6: Bü. 62; L5: Tom. 135, fol. 178; L6.22.6.35; C14: Bü. 56; Neipperg, *Kaiser und schwäbischer Kreis*, pp. 105–8. The money was termed Breisacher Concurrenzgelder.

to continue to maintain the garrison and fortifications. Coming alongside his apparent willingness to concede imperial demands for money for Breisach as well, this seriously undermined his efforts to pose as the defender of Swabian interests.

The duke's attempt to enhance his freedom of action by consolidating his position in Swabia failed for two reasons. First, the Kreis structure, with its multitude of small territories and close proximity to Austrian possessions, gave the emperor numerous opportunities to exert influence. For the price of a few minor concessions, the emperor achieved his limited objective of safeguarding Austria's regional interests. Second, the absence of serious French interest in the region in 1714–26 prevented Eberhard Ludwig playing Austria off against France. Only through this could he hope to reverse his dependence on the major powers and force them to make real concessions in return for his support.

Such an opportunity arose in 1726 following an international crisis resulting from a short-term reversal of alliances which saw Austria siding with Spain against an unusual coalition of the French, Dutch and English. War seemed imminent and both coalitions began diplomatic offensives in the Reich to secure the support of as many of the smaller territories as possible.

Conscious of his weakness in Mömpelgard, Eberhard Ludwig seized the opportunity to sell his support to the anti-Habsburg faction in return for full restitution of the occupied lordships. From March 1726 he offered to join the Herrenhausen powers (Britain, France, Prussia, Sweden, Denmark and the Dutch Republic) on this condition. To improve his chances, the duke compelled the Kreis Assembly to repay a large Dutch loan that dated back to 1708. Throughout 1726 and early 1727 he also successfully held back Austrian attempts to reactivate the Kreis Association.[109]

His efforts to pose as the Swabian power obviously had some effect, for the French representative, Chavigny, became convinced that an alliance with Württemberg would win over the rest of the region. This had assumed great importance in French calculations given their attempts to win back Bavaria, recently enticed into the imperial camp by Spanish subsidies. On the basis of Chavigny's optimistic assessment of Württemberg's potential, the French opened negotiations for a subsidy treaty at the beginning of 1727. By February these had extended to include Bavaria. Both German states agreed the following month to co-operate in enforcing an armed neutrality in southern Germany in the event of war.[110]

From this promising start the duke's position rapidly crumbled when Paris began to have doubts whether Württemberg could really carry the rest of the Swabian

---

[109] Neipperg, *Kaiser und schwäbischer Kreis*, pp. 58, 117–18, 125.
[110] A. M. Wilson, *French foreign policy during the administration of Fleury 1726–1743* (Cambridge, MA, 1936), pp. 156–7; Hughes, *Law and politics*, pp. 201, 204–5; Hartmann, *Geld*, pp. 101–12.

states. To avoid being completely isolated, Eberhard Ludwig hastened to rebuild his links to Vienna. His efforts to persuade the Kreis to mobilise for armed neutrality were now portrayed as moves to support the emperor. Württemberg now lessened its opposition to a renewal of the Kreis Association which finally went through on 31 May 1727.[111]

Meanwhile, the duke sought to compensate for his loss of influence in Swabia by establishing links with princes in a similar predicament. On 24 July he formed a secret alliance with Braunschweig-Wolfenbüttel, which was later extended to include Sachsen-Gotha, Hessen-Kassel, Denmark and Sweden. The intention was to extract concessions from the major powers by developing a rival 'third force' in the Reich. It failed. The attraction of separate deals with the major powers proved too strong for this combination of smaller states to operate effectively. Following Wolfenbüttel's treaty with Hanover (6 December), the new league was rendered ineffective by the efforts of George II to make it the core of a wider, Protestant alliance.[112]

Eberhard Ludwig himself had already followed the path of separate negotiation and despatched Victor Sigismund von Grävenitz (died 1766) to London on George II's accession. In his instructions of 4 August Grävenitz was told to ask the English for a *union und traittes d'alliance*, together with a subsidy agreement in a secret clause. In addition, he was to solicit English support for Württemberg electoral status and ask the new king to use his good offices with the French over Mömpelgard. However, by now it was too late as Britain, along with France, Austria, Spain and the Dutch had already signed peace preliminaries in May 1727. Although the British did exert pressure on France to settle the Mömpelgard dispute, nothing came of it.[113] The duke's other aims were ignored. In a final attempt in May 1730, he even sent the abbot of Mömpelgard to London, but equally without result.[114]

In desperation the duke approached the Austrians with an identical set of demands.[115] In addition, he included traditional Württemberg request for a Reichstag vote for Teck as well as a favourable verdict in the imperial courts in the duchy's dispute with Baden-Durlach.[116] Significantly, the emperor was not only asked to turn a blind eye to Württemberg transgressions against the imperial knights, but was to promise in a secret article to reject any complaint from the

---

111 Neipperg, *Kaiser und schwäbischer Kreis*, pp. 125–43; D. Münch, 'Die Beziehungen zwischen Württemberg und Österreich bzw dem Kaiser 1713–1740' (Innsbrück Ph.D., 1961), pp. 55–78.
112 Wilson, *French foreign policy*, p. 193; Hughes, *Law and politics*, pp. 218–19.
113 HSAS, A6: Bü. 59; PRO, SP102/25. The existence of this mission was previously undiscovered.
114 PRO, SP102/25.
115 HSAS, A74: Bü. 100, 102, 109–11; A202: Bü. 1157; LBS, cod. hist. fol. 647.
116 The court case resulted from conflicting claims to the Württemberg Ämter Besigheim and Mundelsheim. It was finally settled in 1753 when Carl Eugen paid 130,000fl. in compensation to Baden-Durlach.

estates over the question of military finance.[117] As the following three chapters will show, these demands were to remain remarkably consistent throughout the eighteenth century. They effectively summarise all that Eberhard Ludwig and his contemporaries among the princes of the Reich were trying to achieve: an internal consolidation of their power at the expense of such groups as the estates and an external expansion at the expense of their smaller neighbours.

As long as the emperor was interested in upholding the system of the Reich, he could never agree to such demands. However, it is typical of Eberhard Ludwig's bad timing that he waited until 1727 before beginning serious negotiations with Vienna. A year before, when the pressure on Austria had been greater, the emperor had agreed to generous terms in order to secure the four Wittelsbach electors.[118] By mid-1727 not only had this pressure eased, but Austria's worsening financial situation forced the emperor to keep his subsidy offer low. This in turn compelled Eberhard Ludwig to reduce his offer of 10,000 men to 6,000. More problems arose over the degree of control the duke was to be permitted to exercise over the corps and the geographical area in which it was to serve. Negotiations dragged on without result despite the fact that the emperor was genuinely interested in a treaty and needed Württemberg agreement to the Pragmatic Sanction.

A final opportunity arose during a second European crisis in 1730. Again the duke attempted to play a double game with both France and Austria, reinforced by his continued membership of the league of princes and his position in Swabia. As in 1726–7, the limits on his freedom of action soon became all too apparent. The emperor won him over by a promise to elevate Christiane Wilhelmine to the status of a princess, but then delayed until Württemberg support secured a further renewal of the Kreis Association. As the elevation still failed to materialise, Eberhard Ludwig began to realise he had been tricked again and his frustration in the matter probably played a role in his decision to banish his unfortunate mistress early in 1731. Meanwhile, all his efforts to please the emperor within the Kreis only served to further undermine his position within Swabia.[119]

The failure of Eberhard Ludwig's policy between 1714 and 1733 highlights Württemberg's weakness. Austria managed to secure its interests in the region without recourse to the subsidies and concessions involved in its contemporary agreements with Prussia (1726, 1728), Mainz, Wolfenbüttel, and the four Wittelsbach electors (all 1726). The duke, in part, only had himself to blame. He

---

[117] The relevant clause is in secret article 1 in the draft treaty of 3 Nov. 1731, and would have obliged the emperor to inform the estates that under the terms of the imperial constitution they had to contribute to the army's upkeep. This was particularly important, because between 1730 and 1733 Eberhard Ludwig was planning to use illegal impressment of militiamen to make up the number of soldiers required by the treaty: HSAS, A28: Bü. 99; A202: Bü. 1157.

[118] Hartman, *Geld*, pp. 108–12.

[119] HSAS, A74: Bü. 102, 109–11, Münch, 'Württemberg und Österreich', pp. 226–315; Braubach, *Prinz Eugen*, IV, pp. 356–7; Neipperg, *Kaiser und schwäbischer Kreis*, pp. 148–57.

was overambitious and rather than settle for a compromise which secured meaningful gains, he held out too long for impossibly high targets. In addition to his poor timing, he seems to have lacked the nerve to hold the diplomatic knife-edge necessary to make political capital out of Württemberg's position. By the end of his life he lost all desire to take risks. In the crisis over the Polish succession in 1733 he negotiated behind the back of his chief minister in the vain hope of securing the duchy's neutrality. This policy collapsed on his death. It would have done anyway, as neither France nor Austria were prepared to allow Württemberg to remain neutral in the developing conflict.[120]

Eberhard Ludwig's contemporaries generally fared much better, though few achieved major political goals. The six princes who secured Austrian subsidies in 1726 found they were owed large arrears when these agreements expired two years later. Bavaria was forced to reduce its army as a result. The Palatinate received only vague guarantees for the disputed territory of Jülich-Berg, while Bavaria was promised only support for its claims in Italy. The others received no political concessions. Not surprisingly the four Wittelsbach states defected to France in 1728–9, where they received a better financial deal but no real political benefits. Bavaria then bound itself still closer to France in an effort to improve its position. The Polish succession crisis exposed this as a serious miscalculation. Bavaria was too weak to side openly with France, but too dependent on French subsidies to go over to the emperor. The result was an expensive armed neutrality, which left the elector heavily in debt and no further towards achieving his political objectives. His relatives in Trier and Cologne had both returned to the imperial fold in 1731 along with Mainz. All received subsidies. In addition, Clemens August of Cologne was rewarded with Austrian help to secure his election as Master of the Teutonic Order in 1732 – a title which brought a considerable increase in land and revenue. He also received imperial backing in his dispute with Hanover over Hildesheim. Emboldened, he overambitiously tried to extract further concessions by threatening to defect to France in 1734 and was punished by the quartering of imperial troops on his territory.[121]

Augustus II of Saxony also suffered setbacks through being overambitious. Neither the Anglo-French alliance (1726) nor Austria (1728) was prepared to concede his high demands. His son fared better and received strong Austrian backing to secure the Polish crown in 1733. Prussia gained little from siding with Austria in 1728 beyond vague assurances over Jülich-Berg, which were in any case contradicted by the emperor's earlier promises to the Palatinate.

---

[120] HSAS, A202: Bü. 1996.
[121] Hartmann, *Geld*; Braubach, *Prinz Eugen*, IV and V, and his *Kurköln: Gestalten und Ereignisse aus zwei Jahrhunderten rheinischer Geschichte* (Münster, 1949); J. Black, 'The problem of the small state: Bavaria and Britain in the second quarter of the 18th century', *European History Quarterly*, 19 (1989), 5–36, and his 'Anglo-Wittelsbach relations 1730–42', *Zeitschrift für bayerische Landesgeschichte*, 55 (1992), 307–45.

Only Hessen-Kassel drew major benefit from these diplomatic manoeuvres. British subsidies paid for its entire army 1726–32, while British diplomatic support eventually helped secure full recognition of its claims to Rheinfels in 1754. However, Hessen was exceptionally fortunate. Its troops had a high reputation – at that time superior to that of the Prussians – and British subsidy payments were both generous and punctual. Geography placed Hessen close to Hanover which constantly needed auxiliaries for its defence. Fortune prevented these actually being required when Prusso-Hanoverian rivalry nearly spilled over into war (1729–30).[122]

THE PROBLEMS OF PEACETIME MILITARY FINANCE

Eberhard Ludwig's lack of success on the international stage was mirrored by an equal failure in his conflict with the estates. As has been mentioned above, this struggle was provoked by the financial problems arising from the duke's ambitious diplomacy and not from 'cultural competition'. At the centre of the dispute was the question of the peacetime finance of the army. Württemberg was faced with this problem for the first time in 1714. Apart from a the brief period of peace, 1698–1701, when the army had been retained, the previous thirty years had been a time of continual warfare and before that the duchy had no regular forces to speak of. Between 1714 and 1733 Württemberg was not involved in any conflict. To the estates this seemed sufficient reason for the army to be disbanded. Eberhard Ludwig, on the other hand, was determined to retain as large a force as possible, to maintain his newly acquired image as an Armierter Fürst in the hope that this would attract foreign subsidies and support for his political ambitions. As these subsidies were not forthcoming and as he was unable to sustain his establishment from his own resources, conflict with the estates was unavoidable.

Part of the trouble was that, in addition to all his other difficulties, Eberhard Ludwig entered the peace with a number of specifically military financial problems which had been exacerbated by the war. These made it difficult for him to reduce costs and so made his tax demands seem all the more unreasonable to the estates. These problems have already been touched upon in the discussion of military finance on pp. 37–42. They included the difficulty of such small states achieving financial economies of scale, the relatively expensive nature of over-officered peacetime cadres and the growing need to mitigate the social problems caused by large numbers of discharged soldiers and invalids by making some form of welfare

---

[122] Black, 'Parliament and foreign policy', pp. 41–54; K. E. Demandt, *Geschichte des Landes Hessen* (Kassel, 1980), pp. 276–7. The 1726 treaty is printed in Frauenholz, *Entwicklungsgeschichte*, pp. 461–3.

payments.[123] Often overlooked is the fact that Eberhard Ludwig as well as his two successors did make genuine attempts to try and reduce these costs, but it usually proved impossible to do so. On no fewer than five occasions, Eberhard Ludwig had the Kriegsrat and its successor agency (after 1719), the *General-Kriegs-Commissariat*, draw up economy proposals.[124] Each time he rejected their suggestions, as they would have involved either a reduction in strength or the problematical discharge of officers. Other forms of economy were virtually impossible.

It was universally agreed that a cut in pay was not practicable, because this would reduce it below subsistence level. In any case, the pay and provision rates of the Kreistruppen could not be altered, as they were specified by Kreis and Reichs ordinances.[125] Just how low these rates already were is shown by the fact that even including food and clothing allowances, a Württemberg private in around 1700 received under 4fl. a month, which had been the standard wage of a soldier 200 years previously. Despite minor improvements under Carl Eugen after 1744, soldiers' wages remained fairly static throughout the century, which, considering that meanwhile both prices and civilian wages increased significantly, represents a decline in real terms. Even among the officers the situation was not much better. Apart from a few favoured exceptions, officers' pay was not over-generous; although it was considerably above that of the lower ranks, the officers' outgoings were generally correspondingly higher. They were expected to pay for their uniforms and equipment out of their own pockets and feed and accommodate themselves, and usually a horse and servant as well.[126] The same situation was to be found in most other armies in Europe at the time.[127] In the long run it added to the problems, as it made recruitment more difficult and encouraged desertion.

---

[123] The policy of making welfare payments called *Invalidengelder* to invalided and discharged soldiers was begun under Eberhard Ludwig in 1704 and extended under his successors. The number of recipients, however, always remained below the number of those in need: HSAS, A5: Bü. 69; A6: Bü. 64; A8: Bü. 59, No. 70, Bü. 60, Nos. 96–101; A30a: Bü. 110, 154; A32: Bd. 154–215; A202: Bü. 2283–4; L6.22.5.83; L6.22.6.38. See also O. Breitenbücher, *Die Entwicklung des württembergischen Militärversorgungswesens nach dem dreißigjährigen Krieg bis zum Jahr 1871* (Tübingen Ph.D., printed 1936). Breitenbücher's work suffers from a number of omissions – particularly his failure to use the Invalidengeld Rechnungen – and his unsubstantiated assertion that prior to 1800 there was no difference in treatment between officers and men.

[124] In 1717, 1719, 1721, 1729, 1732. For the plans drawn up see HSAS, A6: Bü. 35, 36; A28: Bü. 99; A202: Bü. 1992, 2205, 2278.

[125] HSAS, A28: Bü. 99. The Kriegsrat rejected 'die retranchierung der gage' on 13 Feb. 1717, because 'der unterofficier und gemeiner Mann zu pferd und zu fuß nicht nur allzu pauvrement, sondern gar nicht würde subsistiren können'.

[126] HSAS, A6: Bü. 35, 67; A8: Bü. 51; A28: Bü. 99; A30a: Bü. 57–60, 63, 66; A30c: Bd. 4, 6; A202: Bü. 1871, 1992, 2206, 2276, 2278; C14: Bü. 334; R. Baumann, *Das Söldnerwesen im 16. Jahrhundert im bayerischen und süddeutschen Beispiel. Eine gesellschaftsgeschichtliche Untersuchung (Miscellanea Bavarica Monacensia*, 79, Munich, 1978), pp. 112–24, and his *Die Landsknechte* (Munich, 1994), pp. 86–91.

[127] HSAS, A6: Bü. 58; A8: Bü. 51; Redlich, *German military enterpriser*, II, pp. 32–46, 231–67. A. J. Guy, *Oeconomy and discipline: officership and administration in the British army 1714–63* (Manchester, 1985), pp. 91–110.

In this context it is worth making a point about uniforms. It is a popular misconception to see eighteenth-century armies, especially those of the small states, as elaborately dressed and therefore as unnecessarily expensive. Apart from the useful functions of enabling a soldier to identify friend from foe and to find his own regiment in the heat of battle, part of the reason for uniforms was that bulk purchase of uniform-coloured clothing kept costs down. Other than a few favoured guard units, which were to be found in every army at the time, Württemberg uniforms were neither over-elaborate nor over-expensive by contemporary standards. In fact, judging by the constant stream of complaints the soldiers were probably very shabbily turned out, as the administration frequently defaulted on the clothing issues.[128] The adoption of Prussian styles in 1748 was accompanied – as elsewhere – not by increased costs, but by economies. By the mid-1750s the uniform coats were cut so tight that they could no longer be buttoned up at the front.[129] Further economies were really only possible among the well-paid and finely dressed guardsmen, whose cost was out of all proportion to their numbers. Under Eberhard Ludwig they consumed nearly a third of the total expenditure on the army although they only made up less than 10 per cent of its strength.[130] However, all the dukes constantly rejected proposals for drastic economies in this area, probably because of the importance of having such units to add a false air of grandeur to the court.[131]

One final area where economies could be made was in the large pay and pensions bill for the general staff, central military agencies and pensioners. This consumed on average around 10 per cent of total expenditure, despite periodic attempts to cut it back.[132] Part of the bill did include non-essential payments such as over-generous salaries to favoured advisers – something which was particularly notable during the Grävenitz–Schütz regime. However, the bulk consisted of the salaries of the overworked Kriegsrat and commissariat officials, who were underpaid in comparison with their colleagues in the civil administration, and the payment to the pensioners. Many of these 'pensioners' were in fact fulfilling indispensable functions as military

---

128 Examples of the complaints in HSAS, A8: Bü. 250, 12 Oct. 1758 and 27 Mar. 1759; A202: Bü. 2257, 13 July 1739; Bü. 2267, 31 July 1749; C14: Bü. 489, Sept. 1739; T. Griesinger, *Geschichte des Ulanenregiments König Karl (1. württ) Nr. 19 von seiner Grundung 1683 bis zur Gegenwart* (Stuttgart, 1883), pp. 39, 41.

129 LBS, cod. milit. qt. 28; G. von Niethammer, 'Die Reichsarmee im Feldzug 1757 mit Rücksicht auf das schwäbische Kreistruppenkorps und das Kreis-Füsilier-Regiments Württemberg . . .', *BMWB*, 9 (1879), 149–204 at p. 154.

130 HSAS, L5: Tom. 139, fols. 388–93; L12: *Kriegsparticulare* 1714/15–1732/3. Between 1714 and 1733 the guards had an average strength of 238 officers and men compared with 1,661 for the Haustruppen and 1,065 for the Kreistruppen.

131 HSAS, A6: Bü. 35, 36; A28: Bü. 99.

132 In 1717 for example, this bill came to the equivalent of two-thirds the annual cost of one of the (then) two Haustruppen foot rgts. The Kriegskasse paid 11,559fl. 41xr. while the Tricesimationskasse paid 11,509fl. 25xr. (L5: Tom. 128, fols. 429b–38b, Tom. 139, fols. 388–93). A Haustruppen IR cost around 35,000fl. while the still 70 per cent mounted dragoon rgt cost about 20,000fl. more (A28: Bü. 99, Lit A).

engineers, fortress commandants or militia captains. Most of the rest were officers who had only joined the list as the result of the reduction of their unit by the duke, who was obliged to pay them half pay until they found other employment.

A particular problem was the wartime arrears which meant the Kriegskasse entered the peace already with a large deficit. This was partly caused by the failure of the Dutch to pay their subsidy in full. The same was to be true under Carl Alexander and the regency of 1737–44 as the result of hire of the troops to the Austrians. These arrears resulted in a constant backlog of payments which it proved impossible to clear. Despite various illegal methods adopted after 1714, such as offloading payment for food and accommodation on to the Ämter and compelling the estates to vote money for uniforms which were then never issued, this backlog continued to grow.[133] By 1722 the Kriegskasse owed 213,723fl. in arrears of pay and clothing allowances alone.[134] This represented two-thirds of the total annual running costs of the army and would have required the estates to double their tax grant to clear it. Although the duke had begun levying the Tricesimation by decree in 1710, the army remained underfunded as the estates' grant continually proved inadequate to cover the difference between the Tricesimation returns and the actual costs.

THE 1724 AGREEMENT

The practice of renegotiating the level of the Extraordinari every six months meant that even this grant was uncertain. As the general staff and commissariat pointed out in March 1721, this uncertainty was detrimental for military *disciplin und oeconomie*.[135] Each time the duke approached the estates' committee for more money, it replied with a demand for a Landtag and claimed that it had not been empowered by the Amtsversammlungen to negotiate on such matters. In 1723 the duke pre-empted this by issuing a circular to each Amt before the committee had convened for the winter round of negotiations. In this circular he asked the Amtsversammlungen to empower the committee to grant long-term funding for a well-trained regular army in return for the abolition of the Tricesimation. The presence of the ducal Amtmann at each Amtsversammlungen helped to secure sufficient numbers of favourable answers. This effectively undermined the committee's position, while the presence there of the conciliatory Osiander also helped achieve a consensus. Agreement was finally reached on 16 March 1724 when

---

[133] HSAS, A6: Bü. 35, 36; A202: Bü. 1992; L5: Tom. 125–41; L6.22.6.1–33; L12: *Kriegsparticulare* 1713/14–1732/3. Note that the military costs quoted by Carsten, *Princes and parliaments*, p. 117 as expenditure are in fact *intended* and not actual expenditure and include the uniform allowance arrears which were actually never paid.

[134] HSAS, L5: Tom. 132, fols. 234b–9b. In addition, the garrison of the Hohentwiel fortress was owed 25,895fl. by March 1722: K. von Martens, *Geschichte von Hohentwiel* (Stuttgart, 1857), p. 160.

[135] HSAS, A6: Bü. 35, 18 Mar. 1721.

the duke accepted the committee's offer of an Extraordinari at the level of an annual tax every six months for three years.[136]

While this agreement was undoubtedly a victory for the duke, it was far from the 'once and for all' acceptance of 'the principle of a permanent army', as has been widely asserted.[137] Neither is it evidence for the supposed conversion of the estates to a tool of absolute government – a theory which appears to be corroborated by the lack of identifiable leaders after the deaths, also in 1724, of Prelate Osiander and legal adviser Johann Dietrich Hörner.[138]

To secure the agreement, Eberhard Ludwig had been forced to halve his original demand for a six-year grant and make important concessions. On 5 February 1724 he stated that as long as a *miles conductus* was maintained by his subjects there was no need for militia recruitment (Auswahl). This statement was to be used as justification for a policy of non-co-operation when he attempted to re-establish the militia in 1726–33.[139] He also failed to secure the estates' agreement to a separate tax grant to cover the *Kreisextraordinari* which regularly took over 10 per cent of the money which could otherwise be devoted entirely to the Württemberg army. Even more significant was the retention by the estates of the right to extend or discontinue the grant. When the first grant expired in 1727, Eberhard Ludwig wanted it extended for four years, but secured only two. When this expired he wanted a further three to four years, but again only received two. On the expiry of this in 1731 he asked for only three, but was granted no extension at all. Instead, the old system of granting a fresh tax every six months was reverted to, despite his continued requests for longer-term funding. Moreover, after the summer of 1732 the estates began granting considerably less than a full annual tax as Extraordinari and specifying that various other ducal monetary requests be met from this and not only the military costs.[140]

Although the estates no longer demanded the disbandment of the entire army in the same strident terms used ten years previously, the return to the old six-monthly funding system indicates that they had not abandoned hope that the next grant might also be the last. The permanence of the standing army was not fully accepted

---

[136] HSAS, L5: Tom. 133, fols. 470–3b, 694–5, 735–7, 740–2, 752b–78b; L6.22.6.29; Carsten, *Princes and parliaments*, pp. 120–1. Vann, *Making of a state*, pp. 183–8. The total value of the grant was around 1.1 million fl.

[137] Vann, *Making of a state*, p. 184 and similar comments in Carsten, *Princes and parliaments*, p. 121; Grube, *Landtag*, pp. 384–5.

[138] This theory is most strongly advanced by W. Grube: see his *Landtag*, pp. 382–8, and 'Die württembergischen Landstände und die Graevenitz', *ZWLG*, 40 (1981), 476–93. It is also followed by Wunder, 'Herzog Eberhard Ludwig', p. 223, but not wholeheartedly by Carsten, *Princes and parliaments*, p. 123. Osiander's death was more a blow than a benefit to ducal absolutist pretensions as it removed the one man in the estates' committee who had been prepared to co-operate.

[139] HSAS, L6.22.6.34.

[140] HSAS, L5: Tom. 135–42. Pfaff, *Militärwesen*, p. 45 is incorrect in saying that the duke got the full 360,000fl. each year until his death in 1733. The *Kreisextraordinari* was an annual payment the duchy was obliged to pay each year to the Kreis military budget.

until the Landtag recess of 1739 when the estates not only voted permanent funding, but also agreed to pay for barracks to accommodate it.[141]

THE DUKE ON THE DEFENSIVE, 1724–33

The reduction not only in the length and size of the estates' grant, but also in Eberhard Ludwig's demands, clearly shows that the ducal ascendancy of 1724 was only temporary and had largely been lost by 1732. The only long-term gain seems to have been that the duke no longer presented a detailed budget for scrutiny by the estates' committee. However, this practice was restored by Carl Alexander in 1734.[142] If anything, Eberhard Ludwig's position after 1724 was weaker than before, as with the abolition of the Tricesimation he no longer had a military tax outside the estates' control. He also missed the opportunity to do without the estates altogether during the period of the grant which would have weakened their influence. The indebtedness of the Rentkammer prevented him from financing the other areas of government without their support. He had to call on them for financial assistance to make good his claims to Mömpelgard after 1723, meet the duchy's share of the Breisach Concurrenzgelder, cover his visit to Berlin in 1731 and pay off Christiane Wilhelmine's claims after he had finally broken off their relationship. Thus, the committee continued to meet regularly both to vote the Ordinari to amortise the debts and to negotiate on these further demands.[143]

Although as late as 1728 Eberhard Ludwig was able to browbeat and bribe the committee into agreement to lavish land grants on the Grävenitz–Schütz clique and to the pawning of a Kammerschreiberei property, he experienced increasing difficulty in security their agreement.[144] It seems likely that this was due to changes in the line of succession in the ruling house. In 1728 Eberhard Ludwig's grandson, Eberhard Friedrich, had died, closely followed by his own son, Friedrich Ludwig, on 23 November 1731. Despite his reconciliation with his 51-year-old wife in May of that year, it was now obvious that Eberhard Ludwig was not going to be succeeded by one of his own line, but by his Catholic cousin, Carl Alexander. The estates had ensured that this prince would be unable simply to carry on where the would-be absolutist Eberhard Ludwig had left off, by binding him to the old constitution through the Reversalien. Already alarmed by Eberhard Ludwig's

---

[141] *Landtagsabschied* 18 Apr. 1739 in Reyscher (ed.), *Gesetze*, II, Nos. 517–36.
[142] The budget proposals are to be found in HSAS L5 and L6 papers. None was presented between winter 1723/4 and summer 1734.
[143] HSAS, L5: Tom. 134–42. On the fall of Christiane Wilhelmine see Pfaff, *Geschichte des Fürstenhauses*, IV, pp. 146–9, 193–4; Kaufmann, *Stetten*, p. 333; S. Stern, *Jud Süss. Ein Beitrag zur deutschen und zur jüdischen Geschichte* (Munich, 1929), pp. 45–6.
[144] HSAS, L5: Tom. 136, fols. 68off.; Grube, *Landtag*, pp. 386–7. The duke obtained 330,000fl. from the estates through the pawning of Weiltingen.

ambiguous attitude towards Lutheranism as the sole permitted religion, the estates had been negotiating with Carl Alexander since 1725. On 11 June 1727 he signed the Reversalien and subsequently confirmed them on many occasions.[145] Backed up by these assurances, the estates began to act with greater confidence, as is borne out clearly in the area of military finance.

Already, one year after the 1724 agreement, all the regimental commanders were complaining of substantial arrears of pay.[146] This failure to balance the budget was largely due to the continued presence of the aspects so criticised in the economy plans of 1716–21: the guards were still too expensive and the pensions bill too high. In addition, the level of the estates' grant was inadequate: something which the duke had pointed out when he accepted it in 1724.[147] Despite further troop reductions in 1728, the arrears had risen to 136,326fl. again by the following summer.[148]

The high command now rebelled and provoked a confrontation with the estates. After the resignation of Josua Albrecht von Boldevin in May 1729 Eberhard Ludwig had offered the *Directorium* in military affairs to General Phull. Phull now refused to accept it until 'der Confusion in Militaribus' and especially the *arrerages* (arrears) had been sorted out. The duke was forced to take action and on 3 February 1730 ordered the Amtsversammlungen to empower the standing committee to grant money to pay off the arrears. Three days later he dissolved the now moribund General-Kriegs-Commissariat and re-established the Kriegsrat with Phull as president. Simultaneously, Phull was appointed to negotiate directly with the estates' delegates.[149]

This form of direct negotiation had already been practised during the troop reductions of 1721–2 when the estates' delegates would suddenly find themselves whisked off by coach to Ludwigsburg, there to be confronted directly by ducal ministers. In 1723 Phull, who enjoyed some credit with the estates for his part in securing the reductions, had successfully obtained their agreement to be disputed *Montourkassen* through such direct talks.[150]

However, times had changed since 1723 and already, in 1727, the committee had refused to be browbeaten by a ducal attempt to approach the Amtsversammlungen directly.[151] The approach in 1730 also failed and it was only out of deference to

---

[145] The best account of the Reversalien negotiation and content is Tüchle, *Kirchenpolitik*, pp. 33–44.

[146] HSAS, A6: Bü. 35, Feb. 1725. The arrears stood at 68,029fl. 38xr.

[147] HSAS, L5: Tom. 133, fols. 774–7.

[148] HSAS, A6: Bü. 35, Aug. 1729. This was owed to the three Hausregimenter and dated back to 1723/24. In addition the Hohentwiel garrison was owed 43 months pay totalling 24,630fl.; Martens, *Hohentwiel*, p. 162.

[149] HSAS, A202: Bü. 2186; L5: Tom. 138, fols. 140b–142; A6: Bü. 36.

[150] HSAS, L5: Tom. 132, fols. 250–1, 260b–2b, 289, 291–2, 516–17, 632; Tom. 133, fols. 562–4. The Montourkassen were special treasuries operating 1720–4 to receive the uniforms allowance payments made by the estates.

[151] Carsten, *Princes and parliaments*, p. 122.

Phull that the committee decided to grant 10,000fl. towards the arrears.[152] This grant was wholly inadequate and, in July that year, Phull was sent again to ask for more money. This time the delegates vehemently attacked this practice of direct negotiation as unconstitutional and insisted on a return to the previous method of communication through the privy council. They also made a formal protest on a wide range of other subjects based on statistics they had collected on their own initiative from the Ämter. Only after Phull took this attack as a personal affront and stormed out did the delegates hurriedly grant a further 10,000fl., which after long negotiations was raised to 25,000fl.[153] All further attempts achieved nothing beyond a further 15,000fl. and by 1732 Eberhard Ludwig had abandoned his unconstitutional tactics and negotiated again through a member of the privy council.[154]

A further sign of the weakening of ducal absolutism is the disappearance of the Grävenitz–Schütz clique which had supported it. By 1731/2 most had died or left ducal service following the banishment of Christiane Wilhelmine.[155] With the failure of the negotiations of the arrears, the numbers were further thinned by the disgrace of J. A. von Boldevin and Privy Councillor von Pöllnitz, while Phull effectively relinquished direction of military affairs when he took up the post of commandant of Kehl. With J. H. von Schütz's death in 1732, the group shrank to a hard core of four with a mere handful of supporters.[156] The lack of new recruits to the clique seems to indicate that the bureaucrats, like the estates, were simply waiting for the change in affairs widely expected to follow the death of the already sickly Eberhard Ludwig.

Eberhard Ludwig's weakness in the last years of his life had set back prospects of establishing the absolute rule he and his successors required if they were to achieve their dynastic and political aims. His failure to seize the opportunity offered by the 1724 agreement to do without the estates had permitted them to regain the influence they had lost earlier in his reign. By 1733 he was effectively back where he had been before the agreement, only now he no longer had the additional income of the Tricesimation. This and his failure to reform the duchy's tax structure had prevented his achieving the financial independence from the estates that was the essential prerequisite to establishing absolute rule. This failure was only

---

152 HSAS, L6.22.6.34; L5: Tom. 138, fols. 142–52b.
153 HSAS, L5: Tom. 138, fols. 299–514.
154 HSAS, L5: Tom. 139, fols. 116–18, 325; Tom. 139, fols. 348–411; Tom. 140, fols. 24b, 26b, 38–9, 265b–320b, 500–29; Tom. 141, unpaginated.
155 Frommann left 1721; Seubert died 1721; Thüngen died 1723; Schunck died or left 1724; Sittmann died or left 1731; C. C. von Boldevin was relieved of the post of army commander in 1721 and died 1732; his brother J. A. was pensioned off in 1729 and disgraced 1732; Pöllnitz was disgraced 1732.
156 F. W. and V. S. von Grävenitz, A. H. and J. P. von Schütz supported by K. von Pfau and General von Wittgenstein. In addition, General Carl Ludwig von Grävenitz and four Grävenitz sons, together with one Boldevin, one Schütz, and one Pöllnitz were still serving in the army, mostly with low ranks.

compounded by his inability to find a foreign sponsor for his ambitions. The weak ducal position he bequeathed to his successor, Carl Alexander, only added to that ruler's already considerable problems. That the new duke proved radically different than anticipated and came far closer to establishing genuine absolute rule could not have been foreseen in 1733.

6

Carl Alexander, 1733–1737

THE STATE OF AFFAIRS IN 1733

When the new duke, Carl Alexander, arrived in Stuttgart on 16 December 1733, the difficulties facing him were considerable. Externally, Württemberg was threatened by war, as a new Franco-Austrian conflict had broken out that October over the Polish succession. On 29 December the French seized the bridgehead at Kehl and were now poised to break through the hastily prepared defensive lines at Ettlingen. Other detachments were already moving into Mömpelgard.[1] The dying Eberhard Ludwig had feared that they would soon 'sweep like a torrent over Swabia'.[2] Meanwhile, Eberhard Ludwig's weakness in the last years of his life had permitted the estates to recover from their earlier setbacks. They consolidated their position by compelling the new duke to sign the Reversalien, limiting his ability to alter the internal structure of the duchy.

To overcome these problems, Carl Alexander turned them to his advantage. By exploiting the emergency resulting from the war, he was able to introduce a wide range of measures that went a long way towards establishing the kind of absolutist rule attempted by his predecessor and his father. These innovations have led to the recent interpretation of his short reign as a break with the past and a departure point for 'new directions of growth', before 'a return to course' under his son and successor Carl Eugen. This view rests on the coincidence of Carl Alexander's accession with the start of Catholic rule in Württemberg, the character of the duke as an outsider, his social and economic innovations and his supposed non-involvement in cultural competition with other states.[3]

This view rather overemphasises the novelty of the changes introduced by Carl Alexander and underestimates the broad continuity between him and his predecessors and immediate successor. Carl Alexander's rule was more a change in style than a true break with the past. It did herald a period of more direct rule by

---

[1] HSAS, A6: Bü. 18; A29: Bü. 168; A202: Bü. 1996; L5: Tom. 142; Lang, *Ettlinger Linien*. On the military operations on the Rhine generally see K.u.K. Kriegs-Archiv, *Feldzüge*, XIX–XXI; J. L. Sutton, *The king's honor and the king's cardinal: the war of the Polish Succession* (Lexington, 1980).

[2] HSAS, A202: Bü. 1996; Eberhard Ludwig to Prince Eugene, 16 Oct. 1733.

[3] Vann, *Making of a state*.

the duke and greater personal participation in policy-making than under Eberhard Ludwig. However, this is due more to Carl Alexander's forceful character than to a change in the policies themselves.[4]

For example, most accounts of Carl Alexander's reign emphasise the novelty of his fiscal measures, although most of these were neither new to Württemberg nor untypical or the rest of Germany. The social implications of these measures, perceived by Vann as unique to Carl Alexander's reign, are not lacking from the fiscal policy of Carl Eugen or Eberhard Ludwig's attempted tax reform. As we shall see, the threat to the worthies' stranglehold of public office presented by the sale of posts by Carl Alexander's *Gratialamt* (see p. 181) is paralleled by a similar development in the 1760s.

The presence of the apparently all-powerful Jewish financial adviser, Joseph Süss Oppenheimer, as instigator of most of these measures is also generally seen as unique to the 1730s. Just as an emphasis on Carl Alexander's military links with the Habsburgs has led to those of his predecessor being ignored, the notoriety of 'Jew Süss' has obscured the existence of other Jewish financiers in Württemberg and the importance of native financial agents.[5]

Similarly, Süss, together with the new Catholic commander-in-chief, General Remchingen, are taken to personify the influx of foreign advisers associated with Carl Alexander.[6] Both the number and influence of these 'foreigners' have been greatly exaggerated by the estates' propaganda and obscure the fact that both Carl Alexander and Süss relied heavily on native Württembergers.[7]

In addition, far from being a 'colonial authoritarian' suddenly arriving to govern a country of which he had little knowledge, Carl Alexander had long and extensive contacts with the duchy.[8] As we have already seen, the prospect that he might one

---

[4] On Carl Alexander's character and reign see Pfaff, *Württembergs geliebte Herren*, pp. 61–4; H. Tüchle, 'Herzog Carl Alexander (1733–1737)', in Uhland (ed.), *900 Jahre Haus Württemberg*, pp. 227–36; Dizinger, *Beiträge*. On his military career see pp. 112–13, 122–4.

[5] More than any other individual, Süss is most closely associated with Carl Alexander's reign and has been the subject of at least one play and two novels, of which Lion Feuchtwanger's has been filmed twice. The most balanced account of his life is Schnee, *Hoffinanz*, IV, pp. 109–48, 277–84. Pages 87–209, 212–18 of this work cover the other Jewish agents in Württemberg. On Süss see also Stern, *Jud Süss* and *The Court Jew*; L. Sievers, *Juden in Deutschland* (Hamburg, 1977), pp. 115–23; C. Elwenspoek, *Jud Süss Oppenheimer, Der große Finanzier und galante Abenteurer des achtzehnten Jahrhunderts* (Stuttgart, 1926, translated as *Jew Süss Oppenheimer*, London, 1931).

[6] Vann, *Making of a state*, p. 223.

[7] Süss' most notorious assistants and political allies *Oberhofkanzler* Dr Johann Theodor Scheffer, *Expeditionsrat* and *Landschreiber* Bühler, *Expeditionsrat* Jakob Hallwachs. *Regierungsrat* Metz and secretaries Thill and Lamprecht were all Württembergers. The duke also favoured native sons in his promotions to the privy council; see Vann, *Making of a state*, p. 212. Although Carl Alexander did bring a large number of army officers from the Austrian forces with him to Württemberg, this was by no means an exceptional development. Many Mecklenburgers had been brought into the army during the Grävenitz–Schütz regime under Eberhard Ludwig. For the composition of the officer corps at this time see HSAS, A30c: Bd. 5–8; Lemcke, 'Württembergisch Offizierskorps', 34–7, 111–17.

[8] Phrase from Vann, *Making of a state*, pp. 258, 263.

day be duke had been a real possibility as early as 1725 and became almost certain with the death of Eberhard Ludwig's only son in 1731. In February 1732 he was officially designated heir-apparent. Through his secretary, Philipp Jacob Neuffer, Carl Alexander had kept in constant touch with matters in the duchy which he also visited on many occasions. As early as 1730, he made contingency plans in the event of Eberhard Ludwig's death and in 1733 Neuffer was on hand in Stuttgart to oversee the transition of government.[9]

His accession certainly did not mark a break in Württemberg's cultural competitiveness. Vann's assertion that this ruler 'showed no interest in personal luxury' and dissolved the court orchestra as 'an unnecessary expense' is simply incorrect.[10] There is no indication that Carl Alexander lessened the element of display at court. On the contrary, during his rule, the court orchestra rose to sixty-three musicians, or equivalent to the high point under his son, while expenditure on it was twice that of 1719/20. The duke was also as passionate an opera lover as his son. He had the old theatre in Stuttgart renovated as the duchy's first opera house and held up to a hundred performances in Ludwigsburg each year.[11] In addition, far from shunning personal luxury, Carl Alexander was an ardent collector of precious stones and works of art. Finally, in spite of his military activities, he also found time to lay out new gardens at the Ludwigsburg palace.[12]

As indicated in the previous chapter, the object of this display was not merely the comfort of the duke himself, but also the maintenance of the duchy's status as the leading power in the south-west of the Reich. After a period of austerity under the regency, this policy was followed with redoubled vigour by Carl Eugen.

In his political aims, Carl Alexander also displayed continuity with the other Württemberg rulers under study here. Like them, he aimed to enlarge his territory and to create a powerful army to increase his 'influence in the important affairs' of the Reich ('einfluß in die Haubtaffairen').[13] There is also nothing different about the methods he used to try and achieve this: new taxes, foreign subsidies and a manipulation of both the duchy's militia system and the opportunities presented him by the system of the Swabian Kreis. What was new was that his Catholic religion made it considerably more difficult to do this than would have been the case had he been Protestant. However, as we shall see, he was quite successful in overcoming this.

---

[9] HSAS, L5: Tom. 141, unpaginated; Tüchle, *Kirchenpolitik*, pp. 33–44; Dizinger, *Beiträge*, I, pp. 7–13.

[10] Vann, *Making of a state*, pp. 221, 260.

[11] HSAS, A256: Bd. 217–22; A282: Bd. 1469x–1472x; N. Stein, 'Das Haus Württemberg, sein Musik- und Theaterwesen', in Uhland (ed.), *900 Jahre Haus Württemberg*, p. 558; R. Krauß, 'Das Theater', *HKE*, I, p. 485; Belschner, *Ludwigsburg*, pp. 154–5.

[12] Fleischhauer, *Barock*, pp. 264, 307; Stern, *Jud Süss*, pp. 48, 327; K. Merten, 'Das Haus Württemberg und seine Schlösser and Gärten', in Uhland (ed.), *900 Jahre Haus Württemberg*, p. 526.

[13] HSAS, A202: Bü. 2230, 30 and 31 Dec. 1735; A28: Bü. 99, 31 Dec. 1735; Pfaff, *Militärwesen*, p. 56.

DUCAL DOMESTIC POLICY, 1733–5

On internal affairs, Carl Alexander's Catholicism tended to cut him off from his subjects and lay him open to the propaganda of his opponents. The same was true of his son, who shared his religion. Under the Reversalien, the Lutheran faith was confirmed as the state religion and Catholic worship was restricted to the ducal family. Any flouting of these restrictions, or open favouritism to Catholics, now brought a swift response from the estates, who were quick to pose as the guardians of the faith. Religious prejudice could easily be whipped up to rally opposition against ducal measures simply by portraying these as purely in the interests of foreign Catholics. This reached its height by the start of 1737, when wild stories circulated about an international papist plot to recatholicise the duchy by force of arms. Some of the pious even regarded the duke's death on 12 March as an act of God, while others thought that he had been whisked away by the devil.[14]

However, it would be wrong to overemphasise this. Eberhard Ludwig's ambiguous attitude towards Catholics, whom he encouraged to settle in his new capital at Ludwigsburg, had already caused disputes with the estates. Such disputes, therefore, were not peculiar to the reigns of Carl Alexander and his son. Furthermore, the differences in religion did not totally preclude an appeal from ruler to subject. On his accession, Carl Alexander was popularly feted as the hero of the storming of Belgrade (1717). Carl Eugen was also able to establish a considerable degree of popularity through his weekly audiences and constant travelling throughout the duchy.[15]

Where religion did represent a more serious obstacle to ducal plans was in the terms of the Reversalien. Nominally, this document was designed to prevent the duke arbitrarily changing the religion of his subjects. However, it also obliged him to confirm all the existing laws and charters of the duchy as well. In itself, this was nothing new, as all new dukes customarily confirmed these on their accession. The novelty lay in the inclusion of two new provisions among these older laws. The first was the transfer of the duke's rights as head of the state church (*Landesbischöfliche Rechte*) to the privy council. This actually took place on 27 March 1734 and represented a new limitation on the duke's power to silence opposition from the prelates and to tap the church revenues.[16] The second was the inclusion of the 1660 Kanzleiordnung among the laws to be confirmed. This

---

[14] Grube, *Landtag*, I pp. 397–8; Dizinger, *Beiträge*, I, pp. 159–62, 181–4. The old theory that the duke was poisoned by an agent of the estates has now been disproved.

[15] Tüchle, *Kirchenpolitik*, pp. 9–12; Belschner, *Ludwigsburg* (1933 edn), pp. 81–9. E. Schneider, 'Herzog Karls Erziehung, Jugend und Presönlichkeit', in *HKE*, I, pp. 43–5.

[16] For a discussion of these limitations and a comparison with similar Reversalien elsewhere see Haug-Moritz, *Württembergischer Ständekonflikt*, pp. 32–9, 172–205.

elevated what had been a ducal administrative guideline to the status of an inalienable part of the constitution and bound Carl Alexander to keep the existing bureaucratic structure intact.[17] The duke suspected that the sheet containing this provision had been slipped in after he had signed the original document. This further soured relations between him and the estates, which were already strained after his discovery of their secret negotiations with his Protestant brother, Prince Heinrich Friedrich, to cut him out of the succession.[18]

The estates also opposed him when he took up his predecessor's demands for a renewal of the 1724 agreement on army funding. It is clear that they intended to capitalise on what they regarded as a weak ducal position. In addition to calling for a Landtag to discuss these, they tried to establish the principle that the army was not to be maintained in peacetime. Although the French were now across the Rhine, the estates were reluctant to fund any troops other than the Kreis contingent the duchy was obliged to provide under imperial law. Carl Alexander's expressions of German patriotism were absent from their phraseology and they showed little support for the idea of collective defence embodied in the imperial military organisation. In their opinion, Württemberg could never raise an army large enough to oppose France and any military activity would only provoke the French into invading as they had done in 1688, 1693 and 1707. Their solution to the duchy's defence problem was to buy security from France by agreeing to Marshal Berwick's demands for contributions.[19]

That, by 1736, Carl Alexander had gone a long way to overcoming their opposition was not owing to any inherent weakness in the Reversalien document itself, but to the estates' inability to compel him to stick to its terms. During his reign, the document was only guaranteed by the Corpus Evangelicorum. This single guarantee was insufficient to deter him from ignoring those terms which stood in his way. His hand was strengthened by his relatively close ties with the emperor who would be called upon to judge any appeal by the estates against arbitrary rule. This loosened the restrictions resulting from the transfer of the Landesbischöfliche Rechte to the privy council. The extent to which he was able to ignore these restrictions is demonstrated by the unprecedented plundering of church revenues to pay court and government salaries.[20] He also disregarded the inclusion of the 1660 Kanzleiordnung and dismissed the officials he held responsible. On 6 June 1735 he reconstituted the cabinet ministry he had agreed to abolish on his accession

---

[17] Wunder, *Privilegierung*, pp. 53–4. On the Kanzleiordnung see pp. 66–7 above.

[18] Dizinger, *Beiträge*, I, pp. 24–6.

[19] HSAS, L5: Tom. 142; L6.22.7.2; Kriegs-Archiv, *Feldzüge*, XIX, pp. 44–5; Sutton, *King's honor*, pp. 75–6. Baden was forced to pay 40,000fl.

[20] HSAS, A282: Bd. 1469x–1472x; Müller, 'Finanzwirtschaft' at p. 306 is incorrect in his statement that Carl Alexander took less money from the Kirchenkasten than Eberhard Ludwig. Müller only looked at the Rentkammer account books and missed the fact that the salaries were paid direct to the individuals concerned.

and so re-established the governmental system used by Eberhard Ludwig to advance absolutist rule.[21]

The emergency brought about by the war also enabled Carl Alexander to force through a number of other measures to ease the financial problem caused by the military buildup he began in December 1733. Here he was greatly assisted by the opportunity to capitalise on the fears of the estates over the possibility of a French invasion. While the outbreak of hostilities had not made them any more prepared to fund the army, they were willing to co-operate, in order to forestall the destruction to property that invasion would inevitably bring, by agreeing to Marshal Berwick's demands for contributions before he actually sent his troops to collect them. On 4 May 1734 the French broke through the defensive Ettlingen lines, forcing Prince Eugene and the imperial army to fall back on Frankfurt. Württemberg was now exposed and on 13 May the alarming news arrived that General Quadt and 10,000 Frenchmen were advancing on the duchy. This prompted the estates' committee to start discussions with the privy council as to the best way to raise the money to buy off the dreaded French. Having considered past precedents, the estates' committee suggested a reintroduction of the Tricesimation for one year.[22]

This was immediately seized upon by the duke. The estates had already gone too far to retract their suggestion and although the situation had now stabilised on the Rhine front, so that French demands could safely be ignored, the duke went ahead and decreed the Tricesimation in July 1734. He also rode roughshod over their claim to administer it and entrusted the overseeing of it to Kriegsrat Hopfenstock, although in 1735 he did consent to their right to check the accounts. At a stroke, the estates had signed away one of their key gains from the 1724 agreement. The collection of the Tricesimation enabled the duke to plug the gaps in his military budget left by the payment of the rising Kreis and Reichs obligations.[23]

The fear of imminent French invasion also prompted the estates to act as guarantors of the loans the duke was negotiating. As with the Tricesimation, they appeared to have considered these as a means of raising money to meet French demands. Instead, the money went to ease the cash-flow problems caused by the slow payment from Vienna and to cover the mobilisation costs of the Kreistruppen.[24]

Contrary to popular belief, Süss played little part in negotiating these loans. Instead, the leading role was taken by a native Württemberger, *Commercienrat*

---

[21] Wintterlin, *Behördenorganisation*, I, pp. 65–73. The officials dismissed were Privy Council President Christoph Peter von Forstner, and the duke's former private secretary, Councillor Philipp Jacob Neuffer.

[22] HSAS, L5: Tom. 142, fols. 413–685.

[23] *Ibid.*, fols. 695–872, 926ff.; Tom. 143, fols. 108b–182, 295–6, 303–4; A202: Bü. 2201; L12: *Kriegsparticulare* 1734/35–1736/37.

[24] HSAS, L5: Tom. 142, fols. 355b–66b.

Egidius Böhm, who was very active in securing money in May 1734. Also instrumental in the negotiations was another native, Professor Georg Bernhard Bilfinger, who soon won the confidence of the duke and was promoted to privy councillor.[25] Most of the money came from Augsburg bankers and various individuals in and around the duchy.

This comparative weakness of the estates also lessened the share of the burden that the ducal Rentkammer had to bear. Between 1733/4 and 1735/6 the estates took on capital totalling 260,980fl. compared with only 110,092fl. by the Rentkammer.[26] The contrast is even greater if the situation under Carl Alexander is compared with that under his predecessor. Poor financial management under Eberhard Ludwig had created over two million florins of Rentkammer debts by 1733. In the year 1732/3 the Rentkammer was forced to raise 162,552fl. in capital alone, while in August 1733 the duke was talking of raising a colossal 300,000fl. to finance his war effort. Through better management at the Rentkammer, together with imperial subsidies and co-operation from the estates, Carl Alexander was able not only dramatically to reduce his borrowing requirements, but also to pay off 187,559fl. of the capital debt of his predecessor.[27]

DUCAL FOREIGN POLICY, 1733–5

As in his domestic policy, Carl Alexander initially encountered considerable problems in his external affairs, caused by his religion. Primarily he lost the sympathy of the Protestant states within the Swabian Kreis, who had traditionally been more prepared to follow the Württemberg line than the Catholics. This was potentially very serious, as it threatened to remove the chance of developing the Kreis as a bulwark against Austrian domination of the duchy. As the Catholic Kreis members were largely Austria's clients, Carl Alexander could not look to them as a substitute for a loss of Protestant support. His Catholic religion also threatened to undermine the monopoly of Kreis military posts built under Eberhard Ludwig. These posts had fallen vacant upon that duke's death. Württemberg's longstanding rival, Baden-Durlach, immediately applied for them and for command of the duchy's two Kreis regiments on the grounds that it was contrary to Kreis rules that Protestant units be commanded by a Catholic. Simultaneously, Carl Alexander encountered the same problem at the Reichstag when he tried to get himself appointed to Eberhard Ludwig's former post as imperial field marshal.[28] To

---

[25] *Ibid.*, fol. 406b. Böhm was a longstanding supplier to both the court and army, especially of uniforms and clothing. On Bilfinger, see E. Schmid, 'Geheimrat Georg Bernhard Bilfinger (1693–1750)', *ZWLG*, 3 (1939), 370–422.

[26] HSAS, A256: Bd. 217–21; L10: *Einnehmerei Rechnungen*, Bd. 1733/4–1735/6.

[27] HSAS, A202: Bü. 1966 esp. ducal resolutions of 12 Aug. and 14 Sept. 1733; A256: Bd. 216–22. See also Müller, 'Finanzwirtschaft', pp. 282–3 and p. 60 above.

[28] HSAS, A6: Bü. 15; C14: Bü. 85, 217, 217a, 490; Griesinger, *Ulanenregiments*, p. 33.

make matters worse, the Prussians entered into the competition with a very strong candidate in the person of Prince Leopold von Anhalt-Dessau (1670–1747).[29]

Nonetheless, Württemberg still possessed considerable weight within the Kreis on account of its position as the most powerful member state. Carl Alexander was also assisted by his undisputed military reputation which, as it was wartime, was much appreciated by the other members.[30] He also went to great lengths to emphasise that these were 'purely military appointments which have no influence on religious matters'.[31] However, the decisive factor was the considerable backing he received from the Austrians, especially at the Reichstag.[32] This secured his appointment in May 1734 as the second most senior imperial field marshal after Prince Eugene.[33] Meanwhile, the decision on the vacant Kreis posts was hustled through the Kreis Konvent in early January when most of the delegates were away still celebrating New Year.[34]

Thereafter, Württemberg experienced little difficulty on religious grounds in maintaining its monopoly of Kreis military appointments. After his death, the delay in transferring Carl Alexander's posts to his son was caused more by the weakness of the regency and the absence of a mature duke than by confessional problems.[35] Religion was thus becoming a less significant political factor than it had been at the time of Carl Alexander's father. While it was still to remain important, other factors were now playing a greater role in determining political alignment, as the discussion on the Seven Years War in Chapter 8 will show.

As indicated in the preceding two chapters, these Kreis posts were not empty titles, but enabled their holder to extend his influence. Carl Alexander was able to ensure that Württemberg escaped the heaviest quartering of the Austrian and allied troops.[36] He also redirected many of the entrenchment workers the duchy was supposed to provide for the building of defensive lines in the Black Forest, to work on his ambitious project to convert the duchy's antiquated castles into

---

[29] HSAS, A6: Bü. 15, Anhalt-Dessau to Carl Alexander, 10 Jan. 1734.

[30] Replies from both Protestant and Catholic Kreis members to his requests for support all praise his military experience: HSAS, A6: Bü. 15, 24.

[31] HSAS, A6: Bü. 15, application to the Reichstag, 2 Jan. 1734; Tüchle, *Kirchenpolitik*, p. 45.

[32] HSAS, A6: Bü. 15 esp. 18 Dec. 1733, 26 May 1734. Both Prince Eugene and the Austrian representative at the Reichstag, Prince Frobian Ferdinand zu Fürstenberg-Meßkirch, gave strong support.

[33] *Ibid.* Fürstenberg to Carl Alexander, 21 May 1734. Ferdinand Albrecht von Brunswick-Lüneburg-Bevern was appointed field marshal junior to Carl Alexander, with Anhalt-Dessau as fourth in seniority. It is interesting to note that by this arrangement the Reich had abandoned the idea of religious parity in military posts, as both Protestants were junior to the two Catholic field marshals.

[34] HSAS, C14: Bü. 217, 217a.

[35] HSAS, A202: Bü. 2274; C14: Bü. 185, 192, 193, 217, 217a, 330, 489.

[36] HSAS, A6: Bü. 9, 18; C14: Bü. 188.

modern fortresses.[37] He even managed to channel Kreis funds into this project and ensured that the Kreis paid for work carried out by Württembergers on the lines.[38]

His monopoly of Kreis posts was probably most useful to him in helping him complete the military plans of Eberhard Ludwig. Ever since his previous attempt in 1726 to reorganise the duchy's militia along traditional lines had ground to a halt after four years, in the face of passive resistance from the estates, Eberhard Ludwig had been secretly planning to transform the force into a manpower reserve for the regular army so that, when needed, the required number of militiamen would be called out to bring the regular units up to field strengths.[39] As early as 1731 he had proposed using this method to mobilise a subsidy corps for the emperor.[40] Lists were prepared of the eligible men in each district and in September 1733 it had been decided to conscript 4,500 men and 1,200 horses by this method. A week before his death, Eberhard Ludwig ordered the call-up and impressment to begin. Three days after his arrival in Stuttgart, Carl Alexander ordered Holle to complete the task.[41]

This was technically illegal as it contravened the terms of the Tübingen Treaty, which had banned impressment. To provide a veneer of legality, ducal representatives at the Kreistag pushed a motion calling for the organisation of a Kreis militia (*Kreislandauswahl*). This was passed on 24 April 1734 and provided cover for the continued call-up of Württembergers and their impressment in the subsidy units. Then, on the grounds that the duchy had not fulfilled its obligations to the Kreis in April, the duke ordered the call-up of a further 3,000 men on 12 November. This was again retrospectively sanctioned by the Kreistag, when the Württemberg representatives secured the call-up of a second Kreis militia contingent on 4 March 1735. This time the duchy did send most of its quota to join other Kreis militia in the Black Forest. However, as the number called up on 12 November was almost twice the size of the Kreis requirements, the duke still had surplus manpower to help with the formation of two more regular regiments. Moreover, when the Kreis gave the order for its militia to stand down in November 1735, the duke promptly converted most of his contingent into a regular *Land* or garrison regiment.[42]

The manipulation of the militia call-up also enabled the duke to extend his influence within the Swabian Kreis. Through a series of agreements, three of the smaller Kreis members paid him to provide Württemberg Kreis militiamen in place

37 HSAS, A30a: Bü. 27, 19 Oct. 1736; L6.22.7.5a; C14: Bü. 307; L5: Tom. 143, fols. 440, 498, 522–524b, 551, 641b; Tom. 145, fol. 546; Tom. 148, fols. 377–80; Tom. 149, fol. 184b; Schempp, *Finanzhaushalt*, pp. 98–102; Weisert, *Sindelfingen*, p. 245.
38 HSAS, C14: Bü. 307; L6.22.7.5a; L12; *Kriegsparticulare*, Bd. 1733/4–1736/7.
39 HSAS, A6: Bü. 40–2, 44; A8: Bü. 99; A202: Bü. 2005; L6.22.6.34.
40 HSAS, A202: Bü. 1157, 1358. These proposals were endorsed by the treaty Carl Alexander signed on 29 Nov. 1733 with the emperor.
41 HSAS, A28: Bü. 99, fol. 80; A6: Bü. 34, 22 Oct. 1733; A202: Bü. 2005, 19 Dec. 1733.
42 HSAS, C14: Bü. 306, 307; L6.22.7.5a.

of their own contingents.[43] Carl Alexander also received imperial permission to provide the contingents of some of the smaller princes to the Reichsarmee in return for payment. Although these measures brought little financial reward, they did enable the duke to increase his active role within Kreis and Reich politics.[44]

However, as we have seen in the preceding chapter, there were limits on Württemberg's ability to manipulate the Kreis system to its advantage. These limits were clearly demonstrated by Carl Alexander's failure to persuade the Kreis to increase its regular forces. Despite considerable efforts, the other Kreis members could not be induced to raise the overall strength of the Kreistruppen. Similarly, his plans to retain a large number of troops upon demobilisation in 1736 also met with an adverse reaction. By May 1737 most of the members had already reduced their contingents well below the level the duke had stipulated.[45]

The duke's intention behind these abortive efforts appears to have been partly to provide a more effective defence against the French threat and partly to please the emperor. As already noted, Carl Alexander's aims did not differ from those of the other Württemberg dukes, and like them he was dependent upon imperial co-operation to realise them. As he had spent his entire life in imperial service it was also natural that he should look in that direction for reward. Like his father, he hoped to provide for his large family by securing them command posts in the Austrian army. He also hoped that his support for the imperial war effort would be rewarded by his enfiefment with Austria's Swabian lordships of Hohenburg, Nellenberg and Buchau.[46]

His existing good relations with Austria, coupled with the emperor's desperate need for troops, led to the signing on 29 November 1733 of the subsidy treaty which Eberhard Ludwig had been negotiating since 1727.[47] This was obviously signed in a hurry, as the news of Eberhard Ludwig's death only reached Vienna on 4 November.[48] In his haste, Carl Alexander failed to write in any of that duke's ambitious political demands or secure a promise of enfiefment with the three

---

[43] HSAS, L6.22.7.5a; L5: Tom. 143, fols. 283b, 287–94b. The treaties were with the cities of Esslingen (eighty men for 5,000fl.) and Bopfingen (seventeen men for 1,000fl.) and the *Reichsgotteshaus* Kaisersheim (fifty men for 3,000fl.). Württemberg actually provided only forty-three, eight and twenty-five men respectively. According to an estates' complaint (L6.22.7.5a, 27 Jan. 1738) the money went to the ducal Chatoule.

[44] HSAS, A6: Bü. 34, 25 June 1735; A74: Bü. 114, reports of *Regierungsrat* Zech. The money, totalling about 143,000fl., was to come from the Relutionen of the dukes of Mecklenburg and East Frisia and the bishops of Liege and Lübeck. In return, Carl Alexander proposed to send his new Leibregiment to serve with the Reichsarmee. According to fragmentary evidence (A7: Bü. 41, No. 37) it appears that the duke was also negotiating to provide the Palatinate contingent.

[45] HSAS, A30a: Bü. 57; C14: Bü. 307, 327, 330, 334, 337.

[46] HSAS, A74: Bü. 114; Schneider, *Württembergische Geschichte*, p. 346.

[47] HSAS, A7: Bü. 10; A202: Bü. 1157, 1358. On the earlier negotiations see pp. 151–3. The treaty was officially called a *Unions-Tractat* and had the character of a formal alliance.

[48] HSAS, A6: Bü. 52, report of *Kriegsagent* Thalheim, 4 Nov. 1733.

lordships. All the emperor was obliged to do was to assist in recovering Mömpelgard, which had now been completely occupied by French troops. In return, Carl Alexander had to recognise the Pragmatic Sanction and provide three regiments totalling 5,700 men as well as his Kreistruppen to the common war effort against France. These three regiments would pass into imperial pay as soon as they were at full strength.[49]

In addition, Carl Alexander would receive an annual subsidy of 75,000fl. for eight years. This subsidy would continue to be paid in peacetime, although the maintenance costs would stop. During such time the duke was to maintain in readiness the three regiments at somewhat reduced strength, should the emperor require them. The treaty was less favourable as far as the mobilisation costs were concerned, The emperor was merely obliged to pay between 75,000fl. and 100,000fl. within fourteen days of ratification. This was considerably short of the Württemberg estimate of 352,488fl. 42xr. for the true cost of raising the corps and still less than half what the imperial commissariat admitted the expenses to be.[50] In any case, the emperor immediately defaulted on those payments he had promised. When the imperial commissariat finally did send payment, instead of sending cash it supplied credit notes which were twice returned unhonoured by the imperial treasury.[51]

This prompted Carl Alexander to complain bitterly to the emperor 'that after more than eight months and despite so many requests, I still have not received any payment on my considerable mobilisation costs. My credit is consequently ruined and because of the loans I have had to raise, I now find myself at a grave disadvantage'.[52] In addition to the loans, the duke was forced to pay out money from his private treasury, the Chatoule. From fragmentary evidence, this paid out at least 40,000fl. during the course of the war to help recruit and maintain the subsidy units.[53]

Although the emperor did eventually pay both the subsidy and the mobilisation money, ducal attempts to secure a retrograde agreement on reimbursement of the true cost met with little response from Vienna. With the troops already in the field at Württemberg's expense, they saw no reason to pay out more money. The shifting factions at the imperial court also made it difficult for the Württemberg representative there to secure a definitive agreement.[54] Much depended on the good

---

[49] Two infantry regiments each 2,300 strong; one dragoon regiment totalling 1,094 officers and men. The units were formed by expanding the existing three regiments inherited from Eberhard Ludwig, see HSAS, A6: Bü. 34.

[50] HSAS, A6: Bü. 34, 3 Mar. 1734. The imperial estimate was 253,087.5fl.

[51] HSAS, A6: Bü. 29, 6 Apr. 1734; Bü. 34; Bü. 36, 2 May 1734.

[52] Carl Alexander to Emperor Charles VI, 22 Dec. 1734: quoted in P. Stark, 'Zur Geschichte des Herzogs Karl Alexander von Württemberg und der Streitigkeiten nach seinem Tode', *WVJHLG*, 11 (1888), at p. 3.

[53] HSAS, L5: Tom. 143, fols. 637–40, 655b–661; A7: Bü. 42, No. 35.

[54] HSAS, A7: Bü. 41; A74: Bü. 114, 117.

will of individual key officials. In October 1737, Regent Carl Rudolph learnt to his horror that the imperial General Kreigs Commissar Baron von Wibmer was 'so jealous that the treaty had not been made with him, that he now intends to deduct over 90,000fl. from the money owed'.[55] It appears that altogether the raising of the units for imperial service cost the duchy 229,842fl. over and above the 150,000fl. it received from the emperor.[56]

This sorry picture was mirrored in the payment of maintenance costs once the units finally entered imperial service. These units still had pay arrears from Eberhard Ludwig's time which were now compounded by additional arrears owed by the imperial commissariat. By July 1735 these stood at 187,373fl. 35xr. for the three subsidy regiments. This figure exceeded any achieved under Eberhard Ludwig, while the officers now had not been paid for an entire year.[57]

The duke was also disappointed in his hope for other concessions. He did, of course, receive strong imperial support on his appointment to Eberhard Ludwig's Kreis and Reichs posts. He also received command of that duke's former Austrian dragoon regiment, succeeded in obtaining high Austrian ranks for Württemberg officers and had his sons appointed colonels of the regiments hired to the emperor. However, this fell short of expectations. The one firm piece of political assistance the Austrians did provide was help in securing a French withdrawal from Mömpelgard in 1736, but not from the nine lordships occupied since 1723. All his hopes to be enfiefed with Austrian territory went unfulfilled. He also failed to secure the position of supreme commander on the Rhine, as this went to Prince Eugene. Meanwhile, the emperor actually ruled against him by siding with the Kreis in condemning his exploitation of Württemberg minting rights which had led to Swabia being flooded with poor-quality coin.[58]

This was poor reward for the great efforts Carl Alexander had made in 1733–5 to please the emperor. In an attempt to demonstrate his zeal for the imperial cause, he outdid all his competitors among the smaller states in raising troops for the emperor's service. A mere week after signing his original treaty, he boldly declared himself ready to raise an additional 700 men. These were to be added as a fourth battalion to the imperial foot regiment of which he was colonel-in-chief. The emperor agreed to reimburse his expenses by paying 34fl. per

---

[55] HSAS, A6: Bü. 34, Regent Carl Rudolph to Baron Gotter, 23 Oct. 1737.

[56] *Ibid.*. Carl Rudolph to Count Sinzendorf, 23 Oct. 1737. The payment of 150,000fl. was for the subsidy corps of 1733 and a further bn hired in 1735. It does not appear to include the 84,000fl. received July 1735 for the new Leibregiment and certainly does not include money for the 4th bn for the Austrian rgt.

[57] HSAS, A6: Bü. 27, 20 July 1735; Bü. 28, 5 July 1735. The imperial commissariat disputed these figures. For the problems this caused the Württemberg commissariat see A6: Bü. 27, 10 and 26 Feb. 1734; Bü. 28, 22 Jan. 1734, 10, 12 and 19 Mar. 1734; Bü. 29, 11 and 14 Mar. 1734.

[58] HSAS, A6: Bü. 27–9, 50, 52; Tüchle, *Kirchenpolitik*, p. 117; Schnee, *Hoffinanz*, IV, pp. 131–2; Stern, *Jud Süss*, pp. 124–9. His Thurn und Taxis relations were instrumental in securing the DR.

man.[59] No sooner was this agreed than Carl Alexander wrote to the imperial ministers offering the services of his elite Garde du Corps cavalry unit. This was accepted by Prince Eugene on 30 January 1734 and the unit entered imperial pay on 1 May, three months after the three subsidy regiments.[60] Almost simultaneously he formed a third 2,300-man infantry regiment which entered imperial service from 1 July onwards.[61]

The duke was on the point of concluding yet another agreement to bring this fully into imperial pay when the armistice of 3 October 1735 prompted the emperor to halt negotiations.[62] Counting a fourth infantry regiment raised later in 1734, as well as hussars and artillery, which the duke had added to the forces still in Württemberg pay,[63] These measures had increased the number of regular soldiers in the duchy's army from just over 3,000 to over 11,100 by late 1735. Of these, 8,158 were directly serving the emperor, in addition to the others assisting his war effort at Württemberg expense and the 700 men raised for the duke's Austrian infantry regiment.[64]

This military buildup represented a considerable strain on Württemberg resources. That it was accomplished with so little conflict with the estates was due not only to the imperial subsidies, but also to the duke's ability to keep costs down, through manipulating the militia system and obtaining additional money from the Kreis. Thus, although the number of regular soldiers nearly quadrupled, the estates' contribution to the ducal Kriegskasse rose by little more than 5 per cent. While the estates did complain each time a new unit was raised, their complaints soon died down once the offending formation passed into imperial pay.[65] The very real threat of a French invasion also heightened their desire to co-operate. A similar desire existed in 1742–8 when they preferred to vote additional taxes to

---

[59] HSAS, A6: Bü. 51, 7 Dec. 1733; Bü. 55. The regiment in question, in 1914 numbered 17, was an Austrian unit and when the 700 recruits left the duchy in April 1734 they ceased to have any connection with the Württemberg forces. The existence of this treaty had been previously unknown. See Table 6.1.

[60] HSAS, A6: Bü. 8, 10 Feb. 1734; Bü. 25, 16 and 30 Jan. 1734. The value of the supplies for this unit provided in summer 1734 by the emperor was 18,674fl. 42.5xr. Its pay, totalling 20,776fl. for the same period, still had to be borne by Württemberg. L12: *Kriegsparticulare* 1734/35; L5: Tom. 142, fols. 656–7. The unit totalled 164 officers and men.

[61] HSAS, A6: Bü. 34, 18 May 1734; A202: Bü. 737, 16 Dec. 1737; L5: Tom. 142, fols. 186, 462b, 620b, 839, 856–91; Tom. 143, fol. 26b; L12: *Kriegsparticulare* 1734/35, fols. 56b, 59; Pfister, *Denkwürdigkeiten*, p. 142; Stadlinger, *Kriegswesens*. pp. 638–9. The new regiment was formed around a cadre of the Leibregiment and was later called Landprinz.

[62] As note 44.

[63] On the artillery, see S. von Weissenbach, *Geschichte der königlichen württembergischen Artillerie* (Stuttgart, 1882), p. 91. On the hussars see HSAS, L6.22.7.2, 25 June 1735; L5: Tom. 143, fols. 427–9b, 641b. The 4th IR was the General Remchingen rgt.

[64] Strengths calculated from HSAS, A6: Bü. 9, 27, 30, 34, 35, 68, 69; A30a: Bü. 57; C14: Bü. 330; L5: Tom. 141, 142, 143; L6.22.7.2; L12: *Kriegsparticulare*, 1732/3–1735/6. See also Table 6.1.

[65] HSAS, L5: Tom. 142, fols. 185–6, 334–570b, 1000–4; Tom. 143, fols. 15–16, 144–641; L6.22.7.2, 19 Oct. 1734; L12: *Kriegsparticulare* 1732/3–1735/6.

support the policy of armed neutrality rather than see the duchy engulfed in the War of the Austrian Succession. The absence of any visible threat, together with great divisions in the Reich, made the estates unwilling to co-operate when called upon by Carl Eugen to support his military buildup on the emperor's behalf during the Seven Years War. As we shall see, lack of co-operation from the estates was going to cause that duke serious problems in the 1760s.

By averting a conflict with the estates over the military budget, Carl Alexander managed to avoid some of the pitfalls of a subsidy treaty and fared considerably better than his neighbour, the elector of Bavaria. The latter's French subsidies proved wholly inadequate to cover the electorate's military expenditure. Moreover, dependence on subsidies from that source automatically made the elector an enemy of the emperor. Although no actual hostilities broke out, the elector felt it necessary to step up his military preparations in order to defend himself from eventual attack, thus causing expenditure and subsidy revenue to diverge still further. Bavaria ended up with even greater debts than before, no political gains and a large army which it could not hope to maintain in peacetime.[66]

This bleak prospect was also suddenly thrust before Carl Alexander when the peace preliminaries of 3 October 1735 heralded an end to both his subsidies and the willingness of the estates to co-operate. To make matters worse, not only were the hired regiments returned in the summer of 1736, thus ending payment of their upkeep by the emperor, but the emperor broke the 1733 treaty by stopping the annual subsidy as well.[67]

Carl Alexander was thus in a similar situation to that of his predecessor in 1697 and 1714, only this time the number of troops was roughly double. Unlike Eberhard Ludwig, Carl Alexander was not prepared to trade partial reductions for tax grants from the estates. Instead, he was determined to maintain the army at its wartime establishment through a combination of tax grants, new fiscal measures and military reforms.

DUCAL POLICY, 1736–7

Almost immediately after the conclusion of the peace preliminaries and in anticipation of the return of his troops, Carl Alexander convened a special deputation on 13 December 1735 to discuss the future maintenance of the army.[68] Up to now,

---

[66] Hartmann, *Geld*, pp. 161–221. According to figures in Hartmann, Bavarian military expenditure exceeded subsidy revenue by more than 200 per cent.

[67] HSAS, A7: Bü. 41, 9 Feb. 1736; A32; Bd. 157; A202: Bü. 1361. The duke realised as early as Feb. 1736 that the rgts would be returned.

[68] HSAS, A202: Bü. 2230. The members of the deputation were Maj. Gen. Baron von Remchingen, Privy Councillor, Prof. Bilfinger, Kriegsrat Vice Pres. von Holle, and Gen. Adj. von Laubsky. Kriegs Commissar Hofstetter was consulted on accounting matters, while Privy Councillor A. H. Baron von Schütz attended on at least one occasion.

discussion has focused on the duke's subsequent demand on New Year's Eve that the estates finance a 12,100-strong army and on the ensuing political conflict.[69] This overlooks both the revolutionary military reforms drawn up by the deputation and the fact that it was never intended that the funding should come solely from the estates. Instead, the ending of the imperial subsidies coincided with the start of the fiscal measures commonly associated with Süss, and it is in this context that their significance emerges. However, before turning to them, it is worth considering the work of the deputation.

This met between mid-December 1735 and mid-February 1736, and the reforms it drew up began to be implemented that summer. The key to these reforms was an adaptation of Eberhard Ludwig's secret reorganisation of the militia of 1730–3. Instead of being used only to mobilise the regiments on the outbreak of hostilities, the militia system was now altered to provide a constant flow of recruits to keep the units up to strength. Simultaneously, in order to save costs, over a third of the establishment was given leave on half-pay, appearing only for one month's annual exercise.[70]

The duchy was to be divided into military districts grouped around the three command points of the district's regiment. The men enrolled in each district were to go to the regiment of that district. This division appears to have prefaced a political reorganisation that the duke had entrusted to General Remchingen. Under this scheme, the duchy was to be divided into twelve provinces (*Obervogteien*), which were perhaps to be synonymous with the recruiting districts. Each provincial governor (*Obervogt*) was to have a staff officer attached. This officer was to act as something of a cross between a French intendant and a communist political commissar in overseeing all decisions affecting ducal interests and ensuring the loyalty of subordinate officials.[71]

Had they been fully implemented, these reforms would have created a new type of army divided into an active force of full-pays (*Gagirten*) and an active reserve of half-pays (*Halbgagirten*) constantly kept up to strength by a limited form of conscription. It would have replaced the previous small force of regulars recruited by voluntary enlistment and backed up by a loosely organised militia. The militia, as such, would have ceased to exist. Carl Alexander's system differed from his father's 'Transmutation' of 1691 in that it converted the militia organisation into a permanent recruitment system, rather than simply a one-off conversion of militia units to regular.

In fact, it bears a striking resemblance to the Kanton system introduced in

[69] Grube, *Landtag*, pp. 391–7; Carsten, *Princes and parliaments*, pp. 125–8. The draft of the demand to the estates is in HSAS, A28: Bü. 99.

[70] HSAS, A30a: Bü. 57, plan of 28 Dec. 1735; A202: Bü. 2230, 2278; L6.22.6.34; L6.22.7.3; L6.22.7.5a.

[71] Dizinger, *Beiträge*, I, pp. 51, 122–3; Stern, *Jud Süss*, p. 155. The exact details of this political reorganisation remain unclear.

Prussia in 1733 and copied in Hessen in 1762. However, there is no evidence to suggest that it was based on the Prussian model. The relations between Carl Alexander and Friedrich Wilhelm I were far from cordial and there is no mention of Prussian examples in either the deputation's documents or the actual decrees. Instead, Eberhard Ludwig's militia reorganisation and the wartime experience clearly provided the basis for a home-grown solution to the financial and recruitment difficulties associated with a small state's drive for a powerful military establishment. The militia element embodied in the system of half-pay reservists also probably owed something to the presence of Professor Bilfinger on the deputation. Bilfinger was an ardent advocate of a mixed system of regulars and militiamen which also found favour under the regency, but was ultimately to be rejected by Carl Eugen.[72]

Carl Alexander's reforms originally intended an army of 12,660 officers and men, but after decrees in November 1736 this was altered to 12,822.[73] Like Carl Eugen's military plan of 1763, this has been misinterpreted in the literature as an increase in overall strength.[74] In fact, the army had already reached roughly this size through the wartime increases. Nonetheless, this represented almost 3 per cent of the duchy's population. This was only slightly less than the ratio in contemporary Prussia, more than double that in the Habsburg empire and over three times that in Bavaria on the eve of the War of Austrian Succession (1740–8).[75]

The overall annual maintenance costs of the army and military installations were estimated at 760,000fl. This was over two-and-a-half times the cost of the army three years previously. If the inactive half-pays were also maintained at full rates, as they would have to be in wartime, these costs would approach one million florins.[76]

---

[72] HSAS, A202: Bü. 2230; L6.22.7.5a. Bilfinger's plans are in A202: Bü. 1993, 2244. See also pp. 79–81.

[73] HSAS, A30a: Bü. 57, plan of 28 Dec. 1735; L6.22.7.3, 5 and 14 Nov. 1736; A202: Bü. 2278, calculations of 29 Mar. 1737 referring to the organisation established the previous year. The army was to consist of 2,432 cavalry, 10,270 infantry, 120 artillery: a total of 12,822, of whom 8,102 would be with the colours and 4,720 would be on unpaid leave. In addition, there were to be garrison companies in the fortresses. The actual strength of the army was 7,862 in April 1737 not including the 186 garrison troops: A202: Bü. 1871.

[74] HSAS, A30a: Bü. 57, 28 Dec. 1735; A202: Bü. 2278, 29 Mar. 1737; Carsten, *Princes and parliaments*, p. 125. The figure of 12,100 cited in the literature as the army's strength was merely the guideline set down by the duke for the deputation to work on.

[75] Figures for Prussia, see Linnebach, *Deutsche Herresgeschichte*, p. 150; for Austria, HSAS, A74: Bü. 202, 16 Aug. 1785; for Bavaria, Staudinger, *Geschichte*, III, pp. 76–7.

[76] HSAS, A202: Bü. 2278. OKC Koch's estimate, 29 Mar. 1737. From calculations made on 19 Feb. 1736, the annual cost was 717,662fl. 4xr., or 986,412fl. if the half-pays received full rates. If the officers were granted horse rations these figures would rise by 30,747.5fl. All these calculations include the cost of the Kreistruppen, general staff, pensions, uniform issues, and other sundry expenditure as well as unit maintenance. They exclude the cost of a full set of equipment, horses and uniforms, estimated at well over half a million more. Although most of this equipment was already paid for and issued, additional costs would be incurred as the deputation considered a battery of twenty field guns a necessary requirement.

In the light of these costs, the members of the deputation were anxious to raise as much money as possible. They believed that it would be very difficult to obtain the necessary money on a permanent basis from the estates without consenting to a Landtag. However, they did believe it was possible to obtain it in the short term from the standing committee alone and that if individual complaints were dealt with, more money would be granted. The privy council doubted the feasibility of this. Councillor von Schütz thought 6,000 men the largest army possible and even if this could be doubled, it would still be too small to deter France and yet large enough to provoke the peace-loving Cardinal Fleury into hostile action. This was particularly dangerous considering that at that time the French still occupied Mömpelgard. The Rentkammer officials, also, doubted whether it was possible to increase revenue.[77]

Carl Alexander and a clique of senior officers were determined to ride roughshod over these pessimistic views of the civil bureaucrats. Vice President von Holle and General Adjutant von Laubsky were particularly hawkish in pressing for as much money as possible. The outspoken Remchingen was entirely against the idea of a Landtag. In reply to such a request from the estates' committee, he thundered: 'What do we want to do with a lot of peasants? The large committee can deal with the matter alone.'[78]

However, their tactics were far more subtle than this blustering would suggest. Carl Alexander stepped up the policy of his predecessor of undermining the social and political aspirations of the peasants through the Amtsversammlungen. In addition, the duke also tried to weaken the opposition at the top by winning over certain members of the estates committee. Through them, he was now informed of the committee's plans.[79]

The success of these tactics was seen in spring 1736. Having already consented in March to the grant of two Ordinari taxes and the Tricesimation for a trial period of three years, the committee was manoeuvred into agreeing to this for a virtually unlimited period on 31 May.[80] Thus, Carl Alexander was not only able to avoid the restrictions placed on his predecessor in his agreement with the estates in 1724, but also secured the continuation of the Tricesimation. In addition, the agreement was not bought with such heavy concessions as those made by Eberhard Ludwig. The few minor taxes which were abolished brought in little revenue in any case,

---

[77] HSAS, A202: Bü. 2230 deputation's protocol, 30 and 31 Dec. 1735; Dizinger, *Beiträge*, I, pp. 22–3.
[78] HSAS, L5: Tom. 144, fols. 287–97: 'Was man mit den Bauern tun wolle? Der größere ausschuß könne es allein verrichten.'
[79] Grube, 'Dorfgemeinde', 194–219. Vann, *Making of a state*, pp. 237–43; Grube, *Landtag*, p. 393. In particular, Prelate Weissensee of Hirsau and the committee's legal adviser Veit Jacob Neuffer were won over.
[80] HSAS, L5: Tom. 144, fols. 2–18, 64–340. The grant was limited solely by the proviso 'so lange die jedesmalige sich hervortunende mißliche Conjuncturen und Zeiten solchen erfordern und es dem Land abzuführen möglich'.

while the other complaints were merely to be considered without a promise of action.[81]

Nevertheless, this agreement only secured approximately 60 per cent of the funding required. The shortfall was now to be made good through a revision of the tax system and a range of new taxes. Meanwhile, the Rentkammer was to be made totally independent of subsidies from the estates by increasing its revenue through a series of fiscal measures devised by Süss.

The revision of the tax system has already been begun by Eberhard Ludwig. In June 1736 Hofkanzler Scheffer and Commerzienrat Böhm produced a scheme for replacing the existing taxes by an all-embracing property tax (*Schütz-Schirm und Vermögensteuer*).[82] This tax was said to be similar to one which had actually been introduced as an emergency measure in 1690–1 and had been intended to produce a revenue of 627,000fl. annually.[83] The process of softening up the Amtsversammlungen into acceptance was begun, but the duke died before this new tax could be implemented. His death also prevented the introduction of the range of lesser taxes intended to supplement it.[84]

In contrast, Süss's fiscal proposals were actually adopted. Prior to late 1735, Süss had only been involved in the not very successful attempt to generate revenue by exploiting the mint and in a few minor monopolies.[85] With the termination of the imperial subsidies, Süss became increasingly more active in promoting a series of measures designed to bolster ducal finances. These began in November 1735 with the introduction of price regulation through a state newspaper. This paved the way for tighter management of the ducal properties and economic interests in 1736. While the majority of the various new monopolistic enterprises failed or produced low returns, the better management of the Kammergut more than doubled the surpluses remitted by the Keller to the Rentkammer.[86]

Although an attempt to increase government borrowing power by controlling the assets of orphans through a new trust fund (*Pupillenkasse*) foundered on estates

---

[81] *Ibid.*, fols. 155, 180, 182, 248b, 303, 306, 327–8, 333b. The values of the abolished taxes (*Ludwigsburger Baugelder, Spazensgelder*), are given in Müller, 'Finanzwirtschaft' at pp. 302–3. On these taxes see also Chapter 5 note 19.

[82] HSAS, L5: Tom. 144, fols. 379–82; Stern, *Jud Süss*, pp. 87–8; Dizinger, *Beiträge*, I, pp. 34–5. On the earlier attempt at revision see p. 138.

[83] HSAS, L5: Tom. 144, fol. 527. According to Dizinger, *Beiträge*, II, pp. 111–15 the plan of 1736 intended that an annual surplus of 120,000fl. was to go to the Kriegskasse.

[84] These included a tax on servants, a tax paid by town dwellers in return for the army taking over civic guard duty, the confiscation of local tax revenue surpluses left over after public works expenditure, a new salt tax, a surcharge on food imports and exports, a flour excise, and a tax on cattle: HSAS, A202: Bü. 2278, 29 Mar. 1737; Dizinger, *Beiträge*, I, pp. 50–1.

[85] HSAS, A7: Bü. 42, No. 28; Schnee, *Hoffinanz*, IV, pp. 130–2; Stern, *Jud Süss*, pp. 75–6, 117–24; Müller, 'Finanzwirtschaft', pp. 291–2, 300.

[86] HSAS, A256: Bd. 218–22; Vann, *Making of a state*, pp. 228–32; Stern, *Jud Süss*, pp. 56–7, 70–82; Elwenspoek, *Jew Süss Oppenheimer*, pp. 76–82, 95–106; Schifferer, 'Entwicklung', 53–81; Schmäh, 'Ludwigsburger Manufakturen', 29–51.

opposition,[87] two other important measures were pushed through by September 1736. The first was the Gratialamt, established to control two new sources of revenue introduced after the example of other states – confirmation of appointment taxes and sale of offices. The first were a form of income tax paid by civil servants, while the second involved the creation of new local and central government posts and their sale to prospective applicants.[88] The second measure was the formation of the Fiscalamt from the existing Landesvisitation. The Fiscalamt extended its supervision to ordinary subjects and exploited it financially by basically extorting money in return for suspending criminal proceedings for tax evasion and other irregularities.[89]

While the actual revenue generated by these two new institutions has been greatly inflated by some accounts, they undoubtedly did contribute to the financial success of the Rentkammer under Carl Alexander.[90] They also represented a further attack on the social position of the worthies. The inquisitorial nature of the Fiscalamt curbed their misuse of public office for private gain, while the sale of new offices by Gratialamt created a new body of civil servants who owed eir appointments to ducal favour and not to the worthies' network of social ties. Naturally, the system created by these institutions was also open and subject to wid pread abuse. Their founder, Süss, particularly benefited from various fees, bribes a. cut of the profits.[91]

Compared with Eberhard Ludwig, Carl Alexander was considerably successul. Through his close ties with the emperor, and helped by the subsidies the emperor paid him, he had not only overcome the difficulties left him by Eberhard Ludwig, but had forced the estates into a corner. By the time of his death on 12 March 1737

---

[87] Dizinger, *Beiträge*, I, pp. 33–4; Schnee, *Hoffinanz*, IV, pp. 137–8; Elwenspoek, *Jew Süss Oppenheimer*, pp. 85–7; Stern, *Jud Süss*, pp. 91–3. Tüchle, *Kirchenpolitik*, p. 125 sees this as an important stage in the deteriorating relations between duke and estates.

[88] LBS, cod. hist. fol. 74, *Controls der Confiscations- und Gratialgelder*, 1736–7; Müller, 'Finanzwirtschaft', pp. 300, 306; Stern, *Jud Süss*, pp. 86–7, 94–8; Schnee, *Hoffinanz*, IV, pp. 135, 138–9.

[89] Stern, *Jud Süss*, pp. 99–104; Schnee, *Hoffinanz*, IV, pp. 139–40. On the Landesvisitation see p. 132.

[90] Elwenspoek, *Jew Süss Oppenheimer*, pp. 93–4 believes the total revenue from the Fiscalamt and Gratialamt was 650,000fl. while another source claims that 372,000fl. was raised in fines and Gnadengelder (Tüchle, *Kirchenpolitik*, p. 124, n. 2). In reality, the Fiscalamt brought in only 29,448fl. between 20 Sept. 1736 and 19 Feb. 1737, while the confirmation taxes also netted relatively low sums (Müller, 'Finanzwirtschaft', pp. 299–300, 306–7). The total money raised by the Gratialamt is difficult to assess as this was paid into the Chatoule. However, Stern, *Jud Süss*, pp. 286–8 quoted an undated document listing remittances to the Chatoule totalling 305,375fl. which appears to come from this source.

[91] While Stern, *Jud Süss* does her best to exonerate Süss from the charge of profiteering, it is clear that he did draw considerable benefit from the fiscal measures. At the time of his arrest in 1737, his property in Frankfurt was valued at 425,138fl. and that in Stuttgart around 85,000fl. while he personally claimed his total assets were worth 400,000fl. Schnee, *Hoffinanz*, IV, pp. 124, 132, 138–41, 282; Dizinger, *Beiträge*, I, p. 159; Pfaff, *Geschichte des Fürstenhauses*, IV, p. 194; G. Emberger, 'Verdruß, Sorg und Widerwärttigkeiten. Die Inventur und Verwaltung der Jud Süßischen Vermögen 1737–1772', *ZWLG*, 40 (1981), 369–75.

he showed signs that he was well on the way to consolidating his success through the introduction of new taxes and measures such as Gratialamt which were undermining the worthies' position.

However, though the imperial subsidies had covered most of the army's maintenance costs between 1733 and 1735, the emperor still owed large arrears, especially on the mobilisation costs. Carl Alexander had neither secured payment of these nor had he received any significant political concessions. More seriously, the duke's close relationship with the emperor threatened to degenerate easily into dependence, especially as there were clear limits to the duke's influence within the Kreis. Moreover, his ability to establish financial independence through his fiscal measures and army reform was by no means certain. While the Rentkammer overspending had been reversed, it was still weighed down by the legacy of Eberhard Ludwig's debts. Carl Alexander had been unable to persuade the estates to amortise these.[92] In the area of military finance, a switch in November 1736 from half-paid to unpaid reservists clearly indicates a shortage of ready cash. This appears to be confirmed by the decision to sell off all the cavalry privates' horses.[93]

As his death was followed by a disputed regency, continuation of his financial policies in any case became politically untenable. This compelled the regency to find a way to disband the army quickly. As the next chapter will show, the method chosen was to have potentially dangerous consequences for the next duke. Meanwhile, the estates seized the opportunity to make good the ground lost under Carl Alexander and, having learnt their lesson, to secure additional guarantees for the Reversalien.[94]

---

[92] HSAS, L5: Tom. 144, fols. 475b–479b, 517b; Grube, *Landtag*, pp. 394–6.
[93] HSAS, A6: Bü. 57, 13 Oct. 1736; A30a: Bü. 27, 19 Oct. 1736. Remchingen argued that most of the horses would soon go blind anyway.
[94] It is interesting to note that Hessen-Kassel also learnt from the Württemberg lesson and immediately sought outside guarantees for a similar agreement made in 1754 when the hereditary prince converted to Catholicism.

Table 6.1. *Auxiliaries raised for imperial service 1733–1735*

State	Infantry	Cavalry	Staff/ artillery	Total
Prussia	7,875	2,253	161	10,289
Württemberg	6,900	1,258	—	8,158
Denmark	4,027	2,024	144	6,195
Hanover	4,296	1,430	—	5,726
Sachsen-Gotha	4,000	1,000	—	5,000
Würzburg-Bamberg	4,600	—	—	4,600
Hessen-Kassel	3,280	—	—	3,280
Brunswick	3,000	—	—	3,000
Sachsen-Weimar	2,000	822	—	2,822
Mainz	2,300	—	—	2,300
Sachsen-Eisenach	2,000	—	—	2,000
Waldeck	1,600	—	—	1,600
Total	45,878	8,787	305	54,970

7

The regency, 1737–1744

THE STRUGGLE FOR POWER 1737–8

Carl Alexander's death was followed by a period of confusion as various groups jostled for power within the duchy. From this situation there emerged a compromise between the regency and the worthies who dominated the estates. This was brought about by the need of both to fight off threats to their positions and solve the politically sensitive question of troop reductions. In this compromise the regency government traded political protection to the worthies for their final recognition of the army's permanence and the estates' obligation to fund it. In many ways this represented the achievement of the aim of the dukes over the last forty years. However, as Carl Eugen was to find out after he achieved his majority in 1744, the framework of this compromise prevented any further expansion of ducal power in the manner attempted by Carl Alexander. In order to understand how this compromise came about and how it affected the duchy's political structure, we need to analyse the respective positions of the various groups in Württemberg in 1737.

Carl Eugen was a mere nine years old when his father died. According to the late duke's will, direction of affairs was entrusted to a tripartite junta of his Catholic wife, Maria Augusta, his friend and adviser Friedrich Carl von Schönborn (1674–1746), bishop of Bamberg and Würzburg and his uncle, Carl Rudolph von Württemberg-Neuenstadt.[1] This arrangement broke down immediately as the Protestant Carl Rudolph, supported by the privy council and the estates, refused to share power with his two designated colleagues. These in turn, supported by General Remchingen and certain sections of the army, sought to seize sole control for themselves.[2]

None of these factions was in a particularly strong position. Carl Rudolph was a seventy-year-old general who openly declared that affairs of state were too much for him, and was heavily dependent on advisers. Indeed, some even doubted his mental capacity and it was widely expected that he would die soon. He was thus in no position to pursue an independent policy as regent.[3]

---

[1] HSAS, L5: Tom. 145, fols. 132b–4b.
[2] On the disputed regency see *ibid.*, fols. 131–381; Dizinger, *Beiträge*, I, pp. 59–92.
[3] See the reports of the Würzburg resident Raab in Stark, 'Streitigkeiten', 1–28.

In the first few weeks following Carl Alexander's death this suited the members of the estates' committee very well. They were able to push through appointments to the privy council of men who were fully integrated in their own network of social ties.[4] At the same time, the outsiders brought in by Carl Alexander were dismissed and show trials began against a number of them in order to boost the new regime's popularity.[5] In the longer term, however, the committee realised that Carl Rudolph was also a liability, as in the event of his death the regency would fall to the Catholic party. This threatened to undo all their work in securing influence over the positions of central government. It was also particularly alarming at this point as the Reversalien were only loosely guaranteed by the Corpus Evangelicorum. Meanwhile, they also realised that their power was being undermined from below. The success of the policies of Eberhard Ludwig and Carl Alexander in encouraging the democratic aspirations of the peasants manifested itself at the Landtag which the committee had persuaded Carl Rudolph to open in July 1737. Here, some of the delegates, particularly those from the more outlying Ämter, challenged the committee's dominance of affairs. There were accusations of mismanagement, even of complicity in the crimes of the past regime. Committee member Prelate Weissensee was jostled in the street and a stone was thrown through his window. More seriously, the Landtag made use of a right not exercised for 183 years and refused to confirm the re-election of three committee members, including Weissensee.[6]

To stave off these threats, the committee needed to find a new figurehead to replace Carl Rudolph as regent. In a secret session in July they chose Carl Friedrich (1690–1761) of the Oels branch of the Württemberg ruling house. Although Carl Friedrich was a younger and more active man than Carl Rudolph, he also was not in a position to follow an independent policy when he took over in August 1738. As ruler of the small Protestant duchy of Oels marooned in the middle of Austrian Silesia, he always had to take account of the wishes of the emperor and also, after 1740, the king of Prussia. He was thus unlikely to want to involve the duchy in any ambitious foreign adventures that might affect the future of his own lands. In addition, his territories were heavily burdened with debt making him more likely to wish to remain on good terms with the committee in the hope of presents and 'gratifications'.[7]

For their part, the Catholic party was also in a weak position, although this was not at first apparent. Both Maria Augusta and Bishop Schönborn had good legal claims to the regency based on Carl Alexander's will and on a set of instructions,

4 Vann, *Making of a state*, pp. 245–6.
5 In addition to the literature on Süss, see Dizinger, *Beiträge*, I, pp. 95–166.
6 HSAS, L5: Tom. 145, fols. 149–52; Grube, *Landtag*, pp. 419–23; Vann, *Making of a state*, pp. 246–9.
7 On this branch of the family see H. Schukraft, 'Die Linie Württemberg-Oels', in Uhland (ed.), *900 Jahre Haus Württemnberg*, pp. 379–89. This arrangement was contrary to Carl Alexander's will which had expressly excluded the Oels branch from the regency.

drafted four days before his death, naming Maria Augusta as head of a civil government staffed with their supporters, and General Remchingen as director of military affairs.[8] In addition, both could expect support from the emperor on the basis of the traditionally close links of their families to the imperial crown.[9] However, the ground was pulled from under their feet when their opponents simply ignored Carl Alexander's will and established a government without them. As a ruler of another state, Bishop Schönborn could make no direct intervention in the duchy's affairs and until his claims as regent were recognised, he was forced to rely on the efforts of Maria Augusta. She was deeply unpopular within the duchy, which prevented her appealing to the Württembergers' loyalty to the ruling house. In fact, popular feeling was so strong that Carl Rudolph had to issue a proclamation forbidding disrespectful talk against her. In the face of such difficulties, Maria Augusta was not the person to force through her will. The Würzburg resident, Raab, complained to Schönborn of her cursoriness (*Fluchtigkeit*) and her inability to keep anything secret.[10] More critically, she was hopelessly in debt and so potentially open to agreement with the estates' committee if this tempted her with bags of gold.

In the week following Carl Alexander's death matters hung in the balance as to which party would gain the upper hand. All realised the importance of securing the support of the army, the future existence of which had now been placed in doubt. The Catholic party sought to win over the officer corps by accusing the estates' committee of wanting to realise their long-stated aim of disbanding the army. To counter this, Carl Rudolph persuaded the committee to declare publicly on 17 March 1737 to the 'well disposed military' that 'they would do all in their power' to maintain the army permanently.[11]

This managed to prevent the wholesale defection of the Protestant officers to General Remchingen, but left the actual question of how the army was to be funded unanswered. The estates' committee had no intention of permitting the regency government to continue the previous duke's fiscal policies as these directly threatened the power and influence of their friends among the worthies. Particularly, the planned property tax threatened to do away with the committee altogether by removing the prime reason for its existence, namely, to negotiate tax grants with the duke. In addition, the committee could hardly condone the new methods of recruitment. The enrolling was widely unpopular with the lower social groups and, given the new democratic movement in the Landtag, the committee had to take their demands seriously.

As Ober-Kriegs-Kommissar Koch reported: 'Because of these circumstances,

---

[8] Dizinger, *Beiträge*, I, pp. 56–7.
[9] Maria Augusta came from the Thurn und Taxis family.
[10] Raab to Bishop Schönborn, 23 and 26 Mar. 1737 in Stark, 'Streitigkeiten', 5–7.
[11] HSAS, L5: Tom. 145, fols. 137–9. This was the so-called *Versicherungs Urkund für das Militär*.

and because there is no hope of foreign subsidies, it is completely impossible for the country to maintain the army at its present establishment.' Accordingly, he proposed reducing costs by discharging about two-thirds of the privates.[12] However, it was realised that in view of the political situation, no complete units could be disbanded, and therefore the expensive officer corps and regimental staff would have to be maintained intact.[13] In any case, the duchy was bound by Carl Alexander's subsidy treaty, which still had four years to run, to maintain three regiments with the number of companies required by the imperial establishment.

It was thus considered 'desirable, if one or two regiments could be transferred to another service, in order to lighten the burdensome quartering, as well as to create some reserves in the Kriegskasse, so that one would always be able to mobilise the troops and provide them with all necessary equipment'.[14] Many high-ranking officers also favoured the transferring of regiments wholesale to other powers rather than have them disbanded. A disbandment threatened not only to deprive them of their source of income, but to destroy the investment in uniforms and equipment made by the more senior ones.[15] The transfers were welcomed by the civil bureaucracy which saw them as an opportunity 'to get rid of all those officers who arouse suspicion as well as the Catholic privates'.[16]

Although this solution was immediately adopted, it took time for such transfers to be negotiated and they also did not cover the entire army. The pressing problem of how this was to be paid for in the meantime still remained. Carl Rudolph's answer to this was to ask the Landtag to confirm the agreement of 31 May 1736 whereby the estates were to pay two Extraordinari ordinari taxes and the Tricesimation each year to the Kriegskasse. He also took up the late duke's demands that they take over Eberhard Ludwig's Rentkammer debts as well as to pay additional sums to build barracks and fortresses.[17] These demands were also pressed by Carl Friedrich, showing a strong continuity in policy between the regency government and that of Carl Alexander. Further, while the regent agreed that the regular army had to be reduced, he called for the creation of a strong militia not only in wartime, but in peace as well. Although this demand owed much to the influence of Privy Councillor Georg Bernhard Bilfinger whose

---

12 HSAS, A202: Bü. 2278, 29 Mar. 1737.

13 The exception to this was the hussar squadron which was completely disbanded in June 1737. This unit was unpopular with the civilian population, contained only a few officers and about half the rank and file voluntarily requested a discharge: HSAS, A202: Bü. 1871; Bü. 2248, 22 Apr. 1737; Bü. 2264, 27 Apr. and 28 June 1737.

14 HSAS, A202: Bü. 2278, 29 Mar. 1737.

15 Both Colonel Graf von Gross (commander of DR Prinz Louis) and Lt Col. von Spitznas (acting commander of IR Remchingen) requested such a move: HSAS, A202: Bü. 2265, 17 Aug. 1737; Bü. 2109, 8 Oct. 1737.

16 HSAS, A202: Bü. 2278, 29 Mar. 1737. This anonymous proposal bears a striking resemblance to the plans known to have been prepared by Privy Councillor Bilfinger.

17 HSAS, L5: Tom. 145, fols. 365b–73, ducal proposition of 4 July 1737.

pet project it was, it was also a demand that had been pressed by Eberhard Ludwig.[18]

The new political circumstances in Württemberg meant that the estates could not oppose these demands when they came from the regency with the same force used when they had come from the past two dukes. Although many of the provincial delegates still called for the complete disbandment of the army, the standing committee thought otherwise. In November 1737 they had scored a considerable success when they managed to settle the dispute over the regency by reaching agreement with Maria Augusta. Frustrated by the lack of support from Würzburg and Vienna and demoralised by the arrest of Remchingen, the dowager duchess had gone behind Raab's back and negotiated secretly with the committee. In return for the largely nominal title of co-regent and control over her sons' education, she relinquished her claims to direct state affairs.[19] The committee then played its part by subsequently taking over 120,000fl. of her debts. Smaller presents were made to the regent.[20]

While this removed the threat of a Catholic regency, the committee's position was still far from secure. The decisive moment came in March 1739. Until then business had dragged on with the usual interminable discussions of long lists of grievances which characterise the history of Württemberg Landtags. To try and bring matters to a conclusion, Carl Friedrich called another plenary session during which the threats to the committee's position became abundantly clear. Not only were three of its members voted off by a popular move from the floor, but by chance a plot was discovered for a military coup to seize power in favour of Maria Augusta. This was particularly worrying as it not only named which members of the estates and civil bureaucracy could be won over, but also highlighted what might happen if the officer corps was not appeased.[21]

THE COMPROMISE OF 1739

In return for confirmation of their dominant position within the estates, the committee now forced through the approval of the regency's main demands.[22] The

---

[18] HSAS, A6: Bü. 44; A28: Bü. 99; L6.22.6.34; L6.22.7.5a.
[19] Reports of Raab to Schörnborn: Stark, 'Streitigkeiten', 21–5; Dizinger, *Beiträge*, I, pp. 87–8.
[20] The estates took over 80,000fl. in 1740 followed by another 40,000fl. four years later. It is significant that repayment of these debts took precedence over some of the Rentkammer debts. In addition she received an annual salary of 31,000fl. from the ducal Landschreiberei and 5,000fl. from the Kirchenkasten. Friedrich Carl received a gift of 4,000fl. in Oct. 1737 followed by 5,000 in Apr. 1738 together with an annual salary as regent of 36,000fl.: HSAS, A256: Bd. 222–9; A282: Bd. 1472x–79x; L5: Tom. 145, fol. 592; Tom. 146, fol. 331; Tom. 148, fols. 84b–90; Tom. 152; L10, Rechnungsjahre 1736/7–1743/4.
[21] The planned coup is detailed in HSAS, L5: Tom. 146, fols. 193b–6b, 354b–85b.
[22] The Landtag recess of 18 Apr. 1739 is printed in Reyscher, *Gesetze*, II, Nos. 517–36. It is significant that the agreement of 31 May 1736 was not expressly revoked.

only important alteration was that the money from the tax grant of May 1736 was no longer to go solely to the Kriegskasse, but also to help amortise the Rentkammer debts. In addition, although the Tricesimation was formally abolished, it was replaced by a 'surrogate' of equal value. This, together with the two Ordinari, was worth 460,000fl. annually of which around 90,000fl. was to be deducted for debt repayment. This left a guaranteed military budget of approximately the same level as that under Eberhard Ludwig. Unlike the 1724 agreement which had been only a temporary grant, with the implication that the army might then be disbanded, that of 1739 recognised that the soldiers were here to stay. Moreover, not only did the estates acknowledge this on paper, but also in bricks and mortar. Between 1739 and 1747 they paid out over 220,000fl. for barracks construction in addition to the annual grants.[23] To help mollify the popular movement within the estates, the enrolling was stopped and a whole range of traditional complaints about labour services, hunting excesses and the behaviour of ducal officials were settled.

The committee's position was now assured in that it had to meet every six months to determine the exact tax burden of each Amt and to supervise the debt repayment. There was no need to call a further Landtag as long as the government remained happy with the size of the tax grant. As Grube points out, there had been no Landtag between 1700 and 1736 as the committee had been unable to persuade the duke to hold one. Now there was to be none for a long time after 1739 as the committee feared it as a limitation on its power.[24]

This compromise between the regency and the committee was further consolidated over the next few years. By now the privy council was fully in the hands of men of the same background as those in the committee. Together they co-operated to counter the threat to the continued dominance of the worthies perceived in the pietist movement by passing legislation that rendered this politically harmless. To prevent this favourable situation being reversed in the future, the committee also pressed for further guarantees for the Reversalien. This would not only help to fend off attacks on their network of social ties by compelling all future ducal officials to at least be Lutherans, but, through the confirmation of the 1660 Kanzleiordnung contained in the Reversalien, it would also guarantee the position of their friends in the privy council as head of the civil bureaucracy. Having already secured the regent's confirmation of the Reversalien in the 1739 recess, guarantees were then obtained from Denmark (1741), England (1743), Prussia (1744) and the emperor (1742).[25] This was of crucial importance as it now gave these powers a legal right to intervene in Württemberg internal affairs. As the next chapter will show, this was to prove decisive in the reign of Carl Eugen.

---

[23] HSAS, L6.22.7.28. The total sum was 220,229fl. 44.5xr. plus 37,300fl. 3xr. from the commissariat and 400fl. from the Ludwigsburger *Kasernenverwaltung*.

[24] Grube, *Landtag*, p. 426.

[25] Fulbrook, *Piety and politics*, pp. 130–52; Vann, *Making of a state*, pp. 250–4; Haug-Moritz, *Württembergischer Ständekonflikt*, pp. 190–7, 205–14.

THE TROOP TRANSFERS, 1737–40

If this internal political compromise had serious consequences for the next reign, those of the troop transfers were no less important. These transfers began early in the regency. A few weeks before Carl Alexander's death, two battalions, one each from the Prinz Friedrich and Kreis infantry regiments, were sent to garrison the imperial fortresses of Philippsburg and Kehl respectively.[26] Then, on 25 March, the emperor asked for two more infantry regiments on the basis of the 1733 subsidy treaty to garrison Freiburg and Alt-Breisach in the Breisgau. He also declared himself interested in negotiating the transfer of one or two additional regiments permanently into his service.[27]

The reason behind this new interest was the emperor's war with the Turks which had begun with high hopes in 1736 and was now going disastrously wrong.[28] This created a need for fresh troops to replace those that were dying by the score on the unhealthy Hungarian battlefields. This new demand came to the rescue of all those states which, like Württemberg, had raised large forces to support the emperor in 1733 only to find themselves lumbered with their expensive upkeep at the end of the Polish War of Succession. In his desperate search for troops, the emperor even helped the Bavarian elector out of his financial crisis by hiring a large part of the army the French had paid to be raised against him four years before.[29]

The regent immediately seized upon the emperor's offer as the ideal solution to the politically sensitive problem of the army's future. Within a month of the emperor's letter, the Leib and Landprinz infantry regiments were despatched to the two Breisgau fortresses where they remained until 1740. Simultaneously, negotiations were started in Vienna to transfer other units complete to the Austrian army. As early as September an agreement was signed to transfer dragoon regiment Prinz Louis, followed a month later by a second convention covering the Remchingen regiment.[30]

However, in its eagerness to find a way out of its financial problems without antagonising the officers, the regency government had rushed headlong into these

[26] HSAS, A202: Bü. 2111, 29 Sept. 1736, 7 Feb. 1737. The fortresses were handed back by the French in Feb. 1737. Initially one bn of Landprinz had been sent to Kehl but this was replaced within a few months by the Kreis bn.

[27] *Ibid.*, Emperor Charles VI to Carl Rudolph and Maria Augusta, 25 Mar. 1737.

[28] On this conflict see L. Cassels, *The struggle for the Ottoman empire, 1717–1740* (London, 1966); K. A. Roider, Jr, *The reluctant ally. Austria's policy in the Austro-Turkish war, 1737–1739* (Baton Rouge, 1972).

[29] Staudinger, *Geschichte*, III, pp. 434–532; H. Helmes, 'Das Regiment Würzburg im Türkenkriege des Jahres 1739', *DBKH*, 13 (1904), 60–93; O. Schuster and F. A. Francke, *Geschichte der sächsischen Armee von deren Errichtung bis auf die neueste Zeit* (Leipzig, 1885), I, pp. 220–5; Roider, *Relucatnt Ally*, pp. 22–3.

[30] HSAS, A202: Bü. 111. The convention for the DR is in A202: Bü. 2265, 16 Sept. 1737, while details of the transfer of IR Remchingen are in A202: Bü. 2109 and papers in the private collection of Dr Hans Bleckwenn, Münster.

agreements without really appreciating the consequences. The emperor already owed large sums of money on the agreement of 1733 as he had stopped paying the annual subsidy when he returned the regiments in 1736. He had also failed to pay a four-month pay bonus promised when the units were handed back and still owed considerable pay arrears to the regiments themselves. There was now the danger that these arrears would be compounded by additional ones if the emperor failed to honour the new conventions. In fact, there was every indication that he would do just that as the added strain of the Turkish war immediately following that of the Polish succession had stretched his resources to breaking-point.[31] If this happened, the regency ran the risk of having large numbers of mutinous soldiery on its hands and even larger debts to pay.

These fears were realised when the two regiments were hired to garrison the two Breisgau fortresses. The Leibregiment had already mutinied rather than go to Alt-Breisach without first receiving its pay arrears. Only after both the imperial and Württemberg commissars promised payment did it finally depart.[32] However, on arrival matters proved otherwise. Neither it nor the Landprinz regiment, which was also owed large arrears, received full pay for the current service. The regent was soon bombarded with desperate pleas from the officers while the NCOs were even reduced to selling the braid from their uniforms in order to survive.[33] To make matters worse, the narrow-minded imperial commandants of the two fortresses refused to permit freedom of worship to the largely Protestant soldiers, as in its haste to hire out the units, the regency had failed to write this into the convention.[34]

However, despite these problems, the regency was forced to accept the emperor's terms. Whereas Carl Alexander had been in a relatively strong position in 1733 and able to demand favourable terms, the regency was not so fortunate. Although it did press the emperor to pay the money he owed and even managed to secure a promise to this effect in the convention of September 1737, it was in no position to implement sanctions if he failed to do this. The units could not be disbanded for fear of antagonising the officer corps, but neither could they be maintained by the Württemberg Kriegskasse, as the continuation of Carl Alexander's financial policies was politically untenable. Therefore, the regency was in no position to put leverage on the Austrians by threatening to withdraw any regiments hired or withhold those about to be transferred.

This point is graphically illustrated with reference to the two battalions in

---

[31] On Austrian finances at this point see Roider, *Reluctant ally*, pp. 12–17. On the money owed to Württemberg see the preceding chapter.

[32] Raab to Schönborn, 27 Apr. 1737: Stark, 'Streitigkeiten', pp. 11–12. No Württemberg records of this mutiny appear to have survived, but Raab's report is corroborated by details of court martials and sentences of execution on mutineers in HSAS, A202: Bü. 2111, 16 and 28 June 1737.

[33] HSAS, A202: Bü. 2110–12; Bü. 2256, esp. 4 Aug. 1738.

[34] HSAS, A202: Bü. 2111–12; Bü. 2254, 22 May 1737; von Kolb, 'Feldprediger in Altwürttemberg', *BWKG*, 9 (1905), 70–85, 97–124 at pp. 99–108.

Philippsburg and Kehl. These two fortresses were Reichsfestungen rather than Austrian installations, and as such payment for their upkeep and for their garrisons was the responsibility of the Reichstag to decide.[35] This had never fully made a decision, as the majority of German princes had little desire to pay for two forts miles from their own territories. Thus, it had fallen to the two nearest and also best functioning imperial circles, Swabia and Franconia, each to provide garrison for the fort that lay in its immediate vicinity: respectively Kehl and Philippsburg. Carl Alexander had been well aware of these problems, and before sending his battalions, he obtained an imperial assurance that he could retain his Römer Monat payments if the Reichstag failed to come up with a final solution.[36] In addition, as senior Reichs-Feld-Marschall and *Oberinspektor* of both fortresses, he was in a position at least to put pressure on Swabia and Franconia to pay for his 'German patriotism' in providing the garrisons. Unfortunately, Carl Alexander was now dead and despite Carl Rudolph's attempts with Prussian support to secure the Oberinspektion, the emperor had given this to his son-in-law, the grand duke of Tuscany. Furthermore, in the light of the Turkish war, he also insisted Württemberg pay its Römer Monate.[37]

Carl Rudolph accordingly threatened to pull out the two battalions by 1 November 1737 unless he was paid. However, this ultimatum was fraught with risks. As the privy council pointed out, by 'an all-too-quick withdrawal of these battalions, the whole business could grind to a halt and easily lead to no indemnification being paid at all'.[38] The regent was forced to extend the deadline and make interim payments himself to maintain the troops.[39] When further negotiations brought no result, Carl Rudolph was forced to make good his ultimatum and ordered the units to leave the forts. Although the Kreis battalion in Kehl managed to leave, the imperial commandant at Philippsburg refused to let the other one out. Carl Rudolph protested that 'this battalion is not in imperial service, but in mine, and is not to take orders from anyone other than myself'.[40] He even threatened to disband it altogether. However, each time a letter from the emperor arrived ordering it to remain where it was and he had no choice but to extend the deadline a further three times. Finally, it was decided the only way out was to sell the entire Prinz Friedrich regiment outright to the Austrians and have done with the whole business.[41]

Unfortunately, this was not an entirely trouble-free solution either. Not only did

---

[35] See Chapter 5, note 100.   [36] HSAS, A202: Bü. 2111, 7 Feb. 1737.
[37] HSAS, A202: Bü. 2111–12.
[38] HSAS, A202: Bü. 2111, 9 Sept. 1737, 24 Oct. 1737.
[39] For details of these payments see A202: Bü. 2111, 4 Oct., 11 Nov., 13 Dec. 1737; A202; Bü. 2196, 17 Mar., 22 Sept. 1738.
[40] HSAS, A202: Bü. 2112, Regent Carl Rudolph to Col. von Kästner, 3 Feb. 1738. This episode is missing in Nopp's history of Philippsburg.
[41] Details on the transfer of IR Prinz Friedrich are in HSAS, A202: Bü. 2255; L6.22.7.3.

it still not provide a guarantee that the emperor would pay what he owed, it also brought an added obligation for Württemberg. None of the army's regiments was currently at a strength acceptable to the emperor as many of the native rank and file had been discharged while some of the foreigners had already been transferred to Austrian service.[42] All three units transferred between 1737 and 1739 therefore had to be brought up to strength by a mixture of new recruits and drafts from other formations.

The former method was slow and expensive, while the latter was also not without its problems. This was discovered in October 1737. The authorities tried to draft the Carabiniers squadron into the Kürassier regiment, which had been weakened through having to transfer men to bring the Prinz Louis dragoons up to the imperial establishment. The Carabiniers flatly refused to join the Kürassiers, claiming that they were all former NCOs of Austrian and other armies who had been made life members of their units, where they enjoyed a higher rate of pay. In fact of this opposition, the regency had to back down and merely ordered the sale of the Carabiniers' horses to the dragoons.[43] A month later the de Witt company of the Remchingen regiment went even further and mutinied rather than be split up and drafted into other units. This time the government took stronger action and completely disbanded the formation.[44] The fact that the men drawn out of the Leib and Landprinz regiments to bring Prinz Friedrich up to strength were sent under heavy escort also seems to indicate that they were unwilling to be drafted.[45]

Despite these problems, the Prinz Louis dragoons were actually transferred in late November 1737, followed by the Remchingen regiment in April and finally by Prinz Friedrich in March 1739.[46] The net result of the transfers was a poor reward for the effort involved. Despite repeated promises, the emperor never made good his obligation to pay the subsidy arrears. The three regiments were transferred for little new payment for men and equipment, while the emperor still owed large sums for their original mobilisation costs. Not only did the duchy lose out financially, but the emperor cheated on his promise to keep the units together. Instead, on their arrival in Hungary, each was disbanded and both officers and men were forcibly

---

[42] Some foreign rank and file had been transferred to the Austrian rgt of the duke of Lorraine in August 1737 (HSAS, A202: Bü. 2298, 5 and 8 Aug.). On 31 Aug. 1737 the decision had been taken to disband the Remchingen rgt and orders had already been issued for this to be carried out before negotiations with the Austrians caused this to be countermanded (A202: Bü. 1871, 2109).

[43] Raab to Schönborn, 22 Oct. 1737: Stark, 'Streitigkeiten', pp. 20–1. See also HSAS, A202: Bü. 2265, 7 and 9 Oct. 1737. The Carabiniers squadron was the former Garde du Corps. Although then 'attached' to the KR 1737–9 it became an independent unit again titled Garde du Corps by order 22 May 1739: A202: Bü. 2263.

[44] HSAS, A202: Bü. 2265, 12 and 15 Nov. 1737; Bü. 2296, 13 Nov. 1737. The company had protested it was 'eine gantzer und geschloßene' unit.

[45] HSAS, A202: Bü. 2255, 10 Mar. 1739.

[46] The nominal strengths of these units upon transfer was respectively: 1,054, 1,600 and 2,300 officers and men. Prinz Friedrich, however, was considerably below its intended establishment.

impressed into existing Austrian formations. Although many officers undoubtedly lost out when their companies were dissolved, most appear to have been content to accept the move in the light of the better promotion prospects presented by Austrian service. It was a different matter for the two colonels-in-chief from the ducal house. As the younger brothers of Carl Eugen, the two princes Ludwig Eugen (Louis dragoons) and Friedrich Eugen (Prinz Friedrich) had been intended for military careers by their father. As commanders of regiments in Austrian service they could expect to rise in due course to general's rank with an income and influence considered appropriate to their noble birth. Now the dissolution of their units appeared to have ruined this rosy future.[47]

The picture with the hired units was not much brighter. The cost of the Kehl and Philippsburg garrisons ran to over 90,000fl. while, by September 1740, the two regiments in Freiburg and Alt-Breisach had arrears of over 140,000fl.[48] The best that Württemberg could achieve was to obtain imperial consent to withhold that year's payment of Römer Monate which amounted to somewhat less than half the total owed.[49]

Although the transfers of 1737–9 reduced the Haustruppen by half, the remainder was still too expensive to be maintained by Württemberg alone. This was realised in August 1740 when the emperor announced his intention to return the two regiments hired to garrison Freiburg and Alt-Breisach.[50] The only solution seemed to be yet another transfer.

On 22 August 1740 the regent wrote to the Württemberg representative in Vienna, Christian Dietrich Keller, instructing him to negotiate the transfer of either one or both these regiments to the Austrians 'or other powers not objectionable to his majesty the emperor'. This time the regent was determined to use the transfer as a means of gaining other advantages and Keller was told to use it to secure payment of the subsidy arrears and Austrian colonelcies for the Württemberg princes. The Austrians were also to be reminded of their obligations under the 1733 treaty which still had one year to run.[51]

Keller's reply was not hopeful. Austrian finances had been ruined by the Turkish war which had now ended with a considerable loss of territory. The Dutch were also not in a position to hire troops, while the English already had agreements with Hessen-Kassel and Denmark. Although the Prussians showed an interest,

[47] HSAS, A202: Bü. 2255, 30 May, 15 June, 8 Oct. 1739; Bü. 2265, 8 Oct. 1739. This problem did not arise in the case of the Remchingen rgt as its commander had now been dishonourably discharged from the Württemberg army.

[48] HSAS, A202: Bü. 2112, 28 Apr. 1740 (94,451fl. 26xr. 4h.); L5: Tom. 152, fols. 305–6b (144,780fl. 48xr.).

[49] HSAS, L5: Tom. 152, fols. 38–9 (69,314fl. 53xr.).

[50] Hofkriegsrat, Vienna to GFZM and Commandant Baron von Rodt, 13 Aug. 1740 (copy), HSAS, A202: Bü. 2110.

[51] Friedrich Carl to Keller, 22 Aug. 1740, HSAS, A74: Bü. 127.

Keller believed it was desirable if the duchy could find some way of maintaining the troops itself in view of the worsening political situation.[52] On 13 September Friedrich Carl replied in terms that clearly sum up the attitude consistently held by the regency:

How useful and necessary it would be for the constitution of this ducal house if an establishment of regular troops could be maintained, if only the complete exhaustion of the treasury, the almost general poverty of the country and the lack of foreign subsidies did not place pure impossibility in the path of this beneficial intention.[53]

THE DRIFT TOWARDS PRUSSIA, 1740–4

Accordingly, Keller continued negotiations with the Prussians. Unknown to him, they were planning something rather different. On 16 December, barely two months after the death of emperor Charles VI, their army invaded Silesia and so began the War of the Austrian Succession. At a stroke, the king of Prussia, far from being a 'power not objectionable to his majesty', had become the enemy of his daughter and heir. In addition, as the Prussian forces rapidly overran Silesia they also surrounded the regent's duchy of Oels.

The Württemberg regime was in a cleft stick. On the one hand it was still in alliance with Austria through Carl Alexander's subsidy treaty, while on the other it had now gone too far in the negotiations with Prussia to pull out. Indeed, it was now virtually impossible to pull out without unpleasant repercussions in Oels. To make matters worse, the French now sided with the Bavarian elector and despatched a large army to make good his claim to the Habsburg territories. With this new Franco-Bavarian alliance, not only were Württemberg's left Rhenish principalities again under threat, but the French would have to march through the duchy itself in order to co-operate with the Bavarians. Had the duchy had the army of Carl Alexander, which had been considerably larger than that of Bavaria in 1740, it might have been able to take up a stronger stance.[54] However, the inability to maintain that army from its own resources had led to Keller's fears being realised and the duchy left almost without troops.

If all this was not bad enough, worse came in January 1741 when Keller reported the terms of the draft convention with the Prussians. The Württemberg negotiators had completely overstepped the mark and not only agreed to hand over the Landprinz regiment, but promised an additional 2,000 recruits and the prospect of

---

[52] Keller to Friedrich Carl, 3 Sept. 1740, HSAS, A74: Bü. 127. Reichsvizekanzler Rudolph Graf Colloredo told the regent on 3 Oct. 1739 that the war had cost 50 million fl.: A202: Bü. 1159.

[53] Friedrich Carl to Keller, 13 Sept. 1740, HSAS, A202: Bü. 1159.

[54] According to Staudinger, *Geschichte*, III, pp. 76–7, the Bavarian army totalled only 7,893 effectives (excl. artillery) in 1740, or only 60 per cent the size of the Württemberg force four years earlier.

having the former Kürassier regiment as well.[55] In vain the regent hurriedly despatched Kriegsrat President von Holle to Berlin to try and repair the damage.[56] With the Prussian rout of the Austrians at Mollwitz (10 April) followed by the Franco-Bavarian invasion of Upper Austria (September), Württemberg was sucked into the slipstream of events. Barely two weeks after Mollwitz, the Landprinz regiment was handed over to the Prussian Brigade-Major von Kalnein.[57]

Friedrich II of Prussia fully exploited the situation. To bind Württemberg further to his system, he offered a 100,000tlr. loan from his full war treasury in the convention of January 1741. Then, by delaying payment, he put pressure on the duchy that proved decisive in the decision to go ahead with the handover of the second regiment in April 1742.[58] Friedrich also used his new-found leverage on Württemberg to mediate a neutrality convention (9 October 1741) between Swabia and France which allowed the latter's troops unhindered passage to Bavaria.[59] On the grounds that the regiments supplied to him suffered from heavy desertion, he then compelled the duchy to consent to a deserter exchange cartel (12 January 1742).[60] Württemberg stood to gain little by this as desertion from its army to the Prussian forces was virtually non-existent. On the other hand Prussia now had grounds to send officers regularly to Württemberg to hunt for deserters from its army. These missions provided an excellent basis for authorised recruiting which Prussia had consistently tried to establish in Swabia over the previous forty years and which Württemberg had equally consistently sought to prevent.[61] This was also politically dangerous as the Austrians claimed the right to recruit as well. It was now difficult to refuse them once the Prussians had got themselves established, without totally dropping the mask of neutrality. Accordingly, Austrian recruiting also had to be tolerated.[62] This not only seriously curtailed Württemberg's right to control

---

[55] HSAS, A202: Bü. 2113, Convention of 10 Jan. 1741. At about the turn of 1740/1 the KR Maria Augusta was converted to a DR. The original motive for the conversion was that after the transfer of DR Prinz Louis in 1737, an appropriate cavalry rgt no longer existed to fulfil the duchy's obligations under the 1733 treaty with Austria.

[56] On Holle's mission see HSAS, A202: Bü. 2113.

[57] IR Landprinz was transferred at a strength of 1,600 officers and men and became Prussian Fusilier rgt No. 41. It was disbanded in 1806. On the transfer see HSAS, A202: Bü. 2254; Anon., *Vollständige Geschichte aller königlichen preußischen Regimenter . . .* , vol. I, *Geschichte und Nachrichten von dem . . . Fuselier Regimente von Lossow . . .* (Halle, 1767; reprint Osnabrück, 1979).

[58] The DR (600 strong) became Prussian DR No. 12 and was disbanded in 1806. On its transfer see HSAS, A202: Bü. 1208, 2113–14.

[59] It is significant that this convention was negotiated by Brigade-Major von Kalnein.

[60] On the cartel of 1742 see HSAS, A202: Bü. 1207; C14: Bü. 597. On the hunting of deserters 1742–3 see also A202: Bü. 2114, 2254. Another reason why Prussian recruiting was permitted was Keller's rash promise in 1741 of 2,000 recruits. For a time, Prussian recruiting officers were even allowed to use the Hohen Neuffen fortress as a secure depot for their recruits, though from mid-1743 attempts were made to restrict this and most official recruiting appears to have stopped.

[61] HSAS, A5: Bü. 64; A6: Bü. 54; A202: Bü. 1210, 2114, 2254; C14: Bü. 597. See also pp. 141–2 below.

[62] HSAS, A202: Bü. 1161; C14: Bü. 586a.

such matters, but made maintenance of neutrality extremely precarious especially when rival recruiting parties came to blows.

Finally, Württemberg subjugation was completed by the despatch, in December 1741, of Carl Eugen and his two brothers to Berlin, ostensibly for their education and safety. While both the privy council and Maria Augusta saw advantages in this move, it is difficult to see them as anything other than as hostages for Württemberg's continued pro-Prussian path.[63] To tie the duchy still further to Prussia, the boys were given colonelcies in Prussian regiments, while even their mother remained honorary colonel of the cavalry regiment now in Prussian service.[64] In order to secure additional political advantage, Friedrich fell in with Maria Augusta's plan to marry Carl Eugen to Princess Frederike von Bayreuth. This was supported by the privy council and the estates in the belief that a marriage to a Protestant would be a way of restricting Catholic influence. However, it also strengthened the Prussian hold over Württemberg, as Frederike was Friedrich's niece.[65]

Indeed, Friedrich held all the cards. Intrigues among the princes' entourage had succeeded in making them so miserable that they openly declared they wanted to go home. However, Friedrich refused to let them leave until Württemberg renewed a treaty of 1716 signed between Eberhard Ludwig and Friedrich's father. In 1716 Prussia had been 'a power not objectionable to his majesty' and Eberhard Ludwig had seen it as a good opportunity to secure further support for his political objectives. The circumstances now were entirely different. Although all the Württemberg advisers believed the duchy's best ally was Austria and that they stood to lose more than they could gain from a treaty with Prussia, they saw no alternative but to sign. The treaty was phrased so as not to openly contradict Württemberg neutrality. However, secret articles not only forbade the duchy from entering into any agreements with Austria, but also obliged it to supply further recruits for Prussia, thus making the continuation of that neutrality very difficult.[66]

---

[63] On the princes' stay in Berlin see: Boepple, *Verhältnis zu Württemberg*, pp. 11–30; R. Béringuier, *Der Besuch der württembergischen Prinzen zur Zeit Königs Friedrich des Grossen in Berlin und ihre Beziehungen zum preussischen Königshause* (Berlin, 1879); Dizinger, *Beiträge*, II, pp. 53–108, 128–38. None of these works mention the Prussian loan of 100,000tlr. nor realise the significance of the troop transfers.

[64] Ludwig Eugen was given Prussian DR No. 2 (8 Sept. 1742) while his brother Carl Eugen received the new IR No. 46 (8 Apr. 1743). On 8 July 1749 the DR of Maria Augusta was transferred to the third brother, Friedrich Eugen. As the Austrians belatedly conferred the former Austrian DR of Carl Alexander on Carl Eugen in 1741, the young duke enjoyed the dubious distinction of simultaneously being colonel-in-chief of regiments on opposing sides in the Second Silesian War, 1744–5.

[65] Frederike was the daughter of Friedrich's favourite sister Wilhelmine and Margrave Friedrich von Bayreuth. Maria Augusta had even originally intended to marry her son to Friedrich's other sister Anna Amelie.

[66] A202: Bü. 1206, treaties 18 Dec. 1716 and 31 Jan. 1744, and protocol 20 Jan. 1744. The treaty of 1744 obliged Württemberg to provide 1,200 recruits in three batches over three years and to allow the two transferred regiments to recruit in the duchy. Boepple's rather lightweight work completely passes over the existence of these treaties. On Eberhard Ludwig's agreements with Prussia, see pp. 141–2.

All Württemberg secured was a vague Prussian promise to co-operate with Bavaria in inducing France to settle over Mömpelgard.

In order not to lose face through the public believing the princes were fleeing from intolerable conditions at his court, Friedrich persuaded the Bavarian elector, now crowned Emperor Charles VII, to declare Carl Eugen of age on 7 January 1744. On his way home the new duke's enforced pro-Prussian stance was cemented with his engagement to Frederike on 21 February.[67]

Usually the regency of 1737–44 is regarded in a positive light in Württemberg historiography. Certainly from the point of view of the estates, the compromise reached with the weak regency government in the Landtag of 1737–9 represents a major achievement. Not only were the estates, or rather the oligarchy which had come to dominate them, saved from political extinction through the innovations of Carl Alexander, but the chances of the new duke following similar policies with any hope of success were seriously curtailed. Much of the reason for this achievement derives from the regency's inability to cope with the problems arising from Carl Alexander's subsidy treaty of 1733. The events of 1737–44 throw the dangers for the smaller states that such treaties could bring into particularly sharp focus.

Carl Alexander had signed his treaty in the hope of gaining imperial hope in realising his political aims and strengthening his position within the empire. This had necessitated the raising of a large army which proved impossible to maintain after his death, both because the imperial subsidies had dried up and because the emergency financial measures devised to replace them had become politically untenable. While the fear of a military putsch and popular pressure from below had enabled the regent to secure the estates' consent to the ducal aims of the last forty years, this had only been at the expense of political concessions to the worthies. These had not only made it difficult for a future duke to overcome their opposition, but also, through the outside guarantees of the Reversalien, made it possible for foreign powers to intervene on their behalf. Moreover, the 1739 recess established a statutory norm of acceptable financial burdens for the duchy which it was going to prove difficult to alter. Finally, in its desire to trim military expenditure to meet this norm, the regency government stumbled into an agreement which had produced a veritable Württemberg *renversement des alliances*. Now, instead of being allied to the Habsburgs who had traditionally been seen as the best means of achieving the duchy's aims, Württemberg was now allied to the Habsburgs' enemy. Altogether, as Keller commented in 1744, it was 'not a good start for the new regime'.[68]

---

[67] HSAS, L5: Tom. 151, fols. 429–30b; Tom. 152, fols. 39b–40b. Although it was issued on 7 Jan. Friedrich delayed handing over the imperial declaration until 5 Feb.

[68] HSAS, A202: Bü. 1206, protocol 20 Jan. 1744.

8

Carl Eugen, 1744–1793

CARL EUGEN: THE TRADITIONAL VIEW REASSESSED

This chapter is centred on Carl Eugen, the last duke in this study, and its length corresponds not so much to the fact that he ruled for nearly fifty years but to the importance and complexity of the events during his reign. It is also a reflection of the fact that, more than any other Württemberg duke, Carl Eugen has featured prominently in the literature on the duchy at this time.[1]

The picture this literature presents has done much to shape not only the general view of Württemberg in the eighteenth century, but also that of other smaller princes in the Reich. Whenever an example is required to reinforce the stereotype of the petty absolutist in eighteenth-century Germany, Carl Eugen is called upon to provide it.[2] Indeed, his reign does appear at first sight to be the heady rush of hunting expeditions, ballets, mistresses and military adventures that is believed to be so typical of this period. The dramatic events of his reign seem to confirm this. Even to many contemporaries, Carl Eugen was a larger-than-life character whose behaviour was scandalous. However, as we have seen in the case of the subsidy treaties, subsequent writers have often interpreted events as they wanted to see them. In the case of the Württemberg literature this does not appear to have been deliberate, but derives from the fact that some of the more influential writers in the field based their work almost entirely on the papers of the estates' archive. This is particularly true of Karl Pfaff and A. E. Adam, who tended to take the estates' complaints at face value without acknowledging that many were simply rhetorical devices masking the worthies' defence of their own interest. This tendency has been

---

[1] There are no biographies of any of the other eighteenth-century dukes, but two on Carl Eugen: G. Storz, *Karl Eugen. Der Fürst und das 'alte, gute Recht'* (Stuttgart, 1981); J. Walter, *Carl Eugen von Württemberg. Ein Herzog und seine Untertanen* (Mühlacker, 1987). See also R. Uhland, 'Herzog Carl Eugen von Württemberg. Persönlichkeit und Werke', *LBGB*, 31 (1979), 39–56; *Herzog Karl Eugen und seiner Zeit* (issued by the Württemberg Geschichts- und Altertumsverein, 2 vols., Esslingen, 1907–9); Pfaff, *Württembergs geliebte Herren*, pp. 65–8.

[2] For example, Childs, *Armies and warfare*, pp. 35–6, 47–8, 56–7, 74; B. Engelmann, *Wir Untertanen. Ein deutsches Anti-Geschichtsbuch* (Frankfurt am Main, 1976), pp. 141–4, 170; T. J. Reed, 'Talking to tyrants: dialogues with power in eighteenth-century Germany', *Historical Journal*, 33 (1990), 63–79.

followed by most subsequent writers.[3] Added to this, some of the early writers simply got some crucial facts wrong and their mistakes have largely been accepted uncritically by their successors.

The intention here, as with this work in general, is to reassess these events. The picture of Carl Eugen that emerges is one very similar to that of both his predecessors and his contemporaries among the other smaller princes in the Reich. The events of his reign bring the points made in the previous chapters even more sharply into focus. In his aims and methods, Carl Eugen fits into the tradition of Württemberg dukes since at least the time of his grandfather, Regent Friedrich Carl. The difficulties he faced highlight not only the internal structure of the duchy, but the limits placed on princely ambitions by the system of the old Reich. The extent to which this system prevented him from achieving his ambitions goes far towards explaining why such princes as his nephew Friedrich II were willing to overturn it in 1803–6.

DUCAL POLICY DURING THE WAR OF THE AUSTRIAN SUCCESSION

In 1744, with the War of the Austrian Succession still raging around Württemberg's borders, the duke's main priority was the survival of the duchy, essential to which was the maintenance of neutrality advised by the privy council. This was seriously threatened by the drift towards Prussia which had begun with the regency's rash troop transfer agreement in 1741 and had continued with the alliance signed in January 1744. Neutrality would be totally lost if Württemberg openly sided with the Prussian party as Friedrich II was now asking Carl Eugen to do by inviting him to join the Frankfurt Union.[4] This also threatened to lead to overdependence on Prussia and to prevent the duke from going elsewhere to seek better terms. A return to Carl Alexander's pro-Austrian policy at this stage was unthinkable given the presence of powerful Franco-Bavarian forces in the neighbourhood.

Given this precarious position, the young duke and his team of privy councillors managed the situation extremely well. First, Württemberg's neutrality was strengthened by making that of the Swabian Kreis more effective. In December 1744 the duke persuaded the Kreis Konvent to pay him to provide an additional 1,690 infantry to help limit the depredations of foreign troops and recruiting parties.[5] Then, in his capacity as Kreis military commander, he held large-scale

---

[3] On this tendency see Haug-Moritz, *Württembergischer Ständekonflikt*, pp. 57–62 and the literature cited there.

[4] *Politische Correspondenz Friedrich's des Grossen* (46 vols., Berlin, 1879–1939), III, pp. 333, 366; Boepple, *Verhältnis zu Württemberg*, pp. 33–4.

[5] HSAS, A202: Bü. 1993, 2256. The text of the agreement is printed in Schempp, *Infanterie-Regiments*, pp. 102–3. The arrangement involved the division of the existing Leib IR into two formations: IR Prinz Louis and Garde zu Fuß.

summer exercises of all Swabian Kreistruppen (1746, 1747) as a further demonstration of this armed neutrality.[6] The Westphalian Kreis followed a similar policy and mobilised its forces in 1744 to prevent the conflict in the Austrian Netherlands from spreading across the frontier.

Second, to halt the drift towards Prussia, he refused to join the Frankfurt Union. Despite mounting pressure following Prussia's re-entry into the war (August 1744) and the French capture of Freiburg (November 1744), he continued to hold out. Outside events came to his rescue with the rapid collapse of Bavaria early in 1745. Although the duchy was punished with heavy quartering by the retreating Franco-Bavarian forces, Prussia had no desire to see Württemberg pushed into the arms of a resurgent Austria. To prevent this, Friedrich II now encouraged continued Württemberg neutrality at a time when his relations with Carl Eugen were otherwise deteriorating.[7] As Friedrich himself then left the war in December 1745, while events on the Rhine quietened down, the duke was able to ride out the war with relative ease.

Already, during the war, Carl Eugen had sought wider freedom of action by using the alliance of 1744 as a means of reaching an agreement with Prussia's own ally, France, thus apparently opening up promising prospects for the realisation of long-term ducal aims. By maintaining good relations with Versailles, Carl Eugen might hope to secure a withdrawal of French troops from the nine Mömpelgard lordships occupied since 1723 and also for compensation for the winter quarterings of 1744/5. His links with Berlin could prove useful both in these aims and in providing support at the Reichstag for Württemberg attempts to round off its territory at the expense of the imperial knights.

On the other hand, prospects of concrete benefits from a rapprochement with Austria seemed less likely, Austro-Württemberg relations having deteriorated steadily since Carl Alexander's death. The regency settlement made with Maria Augusta had been concluded without imperial approval.[8] The 1733 treaty had expired with Austria owing large sums of money and there now seemed little likelihood of these ever being paid. Vienna had also broken its agreements with the regency and disbanded the regiments transferred to its service.[9] Moreover, as an enemy of France, Austria was in no position to put in a good word at Versailles over

---

[6] HSAS, A202: Bü. 2274; C14: Bü. 638–9.

[7] HSAS, A202: Bü. 2022, 2115–17; L6.22.7.23; *Politische Correspondenz Friedrich's*, III, pp. 271, 278, V, pp. 8, 32; Boepple, *Verhältnis zu Württemberg*, pp. 34–5; Kriegs-Archiv, *Oesterreichischer Erbfolgekrieg*, VI, pp. 162–259. Carl Eugen's deteriorating relations with Prussia are shown by his decreasing cooperativeness over Prussian recruiting in Swabia: HSAS, A202: Bü. 1207, 1210, 2299; C14: Bü. 68, 69, 597.

[8] Dizinger, *Beiträge*, I, pp. 87–90. The emperor only retrospectively confirmed the agreement on 12 July 1738, nine months after it had been concluded. On the deteriorating relations see HSAS, A74: Bü. 116–20.

[9] In November 1741 the regency government calculated that the emperor owed Württemberg a total of 1,306,810fl. 30xr.: HSAS, A202: Bü. 1361.

the Mömpelgard dispute and the question of compensation. The emperor was still less likely to help Württemberg against the imperial knights as these were his traditional supporters. Indeed, from 1749 Carl Eugen ran up against increasing opposition in Vienna over his plan to compel the Swabian knights to recognise the Württemberg overlordship they had thrown off at the beginning of the sixteenth century.[10]

Under these circumstances it is hardly surprising that Carl Eugen began negotiating with France as early as 1745.[11] Three years later he went personally to Paris where his two younger brothers had been since July 1747. It is possible that the question of a French subsidy was discussed during this visit, but at this point France was in no position to pay one. It is, however, significant that as early as 1748 the French foreign ministry considered Württemberg already won over, while on 1 February 1749 the new relationship was symbolised by the conferment of a French regiment on Prince Louis.[12]

This new pro-French orientation also brought material results. In 1748 a convention was signed whereby Württemberg at last regained possession of the disputed lordships, albeit under recognition of French overlordship.[13] With Prussian assistance, Privy Councillor Georg Philipp von Werneck then secured 160,000fl. in 1751 as payment for the winter quarters. Although this was only about 40 per cent of the estimated actual cost, it still represented a better deal than the duchy had ever received from the Austrians.[14] The Prussian assistance on this matter also helped to compensate for disappointingly weak support at the Reichstag for the Württemberg offensive against the imperial knights.[15] Carl Eugen returned this Franco-Prussian co-operation by rejecting Austrian overtures to renew the Kreis Association and opposing Vienna's attempts to win over his brother, Prince Louis. Friendship treaties with Bayreuth and the Palatinate, both recipients of French subsidies, tied Württemberg closer to the Franco-Prussian orbit. The

---

[10] Press, 'Angriff auf die Reichsritterschaft', pp. 329–48.

[11] HSAS, A202: Bü. 2118; L5: Tom. 156, 158, 159, 162. Negotiations were conducted by estates commissary J. F. Spittler (1745–7), envoy J. R. Fesch (1745–7), Privy Councillor Baron D. C. von Keller (1748), Privy Councillor Baron F. C. von Montolieu (1748–50), Privy Councillor G. P. von Werneck (1749–52). All negotiators were assisted by *Legationssekretär* C. W. Metz who had been in Paris since 1736.

[12] Ebbecke, *Frankreichs Politik*, p. 41; A. J. Frhr Zorn von Bulach, *Der Fähnrich Zorn von Bulach vom Regimente Württemberg zu Pferd im siebenjährigen Kriege 1757–1758 nach seinem Tagebuche* (ed. K. Engel, Strasbourg, 1908), p. 6.

[13] Scherb, *Mömpelgard*, pp. 237–40.

[14] HSAS, A202: Bü. 2118; L5: Tom. 159, fols. 445–7b. In 1747 the total cost of the French quartering 1744/5 had been put at 411,686fl. 21xr. As late as 1750 the French had only offered 120,000fl. The compensation was paid by the French between 1752 and 1754 to the estates' treasury and thence to the individual Ämter concerned; see L12: *Kriegsparticulare 1752/3–1754/5*. On the problems of securing compensation from the Austrians for their quartering during 1743 see L6.22.7.26.

[15] Press, 'Angriff auf die Reichsritterschaft', pp. 340–5.

Prussian alliance was further strengthened in 1753 with the marriage of his other brother to Friedrichs II's second niece.[16]

Although thus achieving some of his more minor aims, Carl Eugen still had not found the means to realise his driving ambition of becoming an elector. For this he needed both money and a powerful sponsor, and the best way to obtain these appeared to be a subsidy treaty. Up to this point, the French had been unwilling to pay subsidies, while the Prussians had little need to hire troops stationed so far from their territory. All this changed with the Hanoverian initiative in 1750 to promote the election of the Austrian Archduke Joseph as King of the Romans. Versailles and Berlin were unanimous in their desire to prevent this potential increase in Austrian influence and in January 1751 Louis XV set aside 10 million livres to secure the German princes before they were bought up by George II.[17] In December 1750, the French had approached Werneck in Paris over the possibility of a Franco-Württemberg subsidy treaty.[18] The negotiations that followed led to such a treaty being signed in 1752.

By that time it was obvious that foreign subsidies offered the only way out of the financial restraints imposed by the regency's agreement with the estates in 1739. Not only was the size of the grant inadequate, but anticipation of revenue begun under the regency made it even more difficult for Carl Eugen to manage on it. Although anticipation of revenue had started well before the regency, the financial demands of the armed neutrality had forced the regent to step it up dramatically. By January 1741, over 8 per cent of that winter's grant had been spent before it had been collected.[19] By 1744 the anticipation of revenue was in full swing and Carl Eugen had little choice but to continue it. This not only created all the usual problems associated with arrears we have already met in this study, but led to trouble with the estates' committee.

Shortage of funds forced the commissariat to default on its share of the barrack-building programme and road maintenance. Completion of barracks was held up, resulting in the continuation of the quartering of soldiers on civilians.[20] Meanwhile,

---

[16] HSAS, A202: Bü. 1157, negotiations 1746–7; Boepple, *Verhältnis zu Württemberg*, pp. 39–40; Anon., *Friedrich August von Hardenberg. Ein kleinstaatlicher Minister des 18. Jahrhunderts* (Leipzig, 1877), p. 82. Copies of the treaties with Bayreuth (16 June 1749) and the Palatinate (28 Aug. 1749) are in LBS cod. hist. fol. 647.

[17] Ebbecke, *Frankreichs Politik*, pp. 45–71; Eldon, *Subsidy policy*, pp. 2–3; Schäffer, *Siebenjährigen Krieges*, I, pp. 50–5. The title King of the Romans was given to the successor designate to the emperor. Archduke Joseph was not actually elected until 1764.

[18] HSAS, A202: Bü. 2218.

[19] HSAS, L5: Tom. 147, 148. For the problems this caused the military administration, see esp. the complaint of General von Wittgenstein, 8 Sept. 1752, in A202: Bü. 2207.

[20] HSAS, A202: Bü. 2206, 2207, 2244, 2257, 2260; L5: Tom. 154–64; L6.22.7.28–29.

Carl Eugen manipulated the vague provisions of the 1739 recess as to how much money was to go from the grant towards repaying the Rentkammer debts. When money was short, he simply redirected funds from this to the commissariat, thereby delaying debt repayment. He was also forced to use money intended for the construction of his new palace in Stuttgart, which slowed down the building work.[21] Unable to comprehend the complexities of military finance and in any case regarding the army as an unnecessary expense, the estates regarded these delays as signs of the duke's untrustworthiness and suspected him of misusing their tax grant. For his part, Carl Eugen regarded their growing complaints as an unreasonable lack of co-operativeness. Gradually the gap widened as more misunderstandings and disagreements further soured relations.[22] This was to have serious consequences in the later 1750s when it contributed to the open break between duke and estates after 1758.

It also played an important part in Carl Eugen's decision to sign the treaty with France. It is with this treaty that the chapter of misconceptions over his policy begins.[23] As these have proved so persistent and have so affected the historical picture of Württemberg at this time, it is worth investigating the negotiations in detail.

First, far from a sudden move on his part, it was the French who approached him, while the negotiations themselves were conducted by Werneck who had been in Paris since July 1749. Second, rather than seizing the French offer blindly, Carl Eugen hung back from such a potentially dangerous alliance. Third, instead of going behind the back of the privy council and negotiating secretly as he is always portrayed as having done, Carl Eugen consulted this body as early as January 1751. While councillors considered a treaty desirable and believed it promised advantages, they also saw it as fraught with potential dangers.[24]

Carl Eugen shared their fears, but thought it too dangerous to refuse the offer outright and ordered Werneck in the meantime to spin out the negotiations ('die Sache noch dilatorisch tractirt').[25] Initially, he was mainly concerned with obtaining further guarantees for Mömpelgard and the compensation for the winter quarters. However, the French pressed him for a more extensive agreement and were eager that he increase his offer of 3,000 troops. Carl Eugen was worried that the mobilisation and maintenance payments they offered were significantly short of the actual costs and on no account did he want to commit himself to

---

[21] HSAS, A202: Bü. 2206, 2207, 2278.

[22] HSAS, L5: Tom. 154–64. On the other misunderstandings and disputes see A. E. Adam, 'Herzog Karl Eugen und die "Landschaft"', *HKE*, I, pp. 193–310; Grube, *Landtag*, pp. 424–9.

[23] For examples of the traditional interpretation of the treaty see Storz, *Karl Eugen*, pp. 60–3; Schempp, *Infanterie-Regiments*, pp. 108–9; Vann, *Making of a state*, pp. 264–5; Pfister, *Denkwürdigkeiten*, pp. 162–9.

[24] HSAS, A202: Bü. 2218, esp. privy council protocol, 12 Jan. 1751.

[25] *Ibid.*

more than 4,000 men. However, as Werneck exceeded his brief and began negotiating on other issues, Carl Eugen became inextricably involved. Also, as the negotiations wore on, he began to see the potential advantages outweigh the disadvantages. This was probably because his attempts to economise were clearly failing,[26] and because the estates' committee was being particularly obstructive on other issues.[27] In August 1751 he accepted the final French offer of 160,000fl. compensation for the winter quarters. Later that year, Prussian mediation secured an improved offer on the subsidies and on 4 February 1752 the treaty was finally signed.[28]

The terms of this treaty are also persistently misquoted in the literature, so it is worth outlining them here. They also give a good indication of the structure of such treaties in general. The document signed in Paris by Werneck and the Marquis de Puysieux was a friendship treaty with a troop convention attached. The eleven public articles provided for extensive Franco-Württemberg co-operation to maintain the peace between Louis XV and the emperor. This was fully in the duchy's own interests as it lay in the middle of the potential war zone. In the event of war between France and the Reich, Württemberg was permitted to provide its contingent to the imperial army without this being considered by Versailles as an act of hostility. Further, the Württemberg subsidy corps was not to serve against the Reich or the emperor in his capacity as *Chef de l'Empire*. This ruled out the possibility of the corps meeting the duchy's Kreistruppen on opposing sides on the same battlefield. Altogether, France would regard the corps as auxiliaries and not consider Württemberg to be directly involved in any conflict. However, if the duchy was attacked, Louis XV promised to come to the duke's aid. In return for this protection, Carl Eugen was to represent French interests at the Reichstag, which in 1752 meant opposing the election of Joseph as King of the Romans.

The troop convention fixed the size of the corps at two infantry regiments of 1,500 men each and not the 6,000 men which otherwise appears in the literature. Thus we can dispense with the myth of the French commissar arriving in Württemberg in 1756 to find only half the troops the duke was supposed to

---

[26] The economy attempts centred on a new system of funding, introduced in 1747 upon the suggestion of the privy council. Under this system, the units of the army were each allotted a fixed budget which the commander was told not to exceed. As early as 1750 this 'Selbst Administration des Oeconomie' was breaking down as it proved impossible for the regiments to manage on their limited allowances, while the central administration lost its overview of financial affairs. In 1752 the system was abandoned altogether. See HSAS, A202: Bü. 2206, 2258, 2262, 2277, 2278. The existing literature, particularly Adam, 'Landschaft', pp. 193–209 ignores these attempts to economise and under-estimates the financial problems of the army administration.

[27] Particularly the question of the quartering of ducal tropps on the Ämter. See note 20 above.

[28] Copies in HSAS, A202: Bü. 2218, 2219 and LBS, cod. hist. fol. 647. Prussian pressure on Württemberg played a considerable part in Carl Eugen's acceptance of the French offer: see Boepple, *Verhältnis zu Württemberg*, pp. 37–8.

provide.[29] As the Haustruppen totalled over 2,800 in that year, Carl Eugen was fewer than 200 short of the required number.[30]

Another misconception concerns the amount of money the duke was to receive. Under article one of the treaty, Carl Eugen was accorded an annual subsidy of 130,000fl. paid in quarterly instalments. The mobilisation and maintenance costs outlined in the military convention were only to commence once the French had called for the corps to take the field and were not additional annual payments as has previously been supposed. In other words, the duke received only a quarter of a third of the amount most accounts credit him with.[31] Although the subsidy was 20,000fl. less than he had hoped for, Carl Eugen fared no worse than the other states that signed with France between 1751 and 1752, and considerably better than his father had done in his agreement with Austria in 1733.[32] In addition, the privy council's fears as to the reliability of the French proved unfounded, as all but one of the twenty-four instalments owed were paid in full.[33]

In attached secret articles, the duke received Louis XV's promise of support in his desire to become an elector, in addition to confirmation of the agreements on Mömpelgard and the winter quarters compensation. Here again he fared considerably better than his father whose treaty with Austria had made no mention of the electoral title. While a promise of support was obviously considerably short of the title itself, there was no reason for the duke to doubt Louis XV's ability to turn it into reality. After all, only a decade before, the French had made the Bavarian elector an emperor.

There were many reasons for Carl Eugen to be satisfied with the agreement. Above all, he had retained some degree of independence in the clause concerning

---

[29] The origins of this myth appear to start with Karl Pfaff in 1842 (*Militärwesen*, p. 65) and derive from a confusion of the convention of March 1757 for 6,000 men with that of 1752 for 3,000. At the very latest, the mistake appears in Stadlinger, *Kriegswesens*, p. 400. Thereafter, despite being mentioned by Eugen Schneider in 1907 ('Regierung', *HKE*, I, pp. 147–67 at p. 150), this mistake appears without exception in every work on the subject.

[30] Wilson, 'Violence and the rejection of authority', 1–26.

[31] Examples of the inflated payments appear throughout the literature as late as 1984: Vann, *Making of a state*, p. 265. They probably originate with confusion over the presence of 'peacetime' payments in the convention. These were, in fact, only to start when the French called for the troops in peacetime. The higher payments were in case of a call-up after war had broken out. Even if the duke had received these payments between 1752 and 1757, they were in any case considerably below what the Kriegsrat estimated the true costs to be (A202: Bü. 2218).

	Paid by France	Actual cost
Mobilisation costs for 1,000 men	48,328fl.	52,212fl.
Annual maintenance cost for 1,000 men	54,473fl.	77,159fl.

[32] For details of other treaties, see Ebbecke, *Frankreichs Politik*, pp. 69–70. Ebbecke's survey does not include the negotiations with Württemberg.

[33] HSAS, A202: Bü. 2208, privy council protocol, 23 Nov. 1752. Part of this document is quoted in Pfister, *Denkwürdigkeiten*, p. 169. On the payment of the subsidy see Anon., 'Fürstenhäuser', 324–40 at pp. 332–4.

the provision of his contingent to the imperial army. In his agreement of March 1751 with Louis XV, Duke Christian IV of Zweibrücken had been obliged to promise not to send his contingent in the event of a war between the Reich and France. Moreover, four years later he was compelled to bow to French pressure and become a Catholic, causing him considerable problems.[34]

It is now time to look at the last misconception arising from the 1752 treaty, namely that the duke squandered the money on personal luxury and failed to build up the army to the required strength.[35] Tables 8.1 and 8.2 show that, while not all the French subsidy was paid directly into the Kriegskasse, the shortfall was more than doubly made good by other payments from ducal hands ('von aigenen höchsten Händen'). Of the 65 per cent of the subsidy for which complete accounts survive, over 67 per cent was paid to the commissariat. The bulk of the rest (payments to the Rentkammer and the estates) was used to help amortise the Rentkammer debts. Of the money paid to the Rentkammer, a mere 2,000fl. was spent on so-called luxury expenditure. Even accounting for the fact that most of the money spent via Werneck in Paris went on presents, tobacco boxes and the like, no more than 7.5 per cent of the total went on luxury items. Meanwhile, two infantry regiments were raised in 1753 with a third added the following year.[36]

FINANCIAL INITIATIVES AND ADMINISTRATIVE CHANGES, 1752–6

The expenditure on the court was actually proportionally lower at this time than under the previous regimes (see Appendix). The civil budget also included a considerable amount of expenditure directed at realising the duke's political ends. Unable to defeat the imperial knights in the courts, Carl Eugen decided simply to buy up their territory to round off his own. Here he was aided by the fact that the knights were chronically short of money, while the estates were willing to see the number of tax payers increased. This policy had been begun under the regency, but was greatly accelerated by Carl Eugen. By the time of his death, Carl Eugen had spent over three million florins on the acquisition of territory and rights (Table 8.3). The money came from considerable loans voted by the estates and others raised

---

[34] K. Baumann, 'Herzog Christian IV. von Pfalz-Zweibrücken 1722–1775', in *Deutsche Westen – Deutsches Reich. Saarpfälzische Lebensbilder* (Kaiserslautern, 1938), I, pp. 103–17; E. Drumm, *Das Regiment Royal-Deuxponts. Deutsches Blut auf fürstlichen Befehl in fremden Dienst und Sold* (Zweibrücken, 1937 edn), pp. 5–6. His lack of independence was further demonstrated by the fact that his subsidy regiment effectively became part of the French army.

[35] Again this misconception is all too prevalent in the Württemberg literature: Marquardt, *Geschichte Württembergs*, pp. 202–3; Walter, *Carl Eugen*, p. 214; Harder, *Militärgeschichtliches Handbuch*, pp. 42–8.

[36] On the new formations see HSAS, A32: Bd. 1, fols. 130–2; A202: Bü. 2208, 2268, 2269; Stadlinger, *Kriegswesens*, pp. 400, 404, 658–60.

outside the duchy.[37] The fact that Carl Eugen resorted to such an expensive method is another indication of the limits placed on princely ambition by the framework of the Reich. Purchase was the only way left open after his failure in the imperial courts, while military aggression was unthinkable. Nonetheless, this policy added some 25,000 new subjects and increased his influence within Swabia.[38]

In order to keep his new source of finance secret from the estates, Carl Eugen drew up two military plans on 15 December 1752. The real one was entrusted only to the military administration. The second, which bore no relation to the true costs, but added up neatly to the official budget, was handed to the estates' committee.[39] It is doubtful that the committee was totally taken in by this devious accounting, but the fact remains that it lost the overview of military funding it had gained in the 1739 recess. From now on it was gradually edged out of its dominant position in the duchy's affairs. The duke was already circumventing it at local level in 1752 by approaching his subjects directly through weekly audiences.

Simultaneously, the same was happening to the committee's friends in the privy council, which had begun to question the duke's military buildup. After 1753 Carl Eugen bypassed the council and issued his orders directly to the committee.[40] Two years later he instituted a major reorganisation in government, the importance of which has previously been overlooked; it was far more than the duke coming of age and wishing to take over the reins of government himself.

Contrary to the Reversalien, Carl Eugen dismantled the administrative structure laid down by the 1660 Kanzleiordnung and destroyed the privy council's control over the other departments. In April 1755 these were subordinated directly to the duke, and the pro-Austrian privy council president, von Hardenberg, was dismissed and not replaced. This may have had something to do with Carl Eugen's dislike of Hardenberg's pedantic and dictatorial tone.[41] However, it also accorded with the duchy's new foreign policy alignment and reduced the ability of the

[37] HSAS, A256: Bd. 229–39. On the duke's foreign loans see also A8: Bü. 66, Nos. 1–35, Bü. 68, Nos. 34–62; A202: Bü. 739. These included a large loan from the French playwright Voltaire. The sources differ as to the actual value of this loan: Adam, 'Landschaft', p. 246; Fauchier-Magnan, *Small German courts*, p. 208; Vann, *Making of a state*, pp. 265–6. (Note: Vann reverses the exchange rate of florins to livres and so inflates his figures by a factor of 2.5.)

[38] Population figures calculated from Röder, *Geographie und Statistik*, I, pp. 489–539. Through the acquisition of Jüstingen, Württemberg gained another vote at the Kreis Konvent.

[39] The idea of drawing up two plans came from the privy council: see HSAS, A202: Bü. 2208, 11 Dec. 1752. Details of the actual plan which budgeted for 540,000fl. expenditure survive with papers relating to the 1755 plan in *ibid*. Details of the false plan, budgeting for only 410,000fl., are in A202: Bü. 2207 and L5: Tom. 160, fols. 385–7. Among the historians deceived by this devious accounting is A. E. Adam ('Landschaft', p. 200).

[40] Grube, *Landtag*, pp. 428–9. Direct communication with the estates was contrary to the 1660 Kanzleiordnung and had been at the centre of the dispute with Eberhard Ludwig 1732: see pp. 160–1.

[41] HSAS, A202: Bü. 2196, 13 Apr. 1755; Pfaff, *Geschichte des Fürstenhauses*, IV, pp. 254–7; Adam, 'Landschaft', p. 206; Vann, *Making of a state*, pp. 269–70. On Hardenberg, see in addition to Anon., *Hardenberg*, the essay in *ADB*, X (1879), 560–2.

council to act independently. The oversight of the remaining councillors was further curtailed by the re-establishment of a private chancellery (*Geheime Kabinettskanzlei*) through which ducal directives now flowed. Control over the lower echelons of the bureaucracy was reinforced by the duke's new habit of riding around the duchy and talking to his officials directly. Finally, the whole reorganisation was accompanied by a new budget plan for both court and bureaucracy, designed to put the Rentkammer on a sounder footing.[42]

The committee men reacted to this offensive with a full-scale retreat behind the walls of the constitution. They resolutely refused any offer of co-operation and boycotted most of the Deputationen Carl Eugen established to improve the administration.[43] They particularly disliked the Commerzien Deputation established to stimulate the economy and ostracised their legal adviser Johann Jakob Moser (1701–85) for so enthusiastically devising schemes for it. The committee had good reason for its stubbornness: the dangerous implication of Carl Eugen's brash new ideas was that existing agreements could be changed if considered out of date. As the whole social, political and economic power of the worthies rested on the sum of these old agreements, the duke's innovations threatened to undermine the very heart of their position.

Forced on to the defensive, the committee was undecided what positive action to take to oppose the duke. From 1753 a rift emerged in its ranks over whether it was permissible to withhold taxes to compel Carl Eugen to honour his constitutional promises. This rift widened with the growing personal animosity between Moser and a faction around Johann Friedrich Stockmayer (1703–82), the estates' other legal adviser and head of an influential worthy dynasty.[44] The committee's weakness is demonstrated by its failure to make effective use of the foreign guarantees of the Reversalien it had expended much effort in securing during the regency. Had Carl Eugen been permitted to continue his innovations he might have finally succeeded in eclipsing the estates altogether.

SHIFTING ALLIANCES AND DUCAL DILEMMA

The events that followed the signing of the Convention of Westminster (16 January 1755) between England and Prussia upset the steady course of ducal

---

[42] HSAS, A8: Bü. 66; Wunder, *Privilegierung*, pp. 53–4.
[43] Söll, *Wirtschaftspolitik*, pp. 98–100, 115–20. For an example of Carl Eugen's interest in stimulating the economy see H. P. Liebel, 'Der Beamte als Untertyp in den Anfangsstadien der Industrialisierung. Johann Friedrich Müller und die Staats- und Wirtschaftsreform Württembergs, 1750–1780', in G. A. Ritter (ed.), *Festschrift für Hans Rosenberg* (Berlin, 1970), pp. 221–60.
[44] Walker, *Johann Jakob Moser*, pp. 4–5, 205–32; A. E. Adam, *Johann Jakob Moser als württembergischer Landschaftskonsulent 1751–1771* (Stuttgart, 1887), pp. 15–52; Haug-Moritz, *Württembergischer Ständekonflikt*, pp. 77–9.

policies. The famous 'reversal of alliances' prompted by the Convention saw the duchy's two allies diverge, with Prussia siding with England and France with Austria. With the French promise to Austria of military aid after Prussia invaded Saxony in August 1756, it looked certain that Carl Eugen's subsidy corps would be used to fight his own ally.

The traditional view is that the duke used the war that broke out in 1756 as an excuse to seek personal glory on the battlefield and to acquire sufficient funds, through foreign subsidies and illegal taxation, to indulge in a life of sumptuous luxury. However, just as the subsidy treaty of 1752 has been misinterpreted, so too has Württemberg's involvement in the war. This misinterpretation derives from the mistaken belief that the duke misappropriated military funds for his luxury expenditure and from a gross underestimate of the difficulties he faced at the outbreak of hostilities. An investigation of these difficulties reveals two important points. First, it explains the true reasons why he involved the duchy so heavily in the war. Second, it shows just how the growing Austro-Prussian dualism had limited the potential of small states such as Württemberg to follow independent policies, or even to remain neutral.

In the months leading up to the actual conflict, France, Austria and Prussia hurriedly sent envoys to Württemberg and other small states to try and win them over before the Reich irrevocably split into two warring camps.[45] Faced with this diplomatic pressure, Carl Eugen had only two choices. He could restrict himself to providing his subsidy corps until the treaty expired (1 December 1757) and, in the event of the Reichstag declaring war on Prussia, send only his Kreistruppen into the field. This, at least, was unavoidable given Württemberg's geographical position in the middle of the Franco-Austrian camp, but would bring him no political gains. Alternatively, he could make the best of a bad situation and throw his lot fully in with the Franco-Austrian cause. He could hope for concessions in the meantime until this unlikely alliance between hereditary enemies fell apart and things returned to normal.

Co-operation with the Anglo-Prussian alliance did not number among the choices open to Carl Eugen. A look at the map is sufficient to see why: Württemberg was open on all sides to pressure from the anti-Prussian coalition. Moreover, at the start of the war there was no compelling reason to believe that the outnumbered and surrounded Prussians were going to be able successfully to defend themselves, let alone come to the aid of distant and isolated allies. This view appeared to be confirmed when they proved incapable of defending Hessen-Kassel

---

[45] Ebbecke, *Frankreichs Politik*, pp. 110–20; Eldon, *Subsidy policy*, pp. 81–92; H. Gerspacher, *Die badische Politik im siebenjährigen Kriege* (*Heidelberger Abhandlungen zur mittleren und neueren Geschichte*, 67, Heidelberg, 1934), pp. 10–24; H. Meyer, *Berichte des preußischen Gesandten Eickstedt. Ein Beitrag zur Politik der deutschen Kleinstaaten während des siebenjährigen Krieges* (Hamburg, 1906); P. F. Stuhr, *Forschungen und Erläuterungen über Hauptpunkte der Geschichte des siebenjährigen Krieges* (2 vols., Hamburg, 1842), I, pp. 315–23.

and Brunswick in 1757, both of which were geographically much closer than Württemberg.

It is clear that Carl Eugen was very reluctant to make a choice at all and delayed as long as possible before committing himself. During the vote at the Reichstag on the declaration of war on Prussia (17 January 1757), Württemberg sided with Baden-Durlach and other Protestant states in calling for an armistice and a *Reichsmediation*. Although Austrian pressure had prompted the Catholic majority at the Swabian Kreis Konvent to order a mobilisation of the Kreistruppen (7 December 1756), Carl Eugen blocked this by failing to issue the necessary orders.[46]

However, it became increasingly difficult to follow such a line into 1757 and the prospects of maintaining the strict neutrality of the 1740s looked slim. Then it had been possible to profit from the mutual hostility of France and Austria, each of whom preferred to see the duchy remain neutral rather than have it go over to the other side. Now that both were on the same side, this was no longer possible, while the declaration of the Reichskrieg against Prussia obliged Carl Eugen to take an active part in the conflict. No such obligation had existed between 1741 and 1748, owing to the emperor's inability to persuade the Reichstag to support him.[47]

As early as August 1756 the French had reminded Carl Eugen of his obligations under the 1752 treaty and told him not to maintain any links with Prussia.[48] By early 1757 he was becoming increasingly out of joint with the other Swabian states which were largely Austria's clients.[49] He now feared that the emperor might punish him by depriving him of the Kreis Direktorium.[50] As Keller commented in 1760, the duke would 'rather relinquish half his territory than lose the Kreis Direktorium'.[51]

There were also other dangers if he did not fall in with the desires of Austria and France. To these powers, Württemberg represented a tempting area for winter quarters. In 1761/2 the margrave of Baden-Durlach was punished for attempting to remain neutral by having French troops quartered on his territory.[52] The fate

---

[46] HSAS, C14: Bü. 77, 87/1; Brabant, *Reich*, I, pp. 79, 93, 101; Kohlhepp, *Militärverfassung*, pp. 67–8. Württemberg's hesitancy is paralleled by similar policies elsewhere, for example Hanover: Press, 'Kurhannover', 53–79 at pp. 66–8.

[47] In 1743 Emperor Charles VII did call upon Swabia to provide its Kreistruppen, but Württemberg avoided actually sending any on the grounds that these were already mobilised and fulfilling their proper function in upholding the neutrality agreed with Bavaria: see HSAS, C14: Bü. 744. On imperial efforts to form a Reichsarmee see also Kriegs-Archiv, *Oesterreichischer Erbfolgekrieg*, IV, pp. 330–2.

[48] HSAS, A202: Bü. 2219, memorandum for the Marquis de Monciel, 7 Oct. 1756.

[49] On the actions of the other Kreis members see E. Meissner, 'Die südwestdeutschen Reichsstände im siebenjährigen Krieg', *Ellwanger Jahrbuch*, 23 (1971), 117–58. Meissner, however, is under the mistaken belief that the war prompted the estates to co-operate with Carl Eugen.

[50] Boepple, *Verhältnis zu Württemberg*, p. 44; Meyer, *Berichte*, pp. 7–22. On the Kreis Direktorium see pp. 117–18.

[51] Quoted in Gerpsächer, *Badische Politik*, p. 48.

[52] *Ibid.*, pp. 77–90. The quartering cost the margrave 100,000fl. A similar fate befell the elector of Cologne in 1734–5: see M. Braubach, *Kurköln: Gestalten und Ereignisse aus zwei Jahrhunderten rheinischer Geschichte* (Münster, 1949), p. 244.

of other states that tried to stay out of the war was also scarcely encouraging. In addition, even if Carl Eugen decided to withdraw from an active role in affairs, he could not expect his rivals to do the same. Baden-Durlach, for example, had long had its eye on the Kreis Direktorium and hoped to profit from Württemberg weakness.[53]

On the other hand, a closer co-operation with the Franco-Austrian coalition offered certain advantages. Already the French had held out the prospect of further support for the electoral title,[54] while their new friendship with Austria permitted Württemberg to resume better relations with the emperor. This also had distinct advantages. The duke could expect imperial confirmation on a compromise he had reached with the imperial knights as well as a favourable judgment in his court case with the so-called 'Mömpelgard bastards'.[55] Finally, it took not only French support, but also imperial agreement to make him an elector and allow him to acquire more territory.

At this point it is worth considering the factor of religion in this choice. There has been a tendency to portray Carl Eugen as somehow betraying his Protestant subjects by taking up arms against Prussia. This is then given as the main reason for the mutiny in the Württemberg forces in June 1757 and their subsequent poor performance in the war.[56] Religion is also widely believed to have been a major factor in the poor performance of the Protestant Reichsarmee contingents from Franconia and Swabia in the campaigns against their Prussian co-religionists.

While religion was a significant factor in the war, its importance has been exaggerated. This is partly due to the success of Prussian propaganda. Prussia lost no time in whipping up Protestant fears that the new Franco-Austrian (Catholic) coalition would start a re-run of the religious conflicts of the seventeenth century. This was particularly awkward for Carl Eugen given the popular rumours still surrounding the plans of his father. However, the geo-strategic reasons outlined above played a far greater role than religion in his decision to join the anti-Prussian coalition. The same was true of the other smaller princes. The Catholic electors of Cologne, Bavaria and the Palatinate, for example, showed considerable reluctance to join the Franco-Austrian coalition and continued negotiations with England well into 1757. However, like Württemberg they too were forced by pressure of events to take sides against Prussia. Just how much pressure was applied is shown by the difficulties faced by the Palatinate when it tried to withdraw its troops in 1763. The same is true for the Protestant princes who also showed no great enthusiasm for the war. Like Württemberg, Hessen-Kassel was caught out by the

---

[53] On the margrave's ambitions plans, see Gerspächer, *Badische Politik*, pp. 42–76.
[54] Ebbecke, *Frankreichs Politik*, pp. 111–20.
[55] HSAS, A74: Bü. 139, 140, reports of *Regierungsrat* Renz, 1756–7.
[56] For the following see Wilson, 'Violence and the rejection of authority' and the literature cited there.

reversal of alliances and found itself dangerously exposed in 1757 with a large part of its army actually stationed in England. Considerable pressure was also applied by the Anglo-Prussian alliance on its weaker members, as Brunswick discovered when it tried to withdraw its troops after the debacle at Hastenbach 1757.

DECISION AND OVERCOMMITMENT, 1757–8

Having renewed his existing subsidy treaty with France on 22 October 1756,[57] Carl Eugen irrevocably committed himself to the Franco-Austrian war effort by making an additional military convention on 20 March 1757.[58] Like the original agreement, this new treaty was not entered into lightly, but followed French pressure to double the size of his corps.[59] It was this second agreement, committing him to provide 6,200 infantry, that prompted the frantic recruiting measures carried out by *Geheime Kriegsrat* Philipp Friedrich Rieger (1722–82), which are cited as evidence for the supposed failure to fulfil the requirements of the original treaty.[60]

Although signed with France, Carl Eugen clearly used the Convention as an opportunity to edge towards a closer understanding with Austria. In December 1756 the Austrians had shown an interest in hiring some Württemberg troops, but hung back because they were not sure how the duke would vote at the Reichstag and because the general staff did not want to see two separate corps, one with their army and one with the French.[61] While negotiating with the French, Carl Eugen repeatedly assured the Austrians that he desired to lead his troops in person to demonstrate his personal commitment to their cause. This made a favourable impression in Vienna and in April arrangements were made for the entire corps to go to Bohemia.[62] On 6 May Carl Eugen went personally to the Austrian capital. Unfortunately, no written records survive of the discussions during this

---

[57] Ebbecke, *Frankreichs Politik*, pp. 119–21. He also left his Hohenzollern-born wife, Elizabeth Sophie Frederike von Brandenburg-Bayreuth, in October 1756, a further sign that he was leaving the Prussian political orbit.

[58] Copy in HSAS, A202: Bü. 2219. Text printed in Pfister, *Denkwürdigkeiten*, pp. 540–4. The treaty of 30 March 1757 actually obliged Carl Eugen to provide five IRs each 1,200 men, or altogether 6,000. It was decided that, for military reasons, it would be better to organise the corps into five IRs, each only 1,000 men, and three grenadier Bns., each 400 men, altogether 6,200. Accordingly, a new agreement was signed on 16 April 1757, the existence of which has been previously unknown. This agreement was identical to that of 30 March except for the new organisation and higher annual payments of 69,473fl. (as opposed to 63,473fl.) per 1,000 men in peace and 83,507fl. (as opposed to 78,507fl.) in wartime. Confusingly, these payments were reckoned on a total of 6,000 men although the corps now totalled 6,200.

[59] HSAS, A202: Bü. 2219: French request for a further 3,000 men, 23 March 1757.

[60] Wilson, 'Violence and the rejection of authority', 17–22.

[61] HSAS, A74: Bü. 139, 23 Dec. 1756; Bü. 140, reports Jan.–Apr. 1757.

[62] HSAS, A74: Bü. 140; A202: Bü. 2219; LBS, cod. hist. fol. 647.

visit, but it was clearly crucial to the new pro-Austrian orientation of Carl Eugen's policy.[63]

The duke gave concrete signs of his new attachment by finally ordering the mobilisation of the Kreistruppen on 5 May 1757 and formally recognising the Reichstag's declaration of war on Prussia at the beginning of 1758.[64] In October 1757 he was honoured by being given command of the Bavarian corps as well as his own and in June the following year was rewarded by a favourable verdict on the Mömpelgard bastards.[65]

Despite this small success, he was still no further towards achieving his main aims. He now faced the characteristic problem of the weaker partner in a subsidy agreement: how to compel his stronger partner to grant the concessions he desired. In contrast to Bavaria, which effectively withdrew from the war in 1759,[66] Carl Eugen committed himself, like his father in the 1730s, to a reckless military buildup in the vain hope of finding favour with the emperor. In doing so he dangerously overreached himself, and merely became still more dependent on imperial good will. The crucial point came in 1758 when the cost of his armaments began to outstrip not only his own resources, but his subsidy income as well.[67] To cover the growing deficit he was forced to resort to a wide range of illegal financial measures which could only be continued as long as they were tolerated by the emperor. Whereas his father had carefully prepared the ground and had had time to bully the estates' committee into agreeing to his emergency financial measures, Carl Eugen was compelled to introduce his quickly and without even a sham of consent. This prompted the final break with the estates which had been on the cards since his innovations of the early 1750s. From 1758 the committee began secretly preparing the case against him which they successfully pressed in the imperial courts after 1764.[68] In order to understand why Carl Eugen embarked on such a risky policy we need to examine his position in 1757.

His troop convention of 1757 with France only gave him the status of a provider of auxiliaries. As such he was neither essential to the success of the war against Prussia, nor had he any say in the decision-making of the Franco-Austrian coalition.

---

[63] HSAS, A8: Bü. 60, No. 108, Carl Eugen to the Württemberg resident in Vienna, von Bühler, 1 Dec. 1784: 'Just two years ago I assured the emperor in Vienna that my promise of 1757 to remain attached to the imperial court, will always remain true. I believe this in the year '84 and will always believe it, in the certain hope to have in the emperor a friend and protector for myself and my house.'

[64] HSAS, C14: Bü. 87/1; Brabant, *Reich*, I, p. 101.

[65] HSAS, A74: Bü. 141; Stadlinger, *Kriegswesens*, p. 407; Scherb, *Mömpelgard*, pp. 245–6.

[66] Bitterauf, *Kurbayerische Politik*, pp. 115–45; A. Schmid, *Max III. Joseph und die europäischen Mächte. Die Außenpolitik des Kurfürstentums Bayerns von 1745–1765* (Munich, 1987), pp. 423–75.

[67] On 6 May 1757 Carl Eugen had realised that the payments specified in the Convention were going to be insufficient to cover the actual costs and had unsuccessfully tried through his representative in Paris, von Thun, to get these increased (HSAS, A202: Bü. 2219). The payments under the convention of 16 April 1757 totalled 531,052fl. a year whereas the Kriegsrat calculated on 4 May that the true cost of the corps of 6,200 men was 1,135,396fl. (A32: Bü. 1).

[68] Haug-Moritz, *Württembergischer Ständekonflikt*, pp. 308–18.

He would also be denied a seat at a future peace conference where he would have had an opportunity to press his demands. Altogether, as an auxiliary he lacked leverage on the Austrians to grant his requests. To achieve this, he needed to raise his status to that of full alliance partner.[69] In particular, he needed to persuade the emperor to sign a treaty with him along the lines of the one he had made with France in 1752. This would give him a written promise of the electoral title he desired.

The difference between subsidy auxiliary and full ally was ill defined. Much depended on the military strength and image of the power concerned. After all, both Austria and Sweden drew subsidies from France, but were both considered full alliance partners – the Swedes even though they scarcely ever had more than 14,000 effectives in the field. To achieve the desired impression, Carl Eugen set about establishing what his chief minister, Count Friedrich Samuel von Montmartin (1712–78) termed a 'stattliche Verfassung'.[70]

In practical terms this meant acquiring a high command for himself and expanding his army so that it could act independently from Austrian and French formations. At the beginning of 1758 he tried to get himself appointed successor to the luckless Prince von Sachsen-Hildburghausen as commander of the Reichsarmee. For a time it looked as if, with French assistance, he would succeed. However, here he met with his first set-back as the Austrians pushed through the appointment of another candidate. Meanwhile, he seized on the French envoy's suggestion that the Württemberg corps might operate in the coming campaign to safeguard the communications between the other allied armies.[71] This idea not only suited the duchy's general geographical position, but would give Carl Eugen a responsible and independent role. No doubt it also flattered him to think that he would no longer be directly subordinate to another commander. However, at this point he was handicapped by his corps' poor performance at the Battle of Leuthen (5 December 1757) and subsequent virtual destruction through sickness in unhealthy winter quarters.[72] When the troops finally took the field again in August

---

[69] This was recognised in contemporary law: see the quotation from J. J. Moser cited in Brauer, *Subsidienverträge*, p. 58. Württemberg's policy is also paralleled by that of Hessen-Kassel which tried to force its English subsidy partners to recognise its status as a full belligerent and not a mere auxiliary: Eldon, *Subsidy policy*, p. 113.

[70] H. Arnold, 'Schwedens Teilnahme am siebenjährigen Kriege', *BMWB*, 12 (1908), 453–82; HSAS, A74: Bü. 143, Montmartin to *Legationsrat* Straube, 25 July 1759.

[71] Brabant, *Reich*, II, pp. 42–3.

[72] Together with the mutinies of 1757, the Battle of Leuthen has contributed greatly to the traditional picture of the Württemberg army under Carl Eugen. This stems partly from the fact that the Austrians offloaded the blame for their defeat on to their Württemberg and Bavarian auxiliaries, who had borne the brunt of the first Prussian attack (see Staudinger, *Geschichte*, III, pp. 991–2). They also prevented the duke from publishing an account of the action as this would inevitably have involved criticism of their own generals. In fact, the Austrians might have avoided defeat if they had heeded the warning of the ADC of the Württemberg commander, F. F. von Nicolai. Nicolai had witnessed the Prussian manoeuvres of 1754 in the area and realised it was possible for the Austrians

1758, it was under the same terms as the 1757 convention, only this time they were assigned to Soubise's army in Hessen.[73]

Carl Eugen did not give up hope that such an opportunity for independent command might arise again, and began expanding his army accordingly. In 1757 it had largely consisted of infantry and the duke had been content to equip his corps with as little artillery as possible on the grounds that the Austrians already had enough cannon.[74] This all changed with plans drawn up early in 1758. These envisaged the expansion of the existing artillery corps of fifteen men to a battalion of 253. In addition, three heavy cavalry regiments were to be raised from scratch and the hussar corps expanded to regiment strength.[75] None of these formations was required by the duchy's existing subsidy convention, but all were essential if the army was to be able to act independently.

Similar increases followed in 1759 and 1760, bringing the total strength up to 16,000 effectives.[76] This was more than any ally of Austria and France possessed, other than the Russians. This alone is sufficient to dispel the traditional view that Carl Eugen was only seeking glory and financial profit. Had he desired only the latter he would not have raised regiments that were not paid for by his subsidy partners. Meanwhile, his entire conduct of operations displays an anxious desire to avoid any action with enemy forces which might inflict heavy losses on his own troops and so remove his only political bargaining counter.[77]

Connected with this military expansion was a conscious attempt to boost his image. While political motives were clearly not the only ones behind Carl Eugen's lavish arts patronage and construction of palaces, they obviously played a major part. Indeed, it is significant that the increase in court expenditure also began in 1757/8 and so coincides with the start of the military buildup.[78] The expansion of the army was mirrored by an explosion of cultural activity that was equally out of all proportion to the size of the duchy. This reached such heights that, by the early 1760s, Stuttgart with scarcely 18,000 inhabitants had an opera, ballet

---

to be outflanked to the left – the decisive move the Prussians actually made (see Nicolai's diary in LBS, cod. milit. qt. 29, fols. 75–89, extracts of which are printed in Stadlinger, *Kriegswesens*, pp. 413–22; also D. Hohrath and R. Henning, *Die Bildung des Offiziers in der Aufklärung. Ferdinand Friedrich von Nicolai (1730–1814)* (Stuttgart, 1990), pp. 10, 13).

[73] HSAS, G230: Bü. 49.

[74] HSAS, A74: Bü. 140, Carl Eugen to *Regierungsrat* Renz, 12 April 1757.

[75] The plan is no longer in existence but details of it are in HSAS, A8: Bü. 51; A32: Bd. 4; Stadlinger, *Kriegswesens*, pp. 427–8.

[76] HSAS, A8: Bü. 51; A32: Bd. 4–5; A202: Bü. 2236, *Feldetat*, 1 July 1760; G230: Bü. 50, 50a, 52; *Etat général des trouppes de S.A.S. Monseigneur le Duc de Virtemberg et Theck sur pié en 1759* (1759).

[77] On Württemberg military operations in the Seven Years War see HSAS, A202: Bü. 2279; G230: Bü. 47–53; Pfister, *Denkwürdigkeiten*, pp. 175–210; Schempp, *Infanterie Regiments*, pp. 107–43; Stadlinger, *Kriegswesens*, pp. 405–45.

[78] HSAS, A19a: Bd. 962–4; A256: Bd. 242–52.

and theatre to rival those of Paris with a population of more than all Württemberg.[79] The general reasoning behind this appears to have been that if the duke could afford both such a lavish court and a large army, he must indeed be a powerful prince and an ally worthy of the major states.

That this was more than mere vain self-indulgence is illustrated by the element of orchestrated image-building that accompanied it. For example, foreign envoys were invited to review the Württemberg troops, while details of every military increase were posted to the imperial ministers. In February 1759 *Legionsrat* Friedrich Straube was sent to Vienna with instructions to demonstrate each day how well Carl Eugen was following Austria's intentions.[80] Carefully worded reports of military actions were drafted to portray the Württemberg corps in the best possible light, while the duke and Montmartin reacted angrily to any derogatory articles appearing in foreign newspapers.[81] They also tried to silence publications criticising the arrest in 1759 of Johann Jakob Moser for protesting against the extraordinary taxation.[82]

The cost of this military and cultural competition was colossal. An examination of the costs illustrates two points. First, it underlines just how dangerously Carl Eugen overreached himself after 1758 in his effort to impress the emperor. Second, it reinforces the point that the expenditure was primarily directed towards political ends. This is shown by the fact the military spending far outstripped court costs. While the total spent on the court was higher than ever before, it was proportionately the same or less than under Eberhard Ludwig or Carl Alexander, owing to an overall increase in revenue and expenditure in the meantime. Moreover, while expenditure on the court increased, it did not grow at the pace of military spending. Between 1757 and 1765 the cost of the court averaged 516,500fl. a year, or 10 per cent above pre-war levels. Military spending during this period averaged 1,606,300fl. or 190 per cent above that of 1751–7.[83] The vast sums consumed by the army dwarfed even Carl Eugen's lavish arts patronage. The cost of the Solitude palace, built between 1763 and 1767, and estimated at a million florins, was matched or exceeded by military expenditure for every year between 1757 and 1765.[84] The 2,200,000fl. consumed by the army in 1759/60 alone was equivalent to the cost

---

[79] Yorke-Long, *Music at court*, pp. 43–70; Krauß, 'Das Theater', 481–554; A. Pfister, 'Hof und Hoffeste', *HKE*, I, 103–18; Klaiber, *Philippe de la Guepière*.

[80] HSAS, A74: Bü. 143. Montmartin's instructions to Straube, esp. 6 Feb. 1759, 1 April, 29 and 30 May 1759.

[81] HSAS, G230: Bü. 50, 'Umständliche und wahre Relation . . . Fulda'. On the attempts to suppress foreign newspaper accounts see A74: Bü. 143, 144.

[82] HSAS, A74: Bü. 143, esp. July–Aug. 1759. Montmartin accused the estates of sympathising with the Prussians.

[83] HSAS, A32: Bd. 3–13. In the absence of expenditure figures for 1757/8 and 1758/9, it has been assumed that all money received by the Kriegskasse was spent.

[84] Kleemann, *Schloß Solitude*, p. 23.

of Eberhard Ludwig's palace at Ludwigsburg which had taken thirty years to build.[85]

A similar picture is revealed by the structure of ducal debts. To a great extent these represent goods and services left unpaid and so in this sense can be considered expenditure. By 1765 they were estimated at between thirteen and fifteen million florins and therefore were at an unprecedented level.[86] While debts arising from overspending in the civil budget exceeded those incurred by military spending, the latter had risen from virtually nothing to total over seven million florins.[87] In addition, not all of Carl Eugen's civil debts were of his own making. As late as 1779 the Rentkammer was still burdened with over a million florins of Eberhard Ludwig's debts.[88]

Finally, the civil treasuries were tapped to an unprecedented degree to fund military expenditure. Not only was the contribution of the estates and the Kirchenkasten far in excess of anything experienced before, but the Rentkammer was brought in for the first time since the 1690s to help pay for the army.[89] Money was even transferred from the palace construction funds to the Kriegskasse, while the duke drew heavily on both the Rentkammer and his private Chatoule to pay his own campaign expenses.[90] The Chatoule was also made to contribute large sums to the construction of barracks and an arsenal in Ludwigsburg between 1761 and 1765.[91]

As was the case with the French subsidy money, the duke did not misappropriate funds from the wartime measures intended for the army to spend on other items. A comparison between the total sums known to have been raised by such measures and the amounts actually paid in the Kriegskasse shows that the overwhelming

---

[85] HSAS, A32: Bd. 3. On the Ludwigsburg palace see Chapter 5. The cost of Carl Eugen's other main building project, the Monrepos palace constructed 1760–5, is said to have been 300,000fl.: Walter, *Carl Eugen*, p. 210.

[86] A reliable Prussian estimate in Zentrales Staatsarchiv Merseburg, Rep. XI., Nr. 298, Fasz. 30, vol. 7, fol. 392 puts the total debt at 15,120,000fl., comprising 420,000fl. contracted on Mömpelgard, 5.7 million demanded by the estates in restitution for illegal war taxes and 9 million other debts. Another Prussian estimate in D. Schulenburg (ed.), *Denkwürdigkeiten des Freiherrn Achatz Ferdinand v.d. Asseburg* (Berlin, 1842), p. 226 n.1 places the total at 13,317,000fl.

[87] In summer 1739 the Kriegskasse debts totalled only 74,348fl. including 19,813fl. in borrowed capital (HSAS, L6.22.7.4a). In May 1764 debts stood at 1,393,818fl. plus 5.7 million in illegal war taxes (L6.22.8.3). (Note: H. P. Liebel-Weckowicz in 'Enlightened despotism and the resistance to arbitrary taxation in Southwest Germany after the Seven Years War', *Man and Nature. Proceedings of the Canadian Society for Eighteenth Century Studies*, 5 (1986), 99–118 at p. 103 misinterprets the debt figure of 1,393,818fl. as in part being expenditure items. They were, in fact, all arrears owed.)

[88] Pfaff, *Geschichte des Fürstenhauses*, IV, p. 393. The 1,046,671fl. was in addition to the 2 million Rentkammer debts taken over by the estates in 1739 and which had virtually been cleared by 1779.

[89] HSAS, A256: Bd. 197–252. See Table 8.7.1.

[90] See Table 8.7.1, the 10,000fl. from the *Residenzbaukasse*. See Tables 8.4 and 8.5.

[91] HSAS, A19a: Bd. 109–16. *Landoberbaucommissariats Rechnungen* 1761–7. The Chatoule contributed about 128,000fl. though some of the money may haven been spent on the laying out of gardens. A further 7,000fl. from the Chatoule went towards the construction of a wall around Ludwigsburg: see A19a: Bd. 1133, 1134.

proportion of the money demanded for military purposes did genuinely go towards the upkeep of the army. This is confirmed by an analysis of Kriegskasse expenditure, while the Rentkammer receipts show no income redirected from any measure ostensibly introduced to pay for the army.[92] The absence of any surviving account books for the Chatoule mean that misappropriation through this channel cannot be ruled out. However, it seems almost certain that the Chatoule received very little from such sources. Most of what it did receive was probably consumed by the duke's campaign expenses and by the barracks construction.

There is considerable evidence that the Austrians deliberately played along with Carl Eugen's policy in order to make him more dependent on them. They certainly gave him ample grounds for his false assessment of his importance to the imperial cause. At the end of December 1757 he returned from a second visit to Vienna boasting that the emperor had just promised him the next electoral title.[93] The fact that his main rival for that title, the landgrave of Hessen-Kassel, was on the opposing side and so stood little chance of winning imperial favour, probably encouraged him to think he was close to reaching his goals.

Meanwhile, he was urged to take tougher action against the estates and those in the bureaucracy who opposed him. Not only would this eliminate elements regarded by Vienna as pro-Prussian, but it would open up Württemberg institutions to infiltration by Austrian placemen. The Austrians had been holding out an offer of support for energetic measures against the estates ever since General Brettlach's mission to Stuttgart in 1756. The next year the emperor had written personally promising the duke his protection in the event of an estates' appeal to the imperial courts. Then, at the height of the 1758 crisis, he sent a document called a *Dehortatorium*. This would have enabled Carl Eugen to suspend the constitution on the grounds that the estates were opposing the imperial war effort. The following year, after Moser's arbitrary arrest, an imperial injunction was sent to the supreme court (Reichskammergericht) at Wetzlar to prevent the estates from prosecuting the duke.[94]

Carl Eugen clearly realised the dangers of accepting too willingly offers of support which the emperor was free to retract at any moment. He had no desire to see himself reduced to duke 'by the grace of Austria'. However, his decision to solve his financial crisis in 1758 by decreeing taxes himself effectively placed him in this position.

The duke's decision was considerably influenced by his new chief minister,

---

[92] HSAS, A32: Bd. 3–13; A256: Bd. 242–52. The small sums received from extraordinary measures (e.g. state lottery) derived from measures not ostensibly introduced for the maintenance of the army.

[93] Brabant, *Reich*, I, pp. 41–2.

[94] HSAS, G230: Bü. 46, 29 June 1757; Haug-Moritz, *Württembergischer Ständekonflikt*, pp. 55–8, 212–13, 220–30, 247–8; A. Schmid, *Das Leben Johann Jakob Mosers* (Stuttgart, 1868), pp. 260–3; Adam, *Moser*, pp. 62–3.

Montmartin. Significantly, Montmartin's appointment derived from his being recommended by the Austrians to Carl Eugen during his second visit to Vienna.[95] Montmartin had already known the duke since 1741 and had gained his confidence by his role in engineering the declaration of his majority in 1744. From April 1756 he had sought to enter Württemberg service as the best way to further his ambitious political career. Having convinced Vienna of his loyalty to the Habsburg cause, he was elevated to the status of count and manoeuvred into the position of Carl Eugen's adviser and Austria's man in Stuttgart. On 11 February 1758 he was appointed to a new three-man state and cabinet ministry (*Etats- und Kabinetts-ministerium*).[96] This was similar to the Konferenzministerium which had existed under Eberhard Ludwig and Carl Alexander, and enabled the duke to bypass the privy council which was no longer prepared to co-operate fully with his ambitions.[97] In June 1758 Montmartin was named president of the *Geheime Regiments-Deputation*, established to govern when Carl Eugen was absent with the field corps. Montmartin also headed this body during the campaigns of the following two years and in 1763 became *Premier Minister* and president of the privy council.[98] Throughout this time he remained in constant touch with leading Austrian ministers, particularly *Reichsvizekanzler* Count Rudolph Joseph Colloredo.[99] From his arrival in Stuttgart he began encouraging Carl Eugen to expand his court and army and to take tough action against the estates.

Additional Austrian influence was exerted through General Franz Baron von Werneck (1707–*c.* 75) who entered Württemberg service in 1734 and had acted as close adviser to Carl Alexander. Werneck had subsequently been entrusted with military and diplomatic missions and his promotion had been greatly favoured by Carl Eugen. He lost the duke's trust in 1757, but was saved from dismissal by the intercession of Montmartin. Thereafter, Vienna regarded him as a key agent at the Württemberg court. He was entrusted with securing the army in a Viennese plot in 1761 to seize Stuttgart in the event of Carl Eugen's death.[100]

Meanwhile, Carl Eugen received similar encouragement from his French subsidy partners. They promised military aid if the estates opposed him and sent Baron Franz Ludwig von Wimpffen (1732–1800) to Stuttgart as a French minder. Wimpffen exercised considerable influence between 1760 and 1776. His sister

---

95 On Montmartin, see Haug-Moritz, *Württembergischer Ständekonflikt*, pp. 81–7 and the literature cited there; G. Haug-Moritz, 'Friedrich Samuel Graf Montmartin als Württembergischer Staatsmann (1758–1766/73)', *ZWLG*, 53 (1994), 205–26.
96 HSAS, L5: Tom. 166, fols. 29b–31b.
97 Vann, *Making of a state*, pp. 270–3.
98 HSAS, E31: Bü. 6, 7. In 1764 Montmartin was also given the title of *Kriegsministre* [sic] and so was official head of the military administration: A202: Bü. 2186.
99 HSAS, A74: Bü. 143, 144, 146.
100 HSAS, A30a: Bd. 7, fol. 370; A202: Bü. 2020, 2021, 2262; I. M. P. Hoch, 'Württembergischen Denkwürdigkeiten aus den Herzoge Carl Alexander und Carl Eugen', *Sophronizon*, 6 (1824), 5. Heft. 16–62; Haug-Moritz, *Württembergischer Ständekonflikt*, p. 86.

Josephine was temporarily the duke's mistress, and by 1774 he had risen to the top of the military administration.[101]

These foreign placemen did much to encourage Carl Eugen's ambitions. However, they also had a vested interest in the success of ducal policy to advance their own careers, and in the case of Werneck, those of his five relations in the Württemberg army. They were in the invidious position of trying to please two masters. None had much room for manoeuvre. Lack of time and the hostility of the native Württemberg elite prevented any of them from developing a local patronage network to secure their position. Werneck had a number of enemies among the officer corps who intrigued for his dismissal, while Montmartin was hindered by a personal vendetta against Rieger who headed the military financial administration. As Montmartin had rightly predicted in 1759, failure to secure what Carl Eugen wanted could lead to his being made the scapegoat for ducal disappointment.[102] Montmartin was dismissed in May 1766, followed by Werneck in January 1767 and Wimpffen in 1776. All of Werneck's relations had left Württemberg service by 1761, while Rieger was imprisoned between 1762 and 1766 for protesting at the military buildup and for corresponding with the duke's brothers.[103]

On 20 March 1758, scarcely a month after Montmartin's appointment, Carl Eugen presented his proposed troop increases to the estates' committee. Simultaneously, he repeated a request made the previous September, that the part of the tax grant intended for debt repayment be redirected to the Kriegskasse for the duration of the war. He also asked the committee to take over the growing Kreis military payments as an additional tax. The committee argued that these proposals were contrary to the terms of the 1739 recess and refused. Tension mounted, because their reply contained phrases considered both rebellious and insulting to Montmartin. Finally Carl Eugen took the law into his own hands. Using the Prussian invasion of neighbouring Franconia as an excuse for emergency measures, he decreed the taxes himself on 26 June.[104]

As he arbitrarily fixed the level of the Kreis payments on that of the duchy's nominal contingent rather than the contingent actually sent to the Reichsarmee, he was able to divert the surplus to pay his new formations. He further demanded that the estates pay the provision allowance on the paper, rather than the effective, strength of the Kriestruppen. The difference, the so-called *Vacant Portionen*, was

101 HSAS, A30c: Bd. 7, fol. 384, Bü. 11; R. Uhland, *Geschichte der Hohen Karlsschule in Stuttgart* (Stuttgart, 1953), pp. 20–1; *ADB*, 43 (1898), 326–7. The promise of military assistance was made in the Feb. 1759 treaty.

102 HSAS, A7: Bü. 143, Montmartin to Straube, 25 Nov. 1759.

103 HSAS, A30c: Bd. 7, fols. 371–4; on Rieger see A8: Bü. 223–52; A202: Bü. 1837; G230: Bü. 12, 43–5; E. Schneider, 'Zur Charakteristik des Oberst Riegers', *LBSAW* (1888), 293–6.

104 HSAS, L5: Tom. 165, fols. 453–4; L6.22.8.1; Adam, 'Landschaft', pp. 214–17; Brabant, *Reich*, II, pp. 97–113; Pfaff, *Militärwesen*, pp. 67–9.

also used to pay the new units. These two forms of additional income brought in the equivalent of over half the value of foreign subsidies received.[105] Finally, he demanded an additional 50,000fl. as 'national defence money' (*Landesdefensions-gelder*).[106] When this was refused he sent his officials to 'inspect' the estates' treasury box and seize what they could find. When the two treasurers resisted they were heavily fined, while opposition in the localities was quelled by further fines and even imprisonment.[107] This was followed by further arbitrary measures between 1759 and 1764.[108]

Just how important these measures were to ducal finances is revealed by the accompanying tables. The breakdown of Kriegskasse income (Tables 8.6 to 8.10) shows that between 1757 and 1765 only just over 17 per cent came from the regular tax grant (*recessmäßige Anlagen*). In contrast, the duke was dependent on outside help for nearly 65 per cent of his military finance, whereby the unconstitutional measures (47 per cent) were clearly more important than the subsidies (17.9 per cent). Over one-third of the remaining money came from government borrowing, while the rest largely derived from other emergency measures which could not be continued indefinitely.[109]

THE FAILURE OF DUCAL POLICY, 1759–65

The political consequences of this dependence became apparent with the failure of ducal policy between 1759 and 1765. Carl Eugen's hopes to be able to profit from tension within the Franco-Austrian alliance were dashed when this was renewed at the end of December 1758.[110] Simultaneously, the French discharged the Württemberg corps, which was then forced to winter in the duchy at the duke's expense. This was part of a general attempt to scale down French subsidy commitments: those to Austria were cut by three-quarters with part of the balance being rescheduled for payment *after* the war.[111] On 9 February 1759 they renegotiated their agreement with the duke and terminated the convention of 1757 altogether. Carl Eugen was now required to hold only 2,000 men in readiness in return for 150,000fl. annual subsidy over the next three years.[112] He was also obliged to make an additional concession to the emperor by rejecting the motion of 29 November

---

[105] Tables 8.6 and 8.8.
[106] HSAS, L6.22.8.1. Further contributions of *Landesdefensionsgelder* were demanded in 1759 and 1762.
[107] On the resistance see HSAS, L6.22.8.1, July 1758; Adam, *Moser*, p. 65; J. Kocher, *Geschichte der Stadt Nürtingen* (2 vols., Stuttgart, 1924), I, p. 127.
[108] HSAS, L6.22.8.1–3; Adam, 'Landschaft', pp. 217–33.
[109] In addition to the figures in the tables, the military administration owed the Ämter at least 171,000fl. for goods and services left unpaid: A32: Bd. 10–14, 183–90.
[110] Schäffer, *Geschichte des siebenjährigen Krieges*, II/I, pp. 209–37.
[111] HSAS, G230: Bü. 49; Dickson, *Maria Theresia*, II, pp. 173–4.
[112] HSAS, A202: Bü. 2219, treaty of 9 Feb. 1759; all maintenance payments from France stopped.

1758 of the Corpus Evangelicorum.[113] The French did renew their promise of support for the electoral title and territorial increase. However, the terms of the new treaty effectively deprived Carl Eugen of the means to achieve this by condemning him to an inactive role in the war. The reduction in the subsidy payments also made the continuation of the unconstitutional financial measures absolutely essential if he was to be able to maintain his army to be ready to rejoin the war when a suitable opportunity appeared ('sich Ihren Hohen Alliirten nach Zeit und Umstanden nüzlich zu machen').[114]

Following this treaty, the duke did his best to remain on good terms with the emperor, and the duchy assiduously followed the imperial line at the Reichstag. Unfortunately, Montmartin's continued assurances that the duke had done far more for imperial interests than other rulers rang rather hollow in view of his failure to provide his full Reichsarmee contingent.[115]

At the same time, Carl Eugen pushed his scheme of early 1758 to use his army as a link between the French and the Reichsarmee. In the negotiations on this suggestion, he pressed Austria for an agreement 'on the same footing' as the one he had with France. This would at last give him the elusive written promise that his requests would be granted. He was so desperate for this that, if subsidies proved a sticking point, he was even prepared to allow the emperor to postpone paying until after the war was over.[116] Finally, in late summer an opportunity presented itself and he was able to spring back into the war.

The general panic among the pro-Austrian states following the French retreat after their defeat at Minden (1 August 1759) created the favourable circumstances. To plug the gap between their forces and the Reichsarmee, the French signed a new military convention on 3 November.[117] Under this, France hired 8,670 men for one year in return for over two million florins. Although still not an agreement with Austria, the convention was financially sound, and at last gave the duke an independent command. He was assigned the apparently easy task of occupying the defenceless bishopric of Fulda on the flank of the enemy army. Given the lateness of the season, he could reasonably expect that both sides would soon enter winter quarters to wait for better weather before renewing operations. Unfortunately, the enemy had other ideas and surprised him on 30 November, driving him back

---

[113] Schäffer, *Geschichte des siebenjährigen Krieges*, II/I, pp. 195–6; Brabant, II, pp. 339ff.; Gerspacher, *Badische Politik*, pp. 28–40.

[114] HSAS, A74: Bü. 143, Montmartin to Straube, 25 July 1759.

[115] HSAS, C14: Bü. 77, 87/I, 568; Brabant, *Reich*, III, pp. 16–17, 79. On the problems over the Reichsarmee contingent see pp. 21–2.

[116] HSAS, A74: Bü. 143, esp. Montmartin to Straube, 12 Aug. 1759: 'daß man nehmlich wünschet, sich auf eben den Fuß mit dem Kayserlichen Hof zuverbinden, wie es mit der Crone Frankreich geschehen.'

[117] HSAS, A202: Bü. 2219, *Militär Convention*, 3 Nov. 1759; Hoch, 'Denkwürdigkeiten', p. 39; Brabant, *Reich*, III, pp. 267–8. The duke actually provided 9,140 men, or more than the convention required, strength tables in G230: Bü. 50.

with heavy loss.[118] In view of the unfavourable opinion following this defeat, Montmartin finally abandoned his attempts to persuade Vienna to sign a full alliance with the duke.[119]

Fortunately, the 1759 convention accorded the duke winter quarters for his corps and so he was able to remain around Würzburg until well into spring 1760.[120] In the meantime he began a publicity campaign to repair his damaged reputation. As he was unable to secure permission from the French commander to continue to act independently, he prepared to return to Württemberg.[121] The Austrians had no desire to see the allied army depleted and sought to prevent this.[122] This possibly increased Carl Eugen's view of his indispensability to the allied cause. In late spring the Austrians at last offered to take over the troops currently in French pay.

Although his corps was already set to march, the duke delayed its departure in the hope that the emperor would offer him better terms. In particular, he wanted a set of secret articles promising him the electoral title and additional territory when peace was made. He also wanted an assurance that his men would be taken over for a full year and not just the six-month campaign season; otherwise he would find himself having to pay for their winter quarters as he had done in 1758/9. To cover his additional expenses, he demanded the same generous mobilisation costs as those accorded him by the French in November 1759.[123]

The Austrians saw through this. On 19 June 1760 the imperial envoy, Rüdt, bluntly pointed out the futility of any further attempts and said that it would only be regarded in Vienna as an excuse to delay the corps' departure.[124] The duke was forced to give in to avoid incurring imperial displeasure and on 23 July, Montmartin signed a treaty on the emperor's terms with Rüdt. The duke got a mere 50,000fl. cash assistance towards mobilisation and was let off that year's Römer Monat payment (worth 56,000fl.). In addition, he was permitted to keep a third of all contributions raised. All other costs were to be borne by him, although food was supplied free of charge from the imperial commissariat. In return, he had to

---

[118] HSAS, G230: Bü. 50, 50a; LBS, cod. milit. fol. 29. The popular myth that Carl Eugen was surprised at a masked ball by the enemy attack is untrue. While some of the Württemberg officers had begun celebrating the Prussian defeat at Maxen, the duke actually worked the night through on military matters. The Württembergers were surprised, because the French brigade assigned to protect their flank retreated before the enemy advance and failed to send a warning: see R. Geiges, 'Mit Herzog Karl Eugen im siebenjährigen Krieg. Nach Tagebuchaufzeichnungen des Leibmedicus Dr. Albrecht Reichart Reuß', *BBSAW* (1928), 185–96. See also R. Waddington, *La guerre de sept ans* (5 vols., Paris, 1899–1914), III, pp. 102–9; C. P. V. Pajol, *Les guerres sous Louis XV* (7 vols., Paris, 1881), IV, pp. 474–8.

[119] HSAS, A74: Bü. 143, Montmartin to Straube, 16 Jan. 1760.

[120] On the winter quarters see HSAS, G230: Bü. 50a, reports of Commissar Potier.

[121] HSAS, G230: Bü. 50, correspondence of Carl Eugen with the duc de Broglie; A74: Bü. 144, Montmartin to Straube, 25 May 1760.

[122] A74: Bü. 144, Straube to Montmartin, 2 June 1760.

[123] *Ibid.*, A202: Bü. 2236, esp. Carl Eugen to Emperor Francis, 22 June 1760.

[124] A202: Bü. 2236. See also Rüdt's memorandum of 21 July 1760.

provide 11,000 men 'for this year's campaign', serving as a separate corps under the overall direction of the imperial high command. None of the duke's political aims was granted, though the emperor did agree to turn a blind eye to Carl Eugen's continued levying of any extraordinary means (*außerordentliche Media*) in Württemberg he found necessary. The duke agreed to these terms in the hope that the emperor would 'remember' his patriotism when the time came.[125]

Although the campaign passed of without any major reverses, the duke's precipitate retreat before a superior Prussian force angered the Austrians.[126] On 24 November the emperor wrote that he could no longer guarantee the Württemberg corps winter quarters on the grounds that insufficient contributions had been collected to pay for them. In the meantime the imperial ministers were instructed to work out how best to employ the troops in the future. Six days later, however, after the duke had retreated still further, the emperor told him it was now better if he withdrew them all the way to Württemberg as he no longer needed them.[127] A month later, the whole corps was back in the duchy. The emperor was glad to see it go, as he had begun to fear that Carl Eugen's method of solving his supply problems by reckless requisitioning would alienate Austria's allies in the area.

Although the duke tried hard to excuse his retreat on the grounds of superior enemy numbers, attitudes in Vienna had turned against him. No one was interested in his appeals for compensation for not receiving winter quarters, or in his proposal to support the emperor with as many as 12,000–15,000 men if given command of the Reichsarmee.[128] Austro-Württemberg relations now cooled dramatically. Montmartin's influence declined and in 1761 he was temporarily exiled on a mission to Vienna. Rüdt was recalled that June and another Austrian envoy did not arrive in Stuttgart until November 1762.[129] Following the Reichsarmee's defeat at Freiberg (29 October 1762), Carl Eugen withdrew his contingent and practically declared neutrality on 4 December.[130] Four months later the emperor punished him for this lack of loyalty by an unfavourable verdict on Württemberg coinage devaluation.[131]

This was just the first in a series of unpleasant verdicts that were to demonstrate just how dependent Carl Eugen had become on imperial good will. Between 1761

---

[125] *Ibid.* Convention of 23 July 1760; ratified by Emperor Francis on 2 Aug. 1760.

[126] Details of the campaign in HSAS, G230: Bü. 51–3, esp. the *Journal du corps d'armee de Württemberg* in Bü. 53. Parts of the journal are printed in German translation in Stadlinger, *Kriegswesens*, pp. 436–45. See also E. Frhr von Ziegesar (ed.), *Zwei Württembergische Soldatenbilder aus alter Zeit* (Stuttgart, 1904), pp. 83–6. Ironically, the Prussian force was commanded by Carl Eugen's younger brother, Friedrich Eugen, who entered Prussian service in 1753.

[127] HSAS, A202: Bü. 2236, imperial letters of 24 and 30 Nov. 1760.

[128] HSAS, A74: Bü. 144, esp. Montmartin to Straube, 21 Dec. 1760.

[129] HSAS, A8: Bü. 5.

[130] HSAS, C14: Bü. 77, 87a, 418; L6.22.8.2.

[131] Haug-Moritz, *Württembergischer Ständekonflikt*, p. 119.

and 1765 he made desperate efforts to free himself by widening his room to manoeuvre through a reduction in military spending, a search for new subsidies and the introduction of new forms of taxation. This was the classic mix of solutions that had been tried by all Württemberg dukes when placed in a similar predicament. However, this time they were attempted too late to avert disaster.

From January 1761 the army was drastically reduced and effectively demobilised by selling off half the cavalry horses and all the transport animals.[132] However, all the officers and regimental staffs were retained and no single formation was entirely disbanded. This permitted the duke to mobilise again should a suitable opportunity to further his political aims present itself. It proved impossible to extend the treaty of 9 February 1759 when this expired at the end of 1761 as the French were in no position to pay further subsidies.[133] A second troop reduction was therefore drafted in March 1762,[134] but not implemented as Carl Eugen believed he could profit from the war between Spain and Portugal that broke out in April. Montmartin used his contacts in Vienna to obtain Austrian support for an attempt to hire a corps to the Spanish.[135] In July, Wimpffen was sent to Madrid to negotiate.

Although short of troops, the Spanish were not interested. The negotiations only lasted so long because Wimpffen mistakenly believed that the Spanish army reorganisation that began later that year had improved the chances of success.[136] The Spanish used the difference of religion as an excuse to reject the offer. As the Austrian ambassador pointed out: 'The real reason, however, is the poor discipline shown by the Württemberg troops with us in Silesia and in Hessen in French service.'[137] Finally, when it was abundantly clear he was never going to succeed, Wimpffen left in June 1763. The duke then tried again to persuade the French to pay, before ultimately giving this up as utterly hopeless at the end of the year.[138]

As the war in Europe had ended with the Peace of Hubertusburg in February 1763, Carl Eugen was free to look outside the ranks of the emperor's allies for a foreign sponsor. In February 1764 he opened negotiations with the English, but was led a merry dance by his representative in London, the self-styled Chevalier William Stapleton. One step ahead of his own creditors, Stapleton spun out his time

---

[132] HSAS, A8: Bü. 51, 53, 54; A32: Bd. 4–7. Adam, 'Landschaft', is incorrect in implying that the army was not reduced after 1760 (p. 230) and claiming that it was later even increased (p. 231).

[133] HSAS, A8: Bü. 8, 58; A74: Bü. 117, reports of Ulrich von Thun, ducal representative in Paris.

[134] HSAS, A8: Bü. 512, *Militär Plan*, 8 March 1762.

[135] HSAS, A74: Bü. 146, Montmartin to Kaunitz and Colloredo, 3 June 1762. It is worth remembering that Spain was allied to France which was still allied to Württemberg.

[136] Report of the Austrian ambassador in Madrid, Count Rosenberg, to Kaunitz, 27 Dec. 1762 in H. Jüretschke (ed.), *Berichte der diplomatischen Vertreter des Wiener Hofes aus Spanien in der Regierungszeit Karl III. (1759–1788)* (14 vols., Madrid, 1970–87), II, pp. 262–4.

[137] Rosenberg to Kaunitz, 23 Aug. 1762, *ibid.*, pp. 186–7.

[138] Rosenberg to Kaunitz, 5 April, 23 May and 13 June 1763, *ibid.*, pp. 314–16, 324, 327; HSAS, A74: Bü. 117.

in London at Württemberg expense by creating the impression that subsidies were just another few days negotiations ahead.[139]

By the middle of 1765, however, it was clear that the attempts to find suitable foreign subsidies had failed. This failure coincided with the failure of his attempts to introduce new taxes. As this sealed his fate and led to the complete collapse of ducal policy, it is worth considering the events in detail.

The duke could go a long way towards solving his problems if he could obtain secure funding from his duchy instead of having to rely on foreign subsidies. While the emergency measures introduced in 1758 provided the necessary money, they only worsened his position as he needed the emperor's co-operation to silence the estates' protests. If he could persuade the estates to agree to the measures, he would be freed from this dependence on outside help. As we have seen in the course of this work, this represented a long-term objective of all Württemberg dukes. The perennial problem was how to obtain the estates' agreement. Ever since Eberhard Ludwig, the standard method had been to undermine the committee's resistance by approaching the Amtsversammlungen directly. This method required ample preparation to be successful, and unfortunately for Carl Eugen, time was now at a premium.

Carl Eugen's first attempt in this direction was the so-called *Gemeinbefehl* of 10 April 1758. This was a call to his subjects to send suggestions for improvements in government policies.[140] It appears to have been an attempt to interest the general population in the kind of innovations he had begun in the mid-1750s. In addition, he tried to settle those grievances that genuinely concerned the well-being of his poorer subjects. These were traditional complaints about the unpaid quartering of military personnel, damage caused by game animals, labour services and the like. Such complaints were seized upon by the estates' committee in their attempt to win popular support. To counter this, Carl Eugen repealed some of the unpopular laws, such as the *Mühlreskript* which had been introduced in 1761 and involved higher fees for the use of ducal mills.[141] However, the shortage of money, especially from 1764/5 onwards, prevented him from doing without the labour services and unpaid quartering. As these formed the bulk of the complaints, their retention limited the success of his efforts to swing opinion.

In 1761 he began another move intended to undermine the estates' opposition. This was the sale of offices (Diensthandel). Just like the similar policy conducted by Carl Alexander through Süss' Gratialamt, this was supposed to both boost ducal

---

[139] HSAS, A8: Bü. 8, Stapleton's reports 1764–5; PRO, SP100/17, Stapleton's letters of 19 Nov. and 30 Dec. 1765, 1 Jan. 1766. The fact that Stapleton came from a family of Jacobites can hardly have improved his chances of success.

[140] Walter, *Carl Eugen*, p. 156. For examples of some of the many suggestions actually sent in see HSAS, A8: Bü. 78.

[141] Adam, 'Landschaft', p. 231; Wintterlin, 'Landeshoheit', p. 177.

revenue and weaken the dominance of the worthies.[142] Not only were their relations excluded from new appointments, but by the creation of the post of *Unteramtmann* on 19 November 1762, the duke tried to break their stranglehold on local administration. The new post involved the redrawing of the Ämter boundaries to create new subdivisions (*Unterämter*), based around villages rather than the district towns (Amtsstädte). The Unterämter were to be integrated into the voting organisation of the Landtag. As the villages lay on the periphery of the influence of the town-based worthies, and as they were also more easily intimidated by ducal officials, the creation of the Unterämter threatened to radically alter the structure of the Landtag.[143]

However, the full potential of these changes was not realised, as the policy was not followed through consistently. In view of the duke's growing budget deficit, the financial aspect of the sale of offices began to take precedence.[144] Large numbers of applicants were accepted on grounds of their purchasing power rather than aptitude.[145] Moreover, public opinion was turned against the Unterämter by compelling the communities to pay large fees for the boundary changes.[146] Under heavy pressure from the estates' committee, which fully appreciated the revolutionary potential of the Unterämter, Carl Eugen was forced to abandon this project. In 1768 the Unterämter were abolished and while the sale of offices continued, returns were lower and the primary motive was now financial.

More significant was the duke's attempt to introduce a new system of taxation. This began in January 1763 with the implementation of a new military plan. Without reference to the committee, Carl Eugen fixed the tax burden at over 1,620,000fl., or three-and-a-half times the level set in 1739. The new figure was the sum required under the plan to maintain the army for one year. The money was to be paid in monthly instalments called *Monatliche Gelder*.[147] This did away with the need for the committee to meet every six months to determine each community's precise tax quota. Further, on 5 February he announced his intention of devising an entirely new method of collection for this tax. This would be placed before the

---

142 Wunder, *Privilegierung*, pp. 71–82; Haug-Moritz, *Württembergischer Ständekonflikt*, pp. 66–70.
143 Grube, 'Dorfgemeinde', 194–219; Vann, *Making of a state*, pp. 278–9.
144 For an assessment of the returns see H. P. Liebel-Weckowicz, 'The revolt of the Württemberg estates', *Man and Nature. Proceedings of the Canadian Society for Eighteenth Century Studies*, 2 (1984), 109–20 at p. 114. Adam, 'Landschaft', p. 262 is incorrect in asserting that the proceeds increased after 1767: sales dropped off dramatically after 1764.
145 For examples, Adam, *Moser*, pp. 13–15; Kleemann, *Solitude*, pp. 25–7.
146 Baur, *Städtischer Haushalt Tübingens*, p. 85. For examples of complaints at the Unterämter see pp. 105–7.
147 HSAS, A8: Bü. 51; A30a: Bü. 59. The new military plan of 1763 has universally been misinterpreted as an increase in strength and costs. In fact it represented a slight reduction in strength over the previous plan (1 June 1761) or 10,290 officers and men as opposed to 10,495. Expenses remained roughly level, while the method of funding was changed. The significance of this change has previously been overlooked.

Landtag which he had agreed would meet in September.[148] The committee simply refused to recognise that any change had taken place and instructed the Ämter to pay the Monatliche Gelder as advances on future legal grants.[149] When the Landtag refused to legitimise the duke's new measure, Carl Eugen followed the example of his two predecessors and approached the Amtsversammlungen directly.

On 31 March 1764 all Amtsversammlungen were summoned at short notice and suddenly confronted with the new proposals.[150] Great efforts were made to present the tax, now called *Militär Steuer*, in a favourable light. The new method of collection, modelled on that actually in use in parts of Austria, did actually shift part of the burden from the poorer subjects to the rich.[151] Unfortunately, the majority of the people who stood to benefit were underrepresented at the Amtsversammlungen. The duke has also been unwise enough not to state clearly whether he intended to abolish the existing taxes or not. The result was that his policy completely backfired.

Despite bullying and threats from ducal officials, many of the Amtsversammlungen rejected the proposals or at least requested alterations. Instead of securing support for his policy, the duke found that the Amtsversammlungen opposition only served to legitimise the committee's stance against him. Rather than being at odds with a democratic movement as it had been during the Landtag of 1737–9, the committee now enjoyed widespread support. This was encouraged by its vocal championing of the small man's complaints and the publication of its correspondence from the years after 1758, providing that it had not abandoned the duchy to ducal absolutism during the war. Opposition to the duke now took on a popular form with a tax strike in the localities, while imprisoned officials such as Moser and Huber became national heroes.[152] When Carl Eugen tried to use military force to break the strike, the public outcry became international.[153]

It has been suggested that Carl Eugen's decision to use force was part of a deliberate policy to provoke an open rebellion.[154] Certainly, the estates' committee, already divided over the course of action to be taken, feared the unrest would spill over into violent popular resistance to ducal policies. On 23 June, the Austrian

---

[148] HSAS, A8: Bü. 386; L6.22.8.2.

[149] On the payment of the Monatliche Gelder see HSAS, A8: Bü. 55, No. 47, Bü. 386; L10: *Einnehmerei Rechnungen* 1762/3, 1763/4.

[150] HSAS, A8: Bü. 55; Weisert, *Sindelfingen*, pp. 267–8.

[151] Contrary to the view presented in the existing literature, the tax was very low by modern standards. Those with an income of under 10fl. a year were to pay 15xr., a rate of 0.25 per cent. Those in higher income brackets generally had to pay around 0.5 per cent.

[152] On the level of opposition see HSAS, A8: Bü. 55–7; Liebel, 'Resistance to arbitrary taxation', pp. 105–11 and 'Revolt', pp. 115–16; Kocher, *Nürtingen*, I, pp. 129–33; Weisert, *Sindelfingen*, pp. 268–9; K. Mayer, *Aus Kirchheims Vergangenheit* (Kirchheim/Teck, 1913), pp. 167–8; J. Forderer, *Tüttlingen im Wandel der Zeiten* (Reutlingen, 1949), p. 181.

[153] HSAS, A8: Bü. 55, Nos. 51–63, Bü. 387; L6.22.8.5.

[154] Haug-Moritz, *Württembergischer Ständekonflikt*, pp. 92–3, 349–51.

representative in Stuttgart, Baron Widmann, reported that the situation was now so serious that he feared to leave the town. Indeed, many contemporaries believed a general uprising was imminent.[155] This would have enabled Carl Eugen to brand his domestic opponents as rebels and law-breakers and have given both France and Austria the ideal excuse to intervene on his behalf.

However, neither power was prepared to take such action. France had remained deaf to ducal appeals for support on the basis of the February 1759 treaty which provided for French military assistance against the estates. The fact that this treaty had expired in January 1762 provided a convenient excuse. The real reason for French inaction was the desire on the part of Paris to do nothing that would further harm its already damaged reputation within the Reich.[156]

This was also the underlying reason behind the Austrian policy of passive delay in the Württemberg question. For example, although the emperor recognised the validity of the estates' request that a Landtag be held, he refused to grant the delegates imperial protection. He also turned a blind eye to the continuation of the emergency financial measures which the estates claimed were unconstitutional. Furthermore, he blocked the intervention of the three Protestant guarantors of the Reversalien, England, Prussia and Denmark, whom the estates had been able to call upon now that the war was over. The Austrian ministers, particularly Reichsvizekanzler Colloredo, hoped that the duke would be able to settle matters at a Landtag and so avoid the estates bringing their complaints to the imperial courts.[157]

The object of this policy was not to disturb Austria's wider interests in the Reich. Chief among these in 1764 was to re-establish the influence and prestige lost as a result of the obvious misuse of the imperial title and institutions in the furtherance of Habsburg Hauspolitik during the Seven Years War. In particular, Austrian ministers wished to avoid any action that would further substantiate Prussian claims that, as both a Catholic and a Habsburg, the emperor was no longer able to act in his traditional capacity as the impartial supreme judge. Though Vienna had no desire to see Carl Eugen's domestic position further restricted, active intervention on his behalf against his (Protestant) estates was sure to be interpreted by Prussia and her supporters as further proof of sinister Austrian designs. This had to be avoided at all costs, given that Austria was still embroiled in negotiations for Archduke Joseph's election as King of the Romans. In addition, by leaving the question of a final judgment open, Austrian ministers hoped to keep the internal situation in Württemberg undecided and thus free to be influenced in the future as it suited them. Similarly, the emperor refused to recognise the right of the

[155] Widmann quoted in Liebel, 'Resistance to arbitrary taxation', pp. 108–9; Schulenburg (ed.), *Asseburg*, p. 206.
[156] HSAS, A202: Bü. 2219; Haug-Moritz, *Württembergischer Ständekonflikt*, pp. 332–49.
[157] Adam, *Moser*, pp. 72–3; Grube, *Landtag*, pp. 433–4; Schulenburg (ed.), *Asseburg*, pp. 205–15.

guarantee-powers to intervene for fear of losing his monopoly of influence in Württemberg internal affairs.[158]

However, the events of spring 1764 made the continuation of this policy untenable. Following the Austrian triumph of Joseph's election on 27 March, Prussia was compelled to take action to bolster its own influence within the Reich. Until then, none of the Protestant guarantee-powers had been particularly active on the estates' behalf. Now Prussia swung over to the offensive and called on the emperor to take action. The duke's military occupation of Tübingen to crush its resistance to the tax finally prompted the hesitant estates' committee to lodge a formal case at the Reichshofrat (Aulic Council) on 30 June. Three days later the ambassadors of England, Prussia and Denmark arrived in Stuttgart.[159]

The pressure was now too strong to be ignored for much longer. On 6 September 1764 the Reichshofrat passed its first verdict ordering Moser's release and an end to the Militär Steuer. After Carl Eugen's attempt to reach an out-of-court settlement at a second session of the Landtag in October failed, there was little stopping the process. Moreover, the three guarantee powers now became firmly embedded in the negotiations as the duke opened separate discussions with them in January 1765. In face of mounting pressure on behalf of the estates, a second verdict became unavoidable.[160] This was passed on 15 May 1765 and its effects were crippling. Until a final settlement was reached, the Reichshofrat instructed the estates to pay only the taxes fixed in the 1739 recess. From these, they were to deduct the Kreisextraordinarium and the Rentkammer debt-amortisation payments, leaving only about 330,000fl. to be paid to the duke. In addition, all the unconstitutional measures were to stop. With one blow, Carl Eugen's financial lifeline was cut. The effects are revealed in Tables 8.6 to 8.10. Average annual income from the measures after 1 May 1765 stood at only 6 per cent of what it had been before. The total income of the Kriegskasse fell by nearly two-thirds to about 545,000fl. This was approximately the pre-war level when the number of soldiers to be maintained was less than half that with the colours in 1765. The consequences were felt immediately. Between July and August 1765, the army was reduced by 36 per cent. Significantly, for the first time, many units were completely disbanded.[161]

The loss of financial support was accompanied by growing political isolation. Despite all Carl Eugen's efforts, the Austrians remained unimpressed as to his value as an alliance partner. With the international outcry at the suppression of the tax strike by ducal troops, he came in for heavy criticism from foreign heads of state. They censured him for his extravagance at a time when his debts were mounting at

---

[158] Haug-Moritz, *Württembergischer Ständekonflikt*, pp. 272–92.

[159] *Ibid.*, pp. 308–73; HSAS, A8: Bü. 387.

[160] Grube, *Landtag*, pp. 436–41; Haug-Moritz, *Württembergischer Ständekonflikt*, pp. 393–404.

[161] HSAS, A8: Bü. 51, 54, 58; A202: Bü. 2207, 2288; L6.22.8.5. Effective strength declined from 7,244 officers and men in June 1765 to 4,652 in September.

an alarming rate and his unconstitutional measures had provoked his subjects almost to the point of open revolt. Even his former protectors, the Austrians, urged economies, while shortly after his accession in 1765, the new emperor, Joseph II, took a particularly dim view of the wild extravagance.[162]

Why then, in the face of this criticism, did Carl Eugen not follow what would appear to be common sense and cut back spending? There appear to be three reasons. First, his obstinate optimism appears to have led him to believe that, despite all the setbacks, the Austrians would not totally abandon him and force him to agree to the estates' terms.[163] Second, the continuation of the lavish court expenditure into the mid-1760s has much akin to an act of defiance. If Carl Eugen could not outdo his rivals by realising his political ambitions, he would at least over-shadow them with a dazzling court. In this sense, his policy at this time accords well with the theory of cultural competition. The court and art patronage were to compensate for his failure to 'cut a dash on the international stage'.[164] Indeed, political failure appears to have motivated the construction of the Solitude palace which began with the downturn of ducal fortunes late in 1763.[165] Carl Eugen's long and expensive visit to the Venetian carnival in 1766/7 appears to be an attempt to flee the realities of political failure.[166] Third, to economise would almost be a public admission of defeat. In any case, it was not easy to economise. As the army was much bigger and contained more officers than at any time in the past, the problems associated with its reduction were correspondingly greater.

Contrary to the prevailing view in the literature, Carl Eugen did, in fact, attempt economies as early as 1761. Their effect, however, was limited by the difficulty in discharging the officers who were already owed arrears from the campaigns of 1757–60. The large-scale reductions in 1765 were only possible because the duke made his recognition of the Reichshofrat verdict dependent on the estates paying 200,000fl. towards the arrears. Two years later, he extracted a further 160,000fl. from them in return for their agreement to a partial settlement. This enabled

---

[162] HSAS, A8: Bü. 387; Conrad (ed.), 'Verfassung und politische Lage', pp. 179–80. It is worth noting, however, that much of the criticism was directed more at Carl Eugen's personal behaviour than his policies: see Walter, *Carl Eugen*, pp. 256–7; F. A. Pottle (ed.), *Boswell on the grand tour. Germany and Switzerland 1764. The Yale editions of the private papers of James Boswell* (5 vols., Melbourne, 1953), IV, pp. 250–1.

[163] Carl Eugen told the Danish ambassador, Baron Asseburg, 'er würde in dem äußersten Nothfall sich in die Arme des Kaisers werfen und von selbigem Recht und Hülfe erwarten': quoted in Schulenburg (ed.), *Asseburg*, p. 205.

[164] This aspect of the 'cultural competition' theory is defined by T. C. W. Blanning in *German History. The Journal of the German History Society*, 6 (1988), 191–2.

[165] Kleemann, *Solitude*, pp. 10–15.

[166] On the visit to Venice see Walter, *Carl Eugen*, pp. 250–4; Adam, 'Landschaft', pp. 258–9. The actual cost of the trip came to 230,910fl. (HSAS, A19a: Bd. 52). The duke did not totally isolate himself from politics, and discussed the army and cost-reduction plans enacted in 1767 while still in Venice: A8: Bü. 51; Anon., 'Fürstliche Reisen im achtzehnten Jahrhundert', *WVJHLG*, NF2 (1893), 222–4.

a second major reduction which, for the first time, brought costs down to approximately the level of available funds.[167] Indeed, the economy measure proved so successful that two new units could be added to the establishment in 1769.[168]

These economies were paralleled by cut-backs in civil expenditure, and together contributed greatly to the duke's ability to stave off the inevitable defeat for another five years. Pressure at home was further relieved by minor concessions to the estates, while by co-operating with Austrian policy in the Swabian Kreis, he was able to win a temporary reprieve.[169] Also, by constantly shifting the negotiations between the imperial courts and various special commissions, he was able to delay any of them reaching a conclusion.

THE SETTLEMENT OF 1770 AND ITS EFFECTS

The fact that a final settlement was reached at all was as much due to changes in attitudes in Vienna as to the exhaustion of the ducal treasury in Stuttgart. Like the three guarantee powers, the emperor ultimately realised that if he recognised the duke's argument that it was wrong to stick with old laws when these were outdated, he would be forced to acknowledge the duke's ability to alter the very laws he himself had guaranteed. His guarantee would thus become unnecessary and he would lose his legal excuse to interfere in Württemberg internal affairs. Having come to this conclusion, the emperor inserted an 'epilogue' into the draft settlement whereby the estates were not obliged to recognise any duke until he had confirmed all existing laws and treaties, including that of Prague 1599.[170] As this concerned the Austrian Anwartschaft, the emperor succeeded in writing into the Württemberg constitution his claims to the duchy and so consolidated his influence over its affairs. Having lost imperial protection and short of money, Carl Eugen had no choice but to accept this 'hereditary settlement' (Erbvergleich) on 1 January 1770.[171]

The Erbvergleich was a crushing blow to ducal ambitions. Nevertheless, it probably would have been much worse had Carl Eugen not been so successful in spinning out the negotiations. In doing so, he effectively fought the estates to a standstill, forcing them to moderate their demands and abandon such projects as a constitutional limit on the size of the army, which would have seriously harmed ducal sovereignty. In its final form, the Erbvergleich represented a slightly more severe version of the 1739 recess. The vague passages in the old laws were restated more precisely, particularly in reference to the Kirchengut, thus making it even

---

[167] HSAS, A8: Bü. 51, 53, 54, 58; A30a: Bd. 60; A202: Bü. 2288; L6.22.8.5; L12: *Kriegsparticulare* 1765/6, 1767/8.
[168] DR Prinz Friedrich Wilhelm and Füsilier Rgt Biedenfeld.
[169] Haug-Moritz, *Württembergischer Ständekonflikt*, pp. 230–40; Adam, 'Landschaft', pp. 265–7.
[170] Adam, 'Landschaft', pp. 270–1; Haug-Moritz, *Württembergischer Ständekonflikt*, pp. 373–453.
[171] Reyscher, *Gesetze*, II, Nos. 550–609.

more difficult for the duke to ignore them. The duke did secure the estates' agreement to take over the increased Kreis and Reichs obligations as an additional tax in the event of war. However, this was small consolation for the repeal of all his financial innovations and an end to his attempts to reform the duchy's tax structure. Moreover, the level of the annual tax grant remained that specified in 1739, despite the fact that the population had increased by at least 12 per cent since then. From the 460,000fl. in taxes, 110,000fl. were to be deducted for debt repayment and the Kreisextraordinari, leaving an estates' contribution to the military budget no bigger than that under Eberhard Ludwig.[172] The duke's freedom to modify these conditions was further curtailed by the presence of the emperor, Prussia, England and Denmark as guarantors of the agreement. Carl Eugen now had to tread very carefully so as not to give these powers further excuse for intervention.

Just how effective the Erbvergleich was as a brake on ducal ambitions is to be demonstrated by the failure of Carl Eugen's policies between 1770 and 1793. This also proves two other important points. First, it shows just how consistent ducal aims were. Second, it indicates that here again the traditional picture of Carl Eugen is misconceived. The existing literature paints a picture of the duke somehow being tamed by his new mistress, the homely Franziska von Hohenheim, and becoming an enlightened and benevolent father-figure to his subjects.[173] Despite such public declarations as his confession of past mistakes, made on his fiftieth birthday (1778), Carl Eugen had far from given up his ambitious plans. The only change was that, under the straitened circumstances imposed by the Erbvergleich, he had still less chance of carrying them out than before.

Contrary to the popular belief that he turned his attention away from the army after 1770,[174] Carl Eugen continued to show just as much interest as before. Summer manoeuvres were held almost every year[175] and wherever possible, new formations were added to the establishment.[176] The problem was, as before, how to pay for them. Money was scraped together from all possible sources, and Carl Eugen even paid in the 'free gift' given him by the estates for signing the Erbvergleich.[177] However, conditions were such that he could hardly hope to find adequate resources within the duchy. Thus, scarcely a year went by without some ambitious project to raise new funds.

Between 1771 and 1774 Carl Eugen even toyed with the idea of utilising the joint

---

[172] HSAS, L12: *Kriegsparticulare 1769/70*, fols. 29–32.
[173] *HKE*, I, pp. 79–102; Marquardt, *Geschichte Württembergs*, pp. 210–17.
[174] Storz, *Karl Eugen*, pp. 233–4.
[175] LBS, cod. milit. fols. 28, 33, 34, 38; qt. 48, 63; A. M. F. Frhr von Buwinghausen-Wallmerode, *Tagebuch des herzoglich württembergischen General-Adjutant Freiherrn von Buwinghausen . . . 1767–1773* (ed. E. Zeigesar, Stuttgart, 1911), pp. 50, 181–9, 248–9.
[176] HSAS, A30a: Bü. 62–6, 119; A32: Bd. 14–37.
[177] HSAS, A32: Bd. 14. The new measures were basically restricted to the pawning of the state lottery to some of the generals and giving large numbers of soldiers lengthy periods of leave.

ducal–estates debt repayment commission as a basis to raise a huge foreign loan. This would have established something approaching a national debt system, but was abandoned as too risky.[178] In 1774 Wimpffen devised a plan to double the army through introducing various economies, but this had broken down by 1776.[179] Attempts were also made to attract foreign subsidies through troop hire. These attempts are already fairly well known and comprised the unsuccessful negotiations with England in 1777, the transfer of about 300 men to the English East India Company in 1771 and the hire of the *Kapregiment* to that company's Dutch counterpart in 1787.[180]

What is less well known are Carl Eugen's other subsidy negotiations which were more specifically linked to advancing his aims. As early as 1773 he made an informal approach to the Austrians for a subsidy treaty for 10,000–15,000 men.[181] Although unsuccessful, he continually tried to make some sort of agreement with the Austrians that would induce them to grant what he wanted. Each time the emperor appeared to be in difficulties, he made an offer of support in the hope of a concession in return. During the War of the Bavarian Succession (1777–8), he wanted the Bavarian lordship of Wiesensteig ceded to Württemberg.[182] In 1782 he went personally to Vienna to ask for an electoral title and pressed this again in 1784–5 when the emperor was faced with the Scheldt crisis and a hostile Prussian-sponsored *Fürstenbund* (League of Princes).[183] Here he played on his new under-standing with Austria's ally, Russia, which he had forged during Grand Duke Paul's visit to Württemberg in September 1782. Although it actually came to a draft Austro-Württemberg treaty on 4 January 1785, Carl Eugen quickly backed out when the French expressed their disapproval at the arrangement.[184] The subsequent wrangle over his claims for compensation for the troops he had started to raise only served to sour relations with the emperor and put him yet another step further from his goal.[185] The duke then approached George III through Francis Viscount Beauchamp MP, who had met him in Stuttgart, in autumn 1788. This was a typical piece of Württemberg bad timing: the overture coincided with the regency crisis which paralysed British foreign policy into 1789.[186] Apparently eternally

---

178 HSAS, A8: Bü. 68, Nos. 63–98. The sum considered varied between 2 and 3 million fl.
179 HSAS, A8: Bü. 83, Nos. 14–138; A30a: Bd. 63.
180 See Chapter 3 above.
181 HSAS, A8: Bü. 5, No. 3.
182 Boepple, *Verhältnis zu Württemberg*, pp. 84–6.
183 HSAS, A8: Bü. 60, Nos. 103–23; A74: Bü. 189, 190, 197; A202: Bü. 2290; Boepple, *Verhältnis zu Württemberg*, pp. 86–9; Burr, 'Reichssturmfahne', at p. 315.
184 HSAS, A74: Bü. 199.
185 HSAS, A74: Bü. 199, 201, 205, *Weiner Berichte* 1785–7. The aborted treaty had led to the formation of the Garde Legion.
186 Beauchamp to Lord Malmesbury, Malmesbury to Pitt, both 14 Nov. 1788, PRO 30/8/155, fols. 89, 91–4. My thanks to Jeremy Black for this reference. The subsequent fruitless correspondence is in HSAS, A8: Bü. 59, Nos. 40–52 (1789). For the situation in Britain see Black, *British foreign policy in an age of revolutions, 1783–93* (Cambridge, 1994).

optimistic, Carl Eugen never gave up hope and died in 1793 in the midst of further subsidy negotiations with the English.[187]

Meanwhile, within the duchy he started a project which potentially had far-reaching effects on the internal balance of power in Württemberg. This was the famous *Carlsschule*, founded in 1771. What started out purely as an officer training school soon developed as an establishment for the education of civil bureaucrats as well. Drawing its students from abroad as well as promising native candidates, the Carlsschule trained them in principles of government radically different from those of Tübingen University, which had traditionally produced most of the duchy's civil servants. As the students were obliged to enter ducal service in return for their education, the duke acquired a cadre of bureaucrats more likely to carry out his commands than the hide-bound traditionalists from Tübingen. Whether, given time, the Carlsschule would have actually shifted the balance of power in the duke's favour can only be speculated upon. To a certain extent, by the time of his death Carl Eugen himself was being overtaken by the students, who had seized on Enlightenment ideas and were demanding reforms rather different from those he had in mind. However, it is significant that the estates continually saw the Carlsschule as a threat and finally managed to have it abolished in 1794 on the grounds that it was too expensive and the duchy did not need a second institution to rival Tübingen.[188]

Carl Eugen's failure, like those of his predecessors, was due to a combination of his own overambitious plans and circumstances beyond his control. His room for manoeuvre was already severely restricted before he achieved his majority in 1744. The weakness of the previous regency government had led to a revival of the estates' influence, deterioration of relations with the emperor and a dangerous dependence on Prussia. Through cautious policies between 1744 and 1745, Carl Eugen had done much to free himself from these restrictions. Neutrality was preserved during the difficult years of the War of the Austrian Succession. Dependence on Prussia was turned to advantage by obtaining the support of Prussia's ally, France. The subsidy treaty of 1752 bound Carl Eugen to only a modest commitment, while giving his finances a welcome cash injection. This eased his dependence on the estates' limited tax grant. Opposition from within the civil bureaucracy was curbed by the new style of government introduced after 1752. The influence of the privy council was reduced and Carl Eugen's personal control strengthened by the re-establishment of cabinet government and the new practice of riding around

---

[187] HSAS, A8: Bü. 59, Nos. 53–9; A202: Bü. 2241. The negotiations appear to have led to the formation of a 200-man light infantry unit which was immediately disbanded after Carl Eugen's death, see A202: Bü. 2291.

[188] On the Carlsschule see Uhland, *Geschichte der Hohen Karlsschule* and in his article in *Ausstellung: Die Hohen Carlsschule 4 November 1959 bis 30 January 1960* (Stuttgart, 1959), pp. 13–33. On its potential to change the balance of power within the bureaucracy, see Wunder, *Privilegiering*, pp. 82–97.

the duchy. The latter also increased his popularity among his ordinary subjects which, to judge by his reception by Black Forest villagers in 1770, remained high despite the troubles of the 1760s.[189] The estates' influence declined considerably. After 1753 a serious rift opened in their committee which threatened to paralyse their political opposition to the duke.

From the ducal perspective this represented a promising start, but Carl Eugen remained a long way from achieving his chief dynastic ambitions. These ambitions conspired with events beyond his control in 1756 to push him into catastrophic involvement in the Seven Years War. Rather than restrict his commitments such as Bavaria, Carl Eugen chose to step them up in the hope of attracting Austrian endorsement for his bid to become an elector. The decision in March 1757 to double his treaty commitment to France was already a dangerous step. His corps' involvement in the Austrian defeat at Leuthen that December revealed the precariousness of his position. Participation in the big powers' wars was a costly business that was getting him nowhere. As in 1756, he was faced with the stark choice of cutting his losses and backing out, or increasing his commitment and becoming more deeply embroiled. That he chose the latter course undoubtedly owes much to Austrian encouragement of his false hopes. His decision to fund his military buildup through unconstitutional taxation, as much as any subsidy treaty, placed him in a position of dependence on Austria. The taxation could only be continued as long as the emperor chose not to respond to the estates' appeals for assistance.

The collapse of Carl Eugen's position in 1765–70 represented not just a return to the situation at the start of his reign, but the end of any real chance of achieving his ambition. It was not just that the Erbvergleich restored the estates' influence; the duke's reputation had also been ruined and his credibility shattered. The failure of his schemes after 1770 was largely due to this loss of prestige.

Prestige was crucial. The whole object of what Montmartin termed a 'stattliche Verfassung', indeed of what all the minor princes were doing, was to convince the major powers that they were credible alliance partners whose political objectives were worth taking seriously. This explains the continuation of Carl Eugen's court expenditure after 1765/70. That it could still have the desired effect is indicated by the negotiations with Britain in 1777. The British took his offer of a subsidy corps seriously because their representative had been so dazzled by the Ludwigsburg court two years previously that he had estimated the army at 5,500, or twice its true strength.[190]

However, the legacy of Carl Eugen's disastrous involvement in the Seven Years War became apparent as soon as the British negotiator arrived in Germany. Colonel Faucitt reported to his superiors that he had 'frequently heard, since I have been in

---

[189] Buwinghausen-Wallmerode, *Tagebuch*, pp. 197–205.
[190] Kapp, *Soldatenhandel*, p. 100.

Germany, of the ruinous condition of His Highness's circumstances'. Carl Eugen's 'credit, as well as his finances are unhappily reduced to so low an ebb' that his treasury was 'exhausted'. Lack of funds had compelled him to retain decrepit veterans in the ranks rather than recruit younger replacements. Apart from the artillery (which the British did not need), the soldiers were armed with worn-out equipment left over from the Seven Years War.[191] The Austrians also remained decidedly unimpressed with the Württemberg troops whom their representative describes as 'behaving like Tartars' during the 1760 Saxon campaign.[192] Carl Eugen thus remained dogged by the poor reputation of his army: unable to attract interest from potential partners because of their dim view of his troops, but equally unable to establish a better reputation without their financial assistance.

The continuation of the lavish court was intended to compensate for the lack of martial glory. However, this only reinforced contemporaries' poor opinion of him. In many ways, Carl Eugen was out of step with his times. On the surface there were signs that he kept abreast of the latest developments. There were elements of 'enlightened' rule, such as the creation of a public library, while the educational innovations of the Carlsschule attracted admiration across Europe.[193] Nonetheless, though he adopted rococo architecture for his new Solitude palace, he remained a prince of the baroque, failing to realise that politics within the Reich had changed. The mounting Austro-Prussian dualism had considerably reduced the role that third-rate states such as Württemberg could play. Moreover, the rules of the political game had changed. Contemporaries, under the influence of the Enlightenment, were no longer as impressed by baroque posturing as they had been in the age of Eberhard Ludwig. Indeed, they were now likely to see it as a sign of weakness rather than strength. Faucitt put the poor condition of the Württemberg army down to the 'totally effeminate amusements' to which 'the Duke has given himself up for some years past'.[194] Giovanni Casanova, who had the misfortune to have a brush with some Württemberg officers in 1760, summed up the general view when he commented:

The great subsidies which the King of France was foolish enough to pay the prince had merely allowed him to indulge in luxury and his debauches. This Württemberg corps was magnificent but throughout the war was only distinguished by its mistakes.[195]

That Carl Eugen failed to adapt is understandable. To have changed style or abandoned his aims would have been an admission of defeat. Despite mounting

---

[191] PRO sp81/186, Faucitt to Suffolk, 7 and 17 Feb. 1777.

[192] HSAS, A202: Bü. 2236, Rüdt's reports, 23 and 28 Nov. 1760.

[193] On the issue of enlightened reform in the small states see the article by C. Ingrao in H. M. Scott (ed.), *Enlightened absolutism* (London, 1990), pp. 221–44 and S. Mörz, *Aufgeklärter Absolutismus in der Kurpfalz während der Mannheimer Regierungszeit des Kurfürsten Karl Theodor (1742–1777)* (*VKGLK*, Reihe B, vol. 120, Stuttgart, 1991).

[194] PRO sp81/186, Faucitt to Suffolk, 17 Feb. 1777.

[195] Quoted in Fauchier-Magnan, *Small German courts*, p. 209.

evidence to the contrary, he remained convinced he would eventually succeed. His inflated opinion of his own importance never left him. During one of his several trips to Italy he was told that if he wanted an audience with the Pope he must kiss the toe of the holy father, which even cardinals were obliged to do. In a characteristic outburst, he replied: 'There are a great many cardinals but only one duke of Württemberg.'[196]

However, even he was aware that the structure of the old Reich posed an obstacle to his aims. The Erbvergleich itself was a classic example of the system of checks and balances built into the Reich and which restrained princely ambition. After 1770 Carl Eugen showed signs of losing interest in maintaining the Reich. He failed to reraise the duchy's Kreistruppen which he had disbanded in 1763. The development of ever-closer links with Russia after 1782 showed that he was beginning to look beyond the emperor for dynastic support.[197] His nephew, Friedrich II, was to go even further and co-operate with the major powers in the destruction of the Reich in 1803–6.

[196] *Ibid.*, p. 182.
[197] On these links see Maurer, 'Haus Württemberg', 201–23.

Table 8.1. *Kriegskasse income 1 May 1751 to 30 April 1757*

Source	Amount (florins)	
Ducal hands (at least)	607,907	18.3%
French subsidy (at the most)	657,998*	19.8%
Estates	2,024,651	61.0%
Ducal departments (estimate)	6,000	0.2%
Capital and loans (estimate)	18,000	0.5%
Other (estimate)	6,000	0.5%
Total	3,320,556	100.0%
Average annual income	533,426	

*including 161,102fl. paid between January and March 1757.
Sources: HSAS, A32: Bd. 1–2; A30a: Bü. 58; A202: Bü. 2207, 2219, 2220; L5: Tom. 160–5, 167 fol. 92b; L12: *Kriegsparticulare* 1751/2–1756/7.

Table 8.2. *French subsidy expenditure 13 May 1752 to 2 June 1755*

Item	Amount (florins)	
Banking costs	806	0.2%
Rentkammer	59,258	14.9%
Estates	37,500	9.4%
Sulz salt works	1,500	0.4%
Diplomacy	1,624	0.4%
Werneck in Paris	10,364	2.6%
To ducal hands	15,000	3.8%
Presents	3,021	0.7%
Total	129,073	32.4%
Oberkriegskommissariat	269,396	67.6%
Grand total	398,469	100.0%

Source: HSAS, A202: Bü. 2220.

Table 8.3. *Property bought by Carl Eugen 1737–1786*

Date	Property	Cost (in florins)
1737	Stammheim and Zazenhausen	110,000
1738	Walddorf by Tübingen	exchanged other territory
1739	Remaining half of Köngen	40,000
1743	Rittergut Pfäffingen ⎫	
1743	2/3 of Rittergut Margolsheim ⎭	53,000
1744	Tithe and revenue rights at Langenau	100,000
1744	Freigut Neuffen	10,578
1746	Herrschaft Aldingen	74,000
1747	Stettenfels, Gruppenbach, and Tondorf	209,323
1749	Herrschaft Sterneck	115,880
1749	Zaberfeld, Michelbach, Ochsenber and Leonbrunn (from Herr von Sternenfels)	300,000
Prior to 1750	Sirgenstein wood and Hohentringen	?
1750	Rights of Herr von Haindel to part of Kleinbottwar	22,000
1750	Privy Councillor Bilfinger's property	6,400
1751	Hofen	?
1751	Freireichsherrschaft Jüstingen	301,000
1751	Captain von Gaisberg's rights to Schaubeck and Kleinbottwar	25,000
1750s	Rights of von Bidenbach in Osweil	?
1750s	Lindach	23,000
1750s	Tithe rights at Heubach and Oberbebingen	?
1753	Farm of Baron von Neuhaus	28,000
1753	Various rights of Baron von Gultingen	16,276
1753	To settle dispute with Baden-Durlach over Besigheim and Mundelsheim	130,000
1759	Altburg-Welfenschwann	19,000
1760s	Rights to vineyards at Plochingen and Ober Esslingen	?
1773	Schwieberdingen	?
1780	Part of Grafschaft Limpurg	160,000
1781	Herrschart Schmiedelfeld (from Limpurg)	375,000
1782	Ober Sontheim (from Limpurg)	100,000
1783	Last remaining tax rights of Herr von Sternenfels	115,000
1783	Geisingen	90,000
1783	Hochberg and Hochdorf	470,000
1784	Herrschaft Bönnigheim	?
1784	Mühlhausen	130,000
1786	Bergschloss Ebersberg	?

Sources: HSAS, A256: Bd. 229–39; Bandel, *Auf eine Lüge eine Maultasche!*, pp. 27–30; Wintterlin, 'Landeshoheit', *HKE*, I, pp. 176, 184; Dizinger, *Beiträge*, II, p. 24; Röder, *Geographie und Statistik*, I.

Table 8.4. *Personal campaign expenses 6 May 1757 to 19 January 1758*

Source	Amount (florins)	
Ducal hands	86,483	22.0%
Loans from officials	290,098	73.5%
Loans from Nürtingen Hospital	10,000	2.5%
Ducal departments	6,485	1.6%
Other	706	0.2%
Total	**393,772**	**100.0%**

Sources: HSAS, A8: Bü. 66, Nos. 36–9; A19a: Bd. 53.

Table 8.5. *Personal campaign expenses 28 October 1759 to 2 January 1761*

Source	Amount (florins)	
Kriegskasse	11,000	6.3%
Rentkammer	123,687	70.9%
Kirchenkasten	24,782	14.2%
Profit from exchange rate	14,865	8.5%
Other	81	0.0%
Total	**174,415**	**99.9%**

Sources: HSAS, A19a: Bd. 54–5.

Table 8.6. *Kriegskasse income 1 May 1757 to 30 April 1759*

Source	Amount (florins)	
French subsidies	1,170,169	49.4%
Estates	783,018	33.0%
Staatskasse (loans)	47,867	2.0%
Salt monopoly	259,311	10.9%
Münzkasse	40,000	1.7%
Taxgelder (estimate)	5,500	0.2%
Extraordinary fines	3,650	0.2%
Capital (estimate)	40,000	1.7%
Profit from exchange rate	10,602	0.5%
Other (estimate)	10,000	0.4%
Total	**2,370,117**	**100.0%**
Average annual income	1,185,058	

Sources: HSAS, A8: Bü. 68, No. 26; A32: Bd. 152; A202: Bü. 2219; L6.22.8.2; L12: *Kriegsparticulare* 1757/8, 1758/9; Anon, 'Was einzelne teutsche Fürstenhäuser innerhalb der zwanzig Jahre von 1750–70 an französischen Subsidien und Geschenken gezogen', *Neues Göttingisches historisches Magazin*, 3 (1794), 324–40; Adam, 'Landschaft', *HKE*, I, p. 220; Wintterlin, 'Landeshoheit', *HKE*, I, p. 179.

Table 8.7. *Kriegskasse income 1 May 1759 to 30 April 1770*

Source	1759–65	1765–70	Total	
Ducal hands	475,284	22,149	497,433	3.9%
Via Rieger	155,068	—	155,068	1.2%
Via Montmartin	39,435	29,835	69,270	0.6%
Subsidies	1,022,825	—	1,022,825	8.1%
Ducal departments	1,256,387	321,115	1,577,502	12.5%
Mömpelgard	333,794	—	333,794	2.6%
Military	191,604	110,998	302,602	2.4%
Capital and loans	573,902	49,202	623,104	4.9%
Kirchenkasten	734,236	5,500	739,736	5.9%
Estates	4,775,009	2,033,106	6,808,115	53.9%
Landkriegskasse	191,503	—	191,503	1.5%
Other	164,007	157,119	321,126	2.5%
Total	**9,913,054**	**2,729,024**	**12,642,078**	**100.0%**
Average annual income	1,652,176	545,805	1,149,280	

Table 8.7.1. *Income from ducal departments 1759–1770*

Source	1759–65	1765–70	Total	
Kammerschreiberei	5,000	1,500	6,500	0.4%
Rentkammer	30,000	123,545	153,545	9.7%
Wildprettschreiberei	—	29	29	0.0%
Residenzbaukasse	10,000	—	10,000	0.6%
Oberlandbaukasse	7,752	—	7,752	0.5%
Oberforstämter	179,407	9,938	189,345	12.0%
Münzkasse	325,594	—	325,594	20.7%
Eisenkasse	159,680	—	159,680	10.1%
Salt monopoly	487,706	152,003	639,709	40.6%
Tobacco monopoly	51,248	34,100	85,348	5.4%
Total	1,256,387	321,115	1,577,502	100.0%

Table 8.7.2. *Income from the military administration 1759–1770*

Source	1759–65	1765–70	Total	
Kreis Rechnung	—	2,889	2,889	1.0%
Feldkriegskasse	15,743	—	15,743	5.2%
Invalidengelder	49,289	22,702	71,991	23.8%
Beurlaubten	8,776	33,043	41,819	13.8%
Equipment sales	81,581	3,587	85,168	28.1%
Kasernen Verwaltung	—	2,787	2,787	0.9%
Militär Taxgelder	36,215	8,402	44,617	14.8%
Minorennen Taxgelder	—	37,588	37,588	12.4%
Total	191,604	110,998	302,602	100.0%

Sources: HSAS, A32: Bd. 3–13; L12: *Kriegsparticulare* 1759/60–1769–70.

Table 8.8. *Estates' contribution to military expenses 1759–1770*

Type of payment	1759–65	1765–70	Total	
To the Kriegskasse				
Recessmässige Anlagen	1,569,143	1,668,166	3,237,309	47.6%
Officers' pay arrears	—	360,000	360,000	5.3%
Kreis payments by decree	751,570	—	751,570	11.0%
Kreis Vacant Portionen	131,275	—	131,275	1.9%
Ditto arrears	170,643	—	170,643	2.5%
Monatliche Gelder	1,119,401	—	1,119,401	16.4%
Militär Steuer	468,920	4,940	473,860	7.0%
Cash advance	116,145	—	116,145	1.7%
Tax arrears of the communes	147,912	—	147,912	2.2%
Landesdefensionsgelder	300,000	—	300,000	4.4%
Total	**4,775,009**	**2,033,106**	**6,808,115**	**100.0%**
To Kreis and Reich				
Römer Monaten*	14,009	2,054	16,063	1.3%
Kreis Extraordinarium	355,560	197,439	552,999	44.1%
Kreis Proviant Umlage	684,313	—	684,313	54.6%
Total	**1,053,882**	**199,493**	**1,253,375**	**100.0%**
Total to Kriegskasse	4,775,009	2,033,106	6,808,115	84.5%
Total to Kreis and Reich	1,053,882	199,493	1,253,375	15.5%
Grand total	**5,828,891**	**2,232,599**	**8,061,490**	**100.0%**

*excluding 56,000fl. for 1760/1 included under subsidies in Table 8.7.
Sources: HSAS, A32: Bd. 4–13; L6.22.8.2; L12: *Kriegsparticulare*, Bd. 1759/60–1769/70.

Table 8.9. *Kriegskasse income from unconstitutional measures 1757–1770*

Source	1757–65	1765–70	Total
Kreis payments by decree	924,880	—	924,880
Kreis Vacant Portionen plus arrears	301,918	—	301,918
Monatliche Gelder	1,119,401	—	1,119,401
Militär Steuer	468,920	4,940	473,860
Cash advance	116,145	—	116,145
Tax arrears of the communes	147,912	—	147,912
Landesdefensionsgelder	300,000	—	300,000
Extraordinary fines	4,150	—	4,150
Loans from officials etc.	127,717	23,300	151,017
Kirchenkasten	734,236	5,500	739,736
Landkriegskasse	191,503	—	191,503
Salt monopoly	747,017	152,003	899,020
Tobacco monopoly	51,248	34,100	85,348
Münzkasse (coinage devaluation)	365,594	—	365,594
Oberforstämter	179,407	9,938	189,345
Total	5,780,048	229,781	6,009,829
Overall total revenue	12,283,171	2,729,024	15,012,195

Sources: As Table 8.6.

Table 8.10. *Summary of Kriegskasse income 1757–1770*

Source	1757–65		1765–70		Total	
Constitutional taxation	2,111,986	(17.2%)	2,028,166	(74.3%)	4,140,152	(27.6%)
Unconstitutional measures	5,780,048	(47.0%)	229,781	(8.4%)	6,009,829	(40.0%)
Foreign subsidies	2,192,994	(17.9%)	—		2,192,994	(14.6%)
Other	2,198,143*	(17.9%)	471,077†	(17.3%)	2,669,220	(17.8%)
Total	12,283,171	(100.0%)	2,729,024	(100.0%)	15,012,195	(100.0%)
Annual average	1,535,396		545,805		1,154,784	

*including 856,272fl. in loans.
†including 79,073fl. in loans.
Sources: As Tables 8.6 to 8.9.

9

Conclusion

This work has used a case study of Württemberg to test theories of state development and to investigate early modern German ruler–estate relations and the structure of the old Reich. It now remains to draw together the findings for these issues in turn.

The Württemberg case bears out James Sheehan's conclusions that 'money – for whatever reason – was the dominant force behind the construction of the modern state'.[1] Both Württemberg's institutional development and its ruler–estate relations were fuelled primarily by the duke's fiscal requirements. As we have seen, the ultimate purpose of these has been the subject of considerable debate, not only for Württemberg, but for early modern state-building in general. The findings of this study tend to support the basic premiss of the 'primary of foreign policy' theory of state development. The dictates of foreign policy, in the sense of relations with other rulers both inside and outside the Reich, shaped Württemberg's internal development through the mechanism of ducal fiscal requirements. However, the findings also indicate that this process was not as straightforward as older studies would suggest.

The duke had to compete in the wider arena of imperial and European politics if he wished to achieve his primary objectives. In these he hardly differed from both his contemporaries among the lesser German princes and the more powerful European monarchs. Like them he desired an elevation in status and an increase in territory. The purpose of this policy was to defend his existing position and enhance his voice in international affairs. Despite the growing disparity in resources after 1648, most lesser German princes were not prepared to surrender the initiative to their more powerful neighbours. The conditions of the post-1648 Reich made it imperative that they continue to play an active role if they wished to maintain their status and autonomy. Though the Reich did provide a protective framework for its weaker components, it did not allow them to retreat into passivity, as has sometimes been suggested. The rights and privileges defining a territory's position had to be protected from the encroachments of predatory neighbours. Rulers wishing to improve their position were obliged to 'live beyond their means' to sustain the appropriate image. Chapter 2 has established that a high level of military,

---

[1] *German history*, p. 33.

247

diplomatic and cultural expenditure was crucial to the creation of this 'imposing state'. Spending on the court and army dwarfed that on all other items. Of the two, military expenditure was the more significant, because of its tendency to escalate in times of crisis and generate considerable debts which overburdened subsequent peacetime budgets.

These factors put cultural competition into perspective as a force behind state development. Alone it is an inadequate explanation for the policies of lesser German princes: it was clearly not an end in itself, but a means to an end. The study of Württemberg's subsidy negotiations reveals its true role as an adjunct to, not a substitute for, political and military competition. At no time was subsidy income diverted to pay for cultural expenditure. More usually, other areas were cut back to pay for the army and demands for military funding provided the chief bone of contention with the estates. The duke's failure to secure meaningful concessions from his treaty partners was due to his poor bargaining position, not lack of political ambition. Moreover, on several occasions (1733, 1752, 1757, 1760) he deliberately entered into agreements which were financially disastrous in the belief that, by making himself militarily indispensable to his sponsor, his requests would be granted.

The changes wrought by the ruler's fiscal and military requirements were less obvious in Württemberg than in larger German states, particularly Prussia. The duchy's bureaucratic structure remained essentially unaltered throughout the period under review. Though significant as attempts to circumvent constitutional restraints, changes at the top, such as the creation of 'cabinet' or 'conference' ministries, did not fundamentally alter the basic structure. Functions and responsibilities remained divided among the various departments as illustrated in fig. 2 until the major reorganisation into separate ministries after 1805.[2] The number of civil servants also did not increase substantially.[3] Nonetheless, the areas of change were those most directly associated with the fiscal and military requirements of dynastic policy – indicating that these, rather than domestic considerations like the need to maintain social order, were the primary motors driving the nascent state. Tax collection and financial management remained the primary tasks of most Württemberg bureaucrats. The only area to experience significant expansion was the military administration which, though still small, grew considerably after being placed on a permanent footing in 1704.[4] Moreover, the absence of an omnipresent and overtly militaristic administrative structure should not automatically be taken as evidence for the limited impact of foreign policy considerations. As John Brewer has demonstrated, although Britain is not normally associated with bureaucracy, it in fact created an efficient fiscal–military apparatus capable of defeating France in

---

[2] Dehlinger, *Württembergs Staatswesen.*
[3] *Württembergische Hof- und Staats-Handbücher 1736–93*; Pfeilsticker, *Dienerbuch.*
[4] HSAS, A30a: Bü. 1, 2, 3, 5, 6, 11, 16; A202: Bü. 225, 227, 2185–95; L6.22.6.39.

the colonial struggles of the eighteenth century.[5] Württemberg's relatively small size enabled it to dispense with a large administrative structure. Bureaucratic growth was in any case impeded by the continued autonomy of the church and estates, both of which retained important functions until King Friedrich I abolished the constitution at the end of 1805.

Fiscal requirements also played a significant part in stimulating wider reforms and innovations. We have seen that the desire to boost revenue was a primary concern behind ducal initiatives to stimulate the economy, introduce new industries, reform the tax structure and update tax registers. Again, the continued influence of the estates, together with often faulty mercantilist calculations, helped limit the overall impact of these changes. Carl Alexander's wide-ranging reform programme of 1736–7, which included new taxes, Prussian-style conscription and the intention to reorganise the duchy's entire administrative structure, gives an indication of how far dynastic ambition might have driven internal development had these limitations not been in place. Ducal efforts to stimulate the Amtsversammlungen also threatened to produce significant shifts in town–country relationships throughout the century.

Of course, dynasticism was not the sole driving-force. Cameralism and the desire to maintain a well-ordered state ('eine gute Polizei') did play a vital part in defining the external reality of the state, especially where it came into contact with its ordinary inhabitants. Throughout the period under review, Württemberg bureaucrats produced a growing volume of ordinances directed at regulating all conceivable aspects of everyday life. Though generally aimed at stabilising and conserving existing structures and attitudes, many decrees were innovations intended to effect change. The bureaucracy even displayed a degree of inner dynamism, incorporating proposals from both civil servants and members of the public in its ordinances and building on past experience to shape future policy.[6]

In this sense, state-building in Württemberg was a group rather than an individual activity. As Vann has identified, the bureaucracy constituted a significant third force alongside duke and estates which helped to shape policy. Though circumstances tended to define the parameters of individual action, personality was still important. The dukes varied in the consistency with which they pursued their objectives. Regent Friedrich Carl and his son Carl Alexander appear far more determined and ruthless than either Eberhard Ludwig or Carl Eugen. Eberhard Ludwig's hesitancy and lack of realism during his search for subsidies was a significant factor in the failure of his foreign policy. Carl Eugen's rashness and inflated sense of self-importance were key elements in his disastrous over-commitment in the Seven Years War. His personal behaviour, like that of Eberhard

---

[5] *Sinews of power.*
[6] HSAS, A39: *Generalrescripte* Bü. 29–49; A8: Bü. 78.

Ludwig, lost him considerable sympathy among his fellow princes, as well as antagonising the estates. Carl Alexander's Catholicism, like that of his son, placed him at a disadvantage, as well as imparting a new style to the court. Chance events were also influential. Both Friedrich Carl's capture and Carl Alexander's sudden death resulted in dramatic reversals of fortune.

Domestic security considerations were not a significant influence on policy. There were tensions within Württemberg society, as there were elsewhere in *ancien régime* Europe[7] but these had little impact on the policy-making of either the duke or other 'elite' groups. It is true that the dukes sought external help against domestic opponents in the estates. Carl Eugen secured vague promises of French and imperial assistance in his treaties of 1759 and 1760, while Eberhard Ludwig asked for it in his unsuccessful attempt to ally with the emperor in the 1720s. The discussion of the Extensionists on pp. 71–2 indicates that other princes thought along similar lines. Equally, the Württemberg estates engaged in a parallel diplomacy of their own to counter ducal attacks on their domestic position. However, at no time did domestic concerns dictate foreign policy to the extent that some historians have found in the 'social imperialism' of Wilhelmine Germany.[8] There was no conception of an 'enemy within' that needed to be combated by the development of an apparatus of internal repression, or deflected outwards through successful foreign conquests. Of course, the duchy's army was used as a police force to contain the level of crime and disorder endemic to pre-industrial society. However, policing was not its primary purpose. Its size and structure as a cadre for a much larger force were determined by the nature of ducal dynastic aims and his dependence on subsidy income. That the dukes attempted to revive the duchy's militia in an effort to boost their military potential is further indication that they were not primarily concerned with creating an instrument of repression. The Reich's structure in any case severely limited the use of force against domestic political opponents, though not against popular unrest.

This is not to deny the presence of challenges to the existing order. For example, Eberhard Ludwig feared that unrest in neighbouring Hohenzollern-Hechingen might spread to Württemberg and readily despatched military assistance to the beleaguered prince in 1732. Later dukes also provided troops.[9] Moreover, there were clear limits to authority, as was dramatically demonstrated by the mutiny of the Württemberg infantry in June 1757. Even in the aftermath, ducal officials were

---

[7] D. W. Sabean, *Power in the blood. Popular culture and village discourse in early modern Germany* (Cambridge, 1984); see also his *Property, production and family in Neckarhausen 1700–1870* (Cambridge, 1990).

[8] Kehr, *Primat der Innenpolitik*; W. Mommsen, 'Domestic factors in German foreign policy before 1914', *Central European History*, 6 (1973), 11–43.

[9] HSAS, A202: Bü. 1383, 2248 (17 Mar. 1737); J. Barth, *Hohenzollernsche Chronik, oder Geschichte und Sage der hohenzollernschen Lande* (Sigmaringen, 1863), pp. 532–8; J. Carmer, *Die Grafschaft Hohenzollern. Ein Bild süddeutscher Volkszustände 1400–1850* (Stuttgart, 1873), pp. 257–412; Press, 'Bauernrevolten', pp. 85–112.

unable to carry out the prescribed punishments for fear of arousing popular hostility.[10] However, such problems do not seem to have been in the forefront of the minds of those in power.

The bureaucratic urge to regulate society derived principally from the moral and religious considerations that so profoundly shaped contemporary attitudes to organised social and political life. Rather than being a device to limit the potential for social upheaval, it indicated an inability to conceive social and political structures in terms other than those of cameralist well-ordered society. Innovation and reform were intended to adjust and improve the existing order, not replace it with something new.[11] In particular, there was no perceived need to shore up the existing order from any impending collapse under popular upheaval. In this sense, the duke and his officials shared the estates' conception of an unchanging world order.

In fact there was little social dimension to the internal Württemberg conflicts throughout this period. Ducal attempts to restructure the duchy's political framework were directed at overcoming obstacles to the pursuit of his ambitions, not at protecting any social elite from a threat from below. In the absence of a native nobility, the worthies constituted the duchy's social and political elite. Though they did not participate in policy-making, they were closely connected with the duchy's clergy and bureaucracy and acted as part of the governing elite in their capacity of civic magistrates. Thus, duke–estate conflict was essentially a struggle within the ruling orders. The worthies' success in restraining ducal ambitions was not a victory of the 'common man' over absolutism, though it undoubtedly brought indirect benefit by keeping tax levels relatively low. Popular anger was often directed as much against them as against the duke; most notably by the provincial delegates at the 1737–9 Landtag, and by the ordinary soldiers who threatened to burn the estates' assembly hall during the June 1757 mutiny.[12] There was no equivalent of the mass participation that characterised the struggles in East Frisia, and especially Mecklenburg, where several thousand peasants joined the dispossessed Duke Carl Leopold in an unsuccessful attempt to recover his duchy in 1733.[13] The worthies were fully conscious of the dangers inherent in involving wider sections of the population in their dispute with the duke. Such action could easily escalate out of control and enable the duke to brand them as rebels. Thus, in no sense can their opposition to the new military tax in 1764 be described as a revolt.[14] Instead, popular anger at ducal tax demands was kept under control by the local magistrates and deflected into a well-orchestrated tax strike.

---

[10] Wilson, 'Violence and the rejection of authority', at pp. 22–6.
[11] M. Walker, 'Rights and functions: The social categories of eighteenth-century jurists and cameralists', *Journal of Modern History*, 50 (1978), 234–51.
[12] Wilson, 'Violence and the rejection of authority', pp. 9, 11–12.
[13] Kappelhoff, *Ostfriesland*, pp. 251–343; Wick, *Versuche zur Errichtung*, pp. 193–248.
[14] As it has been by Liebel-Weckowicz, 'The revolt of the Württemberg estates', 109–20.

The emphasis on the role of foreign-policy objectives in shaping internal development should not lead us to return to older concepts of absolutist state-building as the product of a grand design. Württemberg dukes no more set out to create absolutism than rulers elsewhere. The new forms of government and new concepts of the state in general emerged gradually as a by-product of the day-to-day business of government. The shifts in Württemberg politics compelled the duke, bureaucrats and estates to redefine their respective positions. These were often retrospectively justified by lengthy arguments drawn from Württemberg custom and tradition, imperial law and various political philosophies. This process was by no means one of linear development, pitting a 'modernising' duke against 'reactionary' estates. Indeed, the dukes often lagged considerably behind elements of their bureaucracy, and even the estates, in their reception of new ideas. As the discussion of the later years of Carl Eugen shows, by the 1770s the duke was not only out of step with developments elsewhere in Germany, but even with those within Württemberg. Many of the duchy's civil servants, educated at the Carlsschule, were developing concepts of loyalty to an abstract and impersonal state at a time when Carl Eugen still regarded himself as the personification of the fatherland.

A similar lack of a simple linear development is revealed in the examination of the role of war in Württemberg development. Broadly speaking, the findings do reinforce the general view that early modern 'state structure appeared chiefly as a by-product of rulers' efforts to acquire the means of war'.[15] However, they also indicate that elements of older political institutions did not automatically disappear as a result of a prince's need to transform administrative structures to sustain the new standing armies. In particular, the survival of the Württemberg estates demonstrates that it was possible for traditional institutions to preserve and even consolidate their position despite the new directions taken by their ruler.[16] The estates' survival prevented fully fledged absolutism, while their opposition to ducal military plans inhibited the establishment of a large standing army. Together with the duke's inability to use force against them, this indicates that absolutism was as much a precondition for the late seventeenth-century European-wide expansion of permanent armies as its consequence.

Traditional interpretations of the estates' role in Württemberg politics do not stand up to scrutiny. Clearly, the estates were not the selfless defenders of popular liberties portrayed by the older folksy–patriotic Württemberg historians and those of the Whiggish tradition. However, neither can they be viewed solely as an impediment to 'progressive' centralising tendencies. Both these interpretations

---

[15] C Tilly, *Coercion, capital and European states AD 900–1990* (Oxford, 1990), p. 14; see also B. M. Downing, *The military revolution and political change in early modern Europe* (Princeton, 1991); D. Kaiser, *Politics and war: European conflict from Philip II to Hitler* (Cambridge, MA, 1990).

[16] For this elsewhere in Europe see Tallett, *War and society*, pp. 188–216.

suffer from their attempt to discuss the estates' role in state-formation in terms of a positive or negative contribution. It is more helpful to see them as either active or passive participants. Those in Württemberg were clearly passive: they preferred to react to ducal policy rather than initiate their own. Whether this attitude assisted or impeded state development depended on the level of co-operation between ruler and estates.

Here a comparison between Württemberg and England is instructive. Like English MPs, the Württemberg estates opposed higher taxes, deficit financing, an expanding civil bureaucracy and a standing army. Both were set against large permanent financial grants which threatened to free their ruler from constitutional restraints. Both also saw each innovation as the thin end of the wedge: a demand for a small sum presaged one for a larger amount; agreeing to the first made it more difficult to reject the second. However, English parliamentarians ultimately came to accept the army and high taxation as necessary evils because they defended the gains of the Glorious Revolution of 1688 and the Act of Settlement of 1701 against a possible Jacobite–Catholic restoration. They gradually lessened attempts to abolish the fiscal–military state altogether and shifted to a policy of containing it and limiting its effects on the country's social and political fabric. Beneath the violent rhetoric, a considerable degree of co-operation between crown and parliament emerged. Parliament's efforts to limit the growth of the state through the imposition of public accountability paradoxically strengthened it by making it less corrupt and more efficient.[17] The situation in Württemberg was entirely different. The key problems were the inflexibility of the duchy's internal arrangements and its position as a constituent part of the Reich. The estates remained resolutely loyal to the concept of the Reich as a protective structure and consequently saw no need for an independent ducal army. The failure of both duke and estates to establish a viable working relationship removed the possibility of mutually beneficial co-operation where public spirit and self-interest could coincide as in England. Given the divergence of outlook, proposals from one side were viewed with suspicion by the other. As time wore on, this mutual distrust became firmly embedded in the framework of duke–estate relations. The addition of a religious difference after 1733 only widened the gap. Despite the temporary successes of Carl Alexander and Carl Eugen in appealing to their subjects' loyalty across the religious divide, the estates' inveterate Lutheranism remained a permanent obstacle to co-operation.

However, it is important to note that conflict was by no means inevitable. There were instances of co-operation where common interest outweighed the differences. All the dukes in this study tolerated the worthies' dominance of the estates through the standing committee in return for a limited measure of support and acquiescence. This was revealed most explicitly during the regency crisis in 1737–9,

---

[17] Brewer, *Sinews of power*, esp. pp. 137–43.

when the committee compromised with the Protestant regent to fight off the provincial radicals. There was also an element of co-operation after 1770 when Carl Eugen permitted the Stockmayer clan to monopolise many of the key positions.[18] Nonetheless, the possibilities for such co-operation remained limited. The lack of participation in policy-making caused a separation of government and representation which prevented the duke exercising patronage in the manner of the English crown. Similarly, it was impossible to develop a government faction, although the attempts to influence the Amtsversammlungen in some way resemble this. Family ties and common interests did forge a bond between the estates and elements of the bureaucracy. However, this was not to the duke's advantage as both were defenders of the internal status quo which protected their vested interests. The committee's hostile reception to Moser's advocacy of ducal projects in the early 1750s illustrates how limited the possibilities for fruitful co-operation were.

The fact that the Württemberg estates were dominated by a social group keen to defend its vested interests is far from unique. The same could be said of the contemporary English parliament. However, whereas the English MPs were prepared to modify their policies to suit changed circumstances, the Württemberg estates clung tenaciously to an unchanging interpretation of their country's constitution and best interests. Change was opposed because it was seen in terms of a threat rather than an opportunity. The Württemberg agreements of 1739 and 1770 were different from the English settlements of 1688 and 1701. They were not designed to limit change and restrict it to what was deemed constitutional, but to prevent it altogether. Although the estates were forced to give ground and grant limited funds for the army, they managed to link this to agreements which further undermined the duke's possibility of modifying 'the good old law'. Thus, while the English constitution became more flexible, that of Württemberg grew increasingly rigid, mirroring developments in the structure of the Reich as a whole.

The duke also played his part in the failure to reach a workable compromise. He did little to involve the worthies in policy-making and regarded their pleas and suggestions as a meddlesome and misinformed intrusion into his prerogative. He made little effort to explain policies beyond haughty proclamations to the effect that he, not they, was the best judge of the country's interests. This proved particularly damaging in 1764 when Carl Eugen's failure to present his new financial demands in a sufficiently favourable light lost him the support of the Amtsversammlungen. This attitude led all dukes to reject the estates' requests to examine the state budget. Though the establishment of a joint duke–estates debt commission following the Erbvergleich did lead to a measure of public accountability, mistrust and suspicion continued to plague Württemberg finance. Practices such as Carl Eugen's devious accounting to conceal his subsidy income did nothing to build

---

[18] Vann, *Making of a state*, pp. 287–94; though Vann probably goes too far when he describes post-1770 relations as 'harmonious' and a 'cosy arrangement'.

confidence. In this atmosphere, wild rumours of corruption, greedy 'evil advisers' and ducal extravagance were given credence they did not deserve.

The study of Württemberg's role within imperial politics indicates that the Reich can be best understood when viewed as a multi-layered structure. The degree to which princes were obliged to operate within this structure was largely determined by the size and geographical position of their territory. As a moderately sized state close to Austrian possessions, Württemberg was more tightly bound within the imperial framework than the larger and more distant north German powers. Compelled to work within the system, ducal policy had to be pursued at the system's many levels. Thus, the duchy's position within the Reich was determined not merely by its relationship with the emperor and other princes, but also with key imperial institutions such as the Reichstag and Reichshofrat and the intermediary level of the Kreise. Given that other states were also operating within this complex matrix, the possibilities for both co-operation and confrontation were numerous. These often cut across the different levels to produce contradictory constellations. For example, Württemberg co-operated with the emperor to induce the Kreis Assembly to pay for the imperial fortress of Kehl, while at the same time posing as the Swabian champion against Habsburg encroachments in the region.

It proved difficult for any one power to secure predominance within this system because of its inherent tendency to produce an equilibrium. The various coalitions tended to balance each other out, as illustrated by the fate of Württemberg's Kreis policy. The Kreis offered a key area for the extension of Württemberg influence and a means of raising its profile within the Reich and among the European powers. Swabia was strategically situated between France, Austria and Bavaria and had considerable war potential through its effective military structure. Württemberg attempted to capitalise on this by consolidating its hold on the key positions within the Kreis structure. This policy ran counter to the interests of the weaker Swabian states who, collectively, could outvote the duke at the Kreis Assembly. Imperial influence acted as a variable with the emperor opposing or supporting Württemberg policy according to his own objectives. Though Friedrich Carl, Eberhard Ludwig and Carl Alexander were able to consolidate Württemberg's position, the emperor was careful never to allow the duchy to totally dominate the Kreis. Instead, Württemberg was often compelled to compromise with other Kreis members in order to maintain its prestige and influence. While this preserved the Kreis as a working institution, it was only at the price of growing Württemberg uninterest in its continued survival. Swabian efficiency was thus as much the product of discord as accord. The same contradictory forces sustained the system of constitutional checks and balances that held the Reich together. The gradual disappearance of this equilibrium after 1740 was a key element in the Reich's ultimate collapse.

A second factor in that collapse was the growing realisation on the part of the lesser princes that the Reich was more a hindrance than a help in the pursuit of their aims. As Sheehan points out, what the Reich 'could do best – restrain, limit and conciliate – seemed less desirable than what states could do – consolidate, expand and initiate.[19] 'The intensity of devotion' to the Reich among its members had always 'tended to be in inverse proportion to the size and power of the territories themselves'.[20] Württemberg had remained roughly on the borderline between those such as Prussia and Bavaria with a chance to pursue independent policies and those like Baden-Durlach and Schaumburg-Lippe which depended on the Reich for protection. The defection of middle-ranking territories such as Württemberg after the 1790s was a serious blow to the Reich from which it never recovered.

[19] *German history*, p. 24.
[20] Gagliardo, *Reich and Nation*, p. 9.

Appendix

EXPENDITURE FROM THE WÜRTTEMBERG CENTRAL TREASURIES IN ANNUAL AVERAGES (FL.)

	Eberhard Ludwig 1714–33		Carl Alexander 1733–7		Carl Eugen I 1737–57		Carl Eugen II 1757–65	
Debt management								
Duke	134,100		93,000		118,500		24,000	
Estates	391,700		364,800		369,700		215,300	
Church	22,000		20,000		25,500		29,000	
	547,800	(34.5%)	477,800	(23.6%)	513,700	(24.4%)	268,300	(9.1%)
General administration								
Duke	78,000		165,700		180,100		114,000	
Estates	49,100		26,100		53,700		42,000	
Church	70,000		132,200		101,600		109,000	
	197,100	(12.4%)	324,000	(16.0%)	335,400	(16.0%)	265,000	(9.0%)
Court								
Duke	294,100		363,200		345,000		400,000	
Estates	17,500		17,500		15,000		9,000	
Church	80,000		74,000		108,700		107,500	
	391,600	(24.7%)	454,700	(22.5%)	468,700	(22.3%)	516,500	(17.6%)
Army								
Duke	55,600		210,300		90,400		816,600	
Estates	345,000		453,000		472,000		694,800	
Church	10,000		—		—		94,900	
	410,600	(25.9%)	663,300	(32.8%)	562,400	(26.8%)	1,606,300	(54.6%)
Surplus								
Duke	17,900		—		29,000		—	
Estates	17,800		102,000		153,700		237,900	
Church	4,500		—		38,500		47,000	
	40,200	(2.5%)	102,000	(5.1%)	221,200	(10.5%)	284,900	(9.7%)

257

Appendix

	Eberhard Ludwig 1714–33	Carl Alexander 1733–7	Carl Eugen I 1737–57	Carl Eugen II 1757–65
Totals				
Duke	597,700	832,200	763,000	1,354,600
Estates	821,100	963,400	1,064,100	1,199,000
Church	186,500	226,200	274,300	387,400
	1,587,300	2,021,800	2,101,400	2,941,000

Sources:
As Tables 8.1–8.10; plus HSAS, A8: Bü. 66; A19a: 50–2, 120–76, 837, 962–4, 970–83, 1109–16; A202: Bü. 737, 1870–4; A256: Bd. 197–257; A282: Bd. 1449x–1505x; L5: Tom. 135–67; L10: *Einnehmerei Rechnungen* 1713/14–1764/5; L13: *Tricesimations Rappiate* 1707/8, 1714/15, 1723–4; ZstA Merseburg Rep. XI, Nr. 298, Fasz. 30, vol. 7.

Notes:
The table shows the approximate annual average outgoings of the duchy's tripartite financial structure. Changes in accounting procedures for the ducal treasuries in 1765 prevent a comparison with later figures. Ducal expenditure figures include the Rentkammer (Landschreiberei), Kriegskasse with its subordinate treasuries, Tricesimationskasse and the Chatoule where known. Expenditure through the lesser treasuries (e.g. Bauverwaltungen) has been ignored, as these drew the bulk of their income from the Rentkammer and so are already included in its expenditure. Foreign subsidies are included in the ducal expenditure on the army. They totalled 483,000fl. over 1734–6, 617,500fl. over 1752–7 and 2,192,994fl. over 1757–65. The second column for Carl Eugen indicates average expenditure during the period of his arbitrary rule. Estates and church expenditure are those of the Landschaftliche Einnehmerei and Kirchenkasten respectively.

The figures for debt management represent loans repaid and interest on those still outstanding. General administration costs include the salaries of the central government agencies and diplomatic representatives, secretarial costs, correspondence etc. Court expenditure includes courtiers' allowances and food, palace construction and maintenance, payments to members of the ducal household and the cost of the orchestra, theatre, ballet and stables. Records for the Chatoule are virtually non-existent. It probably added a further 50,000–100,000fl. to annual court expenditure between 1714 and 1737. Thereafter it was increasingly drawn on to cover military outgoings and has been included in the totals for this rubric where known. The upkeep of the fortresses and military administration are also included in the totals for the army. These figures do not include payments made directly to Württemberg units from foreign commissariats for which only incomplete data survive. There were 2,300 infantry in direct imperial pay in 1716–20, and another 1,258 cavalry and about 6,600 infantry in 1734–6. Payments to these would have been worth 765,000fl. over the four-and-a-half years from 1716 to 1720, and 1,343,000fl. over the two years from 1734 to 1736. Further unknown payments were made by the French and Austrian commissariats in the Seven Years War. Württemberg units also extorted considerable sums from Hessian and Saxon towns and villages between 1758 and 1760. Finally, the surplus figures are deceptive.

They obscure the fact that considerable items were left unpaid each year. This was particularly the case after 1757 when the ducal Rentkammer and Kriegskasse virtually suspended debt repayment and left much of their current outgoings (especially food and officers' and civil bureaucrats' salaries) unpaid. This deficit could have been as large as one million florins a year between 1757 and 1765.

Bibliography

MANUSCRIPT SOURCES

Hauptstaatsarchiv Stuttgart

Papers of ducal departments
A5: Kabinettsakten II, 1
  Bü. 42, 43, 62–72
A6: Kabinettsakten II, 2
  Bü. 1, 7–9, 15, 19, 23–30, 32–6, 40–2, 44, 50–69, 75
A7: Kabinettsakten II, 3
  Bü. 10, 13, 41–2, 54–6
A8: Kabinettsakten III
  Bü. 3, 5, 8, 40, 51–60, 66–8, 78–9, 83, 223–52, 386–7, 391–2, 397
A14a: Kabinett: Militärangelegenheiten
  Bü. 1–2
A19a: Rechnungen altwürttembergischen Hof- und Residenzbehörden
  Bd. 41–6, 50–5, 120–76, 470, 837, 927, 962–4, 970–83, 1109–16, 1133–4, 1382
A28: Kriegsakten I
  Bü. 92, 93, 99
A29: Kriegsakten II
  Bü. 168
A30a: Kriegsrat
  Bü. 1–3, 5–7, 11, 16, 27–8, 57–67, 82, 85–9, 95, 105–6, 110–11, 119, 126–9, 133–4, 136–7, 140, 154–6, 159–62, 180, 192–3, 203, 231
A30b: Württembergische Kommandobehörden
  Bü. 33
A30c: Oberauditoriat und Truppen
  Bü. 1–8, 10–13; Bd. 5–8
A32: Rechnungen der Militärverwaltungsbehörden vor 1806
  Bd. 1–39, 80–114, 152, 154–215, 226–35, 241–2, 244–51; Bü. 1, 37
A39: Generalrescripte
  Bü. 29–46
A74: Berichte Württ. Gesandter und Agenten vor 1806 (Wiener Berichte)
  Bü. 100, 102, 109–51, 189–90, 197, 199, 201–2, 205
A202: Geheimer Rat I
  Bü. 225, 227, 242, 736–7, 739, 863–4, 1156–7, 1159, 1161, 1177, 1192, 1206–11, 1314,

1345, 1358, 1361–2, 1383, 1820–1, 1837, 1870–4, 1982–96, 2005–7, 2017–22, 2102–4, 2108–18, 2186–96, 2199, 2201–8, 2218–21, 2224, 2226, 2228, 2230, 2235–42, 2244, 2246, 2248, 2250–8, 2260–71, 2273–9, 2281–91, 2294, 2296, 2298–9, 2302, 2418, 2462–72, 2776

A203: Geheimer Rat II
Bü. 162
A211: Generalia
Bü. 139, 484
A256: Landschreiberei Rechnungen
Bd. 197–257
A257: Generalkasse Jahresrechnungen
Bd. 1–3
A282: Kirchenrat (Kirchenkastensverwaltung Rechnungen)
Bd. 1449x–1505x
E31: Königlicher Geheime Rat I
Bü. 6, 7, 1324

Papers of Kreis Institutions
C14: Schwäbischer Kreis: Militärakten
Bü. 56, 68–70, 77, 84–6, 87/I, 87/II, 87a, 121–3, 123a, 180, 185, 188–94, 217, 217a, 220, 300a, 305–8, 327, 330, 332, 334, 336, 336a, 337, 338, 418, 488–90, 499, 512, 530a, 567–8, 586, 586a, 587–90, 595, 597, 637–9, 713–14, 740, 743–4, 875–6

Hausarchiv
G164: Herzog Eberhard Ludwig
Bü. 18–23
G196: Herzog Karl Alexander
Bü. 11, 16
G230: Herzog Karl Eugen
Bü. 12, 38, 43–50, 50a, 51–4
G236: Herzog Friedrich Eugen
Bü. 8–18, 21, 21a–c, 22–62

Papers of the estates
L5: Tomi Actorum Provincialium Wirtembergicorum
Tom. 86–90, 102–17, 125–67
L6: Materienregistratur
L6.4.13.3, 4.13.9, 4.13.10
L6.10.2.1–2
L6.22.2.27, 22.2.32, 22.2.49
L6.22.3.1, 22.3.3–21
L6.22.4.4–33
L6.22.5.2–10, 22.5.11–14, 22.5.19–20, 22.5.78–80, 22.5.83, 22.5.85
L6.22.6.1–35, 22.6.38–40, 22.6.47–8
L6.22.7.2–3, 22.7.4a, 22.7.5a, 22.7.21–9

L6.22.8.1–3, 22.8.5–6, 22.8.14–16
L6.22.9.13
L10: Einnehmerei Rechnungen
Bd. 1713/14–1770/1
L12: Kriegsparticulare
Bd. 1713/14–1771/2
L13: Verschiedene Rechnungen
Tricesimations Rappiate 1707/8, 1714/15, 1723/4

Landesbibliothek Stuttgart

Handschriftliche Abteilung
Cod. milit. fols. 16, 30–2, 39
Cod. milit. oct. 14
Cod. milit. qt. 28–9
Cod. hist. fols. 74, 636, 647

Privatarchiv Dr Hans Bleckwenn, Münster
Papers relating to the transfer of regiments to Austrian service, 1737–40

Zentrales Staatsarchiv Merseburg
Rep. XI, Nr. 298, Fasz. 30, vol. 7

The Public Record Office
SP30/8/155
SP81/186, Faucitt's correspondence
SP100/14–17, German foreign ministers in England 1689–1779
SP102/25, royal letters

The British Library
Add. Mss. 23680, No. 1, Colonel Felix Frederick

PRINTED SOURCES

Alberti, Otto von, *Württembergisches Adels- und Wappenbuch* (2 vols., Stuttgart, 1889–1916; repr. in one volume, Neustadt an der Aisch, 1975).
Anon., 'Fürstliche Reisen im achtzehnten Jahrhundert', *WVJHLG*, NF2 (1893), 222–4
    List- und Lustige Begebenheiten derer Herren Offiziers auf Werbungen (1741; repr. Osnabrück, 1971).
    Vollständige Geschichte aller Königlichen preußischen Regimenter . . . , vol. I, *Geschichte und Nachrichten von dem . . . Fuselier Regimente von Lossow* . . . (Halle, 1767; repr. Osnabrück, 1979).
    'Was einzelne teutscher Fürstenhäuser innerhalb der zwanzig Jahre von 1750–1770 an französischen Subsidien und Geschenken gezogen', *Neues Göttingisches historisches Magazin*, 3 (1794), 324–40.

Bibliography

Bandel, Joseph Anton von, *Auf eine Lüge eine Maultasche! Oder: der bey Bestürmung der herzogl. würtemb. Ehre zurükgeschlagene Feind* (1766)

Becke-Klüchtzner, Edmund von der (ed.), *Der Adel des Königreiches Württemberg. Neu bearbeitetes Wappenbuch mit genealogischen und historischen Notizen* (Stuttgart, 1879).

Belschner, Christian, 'Ludwigsburg ums Jahr 1730. Nach den Memoiren des Barons von Pöllnitz', *LBGB*, 3 (1903), 81–96.

Bevölkerungs-Ploetz: *Raum und Bevölkerung in der Weltgeschichte* (4 vols., Würzburg, 1956).

Boelcke, Willi A., *Handbuch Baden-Württemberg Politik, Wirtschaft, Kultur von der Urgeschichte bis zur Gegenwart* (Stuttgart, 1982).

Bredow [Christian Werner] Claus von, *Historische Rang- und Stammliste des deutschen Heeres* (Berlin, 1905).

Brodrück, Karl, *Quellenstücke in Studien über den Feldzug der Reichsarmee von 1757* (Leipzig, 1858).

Burgoyne, Bruce E. (ed.), *A Hessian diary of the American Revolution by Johann Conrad Döhla* (Norman/London, 1990).

Büsching, Anton Friedrich, *Erdbeschreibung* (9 vols., Hamburg, 1788–92, vol. VII, 1790)

Buwinghausen [sic]-Wallmerode, Alexander Maximilian Friedrich Freiherr von, *Tagebuch des herzoglich württembergischen General-Adjutant Freiherrn von Buwinghausen-Wallmerode über die 'Land Reisen' des Herzogs Karl Eugen von Württemberg in der Zeit 1767 bis 1773* (ed. Ernst von Ziegesar, Stuttgart, 1911).

Cast, Fr., *Historisches und genealogisches Adelsbuch des Königreichs Württemberg* (Stuttgart, 1839).

Conrad, Hermann (ed.), 'Verfassung und politische Lage des Reiches in einer Denkschrift Josephs II von 1767–1768', in (Louis) Carlen and (Fritz) Steinegger (eds.), *Festschrift für Nicolaus Grass zum 60. Geburtstag* (2 vols., Innsbrück, 1974), I, pp. 161–85.

Etat général des trouppes de S.A.S. Monseigneur le Duc de Virtemberg et Theck sur pié en 1759 (1759).

Frederick the Great, *Geschichte des siebenjährigen Krieges* (Munich, no date).

Politische Correspondenz Friedrich's des Grossen (46 vols., Berlin, 1879–1939).

Geiges, Robert, 'Mit Herzog Karl Eugen im siebenjährigen Krieg. Nach Tagebuchaufzeichnungen des Leibmedicus Dr Albrecht Reichart Reuß', *BBSAW* (1928), 185–96.

Georgii-Georgenau, Eberhard Emil von, *Fürstlich-Württembergisches Dienerbuch vom IX, bis zum XIX. Jahrhundert* (Stuttgart, 1877).

Grube, Walter (ed.), *Der Tübinger Vertrag vom 8 July 1514. Faksimile Ausgabe mit Transkription und geschichtlicher Würdigung* (Stuttgart, 1964).

Jüretschke, Hans (ed.), *Berichte der diplomatischen Vertreter des Wiener Hofes aus Spanien in der Regierungszeit Karl III. (1759–1788)* (14 vols., Madrid, 1970–87), vol. II (1971).

Kulpis, Johann Georg, *Eines hochlöbl. schwäbischen Crayses alte und neue Kriegsverordnungen und Reglementen wie solche nunmehr zusammen gerichtet und in öffentlichen Druck zu bringen befohlen worden* (Stuttgart, 1737 edn).

Militär-Handbuch des Königreichs Württemberg. Amtliche Ausgabe (8 vols., Stuttgart, 1836–1908).

Pfeilsticker, Walter, *Neues württembergisches Dienerbuch* (3 vols., Stuttgart, 1957–74).

Pottle, F. A. (ed.), *Boswell on the grand tour. Germany and Switzerland 1764. The Yale editions of the private papers of James Boswell* (5 vols., Melbourne, 1953).

Bibliography

Reyscher, A. L. (ed.), *Vollständige, historisch und kritisch bearbeitete Sammlung der württembergischen Gesetze* (29 vols., Stuttgart/Tübingen, 1828–51).

Röder, Philipp Ludwig Hermann, *Geographie und Statistik Wirtembergs* (2 vols., Laibach in Krain/Ulm, 1787–1804).

Schneider, Eugen (ed.), *Augsgewählte Urkunden zur württembergische Geschichte* (*Württembergische Geschichtesquellen*, vol. XI, Stuttgart, 1911).

Snyder, Henry L. (ed.), *The Marlborough–Godolphin correspondence* (Oxford, 1975).

Stark, Paul, 'Zur Geschichte des Herzogs Karl Alexander von Württemberg und der Streitigkeiten nach seinem Tode', *WVJHLG*, 11 (1888), 1–28.

Steininger, Johann, *Leben und Abenteuer des Johann Steininger, ehemaligen herzoglich württembergischen und kaiserlich österreichischen Soldaten von 1779–1790, späteren Tambourmaîtres und Kannoniers unter der französischen Republik und dem Kaiserreich von 1791–1815, nachherigen königlich württembergischen Regiments-Tambours und jetzigen 79 jährigen Invaliden auf Hohenasperg* (Stuttgart, 1841).

Stotzingen, O. Freiherr von, 'Beiträge zur Geschichte der Reichsarmee', *WVJHLG*, NF20 (1911), 71–112.

Thürriegel, J. C. von, *Merckwürdige Lebensgeschichte des berüchtigen Königliche Preußischen Generalmajors Herrn von Gschray* (Frankfurt/Leipzig, 1766, repr. Osnabrück, 1974).

Volz, Gustav Berthold and Küntzel, Georg, *Preußische und Österreichische Acten zur Vorgeschichte des siebenjährigen Krieges* (Leipzig, 1899).

Württembergische Hof- und Staats-Handbücher (Stuttgart, 1736–1918); title varied in eighteenth century: *Hof- und Staatsbuch; Hofkalender; Hof- und Staatskalender; Adress-Calender*, etc.

Zeumer, Karl (ed.), *Quellensammlung zur Geschichte der deutschen Reichsverfassung in Mittelalter und Neuzeit* (Tübingen, 1913 edn).

Ziegesar, Ernst Freiherr von (ed.), *Zwei württembergische Soldatenbilder aus alter Zeit* (Stuttgart, 1904).

Zorn von Bulach, Anton Joseph Freiherr von, *Der Fähnrich Zorn von Bulach vom Regimente Württemberg zu Pferd im siebenjährigen Kriege 1757–1758 nach seinem Tagebuche* (ed. Karl Engel, Strasbourg, 1908).

Secondary works

Adam, Albert Eugen, 'Herzog Karl Eugen und die Landschaft', *HKE*, I, pp. 193–310.

Johann Jakob Moser als württembergischer Landschaftskonsulent 1751–1771 (Stuttgart, 1887).

'Württemberg vor dem siebenjährigen Krieg geschildert in einem Gutachten Johann Jakob Mosers von 9. November 1752', *WVJHLG*, NF12 (1903), 205–26.

Anderson, M. S. *Europe in the eighteenth century 1713–1783* (3rd edn, London, 1987).

War and society in Europe of the old regime, 1618–1789 (London, 1988).

Anderson, Perry, *Lineages of the absolutist state* (London, 1974).

Andler, Rudolf von, 'Die württembergischen Regimenter in Griechenland, 1687–89', *WVJHLG*, NF31 (1922–24), 217–79.

Anon., *Friedrich August von Hardenberg. Ein kleinstaatlicher Minister des 18. Jahrhunderts* (Leipzig, 1877).

Bibliography

Aretin, Karl Otmar Freiherr von, *Heiliges römisches Reich 1776–1806. Reichsverfassung und Staatssouveränität* (2 vols., Wiesbaden, 1967).

Arndt, Johannes, *Das Niederrheinisch-Westfälische Reichsgrafenkollegium und seine Mitglieder (1653–1806)* (Mainz, 1991).

Arnold, Hauptmann, 'Schwedens Teilnahme am siebenjährigen Kriege', *BMWB*, 12 (1908), 453–82.

Asch, Ronald G., 'Estates and princes after 1648: the consequences of the Thirty Years War', *German History*, 6 (1988), 113–32.

Asch, Ronald G. and Birke, A. M. (eds.), *Princes, patronage and the nobility. The court at the beginning of the modern age* (Oxford, 1991).

Atwood, Rodney, *The Hessians. Mercenaries from Hessen-Kassel in the American Revolution* (Cambridge, 1980).

Ausstellung: Die Hohe Carlschule 4. November 1959 bis 30. Januar 1960 (Stuttgart, 1959).

Bader, Karl Siegfried, *Der deutsche Südwesten in seiner territorialstaatlichen Entwicklung* (Sigmaringen, 1978 edn).

'Die Reichsstädte des schwäbischen Kreises am Ende des Alten Reiches', *Ulm und Oberschwaben*, 32 (1951), 47–70.

Barker, Thomas, 'Military enterprisership and absolutism. Habsburg models', *Journal of European Studies*, 4 (1974), 19–42.

Barth, J., *Hohenzollernsche Chronik, oder Geschichte und Sage der hohenzollernschen Lande* (Sigmaringen, 1863).

Barthold, Friedrich Wilhelm, *Geschichte der Kriegsverfassung und des Kriegswesens der Deutschen* (2 vols., Leipzig, 1864).

Batori, Ingrid (ed.), *Städtische Gesellschaft und Reformation* (*Spätmittelalter und frühe Neizeit, Tübinger Beiträge zur Geschichtsforschung*, 12, Stuttgart, 1980).

Baumann, Kurt, 'Herzog Christian IV. von Pfalz-Zweibrücken 1722–1775', in *Deutsche Westen – Deutsches Reich. Saarpfälzische Lebensbilder* (Kaiserslautern, 1938), I, pp. 103–17.

Baumann, Reinhard, *Das Söldnerwesen im 16. Jahrhundert im bayerischen und süddeutschen Beispiel. Eine gesellschaftsgeschichtliche Untersuchung* (*Miscellanea Bavarica Monacensia*, 79, Munich, 1978).

Die Landsknechte (Munich, 1994).

Baur, Ludwig, *Der städtischer Haushalt Tübingens vom Jahre 1750 bis auf unsere Zeit* (Tübingen, 1863).

Beales, Derek, *Joseph II: in the shadow of Maria Theresa 1741–1780* (Cambridge, 1987).

Becker, Constantin, 'Die Erlebnisse der kurkölnischen Truppen im Verbande der Reichsarmee während des siebenjährigen Krieges', *Annalen des historischen Vereins für den Niederrhein*, 91 (1911), 63–108.

Belschner, Christian, *Ludwigsburg im Wechsel der Zeiten* (3rd edn, Ludwigsburg, 1969).

Benecke, G., *Society and politics in Germany 1500–1750* (London, 1974).

Béringuier, Richard, *Der Besuch der württembergischen Prinzen zur Zeit Königs Friedrich des Grossen in Berlin und ihre Beziehungen zum preussischen Königshause* (Berlin, 1879).

Best, Geoffrey, *War and society in revolutionary Europe, 1770–1870* (London, 1982).

Die Bewaffnung und Ausrüstung der Armee Friedrichs des Großen. Eine Dokumentation aus Anlaß seines 200. Todesjahres (Rastatt, 1986).

265

Bibliography

Bezzel, Oskar, *Geschichte des kurpfälzischen Heeres von seinen Anfängen bis zur Vereinigung von Kurpfälz und Kurbayern 1777* (2 vols., Munich, 1925–8).

Die Haustruppen des Letzten Markgrafen von Ansbach-Bayreuth unter preußischer Herrschaft (*Münchener historische Abhandlungen* 2. Reihe, vol. II, Munich, 1939).

Biedermann, Karl, *Deutschland im achtzehnten Jahrhundert* (5 vols., 2nd edn, Leipzig, 1880).

Birtsch, G., 'Die landständische Verfassung als Gegenstand der Forschung', in D. Gerhard (ed.), *Ständische Vertretungen in Europa im 17. und 18. Jahrhundert* (Göttingen, 1969), pp. 32–71.

Bitterauf, Theodor, *Die kurbayerische Politik im siebenjährigen Krieg* (Munich, 1901).

Black, Jeremy, 'Anglo-Wittelsbach relations 1730–42', *Zeitschrift für bayerisches Landesgeschichte*, 55 (1992), 307–45.

'Parliament and foreign policy in the age of Walpole: the case of the Hessians', in J. Black (ed.), *Knights errant and true Englishmen: British foreign policy, 1660–1800* (Edinburgh, 1989), pp. 41–54.

'The problem of the small state: Bavaria and Britain in the second quarter of the 18th century', *European History Quarterly*, 19 (1989), 5–36.

Blanning, T. C. W., *Reform and revolution in Mainz 1743–1802* (Cambridge, 1974).

Blickle, Peter, 'Communalism, parliamentarism, republicanism', *Parliaments, Estates and Representation*, 8 (1986), 1–13.

Boepple, Ernst, *Friedrich des Grossen Verhältnis zu Württemberg* (Strasbourg Ph.D., printed Munich, 1915).

Boguslawski, A. von, 'Soldatenhandel und Subsidienvertrage', *BMWB*, 7 (1885).

Böhme, Hans-Georg, *Die Wehrverfassung in Hessen-Kassel im 18. Jahrhundert bis zum siebenjährigen Kriege* (Kassel/Basle, 1954).

Bolay, Theodor, *Chronik der Stadt Asperg* (Bietigheim-Bissingen, 1978).

Borck, Heinz-Günther, *Der schwäbische Reichskreis im Zeitalter der französischen Revolutionskriege (1792–1806)* (*VKGLK*, Reihe B, vol. 61, Stuttgart, 1970).

Brabant, Artur, *Das heilige römische Reich teutscher Nation im Kampf mit Friedrich dem Großen* (3 vols., Berlin, 1904–31).

Braubach, Max, *Die Bedeutung der Subsidien für die Politik im spanischen Erbfolgekrieg* (Bonn, 1923).

Kurköln: Gestalten und Ereignisse aus zwei Jahrhunderten rheinischer Geschichte (Münster, 1949).

Prinz Eugen von Savoyen: Eine Biographie (5 vols., Munich, 1963–5).

Brauer, Gert, *Die hannoversch-englischen Subsidienverträge 1701–1748* (*Untersuchungen zur deutschen Staats- und Rechtsgeschichte*, NF vol. I, Aalen, 1962).

Breitenbücher, Otto, *Die Entwicklung des württembergischen Militärversorgungswesens nach dem dreißigjährigen Krieg bis zum Jahr 1871. Ein Beitrag zur Geschichte des württembergischen Staats- und Verwaltungsrechts* (Tübingen Ph.D., printed 1936).

Breitling, Richard, 'Kehl und die süddeutsche Kriegsvorbereitung 1792', *ZGO*, NF43 (1930), 107–37.

Brewer, John, *The sinews of power. War, money and the English state 1688–1783* (New York, 1989).

Burke, P., *The fabrication of Louis XIV* (New Haven, 1992).

Bibliography

Burkhardt, Felix, 'Soldatenwerbung im 18. Jahrhundert. Auch im Limpurger Land Lange Kerls gesucht', *Der Haalquell, Blätter für Heimatkunde des Haller-Landes*, 31 (1979), 20.

'Wie der Herzog seine Soldaten bekam', *Der Haalquell, Blätter für Heimatkunde des Haller-Landes*, 29 (1977), 51–2.

Bürlen-Grabinger, Christine, *Verkauft und Verloren. Das württembergische 'Kapregiment' in Südafrika, Ceylon und Java 1787–1808. Ausstellung des Hauptstaatarchivs Stuttgart* (Stuttgart, 1987).

Burr, Wolfgang, 'Die Reichssturmfahne und der Streit um die hannoversche Kurwürde', *ZWLG*, 27 (1968), 245–316.

Büsch, Otto, *Militärsystem und Sozialleben im alten Preussen 1713–1807. Die Anfänge der sozialen Militärisierung der preussisch-deutschen Gesellschaft (Veröffentlichungen der Berliner historischen Kommission beim Friedrich-Meinicke Institut der freien Universität Berlin*, vol. VII, Berlin, 1962).

Carsten, F. L., *Princes and parliaments in Germany from the fifteenth to the eighteenth century* (Oxford, 1959).

Caspary, Hermann, *Staat, Finanzen, Wirtschaft und Heerwesen im Hochstift Bamberg (1672–1693) (Historischer Verein für die Pflege der Geschichte des ehemalige Fürstbistums Bamberg*, Beiheft 7, Bamberg, 1976).

Cassels, Lavender, *The struggle for the Ottoman empire, 1717–1740* (London, 1966).

Childs, John, *Armies and warfare in Europe 1648–1789* (Manchester, 1982).

Corvisier, André, *Armies and societies in Europe 1494–1789* (trans. Abigail T. Siddall, Bloomington/London, 1976).

Cramer, J., *Die Grafschaft Hohenzollern. Ein Bild süddeutscher Volkszustände 1400–1850* (Stuttgart, 1873).

Czok, Karl, *Am Hofe Augusts des Starkens* (Stuttgart, 1990).

Dalwigk, von, 'Der Anteil der hessischen Truppen am österreichischen Erbfolgekriege (1740–48)', *Zeitschrift für hessische Geschichte und Landeskunde*, 42 (1908), 72–139; 45 (1911), 138–201.

Decker-Hauff, Hans Martin, 'Die geistige Führungsschicht Württembergs', in Günther Franz (ed.), *Beamtentum und Pfarrerstand 1400–1800. Büdinger Vorträge 1967* (Limpurg, 1972), pp. 51–80.

Dehlinger, Alfred, *Württembergs Staatswesen in seiner geschichtlichen Entwicklung bis heute* (2 vols., Stuttgart, 1951–3).

Demandt, Karl E., *Geschichte des Landes Hessen* (Kassel, 1980).

Demeter, Karl, *The German officer-corps in society and state, 1650–1945* (English translation, London, 1965).

Dickson, P. G. M., *Finance and government under Maria Theresia 1740–1780* (2 vols., Oxford, 1987).

Dipper, Christof, *Deutsche Geschichte 1648–1789* (Frankfurt am Main, 1991).

Dizinger, Karl Friedrich, *Beiträge zur Geschichte Würtembergs und seines Regentenhauses zur Zeit der Regierung Herzogs Karl Alexander und während der Minderjährigkeit seines Erstgeboren* (2 vols., Tübingen, 1834).

Dorpalen, Andreas, *German history in Marxist perspective. The East German approach* (London, 1985).

Bibliography

Downing, Brian M., *The military revolution and political change in early modern Europe* (Princeton, 1991).

Dreitzel, Horst, *Absolutismus und ständische Verfassung in Deutschland. Ein Beitrag zu Kontinuität und Diskontinuität der politischen Theorie in der frühen Neuzeit* (Mainz, 1992).

Drumm, Ernst, *Das Regiment Royal-Deuxponts. Deutsches Blut auf fürstlichen Befehl in fremden Dienst und Sold* (Zweibrücken, 1937 edn).

Du Boulay, F. R. H., *Germany in the later middle ages* (London, 1983).

Duchhardt, Heinz, *Altes Reich und Europäische Staatenwelt 1648–1806* (Munich, 1990).

Deutsche Verfassungsgeschichte 1495–1806 (Stuttgart, 1991).

Duffy, Christopher, *The army of Frederick the Great* (Vancouver/London, 1974).

The army of Maria Theresa. The armed forces of imperial Austria 1740–80 (New York, 1977).

Duvernoy, Max von, *Württembergische Heeresgeschichte* (Berlin, 1893).

Ebbecke, Otto Carl, *Frankreichs Politik gegenüber dem deutschen Reiche in den Jahren 1748–1756* (Freiburg i.Br. Ph.D., printed 1931).

Ehlers, J., *Die Wehrverfassung der Stadt Hamburg im 17. und 18. Jahrhundert* (Boppard, 1966).

Eicken, Heinrich von, 'Die Reichsarmee im siebenjährigen Krieg. Dargestellt am Kurtrierischen Regiment', *PJb*, 41 (1879), 1–14, 113–35, 248–67.

Eldon, Carl William, *England's subsidy policy towards the continent during the Seven Years War* (Philadelphia, 1938).

Elwenspoek, Curt, *Jud Süss Oppenheimer. Der große Finanzier und galante Abenteurer des achtzehnten Jahrhunderts* (Stuttgart, 1926. Trans. E. Cattle as *Jew Süss Oppenheimer*, London, 1931).

Emberger, Gudrun, 'Verdruß, Sorg und Widerwärttigkeiten. Die Inventur und Verwaltung der Jud Süßischen Vermögen 1737–1772', *ZWLG*, 40 (1981), 369–75.

Engelmann, Bernd, *Wir Untertanen. Ein deutsches Anti-Geschichtsbuch* (Frankfurt am Main, 1976).

Essig, Heinrich, *Die Letzten Krieger Württembergs. Gedrängte Übersicht der Affairen und Schlachten württembergischer Truppen* (Leonberg, 1840).

Evans, R. J. W., *The making of Habsburg monarchy 1550–1700* (Oxford, 1979).

Fann, Willerd, R., 'On the infantryman's age in eighteenth century Prussia', *Military Affairs*, 41 (1977), 165–70.

'Peacetime attrition in the army of Frederick William I 1713–1740', *Central European History*, 11 (1978), 323–34.

Fauchier-Magnan, Adrien, *The small German courts in the eighteenth century* (trans. Mervyn Savill, London, 1958).

Fester, Richard, *Die armirten Stände und die Reichskriegsverfassung 1681–1697* (Frankfurt am Main, 1886).

Fischer, Carl August, *Geschichte der Stuttgarter Stadtgarde zu Pferde* (Stuttgart, 1887).

Fitte, Siegfried, *Religion und Politik vor und während des siebenjährigen Krieges* (Berlin, 1899).

Fleischhauer, Werner, *Barock im Herzogtum Württemberg* (2nd edn, Stuttgart, 1981).

Ford, Franklin L., *Strasbourg in transition 1648–1789* (Cambridge, 1958).

Forderer, Josef, 'Das Bürgermilitär in Württemberg. Von dem Milizen, Bürgergarden und Bürgerwehren in Tübingen', *Tübinger Blätter*, 23 (1932), 1–27.

Tüttlingen im Wandel der Zeiten (Reutlingen, 1949).

Bibliography

Forst, Hermann, 'Die deutschen Reichstruppen im Türkenkriege 1664', *Mitteilungen des Instituts für österreichische Geschichtsforschung, Ergänzungsband*, 6 (1901), 635–48.

Förster, Gerhard, *Kurzer Abriß der Militärgeschichte von den Anfängen der Geschichte des deutschen Volkes bis 1945* (Berlin, DDR, 1974).

Frauenholz, Eugen von, *Die Eingliederung von Heer und Volk in den Staat in Bayern 1597–1815 (Münchener historischen Abhandlungen*, 2. Reihe, vol. 14, Munich, 1940).

Entwicklungsgeschichte des deutschen Heerwesens, vol. IV, *Das Heerwesen in der Zeit des Absolutismus* (Munich, 1940).

Fuchs, Th., *Geschichte des europäischen Kriegswesens* (3 vols., Munich, 1972–6).

Fulbrook, Mary, *Piety and politics. Religion and the rise of absolutism in England, Württemberg and Prussia* (Cambridge, 1983).

Gaese, Heinrich, 'Zur Gründung der Stadt Ludwigsburg', *LBGB*, 20 (1968), 7–30.

Gagliardo, John, *Germany under the old regime 1600–1790* (Harlow, 1991).

Reich and nation: the Holy Roman Empire as idea and reality, 1763–1806 (Bloomington, 1980).

Galperin, Peter, *In Wehr und Waffen: Wehrbürger, Söldner und Soldaten in Oldenburg und den Hansestädten* (Stuttgart, 1983).

Gebauer, Ruth, *Die Außenpolitik der schwäbischen Reichskreises vor Ausbruch des spanischen Erbfolgekrieges (1697–1702)* (Marburg Ph.D., printed 1969).

Gembruch, Werner, 'Zur Diskussion um Heeresverfassung und Kriegsführung in der Zeit vor der Französischen Revolution', in Wolfgang von Groote and Klaus-Jürgen Müller (eds.), *Napoleon I. Von der Militärwesen seiner Seit* (Freiburg i.Br., 1968), 9–28.

Generalquartiermeisterstab, Königlich-württembergischer (eds.), 'Quellenstudien über die Kriegsgeschichte der württembergischen Truppen von 1792 an', *WJb* (1845), 211–35.

Generalstab, Großer (Prussian) (eds.), *Der erste schlesische Krieg 1740–1742* (3 vols., Berlin, 1890–3).

Der siebenjährige Krieg 1756–1763 (12 vols., Berlin, 1901–13).

Der zweite schlesische Krieg 1744–1745 (3 vols., Berlin, 1895).

Gerspacher, Hans, *Die badische Politik im siebenjährigen Kriege (Heidelberger Abhandlungen zur mittleren und neueren Geschichte*, 67, Heidelberg, 1934).

Gessler, Tognarelli, Ströbel, *Geschichte des 2. Württembergischen Feldartillerie-Regiments Nr. 29 Prinzregent Luitpold von Bayern und seiner Stammtruppenteile* (Stuttgart, 1892).

Gilbert, Arthur N., 'Military recruitment and career advancement in the 18th century: two case studies', *Journal of the Society for Army Historical Research*, 57 (1979), 34–44.

Gönner, Eberhard, 'Hohenzollern und Württemberg', in *Bausteine zur geschichtlichen Landeskunde von Baden-Württemberg* (Stuttgart, 1979), pp. 239–59.

Gönner, Eberhard and Haselier, Günther, *Baden-Württemberg. Geschichte seiner Länder und Territorien (Territorien-Ploetz*, Würzburg, 1975).

Göz, von, 'Feldmarschall Villiars in Württemberg Juni 1707', *BBSAW* (1911), 121–5.

Graevenitz, Fritz von, *Die Entwicklung des württembergischen Heerwesens, inbesondere im Rahmen des deutschen Reichsheeres* (Stuttgart, 1921).

Griesinger, [Theodor], *Geschichte des Ulanenregiments König Karl (1. Württembergischen) Nr. 19 von seiner Grundung 1683 bis zur Gegenwart* (Stuttgart, 1883).

Groehler, Olaf, *Die Kriege Friedrichs II.* (Berlin, DDR, 1966).

Bibliography

Grothe, Ewald, 'Der württembergische Reformlandtag 1797–1799', *ZWLG*, 48 (1989), 159–200.

Grube, Walther, 'Dorfgemeinde und Amtsversammlungen in Ältwürttemberg', *ZWLG*, 13 (1954), 194–219.

'Herzog Eberhard Ludwig. Betrachtungen zum 300. Geburtstag des Stadtgründers', *Hie gut Württemberg*, 27 (1978), 33–5.

Der Stuttgarter Landtag 1457–1957. Von dem Landständen zum demokratischen Parlament (Stuttgart, 1957).

'Die württembergischen Landstände und die Graevenitz', *ZWLG*, 40 (1981), 476–93.

'Württemberg's erster Barockfürst. Im Zeichen des Absolutismus – Politische Aspekte der Regierung Eberhard Ludwigs', *Beiträge für Landeskunde*, 6 (1976), 1–4.

Güssregen, Josef, *Die Wehrverfassung der Hochstiftes Bamberg im achtzehnten Jahrhundert* (Erlangen Ph.D., printed Bamberg, 1936).

Gutkas, Karl (ed.), *Prinz Eugen und das barocke Österreich* (Salzburg/Vienna, 1985).

Gutmann, Myron P., *War and rural life in the early modern Low Countries* (Princeton, 1980).

Guy, Alan James, *Oeconomy and discipline: officership and administration in the British army 1714–63* (Manchester, 1985).

Haering, Hermann, 'Württemberg und das Reich in der Geschichte', *ZWLG*, 7 (1943), 294–332.

Hagen, Eduard, 'Die fürstlich würzburgische Hausinfanterie vom Jahre 1757 bis zur Einverleibung des Fürstbistums in Bayern 1803', *DBKH*, 20 (1911), 1–142.

'Die fürstlich würzburgische Hausinfanterie von ihren Anfängen bis zum Beginne des siebenjährigen Krieges 1636–1756', *DBKH*, 19 (1910), 69–203.

Hahn, Herbert, 'Das Ende des schwäbischen Kreiskontingents', *Zeitschrift für Heereskunde*, 37 (1973), 52–7, 123–31.

'Die württembergische Heeresentwicklung', *Zeitschrift für Heereskunde*, 37 (1973), 165–73, 220–5; 38 (1974), 21–32.

Hale, J. R., *War and society in Renaissance Europe, 1450–1620* (London, 1985).

Handbuch zur deutschen Militärgeschichte 1648–1939 (issued by the Militärgeschichtliches Forschungsamt, 11 vols., Frankfurt am Main, 1964–81).

Hansen, Ernst Willi, 'Zur Problematik einer Sozialgeschichte des deutschen Militärs im 17. und 18. Jahrhundert. Ein Forschungsbericht', *Zeitschrift für historische Forschung*, 5 (1979), 425–60.

Harder, Hans-Joachim, *Militärgeschichtliches Handbuch Baden-Württemberg. Herausgegeben vom Militärgeschichtlichen Forschungsamt* (Stuttgart, 1987).

Harms, Richard, 'Landmiliz und stehendes Heer in Kurmainz namentlich im 18. Jahrhundert' (Göttingen Ph.D., printed in *Archiv für hessische Geschichte und Altertumskunde*, NF6 (1909), pp. 359–430).

Hartmann, J., 'Württemberg im Jahr 1800', *WNJB*, NF5 (1900).

Hartmann, Peter Claus, 'Die französischen Subsidienzahlungen an den Kurfürsten von Köln, Fürstbischof von Lüttich, Hildesheim und Regensburg, Joseph Clemens, im spanischen Erbfolgekrieg (1701–1714)', *Historische Jahrbücher*, 92 (1972), 358–71.

Geld als Instrument europäischer Machtpolitik im Zeitalter des Merkantilismus 1715–1740 (*Studien zur bayerischer Verfassungs und Sozialgeschichte*, 8, Munich, 1978).

Bibliography

Karl Albrecht – Karl VII. Glücklicher Kurfürst unglücklicher Kaiser (Regensburg, 1985).

Das Steuersystem der europäischen Staaten am Ende des Ancien Régime. Eine offizielle französischen Enquête (1763–1768) (*Beiheft Francia*, 7, Munich, 1979).

Hasselhorn, Martin, *Der Altwürttembergische Pfarrstand im 18. Jahrhundert* (*VKGLK*, Reihe B, vol. 6, Stuttgart, 1958).

Haug-Moritz, Gabriele, 'Friedrich Samuel Graf Montmartin als Württembergischer Staatsmann (1758–1766/73)', *ZWLG*, 53 (1994), 205–26.

Württembergischer Ständekonflikt und deutscher Dualismus. Ein Beitrag zur Geschichte des Reichsverbands in der Mitte des 18. Jahrhunderts (*VKGLK*, Reihe B, vol. 122, Stuttgart, 1992).

Heinl, Otto, *Heereswesen und Volksbewaffnung in Vorderösterreich im Zeitalter Josefs II. und der Revolutionskriege* (Freiburg i.Br. Ph.D., printed 1941).

Hellstern, Dieter, *Der Ritterkanton Neckar-Schwarzwald 1560–1805* (*Veröffentlichungen des Stadtarchivs Tübingen*, 5, Tübingen, 1971).

Helmes, Hermann, 'Die fränkischen Kreistruppen im Kriegsjahre 1758 und im Frühjahrsfeldzuge 1759', *DBKH*, 17 (1908).

'Kurze Geschichte der fränkischen Kreistruppen 1714–56 und ihre Teilnahme am Feldzuge von Rossbach 1757', *DBKH*, 16 (1907).

'Das Regiment Würzburg im Türkenkriege des Jahres 1739', *DBKH*, 13 (1904), 60–93.

'Übersicht zur Geschichte der fränkischen Kreistruppen 1664–1714', *DBKH*, 14 (1905).

Henle, Julius, 'Über das Heerwesen des Hochstifts Würzburg im 18. Jahrhundert', *DBKH*, 7 (1898), 1–20.

Hermann, Carl Hans, *Deutsche Militärgeschichte. Eine Einführung* (Frankfurt am Main, 1968 edn).

Hermelink, Heinrich, 'Geschichte des allgemeinen Kirchenguts in Württemberg', *WJSL* (1903), 78–101, and part II, pp. 1–81.

Herzog Karl Eugen und seine Zeit (issued by the Württembergischer Geschichts- und Altertumsverein, 2 vols., Esslingen, 1907–9).

Hildenbrand, Manfred, 'Die kriegerischen Auseinandersetzungen im 17. und 18. Jahrhundert, 1672–1748', in Kurt Klein (ed.), *Land um Rhein und Schwarzwald. Die Ortenau in Geschichte und Gegenwart* (Kehl, 1978), pp. 103–11.

Hintze, Otto, *The historical essays of Otto Hintze* (ed. F. Gilbert, Oxford, 1975).

Hittle, J[ames] D[onald], *The military staff. Its history and development* (Harrisburg, PA, 1949 edn).

Hoch, Immanuel Math. Peter, 'Württembergische Denkwürdigkeiten aus den Herzoge Carl Alexander und Carl Eugen, nach Aufzeichnungen von General Wolf und dessen Sohn', *Sophronizon*, 6 (1824), 5. Heft, 16–62.

Hochheimer, Albert, *Verraten und Verkauft. Die Geschichte der europäischen Söldner* (Stuttgart, 1967).

Hofacker, Hans-Georg, 'Die schwäbische Herzogswürde. Untersuchungen zur Landfürstlichen und kaiserlichen Politik im deutschen Südwesten im Spätmittelalter und in der frühen Neuzeit', *ZWLG*, 47 (1988), 71–148.

Hofmann, Johannes, *Die kursächsische Armee 1769 bis zum Beginn des bayerischen Erbfolgekrieges* (Leipzig, 1914).

Bibliography

Hohrath, Daniel and Henning, Rudolf, *Die Bildung des Offiziers in der Aufklärung. Ferdinand Friedrich von Nicolai (1713–1814) und seine enzyklopädischen Sammlungen* (Stuttgart, 1990).

Hossbach, Friedrich, *Die Entwicklung des Oberbefehls über das Heer in Brandenburg, Preussen und im Deutschen Reich von 1655–1945. Ein kurzer Überblick* (Würzburg, 1957).

Hsia, R. Po-Chia, *Social discipline in the Reformation: central Europe 1550–1750* (London, 1989).

Huber, Ernst Rudolph, *Heer und Staat in der deutschen Geschichte* (Hamburg, 1943 edn).

Hughes, Michael, *Early modern Germany 1477–1806* (London, 1992).

Law and politics in eighteenth-century Germany: The Imperial Aulic Council in the reign of Charles VI (Woodbridge, 1988).

Ingrao, Charles W., '"Barbarous strangers": Hessian state and society during the American Revolution', *American Historical Review*, 87 (1982), 954–76.

The Hessian mercenary state. Ideas, institutions and reform under Frederick II 1760–1785 (Cambridge, 1987).

'Kameralismus und Militärismus im deutschen Polizeistaat: Der hessische Söldnerstaat', in G. Schmidt (ed.), *Stände und Gesellschaft im Alten Reich* (Stuttgart, 1989), pp. 171–86.

J. N., 'Über Soldtruppen. Vortrag, dem Offiziercorps gehalten den 18. März 1881', *BMWB*, 4 (1984), 330–53.

Jäger, Edmund, *Das Militärwesen des Königreiches Württemberg* (Stuttgart, 1869).

Jähns, Max, *Geschichte der Kriegswissenschaften vornehmlich in Deutschland* (3 vols., Munich, 1889–91).

Heeresverfassung und Völkerleben (Berlin, 1885).

'Zur Geschichte der Kriegsverfassung des deutschen Reiches', *PJb*, 38 (1877), 1–28, 114–40, 443–90.

Jänichen, H., 'Zur Landwirtschaftlichen Ertragsbewertung vor 200 Jahren. Erläutert am Beispiel von Dömuch, Kr. Tübingen', *ZWLG*, 26 (1967), 113–20.

Janssen, K. H., *Macht und Verblendung: Kriegzielpolitik der deutschen Bundesstaaten 1914–1918* (Göttingen, 1963).

Jany, Curt, *Geschichte der königlich-preußischen Armee vom 15. Jahrhundert bis 1914* (4 vols., Osnabrück, 1967).

'Die Kantonverfassung Friedrich Wilhelms I', *Forschungen zur brandenburgischen-preußischen Geschichte*, 38 (1926), 225–72.

Jutz, K. H., and Fieser, J. M., *Geschichte der Stadt und ehemaligen Reichsfestung Philippsburg* (Philippsburg, 1966).

Kahlenberg, Friedrich Peter, *Kurmainzische Verteidigungseinrichtungen und Baugeschichte der Festung Mainz in 17. und 18. Jahrhundert* (*Beiträge zur Geschichte der Stadt Mainz*, 19, Mainz, 1963).

Kaiser, David, *Politics and war: European conflict from Philip II to Hitler* (Cambridge, MA, 1990).

Kallenberg, Fritz, 'Spätzeit und Ende des schwäbischen Kreises', *Jahrbuch für Geschichte der oberdeutschen Reichsstädte*, 14 (1968), 61–93.

Kampmann, Christoph, *Reichsrebellion und kaiserliche Acht. Politische Strafjustiz im Dreißigjährigen Krieg und das Verfahren gegen Wallenstein 1634* (Münster, 1992).

Bibliography

Kapff, C[arl Christian], *Hohen-Neuffen, geschichtlich und geographisch geschildert* (Reutlingen, 1882).

Kapff, Paul, 'Schwaben in Amerika seit der Entdeckung des Weltteils', *WNJB*, 10 (1893).

Kapp, Friedrich Christian Georg, *Soldatenhandel deutscher Fürsten nach Amerika (1775 bis 1783)* (Berlin, 1874 edn).

Kappelhoff, B., *Absolutisches Regiment oder Ständeherrschaft? Landesherr und Landstände in Ostfriesland im ersten Drittel des 18. Jahrhunderts* (Hildesheim, 1982).

Kaufmann, Adolf, *Geschichte von Stetten im Remstal* (Stetten, 1962).

Kehr, Eckhart, *Der Primat der Innenpolitik: gesammelte Aufsätze zur preussisch–deutsch Sozialgeschichte im 19. und 20. Jahrhundert* (Berlin, 1970).

Kennett, Lee, *The French armies in the Seven Years War. A study in military organisation and administration* (Durham, NC, 1967).

Kessel, Eberhard, 'Der deutsche Soldat in den stehenden Heeren des Absolutismus', in Bernhard Schwertfeger and Erich Otto Volkmann (eds.), *Die deutsche Soldatenkunde* (2 vols., Berlin/Leipzig, 1937), I, pp. 63–93.

Kiernan, V. G., 'Foreign mercenaries and absolute monarchy', *Past and Present*, 11 (1957), 66–86.

Kitchen, Martin, *A military history of Germany from the eighteenth century to the present day* (London, 1975).

Klaiber, Hans Andreas, *Der württembergische Oberbaudirektor Philippe de la Guêpière. Ein Beitrag zur Kunstgeschichte der Architektur am Ende des Spätbarock* (*VKGLK*, Reihe B, vol. 9, Stuttgart, 1959).

Kleemann, Gotthilf, *Schloß Solitude bei Stuttgart. Aufbau, Glanzzeit und Niedergang* (Stuttgart, 1966).

Klein, Hans H., *Wilhelm zu Schaumburg-Lippe. Klassiker der Abschreckungstheorie und Lehrer Scharnhorst* (*Studien zur Militärgeschichte, Militärwissenschaft und Kontliktforschung*, 28, Osnabrück, 1982).

Knüppel, Günter, *Das Heerwesen des Fürstentums Schleswig-Holstein-Gottorf, 1600–1715. Ein Beitrag zur Verfassungs- und Sozialgeschichte territorialstaatlicher Verteidigungseinrichtungen* (*Quellen und Forschungen zur Geschichte Schleswig-Holsteins*, 63, Neumünster, 1972).

Koch, Arwed, 'Beiträge zur Geschichte des Schlosses HohenTübingen', *WVJHLG*, NF6 (1897), 192–240.

Kocher, J., *Geschichte der Stadt Nürtingen* (2 vols., Stuttgart, 1924), vol. I.

Kohlhaas, Wilhelm, *Candia. Die Tragödie einer abendländischen Verteidigung und ihr Nachspiel in Morea 1645–1714* (Osnabrück, 1978).

Kohlhepp, Armin G. W., *Die Militärverfassung des deutschen Reiches zur Zeit des siebenjährigen Krieges* (Griefswald Ph.D., printed Stralsund, 1914).

Kolb, von, 'Feldprediger in Altwürttemberg', *BWKG*, 9 (1905), 70–85, 97–124; 10 (1906), 22–51, 117–42.

Kopp, Walter, *Würzburger Wehr. Eine Chronik zur Wehrgeschichte Würzburgs* (Mainfränkische Studien, 22, Würzburg, 1979).

Kraus, Jurgen, *Das Militärwesen der Reichsstadt Augsburg, 1548–1806. Vergleichende Untersuchungen über städtische Militäreinrichtungen in Deutschland vom 16.–18. Jahrhundert* (*Abhandlungen zur Geschichte der Stadt Augsburgs*, 26, Augsburg, 1980).

Bibliography

Krauß, Rudolph, *Das Stuttgarter Hoftheater von den ältesten Zeiten bis zur Gegenwart* (Stuttgart, 1908).

'Das Theater', *HKE*, I, pp. 481–554.

Krauter, Gerhard, 'Die Manufakturen des Herzogtums Wirtemberg in der zweiten Hälfte des 18. Jahrhunderts', *WJSL*, I (1954/5), 260–77.

Kress, W., 'Einwanderings- oder Auswanderungsland?', *Stuttgarter Illustrierte*, 12 (1986).

Kriegs-Archiv, Kriegsgeschichtliche Abtheilung des K.u.K. (Austrian), *Feldzüge des Prinzen Eugen von Savoyen* (21 vols., Vienna, 1876–96).

Krieg gegen die französische Revolution 1792–1797 (2 vols., Vienna, 1905).

Oesterreichischer Erbfolgekrieg 1740–48 (9 vols., Vienna, 1896–1914).

Kroener, Bernhard R., 'Soldat oder Soldateska? Programmatischer Aufriß einer Sozialgeschichte militärischer Unterschichten in der ersten Hälfte des 17. Jahrhunderts', in Manfred Messerschmidt (ed.), *Militärgeschichte. Probleme, Thesen, Wege* (Stuttgart, 1982), pp. 100–23.

(ed.), *Europa im Zeitalter Friedrichs des Großen. Wirtschaft, Gesellschäft, Kriege (Beiträge zur Militärgeschichte*, 26, Munich, 1989).

Kunisch, Johannes, *Absolutismus. Europäische Geschichte vom Westfälischen Frieden bis zur Krise des Ancien Regime* (Göttingen, 1986).

Fürst – Gesellschaft – Krieg. Studien zur bellizistischen Disposition des absoluten Fürstenstaates (Cologne/Weimar/Vienna, 1992).

Der kleine Krieg. Studien zum Heerwesen des Absolutismus (Frankfurter historischen Abhandlungen, 4, Wiesbaden, 1973).

(ed.), *Prinz Eugen und seine Zeit. Eine Ploetz-Biographie* (Freiburg/Würzburg, 1986).

Kunisch, Johannes and Stollberg-Rillinger, Barbara (eds.), *Staatsverfassung und Heeresverfassung in der europäischen Geschichte der frühen Neuzeit (Historische Forschungen*, 28, Berlin, 1986).

Das Land Baden-Württemberg. Amtlich Beschreibung nach Kreisen und Gemeinden (issued by the Staatlichen Archivverwaltung Baden-Württembergs, Stuttgart, 1974), vol. I.

Lang, K[arl], *Die Ettlinger Linien und ihre Geschichte (Beiträge zur Geschichte der Stadt Ettlingen 5*, Ettlingen, 1965 edn).

Lanter, Max, *Die Finanzierung des Krieges. Quellen, Methoden und Lösungen seit dem Mittelalter bis Ende des zweiten Weltkrieges 1939 bis 1945* (Zürich Ph.D., printed Lucerne, 1950).

La Roche, Carl du Jarrys Baron de, *Der deutsche Oberrhein während der Kriege seit dem westphälischen Frieden bis 1801* (Stuttgart/Tübingen, 1842).

Laufs, Adolf, *Der schwäbische Kreis. Studien über Einungswesen und Reichsverfassung im deutschen Südwesten zu Beginn der Neuzeit (Untersuchungen zur deutschen Staats- und Rechtsgeschichte*, NF16, Aalen, 1971).

Lehmann, Max, 'Werbung, Wehrpflicht und Beurlaubung im Heere Friedrich Wilhelm I', *Historische Zeitschrift*, 67 (1891), 254–89.

Lemcke, 'Ein Blick in das herzoglich württembergisch Offizierskorps des vorigen Jahrhunderts', *WVJHLF*, 2 (1879), 34–7, 111–17.

Leube, Martin, 'Die fremden Ausgaben des altwürttembergischen Kirchenguts', *BWKG*, NF29 (1925), 168–99.

Bibliography

Liebel-Weckowics, Helen P., 'Enlightened despotism and the resistance to arbitrary taxation in Southwest Germany after the Seven Year War', *Man and Nature. Proceedings of the Canadian Society for Eighteenth Century Studies*, 5 (1986), 99–118.

'The revolt of the Wuerttemberg estates', *Man and Nature. Proceedings of the Canadian Society for Eighteenth Century Studies*, 2 (1984), 109–20.

Linnebach, Karl (ed.), *Deutsche Heeresgeschichte* (Hamburg, 1935 edn).

Losch, Philipp, *Soldatenhandel* (Kassel, 1974 edn).

Maçzak, Antoni (ed.), *Klientelsysteme im Europa der frühen Neuzeit* (Munich, 1988).

Marquardt, Ernst, *Geschichte Württembergs* (Stuttgart, 1985 edn).

Martens, Karl von, *Geschichte der innerhalb der gegenwärtigen Gränzen des Königreichs Württemberg vorgefallene kriegerischen Ereignisse vom Jahr 15 von Christi Geburt bis zum Friedensschlusse 1815* (Stuttgart, 1847).

Geschichte von Hohentwiel (Stuttgart, 1857).

Maurer, Hans-Martin, 'Das Haus Württemberg und Rußland', *ZWLG*, 48 (1989), 201–22.

'Das Württembergische Kapregiment. Söldner im Dienste früher Kolonialpolitik (1787–1808)', *ZWLG*, 47 (1988), 291–308.

Mayer, Karl *Aus Kirchheims Vergangenheit. Auf Grund handschriftlicher und gedruckter Quellen* (Kitchheim/Teck, 1913).

'Württembergisches Militärwesen im 17. Jahrhundert', *Der Schwabenspiegel*, 6 (1912/13), 140–2.

Mehring, Gebhard, 'Aus des Franzosenkriegen 1688–97', *LBSAW* (1904), 57–62.

'Wirtschaftliche Schäden durch den dreißigjährigen Krieg im Herzogtum Württemberg', *WVJHLG*, NF30 (1921), 58–89.

Meier-Welcker, Hans, *Deutsches Heerwesen im Wandel der Zeit. Ein Überblick über die Entwicklung vom Anfangen der stehender Heere bis zur Wehrfrage der Gegenwart* (Frankfurt am Main, 1956).

(ed.), *Untersuchungen zur Geschichte der Offizierkorps. Anciennität und Beförderung nach Leistung* (*Beiträge zur Militär-und Kriegsgeschichte*, 4, Stuttgart, 1962).

Meissner, Erhard, 'Die südwestdeutschen Reichsstände im siebenjährigen Krieg', *Ellwanger Jahrbuch*, 23 (1971), 117–58.

Merx, O., 'Zur Geschichte des fürstbischofliche Münsterischen Militärs in der ersten Hälfte des 18. Jahrhunderts', *Westfälische Zeitschrift*, 67 (1909), 168–211.

Metz, F. (ed.), *Vorderösterreich* (2nd edn, Freiburg, 1967).

Meyer, H., *Berichte des preußischen Gesandten Eickstedt. Ein Beitrag zur Politik der deutschen Kleinstaaten während des siebenjährigen Krieges* (Hamburg, 1906).

Mielsch, Rudolf, 'Die Kursächsische Armee im bayerischen Erbfolgekriege 1778/79', *Neues Archiv für sächsische Geschichte*, 53 (1932), 73–103; 54 (1933), 46–74.

Mommsen, Wolfgang J., 'Domestic factors in German foreign policy before 1914', *Central European History*, 6 (1973), 11–43.

Mörz, Stefan, *Aufgeklärter Absolutismus in der Kurpfalz während der Mannheimer Regierungszeit des Kurfürsten Karl Theodor (1742–1777)* (*VKGLK*, Reihe B, vol. 120, Stuttgart, 1991).

Müller, Hermann, *Das Heerwesen im Herzogtum Sachsen-Weimar von 1702–1775. Ein Beitrag zur thüringischen Geschichte des 18. Jahrhunderts* (Jena, 1936).

Müller, Karl Otto, 'Die Finanzwirtschaft in Württemberg unter Herzog Karl Alexander (1733–1737)', *WVJHLG*, NF38 (1932), 276–317.

Münch, Doris, 'Die Beziehungen zwischen Württemberg und Österreich bzw dem Kaiser 1713–1740 unter Berücksichtigung ihrer historischen Entwicklung' (Innsbrück Ph.D., 1961).

Münich, Friedrich, *Geschichte der Entwicklung der bayerischen Armee seit zwei Jahrhunderten* (Munich, 1864).

Mürmann, Franz, 'Das Militärwesen des ehemaligen Hochstiftes Paderborn seit dem Ausgange des dreißigjährigen Krieges', *Westfälische Zeitschrift*, 95 (1939), 3–78.

Musall, Heinz and Scheuerbrandt, Arnold, 'Die Kriege im Zeitalter Ludwigs XIV und ihre Auswirkungen auf die Siedlungs-, Bevölkerungs- und Wirtschaftsstruktur der Oberrheinlande', in *Hans Graul-Festschrift* (*Heidelberger geographische Arbeiten*, 40, Heidelberg, 1974), pp. 357–78.

Neipperg, Reinhard Graf von, *Kaiser und schwäbischer Kreis (1714–1733). Ein Beitrag zu Reichsverfassung, Kreisgeschichte und kaiserlicher Reichspolitik an Anfang des 18. Jahrhunderts* (*VKGLK*, Reihe B, vol. 119, Stuttgart, 1991).

Niemayer, J. and Ortenburg, G., *Die Churbraunschweig–Lüneburgische Armee im Siebenjährigen Kriege* (2 vols., Beckum, 1976).

Niethammer, Georg von, 'Aus der Geschichte des Grenadier-Regiment Königin Olga (1. Württembergisches) Nr. 119. Türkenkriege. Nach bis jetz unbenutzten Akten des schwäbischen Kreis-Archivs in Ludwigsburg', *BMWB*, 1 (1877), 7–36.

Geschichte des Grenadierregiments Königin Olga (Stuttgart, 1886).

'Die Reichsarmee im Feldzug 1757 mit Rücksicht auf das schwäbische Kreistruppenkorps und das Kreis-Füsilier-Regiments Württemberg', *BMWB*, 9 (1879), 149–204.

Niethammer, Hermann von, 'Alexander Freiherr von Bouwinghausen-Wallmerode, Generaleutnant 1728–1796', *Schwäbische Lebensbilder*, 3 (Stuttgart, 1942), 17–32.

Nopp, H., *Geschichte der Stadt und ehemaligen Reichsfestung Philippsburg* (Speyer, 1881).

Oestreich, Gerhard, 'Zur Heeresverfassung der deutschen Territorien von 1500 bis 1800. Ein Versuch vergleichender Betrachtung', in R. Dietrich and G. Oestreich (eds.), *Forschungen zu Staat und Verfassung. Festgabe für Fritz Hartung* (Berlin, 1958), pp. 419–39.

Pajol, Carles Pierre Victor, *Les guerres sous Louis XV* (7 vols., Paris, 1881).

Parker, Geoffrey, 'The military revolution 1560–1660 – a myth?', *Journal of Modern History*, 47 (1976), 195–314.

The military revolution. Military innovation and the rise of the west 1500–1800 (Cambridge, 1988).

Parker, Geoffrey et al., *The Thirty Years War* (London, 1987).

Pfaff, Karl, *Geschichte des Fürstenhauses und Landes Wirtenberg nach den besten Quellen und Hülfsmitteln neu bearbeitet* (4 vols., Stuttgart, 1850).

Geschichte des Militärwesens in Württemberg von der ältesten bis auf unserere Zeit und der Verhandlungen darüber zwischen der Regierung und den Landständen (Stuttgart, 1842).

Geschichte der Stadt Stuttgart, nach Archival-Urkunden und andern bewährten Quellen . . . (2 vols., Stuttgart, 1845).

Württembergs geleibte Herren. Biographie der Regenten von Württemberg von Herzog Eberhard im Bart bis zum König Friedrich (ed. P. Lahnstein, Stuttgart, 1965).

Bibliography

Pfister, Albert von, *Denkwürdigkeiten aus der württembergischen Kriegsgeschichte des 18. und 19. Jahrhunderts im Anschluß an die Geschichte des 8. Infanterie-Regiments* (Stuttgart, 1868).

Das Infanterieregiment Kaiser Wilhelm, König von Preussen (2. Württ.) No. 120. Eine Soldatengeschichte aus drei Jahrhunderten (Stuttgart, 1881).

'Militärwesen', in *HKE*, I, pp. 119–43.

Der Milizgedanke in Württemberg und die Versuche zu seiner Verwirklichung (Stuttgart, 1883).

'Das Regiment zu Fuß Alt-Württemberg im kaiserlichen Dienst auf Sicilien in den Jahren 1719 bis 1720', *BMWB*, 5/6 (1885), 157–268.

'Aus den Tagen des Herzogs Ludwig Eugen von Württemberg', *WVJHLG*, NF3 (1894), 94–192.

Pflichthofer, Erwin, *Das Württembergische Heerwesen am Ausgang des Mittelalters* (Tübingen Ph.D., printed 1938).

Press, Volker, 'Von den Bauernrevolten des 16. zur konstitutionellen Verfassung des 19. Jahrhunderts. Die Unterkonflikte in Hohenzollern-Hechingen und ihre Lösungen', in H. Weber (ed.), *Politische Ordnungen und soziale Kräfte im alten Reich* (Wiesbaden, 1980), pp. 85–112.

'Ein Epochenjahr der württembergischen Geschichte. Restitution und Reformation 1534', *ZWLG*, 47 (1988), 203–34.

'Friedrich der Große als Reichspolitiker', in Heinz Duchhardt (ed.), *Friedrich der Große, Franken und das Reich* (Vienna, 1986), pp. 25–56.

'The Holy Roman Empire in German history', in E. I. Kouri and T. Scott (eds.), *Politics and society in Reformation Europe* (London, 1987), pp. 51–77.

'Die kaiserliche Stellung im Reich zwischen 1648 und 1740 – Versuch einer Neubewertung', in G. Schmidt (ed.), *Stände und Gesellschaft im alten Reich* (Stuttgart, 1989), pp. 51–80.

'Kurhannover im System des alten Reiches 1692–1806', in *Prinz-Albert-Studien*, 4 (Munich, 1986), 53–79.

'Das Römische–Deutsche Reich – ein politisches system in verfassungs- und sozialgeschichtlicher Fragestellung', in G. Klingenstein and H. Lutz (eds.), *Spezialforschung und 'Gesamtgeschichte'* (Vienna, 1981), pp. 221–42.

'Der württembergische Angriff auf die Reichsritterschaft, 1749–1754 (1770)', in Franz Quarthal (ed.), *Zwischen Schwarzwald und Schwäbischer Alb. Das Land am oberen Neckar* (*Veröffentlichungen des alemannischen Instituts Freibugs im Breisgau*, 52, Sigmaringen, 1984), pp. 329–48.

'Der württembergische Landtag im Zeitalter des Umbruchs 1770–1830', *ZWLG*, 42 (1983), 255–81.

Presser, Carl, *Der Soldatenhandel in Hessen. Versuch einer Abrechnung* (Marburg, 1900).

Priesdorff, Kurt von, *Soldatisches Führertum* (10 vols., Hamburg, 1936–41).

Prinz, Johannes, *Das württembergische Kapregiment 1786–1808. Die Tragödie einer Söldnerschars. Unter Benützung des von L. Roser bearbeiteten württembergischen Archivmaterials* (Stuttgart, 1932 edn).

Raeff, Marc, *The well-ordered police state. Social and institutional change through law in the Germanies and Russia 1600–1800* (New Haven/London, 1983).

Reden-Dohna, Armgard von, 'Problems of small states of the Empire. The example of the Swabian imperial prelates', *Journal of Modern History*, 58 (1986), supplement 76–87.

Redlich, Fritz, *The German military enterpriser and his workforce. A study in European economic and social history* (2 vols., *Vierteljahreshefte für Sozial- und Wirtschaftsgeschichte*, Beihefte 47 and 48, Wiesbaden, 1964–5).

Reed, T. J., 'Talking to tyrants: dialogues with power in eighteenth-century Germany', *Historical Journal*, 33 (1990), 63–79.

Regele, Oskar, 'Zur Militärgeschichte Vorderösterreichs', in F. Metz (ed.), *Vorderösterreich Eine geschichtliche landeskunde* (2nd edn, Freiberg, 1967), pp. 123–37.

Reitzenstein, Karl Freiherr von, 'Kurze Lebensabrisse der bayerischen Generale und Obristen', *DBKH*, 13 (1904), 1–59.

Richter, Gregor, 'Die württembergischen Reichstagstimmen von der Erhebung zum Herzogtum bis zum Ende des alten Reiches. Ein Beitrag zur Frage der Reichsstandschaft von Württemberg, Mömpelgard und Teck', *ZWLG*, 23 (1964), 345–73.

Riecke, K. V., 'Das evangelische Kirchengut des vormaligen Herzogthums Württemberg', *BBSAW*, 13 (1876), 129–35, 167–74.

Ritter, G. A. (ed.), *Festschrift für Hans Rosenberg* (Berlin, 1970).

Roberts, Michael, *Essays in Swedish history* (London, 1967).

Rocholl, Ottoheinz, 'Das stehende Heer als Stütze der feudale Reaktion. Ein Beitrag zur Heeresgeschichte vornehmlich des 17. Jahrhunderts', *Wissenschaftliche Zeitschrift der Karl-Marx-Universität Leipzig, Gesellschafts- und staatswissenschaftliche*, Reihe 1, 9/10 (1952/53), 499–510.

Roider, Karl A., Jr, *The reluctant ally. Austria's policy in the Austro-Turkish war 1737–1739* (Baton Rouge, 1972).

Rosenberg, Rainer Freiherr von, *Soldatenwerbung und militärisches Durchzugsrecht im Zeitalter des Absolutismus. Eine rechtsgeschichtliche Untersuchung* (Berlin, 1973).

Rümelin, G., 'Altwürttemberg im Spiegel fremder Beobachtung', *WJSL* (1864).

Russell, C., 'Monarchies, war and estates in England, France and Spain c. 1580 to c. 1640', *Legislative Studies Quarterly*, 7 (1982), 205–20.

Sabean, David Warren, *Power in the blood. Popular culture and village discourse in early modern Germany* (Cambridge, 1984).

Property, production and family in Neckarhausen 1700–1870 (Cambridge, 1990).

Sante, G. W. (ed.), *Die Territorien bis zum Ende des alten Reiches* (*Territorien Ploetz*, Würzburg, 1964).

Sauer, Paul, *Affalterbach 972–1972* (Affalterbach, 1972).

'Die Neuorganisation des württembergischen Heerwesens unter Herzog, Kurfürst und König Friedrich 1797–1816', *ZWLG*, 26 (1967), 395–420.

Das württembergische Heer in der Zeit des Deutschen und des Norddeutschen Bundes (*VKGLK*, Reihe B, vol. 5, Stuttgart, 1958).

Savory, Sir Reginald, *His Britannic Majesty's Army in Germany during the Seven Years War* (Oxford, 1966).

Schäffer, Arnold, *Geschichte des siebenjährigen Krieges* (2 vols. in 3, Berlin, 1867–74).

Schempp, Adolf von, 'Die Beziehungen des schwäbischen Kreises und Herzogtums Württemberg zu der Reichsfeste Kehl während der ersten Hälfte des 18. Jahrhunderts', *WVJHLG*, NF18 (1909), 295–334.

Bibliography

'Die Entwaffnung und Auflösung des schwäbischen Kreiskorps am 29. Juli 1796', *BBSAW*, 14 (1911), 209–15.

Der Feldzug 1664 in Ungarn unter besonderer Berücksichtigung der herzoglichen württembergischen Allianz- und schwäbischen Kreistruppen. Ein militärisches Kulturbild. Auf Grund zum Teil unveröffentlichen Originalquellen bearbeitet (Stuttgart, 1909).

Geschichte des 3. württembergischen Infanterie-Regiments Nr. 121, 1716–1891. Auf Befehl des Königlichen Regiments zu Feier seines 175 jährigen Bestehens zusammengestellt (Stuttgart, 1891).

'Kehls Ende als Reichsfeste', *WVJHLG*, NF22 (1913), 336–50.

'Kehl und der schwäbische Kreis gegen Schluß des 18. Jahrhunderts', *WVJHLG*, NF28 (1919), 167–264.

Schempp, Walter, *Der Finanzhaushalt der Stadt- und Amtspflege Tübingen unter Herzog Karl Alexander, Rechnungsjahre 1732 bis 1737* (Würzburg, 1938).

Scherb, Wolfgang, *Die politischen Beziehungen der Grafschaft Mömpelgard zu Württemberg von 1723 bis zur französischen Revolution* (Tübingen Ph.D., printed 1981).

Schifferer, Otto, 'Die wirtschaftliche Entwicklung Ludwigsburgs von der Grundung der Stadt bis zum Beginn des 2. Weltkrieges', *LBGB*, 20 (1968), 53–81.

Schindling, A. and Ziegler, W. (eds.), *Die Kaiser der Neuzeit 1519–1918* (Munich, 1990).

Schmäh, Hans, 'Ludwigsburger Manufakturen im 18. Jahrhundert', *LBGB*, 15 (1963), 29–51.

Schmid, Alois, *Max III. Joseph und die europäischen Mächte. Die Außenpolitik des Kurfürstentums Bayerns von 1745–1765* (Munich, 1987).

Schmid, August, *Das Leben Johann Jakob Mosers. Aus seiner Selbstbiographie, den Archiven und Familienpapieren dargestekkt* (Stuttgart, 1868).

Schmid, Eugen, 'Geheimrat Georg Bernhard Bilfinger (1693–1750)', *ZWLG*, 3 (1939), 370–422.

Schmidt, Hans, 'Die Verteidigung des Oberrheins und die Sicherung Süddeutschlands im Zeitalter des Absolutismus und der französischen Revolution. Zur Problematik krieggeschichtlicher Beurteilung', *Historisches Jahrbuch*, 104 (1984), pp. 46–62.

Schmierer, Wolfgang, 'Zur Entstehungsgeschichte von Ludwigsburg', *LBGB*, 32 (1980), 79–94.

Schmitt, Heinrich, 'Ulm und sein Militär, besonders 1757', *WVJHLG*, NF4 (1895), 141–61.

Schmolz, Helmut, 'Die "Werbung" eines "Langen Kerls". Werbermethoden fremder Mächte in der Reichsstadt Heilbronn', *Schwaben und Franken. Heimatgeschichtliche Beilage der Heilbronner Stimme*, 14 (1968), issue 7.

Schnackenburg, E., 'Die Freicorps Friedrichs des Grossen. Ein Beitrag zur Preußens Heeresgeschichte', *BMWB*, 4 (1883).

Schnee, Heinrich, *Die Hoffinanz und der moderne Staat. Geschichte und System der Hoffaktoren an deutschen Fürstenhöfen im Zeitalter des Absolutismus* (6 vols., Berlin, 1953–67), vol. IV.

Schneider, Eugen, 'Zur Charakteristik des Oberst Riegers', *LBSAW* (1888), 293–6.

'Regierung', *HKE*, I, pp. 147–67.

Württembergische Geschichte (Stuttgart, 1896).

'Die württembergische Reichssturmfahne', *WVJHLG*, NF30 (1921), 30–5.

Bibliography

Schnitter, Helmut. 'Zur Funktion und Stellung des Heeres im feudalabsolutistischen Militarismus in Brandenburg-Preussen (17./18. Jahrhundert)', *Zeitschrift für Militärgeschichte*, 10 (1971), 306–14.

Volk und Landesdefension (*Militärhistorische Studien*, NF18, Berlin, DDR, 1977).

Schnitter, Helmut and Schmidt, Thomas, *Absolutismus und Heer* (*Militärhistorische Studien*, NF25, Berlin, DDR, 1987).

Schön, Theodor, 'Die Staatsgefangenern von Hohenasperg', *WNJB*, NF4 (1899).

Schott, Theodor, 'Württemberg und die Franzosen im Jahr 1688', *WNJB*, 5 (1888), 1–52.

'Württemberg und Gustav Adolf 1631 und 1632', *WVJHLG*, NF4 (1895), 343–402.

Schreiber, Guido, *Der badische Wehrstand seit dem 17. Jahrhundert bis zu Ende der französischen Revolutionskriege* (Karlsruhe, 1849).

Schremmer, E. (ed.), *Handelstrategie und betriebungswirtschaftliche Kalkulationen im ausgehenden 18. Jahrhundert. Der süddeutsche Salzmarkt. Zeitgenössische qualitive Untersuchungen* (Wiesbaden, 1971).

Schulenberg, D. (ed.), *Denkwürdigkeiten des Freiherrn Achatz Ferdinand v.d. Asseburg aus dessen Papieren bearbeitet* (Berlin, 1842).

Schulte, Aloys, *Markgraf Ludwig Wilhelm von Baden und der Reichskrieg gegen Frankreich 1693–1697* (2 vols., Heidelberg, 1901).

Schultz, W., *Die preussischen Werbungen unter Friedrich Wilhelm I und Friedrich dem Grossen bis zum Beginn des Siebenjährigen Krieges, mit besonderer Berücksichtigung Mecklenburg-Schwerin* (Schwerin, 1887).

Schulz, T., 'Die Mediatisierung des Kantons Kocher. Ein Beitrag zur Geschichte der Reichsritterschaft am Endes des alten Reiches', *ZWLG*, 47 (1988), 323–57.

Schüssler, Walter, 'Das Werbewesen in der Reichsstadt Heilbronn vornehmlich im 18. Jahrhundert' (Tübingen Ph.D., 1951).

Schuster, Oscar and Franke, F. Adolf, *Geschichte der sächsischen Armee von deren Errichtung bis auf die neueste Zeit. Unter Benützung handschriftlicher und urkundlicher Quellen dargestellt* (3 vols., Leipzig, 1885).

Schwarz, Paul, 'Die Werbung langer Kerls im 18. Jahrhunderts', *Reutlinger Geschichtsblätter*, NF11 (1973), 45–54.

Scott, H. M. (ed.), *Enlightened absolutism. Reform and reformers in later eighteenth century Europe* (London, 1990).

Seeger, Karl von, *Zweitausendjahre schwäbisches Soldatentum* (Stuttgart/Berlin, 1937).

Sheehan, James, *German history 1770–1866* (Oxford, 1989).

Siben, Arnold, 'Der Kontributionszug des französischen Generals Marquis de Feuquière durch Franken und Schwaben im Herbst 1688', *ZGO*, NF54 (1941), 108–91.

Sichart, L[uis Heinrich Friedrich] von, *Geschichte der königlich-hannoverschen Armee* (5 vols., Hanover, 1866–98).

Sicken, Bernhard, 'Residenzstadt und Fortifikation. Politische, soziale und wirtschaftliche Probleme der barocken Neubefestigung Würzburgs', in Hans-Walter Herrmann and Fritz Irsigler (eds.), *Beiträge zur Geschichte der frühneuzeitlichen Garnisons- und Festungsstadt* (*Veröffentlichungen der Kommission für saarländische Landesgeschichte und Volksforschung*, 13, Saarbrücken, 1983), pp. 124–48.

'Die Streitkräfte des Hochstifts Würzburg gegen Ende des ancien regime', *Zeitschrift für bayerische Landesgeschichte*, 47 (1984), 691–744.

Bibliography

Das Wehrwesen des fränkischen Reichskreises. Aufbau und Struktur (1681–1714) (2 vols., Würzburg Ph.D., printed Nuremberg, 1967).

Sievers, Leo, *Juden in Deutschland. Die Geschichte einer 2000 jährigen Tragödie* (Hamburg, 1977).

Soliday, Gerald Lyman, *A community in conflict: Frankfurt society in the 17th and 18th century* (Hanover, NH, 1974).

Söll, Wilhelm, *Die staatliche Wirtschaftspolitik in Württemberg im 17. und 18. Jahrhundert* (Tübingen Ph.D., printed 1934).

Stadlinger, Leo Ignaz von, *Geschichte des württembergischen Kriegswesens von der frühesten bis zur neuesten Zeit* (Stuttgart, 1856).

Stark, Paul, *Fürstliche Personen des Hauses Württemberg und ihre bewährten Diener im Zeitalter Friedrichs des Grossen* (Stuttgart, 1876).

Staudinger, Karl, *Geschichte des bayerischen Heeres* (5 vols., Munich, 1901–9).

Stern, Selma, *The court Jew* (Philadelphia, 1950).

Jud Süss. Ein Beitrag zur deutschen und zur jüdischen Geschichte (Munich, 1929).

Stiefel, Karl, *Baden 1648–1952* (2 vols., Karlsruhe, 1977), vol. II.

Stoffers, Albert, 'Das Hochstift Paderborn zur Zeit des siebenjärigen Krieges', *Zeitschrift für vaterländische Geschichte und Altertumskunde Westfalens*, 69 (1911), 1–90; 70 (1912), 68–182.

Storm, Peter-Christoph, *Der schwäbische Kreis als Feldherr. Untersuchungen zur Wehrverfassung des schwäbischen Reichskreises in der Zeit von 1648–1732* (Berlin, 1974).

Storz, Gerhard, *Karl Eugen. Der Fürst und das 'alte gute Recht'* (Stuttgart, 1981).

Stuhr, P. F., *Forschungen und Erläuterungen über Hauptpunkte der Geschichte des siebenjährigen Krieges* (2 vols., Hamburg, 1842).

Stutzer, Dietmar, 'Das preußische Heer und seine Finanzierung in zeitgenössischer Darstellung 1740–1790', *Militärgeschichtliche Mitteilungen*, 24 (1978), 23–47.

Sutton, J. H., *The king's honor and the king's cardinal: The War of the Polish Succession* (Lexington, 1980).

Tallett, Frank, *War and society in early modern Europe 1495–1715* (London/New York, 1992).

Taylor, Peter Keir, 'The household's most expendable people: The draft and peasant society in 18th-century Hessen-Kassel' (University of Iowa Ph.D., 1987).

Taylor, Peter Keir and Rebel, Hermann, 'Hessian peasant women, their families and the draft: A social–historical interpretation of four tales from the Grimm collection', *Journal of Family History*, 6 (1981), 347–78.

Tessin, Georg, *Mecklenburgisches Militär in Türken- und Franzosenkriegen 1648–1718* (*Mitteldeutsche Forschungen*, 42, Cologne/Graz, 1966).

Thenius, Walther, *Die Anfänge des stehenden Heerwesens in Kursachsen unter Johann Georg III. und Johann Georg IV* (*Leipziger historische Abhandlungen*, 31, Leipzig, 1912).

Thum, Walter, *Die Rekrutierung der sächsischen Armee unter August dem Starken (1694–1733)* (*Leipziger historische Abhandlungen*, 29, Leipzig, 1912).

Thüna, Lothar, Freiherr von, *Die Würzburger Hilfstruppen im Dienste Österreichs 1756–1763* (Würzburg, 1893).

Tilly, Charles, *Coercion, capital and European states AD 990–1990* (Oxford, 1990).

Bibliography

Tüchle, Hermann, *Die Kirchenpolitik des Herzogs Karl Alexander von Württemberg 1733–1737* (Würzburg, 1939).

Tumbült, Georg, 'Das fürstenbergische Kontingent des schwäbischen Kreises', *Schriften des Vereins für Geschichte und Naturgeschichte der Baar und der angrenzenden Landesteile*, 17 (1928), 3–12.

Uhland, Robert, *Geschichte der Hohen Karlsschule in Stuttgart* (Stuttgart, 1953).

'Geschichte des Hohen Carlsschule', in *Ausstellung: Die Hohen Carlsschule 4 November 1959 bis 30 Januar 1960* (issued by Wurttembergisches Landesmuseum Stuttgart, 1959), pp. 13–33.

'Herzog Carl Eugen von Württemberg. Persönlichkeit und Werke', *LBGB*, 31 (1979), 39–56.

(ed.), *900 Jahre Haus Württemberg. Leben und Leistung für Land und Volk* (Stuttgart, 1985 edn).

Ühler, H., 'Der Aufstand des Armen Konrad im Jahr 1514', *WVJHLG*, NF38 (1932), 401–86.

Vann, James Allen, *The making of a state. Württemberg 1593–1793* (Ithaca/London, 1984).

The Swabian Kreis. Institutional growth in the Holy Roman Empire, 1648–1715 (Brussels, 1975).

Vann, James Allen and Rowan, Steven W. (eds.), *The old Reich. Essays on German political institutions 1495–1806* (*Studies presented to the International Commission for the History of Representative and Parliamentary Institutions*, 48, Brussels, 1974).

Waddington, Richard, *La guerre de sept ans* (5 vols., Paris, 1899–1914).

Wagner, Fritz, *Kaiser Karl VII. und die Grossen Mächte 1740–1745* (Stuttgart, 1938).

Walker, Mack, *German home towns. Community, state and general estate 1648–1871* (Ithaca, 1971).

Johann Jakob Moser and the Holy Roman Empire of the German Nation (Chapel Hill, 1981).

'Rights and functions: the social categories of eighteenth-century German jurists and cameralists', *Journal of Modern History*, 50 (1978), 234–51.

Walter, Jürgen, *Carl Eugen von Württemberg. Ein Herzog und seine Untertanen* (Mühlacker, 1987).

Weber, Gerhard, 'Die Eppinger Linien', *Kraichgau. Heimatforschung im Landkreis Sinsheim unter Berücksichtigung seiner Nachbargebiete*, 3 (1972), 179–87.

Weber, Hermann, *Die Politik des Kurfürsten Karl Theodor von der Pfalz während des österreichischen Erbfolgekrieges (1742–1748)* (Bonn, 1956).

Weisert, Hermann, *Geschichte der Stadt Sindelfingen 1500–1807* (Sindelfingen, 1963).

Weissenbach, Strack von, *Geschichte der königlichen württembergischen Artillerie* (Stuttgart, 1882).

Weller, Karl and Weller, Arnold, *Württembergische Geschichte im südwestdeutschen Raum* (Stuttgart/Aalen, 1972 edn).

Wessling, Mary Nagle, 'Medicine and government in early modern Württemberg' (University of Michigan Ph.D., 1988).

Whitman, James Q., *The legacy of Roman law in the German Romantic era* (Princeton, 1990).

Wick, Peter, *Versuche zur Errichtung des Absolutismus in Mecklenburg in der ersten Hälfte des*

18. Jahrhunderts. Ein Beitrag zur Geschichte des deutschen Territorialabsolutismus (Berlin, DDR, 1964).

Wilson, Arthur McCandless, *French foreign policy during the administration of Fleury 1726–1743* (Cambridge, MA, 1936).

Wilson, Peter H., 'The power to defend, or the defence of power: the conflict between duke and estates over defence provision, Württemberg 1677–1793', *Parliaments, Estates and Representation*, 12 (1992), 25–45.

'Violence and the rejection of authority in 18th-century Germany: the case of the Swabian Mutinies in 1757', *German History*, 12 (1994), 1–26.

Wintterlin, Friedrich, 'Die altwürttembergische Verfassung am Ende des 18. Jahrhunderts', *WVJHLG*, NF23 (1914), 195–209.

'Die Anfänge der landständischen Verfassung in Württemberg', *WVJHLG*, NF23 (1914), 327–36.

Geschichte der Behördenorganisation in Württemberg (2 vols., Stuttgart, 1904–6).

'Landeshoheit', *HKE*, I, pp. 168–90.

'Wehrverfassung und Landesverfassung im Herzogtum Württemberg', *WVJHLG*, NF34 (1928), 239–56.

Witzleben, A. von, *Der Wasunger Krieg zwischen Sachsen-Gotha-Altenberg und Sachsen-Meiningen 1747 bis 1748* (Gotha, 1855).

Wrede, A. von, *Geschichte der kaiserlichen und königlichen Wehrmacht von 1618 bis zum Ende des XIX. Jahrhunderts* (5 vols., Vienna, 1898–1905).

Wunder, Bernd, 'Der Administrator Herzog Friedrich Karl von Württemberg (1652–1698)', *ZWLG* 30 (1971), 117–63.

Frankreich, Württemberg und der schwäbische Kreis während der Auseinandersetzungen über die Reunionen (1679–97). Ein Beitrag zur Deutschlandpolitik Ludwigs XIV. (Stuttgart, 1971).

'Die französisch–württembergischen Geheimverhandlungen 1711', *ZWLG*, 28 (1969), 363–90.

'Joseph II., der Reichshofrat und die württembergischen Ständekämpfe 1766/67', *ZWLG*, 50 (1991), 382–9.

Privilegierung und Disziplinierung. Die Entstehung des Berufsbeamtentums in Bayern und Württemberg, 1780–1825 (*Studien zur modernen Geschichte*, 21, Munich, 1978).

Yorke-Long, A., *Music at court: four eignteenth century studies* (London, 1964).

Index

Index

soldier trade of, 85n, 86–96, 145–6, 215
see also emperor, Württemberg
Austrian Netherlands, *see* Belgium
Austrian Succession, War of (1740–8), 103–4,
    175–6, 178, 195–6, 200–1, 211, 236

Baden, 13, 167n
    estates in, 69
Baden-Durlach, 29, 30, 43, 118, 131, 151, 169,
    211–12, 255
    soldier trade of, 146
Bamberg, bishopric
    finances of, 36, 41, 47
    see also Schönborn
Bandel, Joseph Anton, courtier, 32
Bar, Count Christian von, 60n
Bavaria, 13
    army of, 42, 80, 121n, 178, 195n, 200–1, 215n
    estates in, 69
    finances of, 36, 41–2, 47–8, 127
    foreign policy of, 26, 37, 103–4, 108, 139–40,
        142, 147, 150, 152–3, 176, 195–6, 198,
        206, 212, 214, 237, 255
    soldier trade of, 76–7, 190
    trade with Württemberg, 45
    see also Wittelsbach dynasty
Bavarian Succession, War of (1777–9), 235
Bayreuth, margraviate, 197, 202
Bayreuth, Elizabeth Sophie Frederike von
    (1732–80), wife of Carl Eugen, 197–8,
    213n
Bayreuth, Wilhelmine von (1709–58), 197n
Bayreuth, Margrave Friedrich von (d. 1763),
    197n
Beauchamp, Francis Viscount, MP, 235
Beilstein, district, 17n
Belfort, 43
Belgium, 24, 86, 123n, 147, 201
Belgrade, siege of (1717), 166
Berg, duchy, 69, 153
Berlin, 142, 159, 197
Berwick, Duke James Fitzjames (1670–1734),
    French general, 167, 168
Besançon, Parliament of, 109
Besigheim, district, 151n
Besold, Christoph (1577–1638), professor, 54,
    55, 59, 63, 70
Bilfinger, Georg Bernhard (1693–1750), privy
    councillor, 169, 176n, 178, 187–8
Black Forest (Schwarzwald), 24, 43, 170–1, 237
Blamont, lordship, 143n
Blaubeuren, district, 17n, 132n
Blenheim, battle of (1704), 33, 131n, 140
Bohemia, 17n
    campaigns in, 213

estates in, 60, 68, 100
Böhm, Egidius, Württemberg merchant, 168–9,
    180
Boldevin, Carl Christoph von (d. 1732), general,
    132–3, 161n
Boldevin, Josua Albrecht von (1670–1740), war
    councillor, 132–3, 135n, 160–1
Bopfingen, imperial city, 172n
Bottwar, district, 17n
Boyne, battle of (1690), 113
Brackenheim, district, 132n
Brandenburg, *see* Prussia
Brandenburg-Schwedt, Henriette Maria von
    (1702–82), 142
Breisach, fortress, 149–50, 159, 190–4
Brettlach, Austrian general, 219
Brunswick-Lüneburg-Bevern, Ferdinand
    Albrecht von (1686–1735), imperial
    general, 170n
Brunswick-Wolfenbüttel, 13, 19, 60, 72, 151,
    152, 211, 213
    army of, 183
Brunswick-Wolfenbüttel, Anton Ulrich
    (1633–1714), duke from 1704, 73
Buchau, lordship, 172
Bühler, councillor, 164n
Burgundy, 43, 107, 109

cabinet ministry (Geheime Konferenz Rat, or
    Ministerium, also Kabinettskanzlei), 134,
    167–8, 208–9, 220, 236, 248
Calw, county, 42, 45
cameralism, 2, 77, 249, 251
Cannstatt, district, 132n
Carl Alexander (1684–1737), duke from 1733
    and army, 30, 133, 159, 170–9, 192
    character and aims of, 24, 37, 71, 162–7, 172,
        181–2, 249–50
    conversion to Catholicism, 73, 123
    court of, 163, 165
    death of, 123n, 124, 166, 181–2, 184–5
    and estates, 64–5, 98
    fiscal policy of, 164, 167–9, 179–82, 186, 214
    foreign policy of, 36–7, 105, 169–76, 200, 255
    and Grävenitz family, 37, 105
    and imperial knights, 120
    military career of, 30, 36–7, 112–13, 122–4,
        166, 169–70, 197n
    soldier trade of, 95, 124, 172
Carl Eugen (1728–93), duke from 1737
    and army, 29–30, 89, 95, 133, 155, 176, 178,
        197n, 205–8, 215–26, 234
    character and aims of, 12, 22–4, 199–200,
        209–10, 214–17, 225–6, 231–2, 234,
        236–9, 249–50, 252

285

Index

Index

Jülich, duchy, 69, 153
Jüngster Reichsabschied (JRA, 1654), 61, 62–3, 68, 71, 75, 115
Jüstingen, lordship, 208n

Kaisersheim, abbey, 172n
Kalnein, von, Prussian officer, 196, 196n
Kammergut (ducal domains), 47–8, 60, 180
Kammerschreibereigut (ducal domains), 47–8, 159
Kanzleiordnung (chancellory ordinance)
  of 1660, 66–7, 107, 166–7, 189, 208
  of 1724, 134
Karlsruhe, 29
Kechler von Schwandorf, Heinrich Friedrich (d. 1733), general, 133n
Kehl, imperial fortress, 20, 147, 149–50, 161, 163, 190, 192, 194, 255
Keller (ducal administrator), 48, 180
Keller, Baron Christian Dietrich von (1699–1766), diplomat, 59, 194–6, 198, 202n, 211
Kirchengut (church property), 49–50, 53, 63, 110, 233
Kirchenkasten (church treasury), 49, 128–9, 167n, 188n, 218
Kirchenrat (church council), 49
Kirchheim/Teck, district, 132n, 135n
Klosterämter (monastical districts), 49, 65
Knittlingen, Swabian town, 116
Koch, Johann Friedrich (1692–1752), war commissar, 186
Konsistorium (consistory), 48
Kreis (imperial circle)
  Austrian, 106
  Franconian, 18, 119, 139, 149, 192, 212, 221
  Lower Saxon, 22
  structure, 8–9, 18, 32
  Swabian, 8–9, 18, 42, 67, 105–8, 117–19, 147–52, 192, 212, 255
  Upper Saxon, 22
  Westphalian, 201
Kreis Association, 18, 119–20, 139, 147, 150–2, 202
Kreis Direktorium, 117–18, 211
Kreisextraordinari (military tax), 158, 234
Kreis militia, 106, 119–20, 171–2
Kreistag, also Konvent, Assembly, 105, 117–20, 136–7, 140, 148, 170–1, 200, 208n, 211, 255
Kreistruppen, 18–19
  in Württemberg, 21–2, 61, 63, 70, 109, 111, 112, 114, 117n, 118–20, 122, 136–7, 148–9, 155, 167, 172, 173, 178n, 190, 192, 200–1, 205, 210–11, 214, 221–2, 239

Kriegskasse (war treasury), 35n, 51, 129, 157, 174, 187, 189, 191, 207, 218–19, 221–2, 231
Kriegsrat, also General-Kriegs-Commissariat (war council), 117n, 131, 132, 140, 145, 155–6, 160, 206n
Kulpis, Dr Johann Georg von (1652–98), privy council president, 135, 139

La Favorite, palace, 36, 127
Lamprecht, secretary, 164n
Landeshoheit (territorial sovereignty), 11, 31
Landesvisitation, 132, 181
Landfrieden (public peace), 65, 100
Landschaft, see estates in Württemberg
Landschaftliche Einnehmerei (estates treasury), 50
Landschreiberei (ducal treasury), 48, 128–9, 143, 188n; see also Rentkammer
Landtag (territorial diet), 114, 137, 157, 166, 179
  function of, 54
  membership of, 46, 49, 54, 56, 58, 63–5, 228
  sessions of: (1457), 35n; (1628), 58, 63–4; (1692), 120; (1698), 58, 63–4; (1737–9), 137, 159, 185–9, 198, 229, 251; (1763), 228–30; (1764), 231
Laubsky, Baron Rudolph von (1700–54), general, 133, 176n, 179
Lauffen, district, 132n
Leiningen-Westerburg, Johann Wilhelm Friedrich, general, 132, 133n
Leonberg, district, 132n
Leopold I (1640–1705), emperor 1658–1705, 62–3, 95, 99, 102
Leuthen, battle of (1757), 215, 237
Levin, financier, 60n
Liege, bishopric, 47, 172n
Lille, 39
Lisbon, 23
London, 147, 151, 226–7
Lorch, district, 132n
Louis XIV (1638–1715), king of France from 1643, 4, 98, 121, 142
Louis XV (1710–74), king of France from 1715, 203, 205–7
Lübeck, bishopric, 172n
Ludwig Eugen ('Prince Louis', 1731–95), brother of Carl Eugen, duke of Württemberg from 1793, 194, 197, 202, 221
Ludwigsburg
  district and town of, 132n, 134, 135n, 160
  foundation of, 28–9, 36, 166
  palace at, 126–8, 140, 165, 218, 237

289

Index

Ludwig Wilhelm ('Türkenlouis', 1655–1707), margrave of Baden-Baden from 1677, 16, 22, 119, 135–6, 148

Madrid, 23, 226
Magdalene Sibylle (1652–1712), coregent, 97, 107, 114, 121, 135
Magdeburg, 39
Mainz, electorate, 13, 43
  army of, 39n, 80, 183
  finances of, 47
  foreign policy of, 34, 61, 152–3
  fortifications of, 39
Mannheim, 29
Maria Augusta von Thurn und Taxis (1706–56), wife of Carl Alexander, 59, 184–6, 188, 197, 201
Maria Theresia of Austria (1717–80), 103
Mark, duchy, 61, 69
Markgröningen, district, 132n
Marlborough, John Churchill (1650–1722), first duke of, 16, 140
Max Emanuel (1662–1726), elector of Bavaria from 1679, 22–3, 40–1, 91
Max Franz, elector of Cologne 1784–1802, 37
Max Joseph (1727–77), elector of Bavaria from 1745, 42
Maxen, battle of (1759), 224n
Mecklenburg, 13, 43–4, 124n, 141
  army of, 71–2, 80, 131n, 172n
  estates in, 61, 63, 68–72, 101, 251
  social structure of, 70
  soldier trade of, 123
Mecklenburg, Carl Leopold, duke of 1713–28/47, 37, 71–2, 251
Mecklenburg, Christian I Louis, duke of 1658–92, 71, 73
Mecklenburg, Christian II Louis, duke of 1747–56, 72
Mecklenburg, Friedrich Wilhelm, duke of 1692–1713, 71
mercantilism, 3, 44, 97, 138–9
Metz, Christoph Wolfgang, diplomat, 202n
Metz, Johann Albrecht Friedrich, councillor, 164n
Milan, duchy, 114
military enterprisers, 4, 16–17, 90–2
military revolution, 4
Mindelheim, lordship, 16
Minden, battle of (1759), 223
Mitscheval, Sigmund Christian von (1667–1740), general, 133n
Mockmühl, district, 16n
Mollwitz, battle of (1741), 196
Mömpelgard (Montbéliard)
  abbot of, 151

acquisition by Württemberg, 142–4, 150–1, 159, 201–2, 204, 206
  dynasty of, 15, 109, 143
  French occupations of, 107–9, 163, 173, 174, 179
  territory and population of, 16n, 24, 43, 45, 218n
'Mömpelgard bastards', 143, 149, 212
Mömpelgard, Leopold Eberhard (1670–1723), count from 1699, 107, 143
Mömpelgard, Ludwig Friedrich (1586–1631), count from 1617, 15
Monrepos, palace, 36, 218n
Montigny, Baron von, general, 133n
Montmartin, Count Friedrich Samuel von (1712–78)
  influence of, 126, 219–21, 225
  policies of, 27, 215, 217, 223, 224, 226, 237
Montolieu, Baron Friedrich Carl von, privy councillor, 202n
Moser, Johann Jakob (1701–85), lawyer, 46n, 75, 209, 217, 219, 229, 231, 254
Mundelsheim, district, 151n
Münsingen, district, 132n
Münster, bishopric, 13, 61, 69

Napoleon Bonaparte (1769–1821), emperor of the French 1804–15, 23
Nellenberg, lordship, 172
Neuenburg, district, 17n
Neuenstadt, district, 16
Neues Schloss, palace, 36, 204
Neuffen, fortress, 61, 132n, 196n
Neuffer, Philipp Jacob (1677–1738), privy councillor, 165, 168n
Neuffer, Veit Jacob (d. 1741), lawyer, 179n
Neu Wied, 33
Nicolai, Ferdinand Friedrich von (1730–1814), military theorist, 215n
Nine Years War (1688–97), 70, 114–15, 135–6, 139
Nuremburg, imperial city, 24
Nürtingen, district, 132n
Nymphenburg, palace, 29

Obervogt, see Amtmann
Oels, duchy, 16, 109, 185, 195
Oetisheim, battle of (1692), 121
Ortenau, 17, 24
Osiander, Johann (1657–1724), abbot of Königsbrunn and Hirsau, 89n, 146–7, 157–8
Öttingen, counts of, 33, 90

Paderborn, bishopric, 47

290

Index

Index

CAMBRIDGE STUDIES IN EARLY MODERN HISTORY

Early Modern Democracy in the Grisons: Social Order and Political Language in a Swiss Mountain Canton, 1470–1620
RANDOLPH C. HEAD
War, State and Society in Württemberg, 1677–1793
PETER H. WILSON

Titles available in paperback marked with an asterisk*

The following titles are now out of print:

French Finances, 1770–1795: From Business to Bureaucracy
J. F. BOSHER
Chronicle into History: an Essay in the Interpretation of History in Florentine Fourteenth-Century Chronicles
LOUIS GREEN
France and the Estates General of 1614
J. MICHAEL HAYDEN
Reform and Revolution in Mainz, 1743–1803
T. C. W. BLANNING
Altopascio: a Study in Tuscan Society 1587–1784
FRANK MCARDLE
Gunpowder and Galleys: Changing Technology and Mediterranean Warfare at Sea in the Sixteenth Century
JOHN FRANCIS GUILMARTIN JR.
The State, War and Peace: Spanish Political Thought in the Renaissance 1516–1559
J. A. FERNÁNDEZ-SANTAMARIA
Calvinist Preaching and Iconoclasm in the Netherlands, 1544–1569
PHYLLIS MACK CREW
The Kingdom of Valencia in the Seventeenth Century
JAMES CASEY
Filippo Strozzi and the Medici: Favor and Finance in Sixteenth-Century Florence and Rome
MELISSA MERIAM BULLARD
Rouen during the Wars of Religion
PHILIP BENEDICT
The Emperor and his Chancellor: a Study of the Imperial Chancellery under Gattinara
JOHN M. HEADLEY
The Military Organisation of a Renaissance State: Venice c. 1400–1617
M. E. MALLETT AND J. R. HALE
Neostoicism and the Early Modern State
GERHARD OESTREICH
Prussian Society and the German Order: an Aristocratic Corporation in Crisis c. 1410–1466
MICHAEL BURLEIGH
The Changing Face of Empire: Charles V, Philip II and Habsburg Authority, 1551–1559
M. J. RODRIGUEZ-SALGADO